LIFE IN A LATE MEDIEVAL CITY
Chester 1275–1520

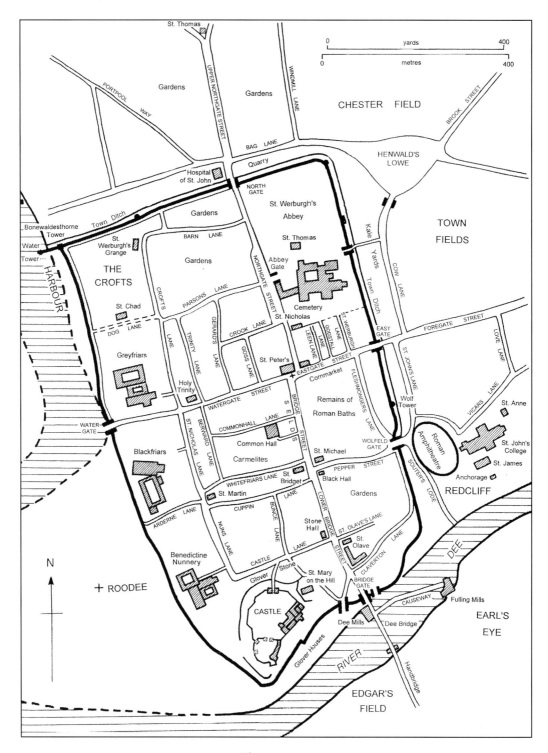

Chester, *c.*1500

Life in a Late Medieval City

Chester 1275–1520

Jane Laughton

Windgather Press
is an imprint of
Oxbow Books

ISBN 978-1-905119-23-3

A CIP record for this book is available from the British Library

This book is available direct from

Oxbow Books, Oxford, UK
(Phone: 01865-241249; Fax: 01865-794449)

and

The David Brown Book Company
PO Box 511, Oakville, CT 06779, USA
(Phone: 860-945-9329; Fax: 860-945-9468)

or from our website

www.oxbowbooks.com

Printed in Singapore by
KHL Printing Co Pte Ltd

Contents

Acknowledgements

This book has been many years in the making and foremost among the pleasures of approaching completion is the opportunity to thank those who have given me guidance and support along the way.

My first thanks are to Dr Margaret Bonney and Professor Barrie Dobson who supervised my post-graduate studies and provided scholarly encouragement at an early stage. I was then fortunate to work on a research project investigating medieval towns in the East Midlands directed by Professor Christopher Dyer. His approach to medieval history has profoundly influenced the way my research interests have developed and I am indebted to him. I am also grateful for his continuing support. Dr Alan Thacker and Dr Chris Lewis have shared their extensive knowledge of medieval Chester with me and have generously provided advice and assistance. I thank them both. Professor David Mills kindly answered my queries about the Corpus Christi procession and plays.

The documentary research on which this book is based was begun in the City Record Office in Chester Town Hall and involved months spent deciphering court rolls with the help of ultra-violet light in a cloakroom surrounded by coats and umbrellas. It was completed in the pleasant surroundings of the Cheshire Record Office. The staff have been constantly welcoming and helpful. Special thanks are due to Jonathan Pepler, the county archivist, for assistance with the illustrations for this book. I have been given great assistance by the librarians and archivists in the British Library, in the Public Record Office at Chancery Lane and at Kew, and in Staffordshire Record Office.

My debt to the archaeologists at Chester is considerable and I have profited from discussions with Mike Morris and his colleagues Julie Edwards, Ian Smith and Simon Ward. It is gratifying to discover that the material and the written evidence so often prove to be complementary. I am grateful to them for sharing their knowledge and for providing some splendid illustrations. Additional images were kindly provided by Jill Collens, Rob Philpott, Mike Shaw and the staff of Earthworks Archaeology. Rob Philpott also provided a map and Mike Shaw has given me information about the small Cheshire towns.

Paul Hyde of Chester City Council has been generous with his advice and encouragement and I am most grateful. Thanks are also due to his colleague David Sejrup for photographing the mayor's sword for me. I have appreciated the guidance, information and support given by Stewart Ainsworth, Ian

Archibald, Paul Booth, Helen and Giles Clarke, Jeremy Goldberg, Jane Grenville, Kathryn Jennings, Brian Rich, Mary Syner and Philip Wright. I should like to thank Richard Purslow of Windgather Press for encouraging me to write this book and Val Lamb of Oxbow Books for seeing it through to publication.

Finally I must thank my husband for his unfailing support over many years. I would have achieved nothing without his help and this book is for him.

List of Figures and Tables

Figures

Tables

CHAPTER ONE

Medieval Towns and Urban Hierarchies

In *c*.1300 the monk Robert of Gloucester began his chronicle with a description of contemporary England. He depicted a 'wel god land' of pastures, meadows, woods and rivers, and he praised the wealth of its agriculture. The land produced an abundance of corn; animals, birds, fish and fruit were plentiful; the quality of English wheat and wool was unsurpassed. Although Robert's England was predominantly rural it nevertheless contained towns. He named 27, fourteen of them 'chef tounes', and noted that there were also 'grete tounes' in Wales. Some English towns had already developed particular specialisms: Gloucester was associated with iron, Worcester with fruit, Coventry with soap, Exeter and its region with lead and tin. Trade played a significant role in the economy. The monk stressed the importance of great rivers like the Severn, Thames and Humber, and named the four major roads, all of Roman origin, which linked towns across the length and breadth of England. Trading networks stretched overseas. Most ships sailed to and from London, but Norwich was described as facing Denmark, Durham as facing Norway, and Chester as facing Ireland.[1]

Recent scholarship has produced a picture of late medieval England which tallies well with this contemporary description. England in 1300 was still overwhelmingly rural, with 80 per cent of the population living in villages and hamlets and earning their living from the land, but one in five of the inhabitants were townspeople. The country was more urban than earlier historians believed. The number of towns in England at the start of the fourteenth century is now thought to have been about 650 and there may have been as many as 200,000 urban households. The difficulties in reaching these figures are recognised and it is acknowledged that they will be improved in the future, but despite these *caveats* they are generally accepted as correct.[2]

The increase in the number of places now recognised as urban stems from the adoption of a new definition of medieval towns. Historians have always found it difficult to identify these places and in particular to differentiate between small towns and rural settlements. They have not been helped by medieval terminology since contemporaries applied the word 'vill' to both types of place.[3] In the first half of the twentieth century a constitutional definition was preferred and towns were equated with boroughs, places which had been granted a charter conferring a variety of privileges. Chief among these was burgage tenure, which allowed the principal inhabitants (the burgesses) to hold their plots of land freely and to sell, sublet or mortgage them at will. Exemption from payment of market tolls was another valued privilege. Historians came to realise, however, that borough status did not guarantee urban success. Some boroughs failed to develop and their economy remained predominantly agrarian; examples in the Midlands include Brailes in Warwickshire, Newborough in Staffordshire, and Mountsorrel in Leicestershire. Conversely, some places that lacked borough status nevertheless became flourishing commercial centres; among these successes were Downham Market and Wymondham in Norfolk, Eastbourne in Sussex, Rugby in Warwickshire, Rugeley in Staffordshire, and Loughborough, Market Harborough and Kettering in Leicestershire.[4]

This realisation has led to the adoption of an alternative definition of medieval towns, based on social and economic criteria. A town is now seen as a place with 'a relatively dense and permanent concentration of residents engaged in a multiplicity of activities, a substantial proportion of which are non-agrarian'.[5] Occupational diversity is now well established as the key urban characteristic. People living in towns pursued a variety of crafts and trades and offered a range of services; people living in rural settlements worked the land. This was true even of those living in market villages. Hundreds of market charters were granted in the thirteenth and early fourteenth century but they did not guarantee the development of an urban economy.[6] Apart from the weekly flurry of commercial activity, market villages remained wedded to agriculture.

The size of urban populations has also been increased as a result of recent research. London, with 80,000 and possibly as many as 100,000 inhabitants in 1300, was the only city in England to compare with great continental cities like Paris, Milan and Bruges, and far outstripped all other English towns. The provincial capitals of York, Norwich and Bristol had populations in the region of 20,000 and below them in the urban hierarchy came the major provincial towns, among them Winchester, Lincoln and Gloucester. In around 1300 the number of inhabitants of Winchester may have been as high as 10,000 but most provincial towns had populations of about 5,000. Major ports such as Newcastle-upon-Tyne, Sandwich and Southampton were of comparable size. The upper-ranking market towns contained 2,000 or more people, and at the bottom of the hierarchy stood the lesser market towns, many with populations numbered only in hundreds. There were about 50 towns with 2,000 or more inhabitants, and some 600 towns with populations below this figure.[7]

Some major towns stood on or close to the sites of Roman predecessors, although none could claim continuous occupation from Roman times. Other towns developed out of the trading centres (*wics*) that had been established on major rivers in the eighth and ninth centuries. A second phase of urbanization began in about 900, and in 1086 some 112 places with urban characteristics were listed in the Domesday Survey. The majority of towns were founded in the third period of urban growth, in the years between 1180 and 1250.[8]

Population figures provide a broad ranking order for medieval towns and occupational diversity corroborates a town's position in the hierarchy. The leading centres provided employment for people pursuing 70 or more different trades and were able to support physicians and lawyers, and merchants who traded in luxury products. People following between 20 and 40 occupations lived in the upper market towns; most inhabitants of the smaller market towns were artisans and petty traders who pursued between 15 and 20 different occupations. Taxable wealth, social structure and range of market contacts also help to place towns in the hierarchy, and material evidence adds to the picture. Since the 1970s the contribution of archaeologists and cartographers has greatly advanced our understanding of medieval towns. The largest places were encircled by walls and contained impressive stone buildings; their street patterns were complex and their market places large. Houses could be three or four storeys high and the grandest were furnished with tiled floors and stained-glass windows. Towns lower down the hierarchy had one or two main streets at most, small market places, and a single parish church. Dwellings were modest and public buildings unpretentious.

The concept of towns as 'central places' has also added to our understanding. Historians have borrowed this concept from geographers, who see towns as focal points within their region, with differing commercial, administrative and religious functions depending upon their size. The leading towns of medieval England served as episcopal seats, contained hospitals and schools, staged elaborate ceremonial, hosted regular sessions of the county court and occasional sessions of parliament. Middle-ranking towns served as hundredal centres and hosted sessions of the justices of the peace from time to time. All towns, large and small, acted as the marketing centres for their immediate rural hinterland, which extended to a radius of about six miles. It is possible that some agricultural produce from the small towns moved up through the urban system to the larger places and, conversely, that merchants based in the leading centres supplied manufactured goods to petty traders operating in the middle-ranking towns. The nature of marketing contacts between towns at different levels and of contacts between town and countryside is, as yet, imperfectly understood.

The 14 'chief towns' named by Robert of Gloucester in 1300 correspond well with the leading towns identified by modern historians. London came first in his list, York second, and Bristol seventh. Indeed, nine of his chief towns and six of those he named later are among the 23 'greater towns' in England listed in the *Cambridge Urban History*.[9] The monk's inclusion of Worcester, Cirencester and Hereford reveals an understandable western bias and also points to the maturity of the urban system in his region at the start of the fourteenth century. The work of Professor Dyer on the small towns has filled in the picture for us and the urban hierarchy of the West Midlands is well understood.[10] Studies of other regions suggest that urban patterns elsewhere in England were also well established by 1300. Many of these patterns are still recognisable today.[11]

Ten market towns have been identified with certainty in Cheshire, giving the county a density of one small town per 62,000 acres, well below the national median of one town per 49,000 acres. Kent, with one small town per 22,000 acres, was the most urbanized county in England and Cambridgeshire, with one small town per 112,000 acres, the least. The towns were unevenly distributed across the country for reasons that remain unclear. They were naturally scarce in thinly populated northern counties but it is not so easy to understand why there were relatively few towns in Nottinghamshire and Northamptonshire. Industrial development may have stimulated the growth of small towns and more towns were perhaps needed in regions where transport was impeded by steep hills and valleys. Alternative explanations connect the distribution of towns to the wealth of the agricultural resources of the area, or to the ambitions of local lords.[12]

Cheshire

Cheshire's ten successful towns emerged from the 22 places in the county which displayed urban characteristics at some point in the medieval period.[13] Each was a borough but among the failures were other places which had been granted borough status, including Halton, Over and Tarporley.[14] Halton lay at a distance from the river Mersey and off the main Chester to Warrington road; this unpromising location on the communications network probably hindered its progress. Over lay only four miles from Middlewich and was an over-optimistic foundation on the part of the lord, the abbot of Vale Royal. Tarporley occupied a favourable location, on a major road midway between Chester and Nantwich, and may perhaps have succeeded as a town but remains invisible to us because of shortage of source material. Tintwistle, in Cheshire's so-called 'pan handle' on the border with Yorkshire, may also have been omitted because of the accident of survival of sources.[15] Burton in Wirral has proved difficult to classify. It was never a borough but when it was granted a market and fair in the late 1290s, it numbered two merchants, two shoemakers, a mercer, a tailor and a smith among its inhabitants.[16] In the fifteenth century it served as an outport for Chester and saw the arrival and departure of traders from Ireland, Wales, the Isle of Man and Yorkshire. Such activity should have enabled Burton to thrive but there is no certain evidence that it became a functioning town. Indeed, it has been suggested that by 1500 Burton's market and fair had probably ceased to operate.[17]

Nantwich was almost certainly the largest of the market towns, as it was in the mid seventeenth century. Knutsford was very small and in 1294 contained just 38 burgages; its population must have been in the low hundreds. The original number of burgages granted out in Stockport in 1260 may have been 60 and there were 93 by 1483, after the creation of additional burgages on one or more subsequent occasions.[18] Frodsham, with 110 burgages, and Macclesfield, with 120 burgages, were slightly larger and the remaining market towns may have been of comparable size.[19] Populations increased as burgages were divided and occupied by newcomers who were not burgesses.

Cheshire, as a county palatine, did not pay parliamentary taxes after 1290 and was therefore excluded from the tax lists of 1334, 1377–81 and 1522–5, the

FIGURE 1.1. The small
towns of Cheshire and
north-eastern Wales. The
Gough Map (*c.*1360)
represented and named
Macclesfield, [ ]wych
(probably Nantwich) and
[Over]ton. Northwich
was perhaps represented
but not named.

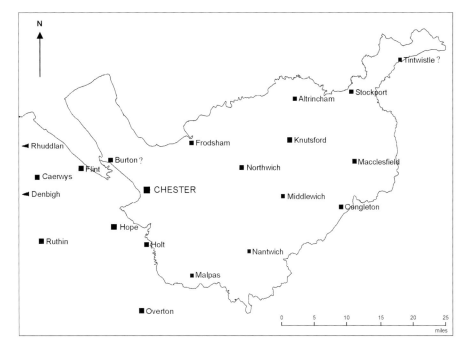

sources used by historians to calculate population size and taxable wealth. Cheshire's own system of taxation, the mize, was established shortly after 1346 and remained fixed at that level in succeeding years. The mize therefore recorded the taxable wealth of individual townships just before the Black Death.[20] England had enjoyed a long period of growth in the twelfth and thirteenth centuries but this ended in the early fourteenth century. A series of bad harvests produced famine in the years 1315–18 and a severe cattle plague in the early 1320s hampered recovery. Demand for manufactured and traded goods fell and urban economies suffered.[21] The mize figures may well reflect this period of crisis. There are problems of interpretation but it seems that Nantwich may have been the wealthiest market town in the mid fourteenth century, with Knutsford and Altrincham at the bottom of the hierarchy.[22] The Black Death in 1348–9 may have reduced the population by 50 per cent.

Domesday Book recorded industrial activity at Nantwich, Northwich and Middlewich but as this focused exclusively on salt extraction the three places were then no more than proto-urban settlements. Stockport's place-name – 'market-place at a hamlet' – indicates that a market was held there by the twelfth century and probably during the Anglo-Saxon period, long before the grant of the borough charter in 1260.[23] Commercial activity at Macclesfield may also date back to the pre-Conquest period, when the place was an important comital estate centre. The large triangular area now known as Park Green possibly originated as a market place fronting the manorial hall, at the junction of the roads from Stockport, Leek and Congleton. The original borough charter of about 1220 does not survive and the confirmation charter granted in 1261 made no mention of a market or fair so it is possible that they were long-established and held by prescriptive right.[24] Borough charters for most of Cheshire's successful towns date from the thirteenth century, several of them after 1260. In other parts of England urbanization came somewhat earlier, with the years between 1180 and 1250 witnessing the greaglyntest period of growth. An early foundation was one of the factors that determined whether a place would develop into a successful town. Other factors included a favourable position on the communications system, a site at the junction of different farming regions or *pays*, and one or more 'central-place' functions.

Each of Cheshire's market towns lay astride an important road. Nantwich, for example, was on the main road from London to Chester and doubtless owed some of its prosperity to its role as a thoroughfare town. Among the most notable travellers was Richard II, who passed through with Bolingbroke in August 1399, *en route* for London and deposition. The duke of Bedford's bearward was there in 1415 and was attacked by a large number of townsmen.[25] Stockport developed at an important crossing point over the Mersey, where the main road to Manchester intersected with a major trans-Pennine route from Yorkshire. Its bridge was probably built in the late thirteenth century and, with Warrington, was one of only two bridging points over the Mersey until a bridge was built near Stretford in the early sixteenth century.[26] In 1463 the duke of Norfolk and his entourage spent 11s on two meals in the town, on their way from Pontefract (Yorkshire) via Tintwistle to Holt (Denbighshire). They continued their journey through Didsbury to Northwich, where they spent almost 12s on food and gave 4d to the fiddler who provided entertainment.[27] The place-name Malpas means 'difficult passage' and in *c*.1360 the road south from Chester to Shrewsbury avoided the town and followed a more westerly route through Overton and Ellesmere. When William of Worcester rode from Bristol to Chester in the late 1470s, however, his route from Shrewsbury went via Whitchurch and Malpas.[28]

A number of indicators in addition to size and taxable wealth point to Nantwich's pre-eminence among Cheshire's small towns. The church, actually a chapel of ease within the parish of Acton, was built on an impressive scale and in *c*.1400 handsome choir stalls were added, with misericords similar to those at St Werburgh's abbey in Chester, albeit carried out by a more provincial team of carvers.[29] St Anne's chapel and four adjacent shops stood next to the bridge and there were two hospitals, the only ones recorded in any small Cheshire town.[30] Nantwich was also the only town apart from Chester where sales of wine were attested. A shop with buildings above and below on the corner of *le fleshrowe* in 1393–4 indicates commercial zoning, as do lost street names including *Melestrete*, *Floureslane*, *Barberslone* and *le Rethermarket* (beast market).[31] The town's mercers and drapers purchased high-quality cloth at Chester, some of which they sold in the smaller centres, including Macclesfield more than 20 miles to the north-east. Traders from larger places did business in Nantwich: a Ludlow draper in 1383, for example, and a Northampton glover in 1488.[32] Cartloads of skins were bought and sold at the Saturday market and at the St Bartholomew fair; this lasted for six days, twice as long as fairs in other towns. Goldsmiths worked in Nantwich and a bonnetmaker was recorded in the 1490s.[33] A study of 400 merchants and craftsmen named in the county court records in the years 1415–25 has shown that almost half came from Chester and that 42 came from Nantwich, more than twice the number from any other market town. Among them were an ironmonger, a grocer, a skinner, a barber and two drapers.[34] Throughout the fifteenth century men from Nantwich were indicted at the county court in larger numbers and more frequently than men from other places and it is clear that the town was particularly prone to outbreaks of violence. Townsmen also enjoyed gentler pursuits. One prominent inhabitant in 1429 owned a book recounting the exploits of Richard the Lionheart.[35]

The other nine towns could be described as lesser market towns and no evidence allows us to place them in ranking order. Stockport perhaps had fewer inhabitants than Macclesfield and Frodsham but it may have ranked more highly in terms of taxable wealth. Other indicators boost its position in the urban hierarchy. There was evidently a vigorous leather-working industry and textile workers included dyers (heusters) who needed expensive raw materials. In 1387 quantities of madder and alum were stolen in the town, together with pepper and saffron. Stockport was sufficiently prosperous to support medical practitioners and goldsmiths; coin clipping and false moneying took place. The town's location enabled its merchants to participate in long-distance trade with Ireland, exporting woollen cloth from Yorkshire and importing linen yarn and cloth. Leading mercantile families lived in timber-framed houses like the three-

FIGURE 1.2. 'The Mapp of Stockport Town', about 1680. This is the earliest plan of the town and shows the church, the market place, the site of the castle and the bridge over the Mersey, known as Lancashire Bridge by the early 16th century. Staircase House occupied a fairly central position on the north side of the market place.

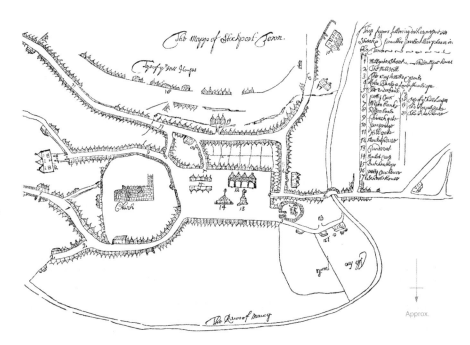

Town	Domesday entry	Charter	Castle	Road/ river	c.1600
Altrincham	-	c.1290	-	y	y
Congleton	y	1272–1274	-	y	y
Frodsham	y	1208–1215	y	y	y
Knutsford	y	c.1292	-	y	y
Macclesfield	y	c.1220	-	y	y
Malpas	[Depenbach]	c.1280	y	y	y
Middlewich	y	1288	-	y	y
Nantwich	y	by 1319–20	y	y	y
Northwich	y	1288	y	y	y
Stockport	-	c.1260	y	y	y

bay Staircase House built in the 1460s on the north side of the market place and which occupied a plot half as wide again as some of its neighbours.[36]

TABLE 1.1 Small towns in Cheshire. (y = yes)

Macclesfield developed at the interface between the Pennine foothills to the east and the Cheshire plain to the west, and served as a centre of exchange for the products of the two contrasting agricultural regions. The borough was sited on the hill to the north of the early medieval manorial centre, at the junction of important north-south and east-west routeways, and was depicted on the Gough Map of c.1360. It was the centre of Macclesfield hundred and the focus of the extensive royal manor and forest of Macclesfield. Edward I and his queen visited the town several times in the late thirteenth century and the queen was instrumental in the enlargement of the town's chapel. The presence of royal officials in later decades – overseeing the Black Prince's horse-breeding enterprise in the park for example – enhanced the status of the town.[37] In the fifteenth century between 20 and 25 occupations were recorded, slightly above the average for a lesser market town. Three roads converged on the central market place, which was flanked on one side by the chapel and on another by the hall of pleas newly erected in 1358–9 using timbers from the house of a disgraced royal servant.[38] Sessions of the borough, manor and hundred courts were held in the upper storey of the hall and below were a dozen or more shops, each rented out for between 6d and 2s a year. Facing them across the market place in the fifteenth century were more shops and three taverns within a structure known as 'the garrets'. Behind those buildings stood a large fortified mansion so imposing that later generations believed (wrongly) that it had once been a castle. Between 20 and 30 market stalls were set up each Monday and grain, foodstuffs, animal hides and fuel were sold, as well as cheap cloth and shoes. Stallage revenues and market tolls fell in the early decades of the fifteenth century and tenants for the shops proved hard to find. In 1448–9 all three taverns stood empty, a truly sobering demonstration of urban decline.[39]

Drapers and 'frysers' worked at Congleton in the 1430s, and red woollen cloth was sold there. The town's mercers traded in Macclesfield, which apparently had no mercers of its own.[40] The inventory of a Malpas mercer drawn up in 1371 reveals the wide range of goods then available in that town: linen cloth, Welsh cloth, blanket, muslin, kerchiefs, green thread, saffron, alum, hides, and two mirrors worth 1d. The indictment of Malpas schoolmaster John Bruyn in 1426 for assaulting a local chaplain raises the possibility that a school may have been associated with the church at that time.[41] By the mid fourteenth century the commercial centre of Middlewich contained a number of butchers' shops and a hall with 12 stalls rented by various merchants. In the 1360s annual revenues from the shops and the hall with its stallage approached £3 but declined sharply in the following decades. By 1414–15 the 'Bothehall' also served as a courthouse and, like the common oven, was in urgent need of repair.[42] From the 1420s a plot of land measuring 40 feet by 12 feet next to the 'Motehalle' was leased for 6s 8d a year, and seven shops produced rental income of about 18s. In subsequent decades, as at Macclesfield, shops stood empty because no-one wanted to lease them and revenues fell.[43] Evidence for other small towns is hard to find. In the 1420s John the leech of Altrincham saved a man's life by staunching a serious wound, and a dyer was recorded at Knutsford. A serious disturbance at Knutsford's fair on 29 June 1422, the feast of the apostles Peter and Paul, was witnessed by some 200 people.[44]

North-east Wales

Towns in north-east Wales lay within Chester's economic hinterland and were closely linked to the city. The county of Flint, newly created in 1284 by the Statute of Rhuddlan, incorporated the cantref of Tegeingl (Englefield), the land of Hope, the land between Rhuddlan and Chester, and Maelor Saesneg (English Maelor). Flintshire was attached to Cheshire for administrative purposes and controlled by a justice based in Chester.[45] Towns in Welsh Maelor and eastern Denbighshire also looked to Chester, which was far larger than any town in north Wales. Chester's own records indicate regular contacts as far west as Denbigh and Ruthin, and as far south as Wrexham.

Many of the towns in north-east Wales were founded in the late thirteenth century. The construction of the castle and *bastide* at Flint began in 1277 and borough status was granted in 1284; the castle and borough of Denbigh were planned in the early 1280s and a charter granted in 1285.[46] Ruthin was already a prosperous administrative centre in 1277 when it was taken by Edward I and the construction of the castle begun. It became a borough in 1282, soon after Dyffryn Clwyd was granted to Reynold de Grey, trusted military commander of the English king.[47] Overton was created a free borough in 1292 and 57 taxpayers were recorded but evidently not all burgage plots were taken up. The following year Grey, now justice of Chester, was ordered to assign to the burgesses or to those who wished to become inhabitants competent lands within the demesnes of Overton castle and timber from the royal forest to build

FIGURE 1.3. Aerial photograph of Flint taken in 1956. The original grid layout of the plantation borough is clearly visible. Eight parallel streets ran down towards the castle and Castle Street and Church Street formed the main axis of the town, leading directly to the outer gate of the castle. Recent development has unfortunately destroyed many of the early streets.

their new houses. They were also given land to cultivate and were to be free of the fee-farm payment to the Crown for the first ten years. The place suffered much destruction during the revolt of Madog ap Llywelyn two years later but it benefited from its location on an important road and residents in the early fourteenth century included Thomas the taverner.[48]

Edward I proclaimed that all burgesses in the new boroughs were to be of English birth but it was common for a minority of early burgesses to be Welsh. At Flint in 1292 three of 70 known burgesses had Welsh names and 22 of the 57 at Overton.[49] Caerwys, midway between Flint and Rhuddlan, received a charter in 1290 and was unusual in that it was always a predominantly Welsh town. At Ruthin in 1324 one third of the 70 burgesses were Welsh, largely grouped together in Welsh Street. Two years later two of the town's tailors and all eleven of its butchers were Welsh.[50] Welsh townsmen shared the trading interests of their English neighbours and prospered as they did. Their reaction to the crisis provoked by Glyn Dŵr's rebellion in the early fifteenth century would have been complex and their loyalties divided.[51] The rebel attacks on Caerwys, Flint, Hope, Holt and Overton contributed to the decline of those towns, and although borough revenues at Denbigh showed signs of economic recovery by the mid 1420s they never again matched the levels of the late fourteenth century.[52] Ruthin's leading officials entered 'truces or agreements of neutrality' with Glyn Dŵr in or before 1409 and the town developed into a significant commercial centre in later decades, with flourishing cloth and shoemaking industries. A weavers' guild was established in 1447 and a shoemakers' guild existed by 1496.[53] Ruthin may have contained only some 70 to 90 families in the later medieval period but the town had a grammar school in 1378 and a bookbinder was recorded in 1493.[54]

Chester

Chester dominated the urban hierarchy of medieval Cheshire and its influence extended beyond the county boundary. It had no rivals closer than Preston to the north, Derby to the east and Shrewsbury to the south, and served as the regional capital of the north-western plain. The city was small in comparison with the great regional capitals of York, Bristol and Norwich and its hinterland less wealthy but its status was enhanced by a number of factors. First and foremost was its role as administrative centre of the palatinate. The castle housed the exchequer and law courts and the large body of officials which staffed them. Cheshire gentlemen and their families were drawn to this mini-Westminster for reasons of business and pleasure and their presence stimulated the urban economy. Chester was also an ecclesiastical capital of some importance. Although its role as seat of a bishopric lasted only from 1075 until 1102 when the see was transferred to Coventry, later bishops continued to style themselves bishops of Chester and maintained a house in the precinct of St John's, the former cathedral. The archdeaconry of Chester enjoyed a semi-independent status and the archdeacon was pre-eminent among the archdeacons of the medieval diocese. The city's religious houses included a wealthy Benedictine abbey, a Benedictine nunnery, three friaries and two hospitals.

Chester regularly served as an important military base. Armies *en route* to Wales or Ireland assembled in or near the city and supplies of foodstuffs, weapons and other military equipment were collected there. This military role was of particular significance during the campaigns against Wales in the late thirteenth century but expeditions to Ireland set out from Chester until the late seventeenth century and a garrison was always maintained in the castle. Chester was a major west-coast port, second only to Bristol in the late medieval period. Its overseas trade was largely restricted to the Irish Sea region but good profits could be made from fish, furs and animal hides. The city acted as a distributive centre for fish, attracting traders from as far south as Worcestershire, and in the thirteenth and early fourteenth century it served as an entrepôt for grain and malt. The scale of malt production made brewing a significant industry. The city's craftsmen produced a wide range of goods and Chester became a major centre for craft manufacture. It also served as a market with an extensive hinterland encompassing west Cheshire and north-east Wales.

The most recent estimates of Chester's medieval population indicate that it was larger than once was thought. There were perhaps up to 3,000 inhabitants in 1066 and 2,000 or more in 1086. Had it been included in the 1377 poll tax then Chester may have been placed around 33rd among English towns, with a population of 4,000 or possibly as high as 4,600.[55] The list of contributors to a tax levied by the city's mayor in 1463 should have allowed us to estimate the population with more certainty. Unfortunately this proves not to be the case. The list survives only in a seventeenth-century transcript and is clearly incomplete. A total of 528 householders were named, 13 of them women.[56] If exempt households are added, the total number of households in Chester in 1463 rises to some 800, amounting to around 3,200 people if the average household size was four, or about 4,000 if it was five. It has been argued that a higher multiplier is required for towns than for villages, because most urban households either employed servants or provided accommodation for lodgers, and wealthier establishments could number up to ten or twelve individuals.[57] If allowance is made for the omissions from the tax list and for the households containing more than five individuals, then Chester's population in 1463 certainly exceeded 4,000. In the 1520s, after serious epidemics of plague in 1506–7 and 1517–18, Chester was among 16 towns with 3,500–5,000 inhabitants. Had the city contributed to the lay subsidy of 1524–5 it may have ranked 23rd among English towns, with a taxable wealth equal to that of Hereford or Lincoln.[58]

Chester's name reveals its Roman origins. Until the eleventh century English speakers called the place 'Legacaestir', the 'fortress-city of the legions'; thereafter it became known simply as 'Chester', *the* Chester, because of its political and commercial importance. From the fourteenth century the alternative name 'Westchester' underlined the city's role as regional capital and principal port of north-western England.[59]

The Romans first established a permanent presence at Chester in the early 70s, building their fortress on a sandstone ridge above the river Dee.[60] The chosen location commanded the river crossing to the south and the natural harbour to the west, in the area now occupied by the Roodee racecourse. It is possible that the original plan was to use Chester as the main base from which to launch campaigns for the conquest of Ireland. The exceptionally large size of the fortress, and unusual features such as its impressive curtain wall and the group of 'special' buildings at its centre, have led to the suggestion that the original intention had been to make Chester the headquarters of the provincial governor. The withdrawal of troops from Scotland and the abandonment of further campaigns of conquest in the late 80s meant that such a plan never materialised. Roman Chester served as a legionary base for some 300 years although there were long periods when many of the fighting troops were absent, leaving only a small garrison to oversee a depot manufacturing and repairing military equipment. Civilian settlements developed outside the fortress on all except its northern side, and the main commercial area appears to have been outside the east gate, close to the amphitheatre and parade ground. By the end of the first century houses, shops and taverns lined the approach road for a distance of 200–300 metres and industrial activities such as metal-working were carried out in yards and workshops to the rear. Bricks and tiles were produced in the vicinity of City Road.

The Romans left Chester for the last time towards the end of the fourth century but the place was not abandoned by the civilian population. The defensive circuit offered security, the commercial centre may have remained important, and Chester perhaps served as the administrative centre of a sub-Roman principality. In the early seventh century it may have played a similar role for a territory associated with the British kingdom of Powys and which encompassed Cheshire and north-east Wales. It was evidently an important ecclesiastical centre and in *c*.600 was chosen as the venue for a synod of the British church. A late tradition records that St John's church was founded by the Mercian king Æthelred in the closing decades of the century. Some years later, in 731, Bede called Chester 'city (*civitas*) of the legions' but although he was evidently well aware of its Roman origins he had nothing to add about its later history. The five centuries that followed the departure of the Romans still remain largely impenetrable and nothing certain is known of the place before the late ninth century.

A Viking raid on the site in 893 indicates the growing importance of Chester, which lay close to the route linking the Scandinavian kingdoms of Dublin and York. There was settlement in the area to the south of the fortress and it seems likely that a mint was operating within the walls in the 890s. The documented history of Chester begins in 907, when the chronicles record the refortification of the site by the Lady Æthelflæd, then ruler of Mercia, at the outset of her campaign against the Danes. Chester was the first of a string of forts (*burhs*) built to protect the northern frontier of Mercia and which eventually extended

FIGURE 1.4. The hypocaust of a chamber attached to the south side of the legionary exercise hall as revealed in 1863. These and other collapsed Roman buildings blocked later development behind the eastern side of Bridge Street.

from north-east Wales to Manchester. The exact nature of the refortification is not known. The most recent study suggests that the Roman walls were repaired where they survived largely intact and that serious breaches were closed with a timber palisade. The north and east walls may have been extended to the river by the construction of earth ramparts, thereby forming an L-shaped enclave protected by the Dee which would have given protection to those living outside the Roman defences in the area of Lower Bridge Street.[61]

Late Anglo-Saxon Chester was the administrative centre of the district responsible for the maintenance of the *burh*. The shire was in existence by 980 and had perhaps originated in the early tenth century. The shire court held its sessions at Chester and there was an exceptionally productive mint, in the early and middle tenth century rivalling London in importance. It was perhaps based in the Roman headquarters building which offered secure storage facilities for the large quantities of bullion required. The mint's output suggests considerable trading activity. Chester was an important regional market for agricultural produce and also a centre for sea-borne trade, particularly with Dublin. The Hiberno-Norse community which handled this trade lived to the south of the legionary fortress near the early harbour. Chester was also an ecclesiastical centre of some importance, with two minsters by 1066. St Werburgh's housed the relics of St Werburg, perhaps brought to Chester at the instigation of Æthelflæd, and royal benefactions ensured that the minster became very wealthy, with a precinct probably occupying the north-eastern quarter of the Roman fortress. The minster of St John's was smaller and lay outside the walls, but by 1066 its precinct contained the subsidiary minster of St Mary's and possibly a hermitage as well.[62]

At the time of the Conquest Chester had three lords, king, bishop and earl, the last of whom wielded most influence. It was a thriving town with perhaps 3,000 inhabitants and rendered a fixed annual payment (fee farm) to the king and the earl of £45 and three timbers of marten pelts (120 skins). There were seven moneyers, indicating that the mint remained important. Chester had its own laws and customs, and offences were dealt with in the city's hundredal court. Those who caused an outbreak of fire were fined and required to give 2s to their neighbour; those who brewed bad ale were either fined or put in the cucking-stool. Overseas trade played a significant role in the economy. Ships entering and leaving the port required a licence from the king; he also had the right of pre-emption of marten skins. Tolls were imposed on out-going cargoes at the rate of 4d per load but incoming cargoes were not subject to tolls, possibly because they included corn, much needed in a city with an unproductive hinterland. Chester in 1066 was the largest settlement in the area and the leading town in western Mercia. Although not among the top-ranking English towns, it was a provincial capital.[63]

The city's close links with the earls of Mercia resulted in its involvement in the rising of 1069–70. Reprisals were swift and savage. William I came with his army and inflicted much destruction; 205 of the city's 487 houses were demolished, some of them to make way for the motte and bailey castle constructed south-west of the Roman fortress.[64] When the Norman earl Hugh was granted the city in 1071 he found it 'greatly wasted'; the value of the farm had fallen to £30 and the population had declined by a third. Ultimately the advent of the Normans proved advantageous. Chester became the *caput* of the new Anglo-Norman earldom, with an enhanced military and administrative role. The earls themselves were not often resident but their leading officials – the justice, two chamberlains and principal clerks – frequently lived in the city, together with large numbers of supporters and servants, and their presence attracted the county élite. The advent of the Normans also initiated important ecclesiastical developments. St John's became the seat of a bishopric in 1075 and retained cathedral status until 1102. Additional buildings in its precinct included the chapel of St James and houses for the bishop and archdeacon. The minster of St Werburgh's was refounded as a Benedictine monastery in 1092, and a Benedictine nunnery was established in the mid twelfth century. The leper hospital of St Giles at Boughton was also founded at that time, and the hospital of St John the Baptist outside the Northgate had been established by *c.*1200. All nine parish churches had been founded by the late twelfth century.[65]

The economy of the twelfth-century city was based on brewing, milling and fishing, and on industrial activities such as leather-working and potting. External trade was of crucial importance. William of Malmesbury noted in *c.*1125 that goods were exchanged with Ireland and that the 'toil of merchants' supplied the corn that could not be grown locally. Some 70 years later the local monk Lucian also praised the 'labour and skill of the merchants' whose efforts, together with God's guidance, enabled ships from Aquitaine, Spain, Ireland and Germany to bring cargoes to the city's harbour.[66] He singled out wine as the pre-eminent import but cereals were doubtless of more significance for most townspeople. Goods exported to Ireland probably included salt and pottery.

Chester was the base for campaigns against the Welsh in the late eleventh and twelfth century and, after 1164, for expeditions to Ireland. Henry II visited Chester in 1165 and his son John was there in 1186. Earl Ranulph III (1181–1232) may have been brought up in Chester and perhaps planned to make it the centre of an independent principality.[67] This ambition remained unfulfilled and after the death of his successor in 1237 the earldom was annexed by the Crown. Earlier visits by English kings had made them aware of the city's importance and royal interest grew in subsequent years. In 1241 Henry III made his first visit to the city, *en route* to and from Rhuddlan to receive the submission of the prince of Gwynedd. His stay at Chester castle evidently inaugurated a programme of refurbishment. A great 'oriel' (a vestibule or covered entrance) was built at the door of the royal chapel and the exquisite wall paintings in the chapel itself may date from that time. A keen patron of wall paintings, Henry ordered the renewal of those in the queen's chamber in 1245.[68] The king was again on his way to Wales, accompanied by a large army, and the supplies needed for the campaign were assembled at Chester. Peas, beans, bacon, cheese, salmon, venison, wine, tallow, wax, pickaxes, hoes, hempen yarn, cables, tanned hides (for slings), quarrels, lead, steel, iron and horseshoes were dispatched to Chester from all over the country. Large sums of money were sent from Ireland and stored in the castle and the abbey. The wardrobe, which administered the royal finances, was temporarily established in the city.[69]

Henry III's military expeditions undoubtedly stimulated Chester's economy and royal interest evidently prompted a growing awareness of civic identity. The office of mayor had perhaps originated in the 1190s when Ranulph III granted the city a guild merchant, but until the mid thirteenth century the mayor ranked below the two sheriffs. From the mid 1240s the mayor became increasingly important. At about this time there was mention of a keeper of the merchants' mark at Chester, paid 9s 2d a year.[70] The first recorded grants of pavage and murage were awarded in 1246 and 1249; the first common hall was perhaps built just before 1250.

In 1254 Henry gave his son Edward, newly created earl of Chester, the county of Chester and the lands in Wales held by the king since 1247, after the submission of the Welsh princes

at the treaty of Woodstock. Edward first visited Chester in 1256 and received the homage and fealty of the nobles of Cheshire and the men of north Wales. A rising in Wales began that year and in 1257 the Welsh reached Chester. Henry and Edward responded by organizing a military campaign in the late summer and Chester once again served as a supply base. The wardrobe was again established in the city and provisions, tents and munitions were assembled there. The English forces achieved very little and by 1258 political difficulties in England precluded further campaigns. That year Llywelyn ap Gruffudd first used the title of prince of Wales. England was engulfed by political turmoil during the Barons' Wars of 1258–65 and during this time Chester was held for the Lord Edward by the justice William la Zouche. In 1264 Zouche began a defensive ditch outside the north wall, destroying in the process houses in Bag Lane belonging to St Werburgh's, but to no avail. City and county were given to Simon de Montfort and in 1265 Simon's son arrived to receive homage from the citizens and the men of the shire. Llywelyn declared his support for de Montfort, receiving in return recognition of his position as prince of Wales and of the lands he had gained. Later that year, however, de Montfort

FIGURE 1.5. The castle mound is the only survival of the motte and bailey castle founded by William I in 1070. The Flag Tower was built on the site of the early keep in the early 13th century. The bailey was probably co-extensive with the later inner ward and the Agricola Tower, built *c.*1210 as the gatehouse and chapel, also survives (not shown).

was defeated and killed at the battle of Evesham and a peace settlement was negotiated with Llywelyn. His title of prince of Wales was acknowledged and his territorial gains were recognised in the treaty of Montgomery in 1267. He in return acknowledged that he owed fealty and homage to Henry III and agreed to pay 25,000 marks in annual instalments. Payments were made to royal representatives at St Werburgh's abbey until 1270 but thereafter Llywelyn refused to pay. He repeatedly ignored summonses to meet Edward and in 1275 failed to appear at Chester to make his submission to Edward, now king.[71] War was inevitable and Chester was on the brink of the period of its greatest prosperity.

Chester 1275–1520

This book aims to describe life in Chester over a period of almost two and a half centuries. It begins with the city poised to become a place of national significance and ends at the close of the 'long' fifteenth century when royal interest had waned and Chester's importance was limited to its relatively underdeveloped region. Many changes occurred over the period. The pendulum of economic fortunes swung from the peak of prosperity in the late thirteenth and early fourteenth century to severe depression and slump in the 1440s, and to a limited recovery by the end of the century. For most of the later medieval period Chester was the most important west-coast port after Bristol but Liverpool began to emerge as a rival in the 1490s. Crafts came and went. Lorimers, who made horse-bits and metal mountings for bridles, may have had their own trading area, Lorimers' Row, in the twelfth century but had more or less vanished from the city by c.1350. Feltcappers and apothecaries appeared in the 1460s and 1470s, and bookbinders and organ-makers in the early sixteenth century.

Chester's townspeople adopted the changes in fashion that swept the country after 1350. Clothes became more tightly fitting and the doublet and hose became the standard male attire; girdles or belts became fashionable accessories for women.[72] The striped fabrics evidently in vogue in the early fourteenth century fell out of favour. From the 1480s there was a decided preference for violet and purple.[73] Relations with the Welsh fluctuated over the period. The local monk Lucian, writing at the end of the twelfth century, although noting that his fellow Cestrians much resembled the Welsh, described attitudes of mutual distrust. The citizens scorned their Welsh neighbours, driven by hunger and cold to haunt the city for supplies; the Welsh for their part nurtured bitter feelings of envy towards the citizens.[74] Regular trading contacts gradually improved relationships and many Welsh migrated to the city in later decades. Edward's wars in the 1270s and 1280s and Glyn Dŵr's revolt at the start of the fifteenth century inevitably produced tensions. In 1403 Chester's authorities were required to expel all Welsh residents and to impose a curfew on Welsh visitors, threatening those who stayed overnight with execution.[75] These were the most extreme measures proclaimed in any English city yet within a year or two men of Welsh descent held high civic office and thereafter the Welsh always formed a significant percentage of the urban community.

Many features remained constant over the years. Chester retained its position as regional capital and administrative centre of the palatinate. Trade continued to play a vital role in the urban economy and trade with Ireland remained crucial, with fish and animal hides always the major imports. The layout of the legionary fortress was recognisable in the street plan of the medieval city. In the Roman period the main commercial and industrial area was located in the civilian settlement outside the east gate; the eastern suburb was the main focus of commerce and industry in the Middle Ages. Bricks and tiles were produced in the vicinity of Cow Lane (Frodsham Street) in Roman times; tiles and tableware were produced on a site east of Cow Lane in the late thirteenth century; the Tile houses stood next to Cow Lane in the 1490s.[76]

Any study of medieval Chester is handicapped by the city's exemption from national taxation. The city's exclusion from the poll taxes of the late fourteenth century and from the lay subsidies of the early sixteenth century makes it impossible to assess its population, and there are no helpful lists naming taxpayers with their occupations. Earlier scholars were gloomy. In 1956 W. G. Hoskins considered that it was impossible to form any certain idea of Chester's economic importance; in 1973 M. W. Beresford and H. P. R. Finberg declared that the palatinate's own surviving records 'did not make up the deficiency.'[77] Their pessimism was misplaced, as is clearly shown by the extensive treatment of medieval Chester in the two volumes recently published by the *Victoria County History*.[78] These scholarly volumes provide the definitive account of the medieval city and will be the point of reference for years to come.

This book has different aims. Professor Palliser has urged us to remember that medieval towns were communities of people and has suggested that, while not ignoring constitutional matters, we should give townspeople central place.[79] The detailed records of proceedings at Chester's local courts, which survive from the 1290s, allow us to do just that. Like all court rolls, they are voluminous yet laconic and they are difficult records to organize. Where they exist, as G. H. Martin advised, they should be 'at the heart of a borough's archives'.[80] Chester's court rolls introduce us to the ordinary men and women who lived in the late medieval city: women like the tapster Alice Dewe whose working life began with the purchase of red cloth (for an eyecatching outfit perhaps) in 1427 and ended 30 years later when she defaulted on a debt; and men like the tailor John Man, a 'neighbour from hell' in the area of Cow Lane throughout the 1480s, stealing, arguing, allowing his pigs to roam, and eventually hanged for theft in 1490. Court rolls have the potential to illuminate social relations in the urban community at an obscure and fascinating neighbourhood level. Personal relationships and the significance of kinship in urban society feature prominently among the issues addressed in this book.

CHAPTER TWO

The Historical Background 1275–1520

Chester's military and political importance was at its height during Edward I's wars against Wales and the city enjoyed its greatest prosperity in the late thirteenth and early fourteenth century. Preparations for the first campaign against Llywelyn began in 1275. Chester was to serve as a major supply base and in November 1276 the earl of Warwick, captain of the king's munitions in Cheshire, was assigned quarters in the castle and authorized to make purveyances. The 'furtherance of the arduous affairs in Wales' required considerable amounts of money and by May 1277 the royal wardrobe was established in the city. Merchants from Ireland were asked to bring provisions and assured of speedy payment, and writs went out to the sheriffs of nine counties to send grain; wine was put in store for the king's use.[1] In July Edward and his troops arrived in the city and ships from the Cinque Ports sailed into the Dee estuary. The army advanced to Conwy via Flint, Rhuddlan and Deganwy, and a contingent reached Anglesey and carried away the harvest. Edward had not intended a campaign of conquest and was willing to accept Llywelyn's offer of surrender. By September the king was back in Chester and in November the peace terms were set out in the treaty of Aberconwy. Castles were built in the aftermath of the campaign: at Flint and at Rhuddlan in north-east Wales, and at Builth and Aberystwyth further south.[2]

When the Welsh rebelled in April 1282 a war of conquest was inevitable. Three military commands were established in the marches, the northernmost at Chester under the command of Reynold de Grey, reappointed justice in 1281. The wardrobe was moved to the city once again and some £38,000 was sent to Chester during the course of the war, this time organized on an unprecedented scale. Foodstuffs were requested from 17 English counties and additional supplies came from Ireland and Gascony. In May 1282 proclamations were made in London and elsewhere asking merchants to bring their goods to Chester. Corn from Ireland had been dried and stored in cellars in the city during the war of 1277 and in 1282–3 the city again served as a major storage depot.[3] Large quantities of weapons and equipment were sent to Chester and workmen assembled there, including 345 carpenters and 1,010 diggers required to build fortifications and dig roads.

The king arrived in June 1282, accompanied by the royal court and chancery. He took over the cavalry, perhaps 600 strong by the end of the month, and advanced into north Wales together with the foot soldiers. Initial success was followed by setbacks, but Llywelyn was killed in battle near Builth in December and by March 1283, after campaigns in Snowdonia, Edward was able to establish his headquarters at Conwy. He returned to Chester after the victory and on 26 May, together with his queen, heard mass at St Werburgh's and offered a valuable cloth.[4] He paid a further visit to the city in the following year, on his way to Wales. The constant comings and goings provided a wealth of commercial opportunities and Chester bustled with activity. The Dee millers ground 1,752 quarters of wheat for the king's use in seven months in 1282–3, for example, and local cartwrights repaired the household's carts.[5] Thirty horses were stabled at the castle in August 1283, including the king's destrier (warhorse), the horse ridden by the queen, and ten great horses from Caernarfon. Grass and litter were purchased daily, and other requirements included cord, canvas, horseshoes and cresset lamps for the stables. In the twelve months from November 1283 up to 65 horses at a time were stabled at the castle and more than £250 was spent on their upkeep. Particular care was lavished on the destriers, extremely valuable animals worth £80 each. Élite citizens who had served as mayor or sheriff supplied goods and so to did the city's craftsmen. Among them were Robert the lorimer who produced

FIGURE 2.1. Finds along the north Wirral shoreline near Meols in the 19th century included Edwardian pennies and 36 crossbow bolts, the majority of them dating from the 13th and 14th centuries. They were perhaps associated with increased military activity during Edward I's Welsh campaigns. (Scale in centimetres)

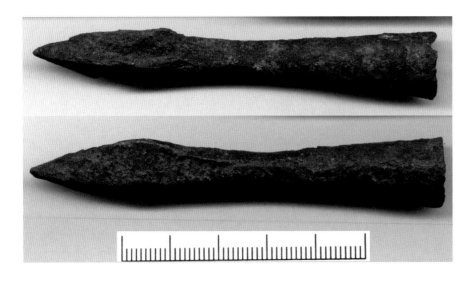

halters and former sheriff Robert of Tarvin who provided blue material for saddle cloths. Litter was purchased from the cellarer of St Werburgh's and in October 1284, when a black warhorse needed a dressing for a leg infection, a monk from the abbey supplied ale, vinegar and olive oil.[6]

Edward consolidated his victory by ringing Snowdonia with castles. Construction work began in March 1283 at Conwy and a few weeks later at Harlech and Caernarfon. Progress was rapid. When the king and queen visited Caernarfon the following spring the Eagle Tower had possibly been completed to first-floor level and their son Edward was perhaps born there on 25 April 1284, as tradition maintains.[7] A decade later, in September 1294, revolt erupted throughout Wales. The new town walls at Caernarfon were thrown down and the castle was put to the flame. Edward's response was swift. Military bases were established at Chester, Cardiff and Brecon and some 35,000 troops were mustered. The greatest danger was in the north and Edward, who had arrived in Chester before 5 December, reached Conwy by Christmas. Government business was carried out there, with provisions arriving by sea. In March 1295 the king commanded his clerk to instruct Chester's mayor and bailiffs to assemble all the city's brewsters (*totes les braceresses*) and order them to brew good ale for him and his army. The supplies were to be shipped to Conwy with all possible speed.[8]

The rebellion began to crumble in the winter of 1294–5 and by April the English had reoccupied the south-eastern coast of Anglesey. Work immediately started on a new castle at Beaumaris and when complete victory was achieved a few weeks later the rebuilding of the town and castle at Caernarfon began. In June 1295 the justice of Chester was ordered to recruit 100 experienced masons in the city and send them with their tools to Caernarfon without delay. The scale of the castle-building programme in the aftermath of all three Welsh wars was colossal and vast numbers of masons, carpenters, smiths, plasterers and navvies gathered at Chester, coming from as far away as Cumberland, Norfolk and Sussex. In the summer of 1295 up to 450 masons and 375 quarriers worked at Beaumaris and, unusually, were kept on over the winter, together with 1,000 carpenters and other workers.[9] The smiths producing the tools and ironwork required vast quantities of fuel and the Flintshire coalminers benefited from the building boom.[10]

Royal visits prompted major works at Chester castle. In 1276–7 the king's and queen's chambers were repaired and a chapel was built in the outer bailey. New domestic buildings were begun in 1284 and Humphrey and William (II) of Doncaster were among those who supplied materials.[11] By 1291 over £1,400 had been spent on the construction of new royal chambers, a chapel and a stable, all apparently in the outer bailey. In 1292–3 a new outer gatehouse was built, with twin drum towers on either side of a vaulted passageway defended by two portcullises.[12] A mason worked from April until December 1293 making a seat for the king in the new chapel and a garden was laid out in front of the building. By the early thirteenth century the architect Richard the engineer was

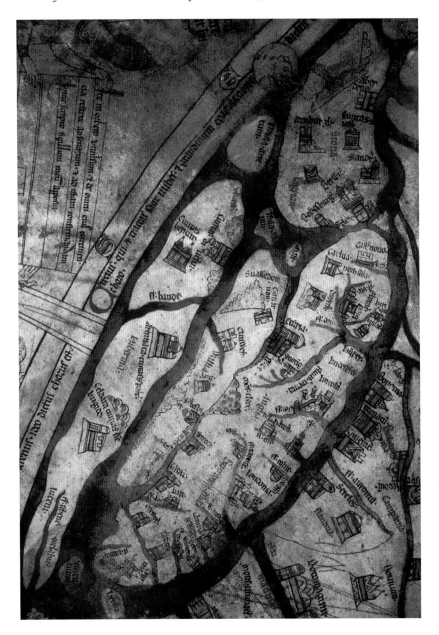

FIGURE 2.2. The British Isles on the Mappa Mundi. (Copyright ownership of The Hereford Mappa Mundi Trust). The map was probably drawn c.1300 and reflects current events. It shows Conwy and Caernarfon, begun in 1277 and 1283, and Berwick-upon-Tweed, sacked by Edward I in 1296 and quickly rebuilt. Chester (centre) is shown as a prominent place, an indication of its strategic importance in the Welsh campaigns, and Berwick is depicted as the most important place in Scotland.

the master of works.[13] A local man who had been involved in the construction of the Welsh castles, he lived in Lower Bridge Street, farming the Dee mills since the early 1270s and serving as mayor in 1305–6. Another prominent citizen was William (III) of Doncaster, active in the city and in royal service by 1295. In 1297 his servants were granted safe conduct to travel through the realm to obtain iron needed for the construction of Beaumaris castle. By 1303–4 he evidently leased the lead mines of Englefield and sold 26 horseloads of lead to the chamberlain; the following year he supplied six cartloads of lead needed to re-roof Gough's tower at the castle.[14] Such activities enabled him to amass a considerable fortune.

Chester's prosperity, coinciding as it did with the availability of skilled building craftsmen, perhaps created favourable conditions for construction work in the city itself. There was evidently considerable activity at the end of the thirteenth century. A three-year murage grant for repairing the walls was made in 1290, and grants of pavage in 1293, 1297 and 1299 enabled the citizens to collect money to pave the streets.[15] A number of townspeople were indicted for constructing steps and shelters in front of their houses and cess-pits in the town ditch in 1293–4.[16] In September 1296 Chester was among the 24 English towns and cities ordered to select two citizens to attend the autumn parliament at Bury St Edmunds. They were to be men 'who shall best know how to dispose and order a new town for the greatest advantage of the king and of merchants coming thither' and their role was to advise on the layout of a new town at Berwick-upon-Tweed, the old one having been sacked during the war with Scotland. Edward evidently believed that men with the relevant knowledge and expertise lived in Chester.[17]

Royal attention was now focused on Scotland and Chester's role in this more distant theatre of war was less significant. The justice Sir John Grey evidently took part in the expedition of 1298 against William Wallace; in the following year he initiated legislation in Chester's Pentice court to recover a lance with a small pennon that had not been returned after the first Scottish

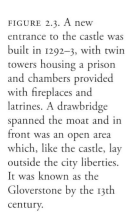

FIGURE 2.3. A new entrance to the castle was built in 1292–3, with twin towers housing a prison and chambers provided with fireplaces and latrines. A drawbridge spanned the moat and in front was an open area which, like the castle, lay outside the city liberties. It was known as the Gloverstone by the 13th century.

war.[18] Recognition of the city's contribution to the conquest of Wales perhaps prompted Edward's grant of a new charter in 1300. It seems that he last visited the city in 1301, the year he created his son Edward of Caernarfon prince of Wales and earl of Chester. The chamberlain's accounts for 1301–2 recorded work on a new great chamber at the castle and payments to Thomas Gardiner and his companion for turfing three gardens in anticipation of the prince's visit.[19] The prince became king in 1307 and the Scottish wars continued throughout much of his reign. Chester remained a base in which supplies could be obtained. William (III) of Doncaster supplied the king with huge quantities of horseshoes and nails in 1309, and two years later the city was asked to provide two ships in the war against Robert the Bruce.[20]

Chester's declining importance coincided with the end of the long period of expansion which England had enjoyed throughout the thirteenth century. The years 1315–18 witnessed the worst famine ever recorded in England, the result of a succession of disastrous harvests caused by exceptionally wet weather. Possibly half a million people died and the north may have suffered more than the south. There were further bad harvests in 1321–2 and 1322–3, accompanied by a serious cattle plague.[21] In 1316 Chester's merchants were among those licensed to go to Ireland to buy corn and other victuals for the king and his lieges, and licences in subsequent years allowed them to purchase grain for the city itself. In May 1322 eight leading citizens, including William (III) of Doncaster, Roger the harper and Richard Russell, were given leave to send their men through the realm to buy corn, wine, victuals and merchandise for the maintenance of their city.[22]

Chester did not escape the political turmoil stirred up by Edward II's quarrel with his cousin Thomas earl of Lancaster. Sir Robert Holland, justice in 1307, 1311 and 1318–19, was Lancaster's chief retainer and owed his appointment to the earl's patronage.[23] Halton, just 13 miles from Chester, was a Duchy of Lancaster manor, and men from there were among the armed group which attacked Chester in August 1318, killing some townsmen and burning houses.[24] There are hints of unrest in the city in the aftermath of Edward II's deposition in 1327. In July the former mayor, Richard le Bruyn, was imprisoned in the castle, accused of supporting the earl of Mar, an 'enemy and a rebel', and was pardoned at the request of Queen Isabella in October. In August the justice was ordered to arrest the large number of outlaws who had congregated in the vicinity of the city.[25]

A new threat faced the government in 1328, posed by Henry earl of Lancaster, heir to the title and vast estates of his brother Thomas, executed for treason in 1322. By the end of 1328 the prospect of civil war loomed and Chester was among the places put in a state of alert. By late December a group of armed knights and 421 hobelars (light horsemen) accompanied by Welsh foot soldiers were based at Chester castle and they remained until 23 January 1329. The king ordered the chamberlain to buy coloured cloth to make 124 short jackets (*courtepys*) for the 100 best archers among the hobelars and for the 24 Welsh foot soldiers carrying lances. Local shearmen finished the cloth and local tailors cut and sewed the garments. The troops evidently left before the work was finished and the jackets were dispatched to Birmingham.[26] Chester's tailors always benefited from military campaigns. They repaired tents for the king's use in 1251 and a century later made the green and white coats worn by the Cheshire archers on campaign with the Black Prince.[27] Chester's role as a military centre perhaps fostered the development of the city's clothing industry, as happened at Winchester.[28]

In 1348–9 the catastrophic outbreak of plague known as the Black Death killed up to half the population of England. Throughout Cheshire holdings were empty and land lay uncultivated because tenants had died during the pestilence. A death rate of some 50 per cent among the manorial tenants at Macclesfield may not be ruled out and in 1350–1 the list of decayed rents at Drakelow (north of Middlewich) was long. Fruit remained unsold because buyers could not be found.[29] Wales was badly affected. The few surviving lead miners at Holywell near Flint refused to work and at Ruthin 77 inhabitants died in two weeks in June 1349.[30] Urban communities, with people living crowded together in often squalid conditions, were particularly vulnerable.

Victims at Chester are said to have included the prioress of St Mary's and the incumbents of three city churches. The abbot of St Werburgh's possibly died in 1349 but as he was buried within the abbey church it has been suggested that he did not die of plague.[31] The revenues from the Dee mills fell sharply; they approached £245 in 1346 but barely exceeded £166 in 1349–50. Building work at the castle more or less ceased and there was a break in the building programme at the abbey. The project initiated in 1346 to rebuild the Dee bridge in stone was evidently interrupted and for several years after 1349 crossings had to be made by ford or by ferry. In 1356–7 the mayor reported empty and ruined tenements throughout the city, among them the important property north of the Stone Hall in Lower Bridge Street and a number of shops.[32] Mayor and commonalty petitioned the Black Prince in May 1357 for a reduction of the fine imposed for the confirmation of their charter, claiming that most of those who would have contributed had died during the plague. The prince's immediate response was to increase the fine but a couple of months later he ordered a proclamation to be made throughout Cheshire forbidding anyone to buy or sell within four leagues of Chester, except in market towns or suitable places ordained from of old. This was perhaps intended to boost the city's trade and suggests that the regular system of markets may have broken down in the aftermath of the Black Death.[33]

By 1360 new tenants had been found for empty properties in prime commercial locations: for a tenement with two shops and two cellars in Flesh-mongers' Row for example, and for a shop in Ironmongers' Row in Northgate Street. Although some properties remained vacant for most of the 1360s, others were re-occupied and repairs undertaken. The civic authorities were anxious to control the labour force and in 1361 petitioned for the right to judge and punish the city's labourers and craftsmen without outside interference.[34] New migrants from the countryside doubtless compensated to some extent for the population losses caused by the Black Death, although further outbreaks of plague in 1361–2, 1369 and 1375 hampered recovery.

People living in the county palatine did not contribute to the poll tax but an insurrection took place close to Chester in July 1381, soon after the Peasants' Revolt in June. A number of villein tenants of the abbot of St Werburgh assembled at Lea by Backford 'to the contempt of the king, to the terror of the king's people in the city and the county of Chester, and to the annihilation and destruction of the abbot and convent.'[35] Lea was only three miles from the city and the 16 men named in the indictment came from villages just north of Chester and were probably known to the townspeople. It has been suggested that the rebels were motivated by local rather than by national issues and that the abbot cunningly linked their conspiracies to the disorder in south-eastern England.[36] There is no evidence that it was anything other than an isolated incident but the government was clearly uneasy. Royal auditors arrived at the castle in December 1381, several months earlier than usual, and they returned in February 1382. Such double scrutiny was unprecedented and was never repeated. It suggests considerable alarm.[37]

In the summer of 1387 Richard II visited Chester for the first time, during the worst crisis of his reign. Grievances against his court had surfaced two years earlier and a commission of leading magnates had been set up to ensure better government. Seeking to evade their control, Richard moved his court to the Midlands in February 1387 and he visited Cheshire a few months later. In September or October he appointed the royal favourite Robert de Vere justice of Chester and north Wales. De Vere established his household at the castle and recruited soldiers on behalf of the king. He enjoyed a scandalous relationship with one of the queen's ladies and lived in considerable style. His furnishings included a bed hanging of blue damask embroidered with *fleur de lys* and a covering of scarlet edged with miniver.[38]

Shortly after his appointment de Vere and other royal favourites were appealed of treason and in December 1387, at Richard's summons, he moved south with 3,000 men. This army was routed at Radcot Bridge in Oxfordshire by the Appellants (the magnates who had made the appeal of treason). De Vere himself escaped and fled to the continent and a copy of the appeal against him was nailed to the door of St Peter's church at Chester, on the orders of the earl of Arundel, one of the three senior Appellants. In January 1388 the Appellants ordered the arrests of the king's leading supporters and at the Merciless Parliament in February charges of treason were brought. Over the next few months a number of men were executed. In May 1389 Richard declared that he had reached the age of maturity and would assume the conduct of affairs.

In 1393 a rebellion broke out in Cheshire. The causes remain uncertain and have been variously explained. One suggestion is that it was linked to current peace negotiations with France, resented by the many Cheshire men who traditionally earned their living as soldiers. Alternatively, there may have been suspicions that palatine liberties were under threat. A third suggestion is that it may have been aimed against the justice Thomas duke of Gloucester, one of the Appellants and, with John of Gaunt, the main negotiator of the peace treaty. The rebellion possibly stemmed from rivalries among the followings of the king (as earl of Chester), of Gaunt (in Lancashire), and of Arundel (in the northern marches of Wales and in Shropshire).[39] There was considerable disorder in Chester in July, August and September 1393, perhaps the result of tensions between the competing affinities. On 8 September, for example, several armed townsmen went to a tavern in Bridge Street intending to ambush and kill a man from Shrewsbury.[40]

In March 1394 Richard II began to consolidate his position in Cheshire, appointing Sir William Bagot deputy justice and commissioning William Lescrope to examine the condition of the royal castles at Chester and in north Wales.[41] Both men became influential royal counsellors and were later considered to be among the agents of Richard's 'tyranny'.[42] Preparations began for an expedition to Ireland, aimed to reassert English control and perhaps provide a new opportunity for military activities. In July 1394 Sir Baldwin Radington, controller of the royal household, arrived in Chester to purvey victuals and transport for the expedition. His men broke into the abbey, seized provisions and imprisoned two townsmen; they raided neighbouring houses and carried off poultry and household herbs. When the mayor John the armourer went to the abbey to seek the release of the townsmen, Radington's household rose 'in manner of armed war' and the cry went up through the city that the mayor had been injured and was in peril of death. The common bell was rung and the townspeople flocked to the abbey to demand the mayor's release. In the ensuing fracas one of Radington's men was killed and in retaliation Radington ordered his supporter Sir John Stanley to collect men-at-arms and archers in Lancashire. For several days this group, several hundred strong, terrorized the neighbourhood within five leagues of the city.[43]

The king arrived in Chester in September 1394, accompanied by the duke of Gloucester and the earls of Nottingham, Arundel, Salisbury, March and Rutland. The following month John the armourer was ordered to arrest ships in the Dee to transport members of the household to Ireland, together with as many mariners as were needed. Two townsmen were among the mariners pressed into service. The following years saw above average expenditure on works at the castle. In December 1396, for example, more than £35 was spent on repairing the two stone towers above the inner gate, in response to a letter from the king which reported that the tower [*sic*] was *molt ruinose et fieble* and on the point of collapse.[44]

Richard was poised to take his long-planned revenge on Arundel, Gloucester and Warwick, the older Appellants. All three were arrested in July 1397 and charged with treason the following month. The case against them was heard in the parliament assembled at Westminster on 17 September. Gloucester was already dead, possibly murdered, Warwick was sentenced to life imprisonment on the Isle of Man, and the king ordered the immediate execution of Arundel. His vast estates in Shropshire and the northern marches of Wales were forfeited and united with Chester. Bagot was appointed steward of these lordships and constable of Holt castle. On 29 September, because of his love for the people of Cheshire, the king raised the enlarged county palatine, which already encompassed Flintshire, to the status of a principality and thenceforth styled himself 'prince of Chester'. A seal was made for the new principality and a city glover made the leather purse in which it was kept.[45]

Richard II looked to the men of his new principality when he began to expand his permanent retinue in September 1397. Within twelve months some 750 men had been retained and this force could be increased to about 2,000 if required. The core of the retinue consisted of a personal bodyguard of 311 archers who accompanied the king wherever he went and who were divided into seven 'watches', one for each day of the week.[46] The Cheshire archers quickly gained a reputation for brutality and the chroniclers considered them instrumental in the king's downfall. For two years the men of the principality basked in the glow of Richard's affection and were showered with offices, pardons and annuities. Among the citizens of Chester favoured by the king were the common clerk John Hatton, appointed yeoman of the livery of the Crown and 6d a day for life in November 1397, and Thomas Cottingham, retained *extra vigilia*.[47] In the autumn of 1398 the sum of 4,000 marks was deposited in St Werburgh's for the Cheshire men who fought for the king at Radcot Bridge and was scrupulously distributed within weeks.[48]

Richard paid several visits to the 'inner citadel' of his kingdom in the final months of his reign. He was at Chester in February, March, April, June and August 1398, immediately before the exile of his cousin Henry Bolingbroke, son and heir of John of Gaunt, in September. For his visit in February 1399 a heated bathroom was constructed in the inner royal chamber, furnished with glass and 'estrichebord' (timber from Norway and the Baltic) and costing almost £70. The royal quarters were luxuriously furnished with tapestry hangings, cushions woven with gold thread, a medley coverlet edged with miniver, and a covering of red tartarin (silk fabric) embroidered with three gold crowns.[49] The king had promised Bolingbroke that he would succeed to his father's duchy of Lancaster but when Gaunt died in March he reneged on that promise, confiscated the duchy and increased Bolingbroke's sentence to exile for life.

A few weeks later, at the end of May, Richard left for a second expedition to Ireland, taking most of his household with him. In late June

FIGURE 2.4. The new great seal of the principality was comparable with the seal of England and its earliest recorded use was 15 October 1397. It was used interchangeably with the old palatinate seal.

Bolingbroke sailed from Boulogne to recover his inheritance and attracted considerable popular support. On 3 July the king's council put Chester castle in a state of defence, installing a garrison of some 30 men-at-arms and archers and organizing supplies of flour, gruel and salt. The citizen John le spicer provided saltpetre and sulphur to make gunpowder.[50] The earl of Salisbury, appointed governor of the principality by Richard, vainly attempted to raise an army to fight for the king but the majority of Cheshire's military men were in Ireland. The county sheriff surrendered the city and its castle to Bolingbroke at Shrewsbury on 5 August. On the same day the chamberlain Robert Parys ordered the new seal of the principality and the old seal of the palatinate to be brought from the exchequer to his home in Lower Bridge Street, former home of Richard the engineer. He fled with them to Wales, in search of the king.[51]

When Bolingbroke entered Chester a few days later he was received in a royal manner with solemn processions of the religious orders, although one chronicler wrote that only God knew the attitude of the citizens. A proclamation at the Cross forbade all retribution but such was the hatred felt for the men of Cheshire that the order went unheeded. The cry of 'havoc' went up and for the next fortnight the surrounding countryside was systematically plundered. During the twelve days that Bolingbroke and his troops spent in the castle the wine was consumed, the brewing equipment destroyed, the bows, bowstrings and arrowheads carried away, as too the towels and cushions from the chapel. Three days after his arrival Bolingbroke ordered the execution of Peter Legh of Lyme, one of the king's favourites, and his head was fixed on a stake outside the Eastgate.[52] Henry Percy the younger (Hotspur) was appointed justice of Chester on 14 August and on 16 August Robert Parys was replaced as chamberlain by John Trevor. On the same day Bolingbroke escorted Richard from Flint to Chester as a prisoner to the sound of trumpets and horns. One of Richard's attendants described the great reverence paid to Bolingbroke by the common people and the mocking shouts with which they greeted the king. Richard was lodged in the donjon of the 'fair and strong' castle and not seen again until he was taken south to London.[53] He was deposed on 30 September and Bolingbroke became king as Henry IV. In his first parliament the status of Chester reverted to that of a county and the annexed lands were restored to the earl of Arundel.[54]

High levels of trade in the years around 1400 brought prosperity to many English towns.[55] At Chester, however, continuing political unrest hindered economic progress. Henry IV had adopted a policy of conciliation towards the county but pro-Ricardian sentiment remained strong and rebellion broke out in Chester on 10 January 1400, during the Saturday market. An armed group of citizens and men of unknown identity appeared on the streets wearing badges of the livery of Richard II and 'other liveries', probably those of the earls who had plotted in December 1399 to seize Henry and his sons at Windsor and restore Richard to the throne. The group marched to the castle and demanded its surrender and,

FIGURE 2.5. The old
Eastgate, demolished
in 1768, was the city's
principal gate. The heads
and quartered remains
of traitors and rebels
were displayed here,
including the head of
'Perkin a Legh' in 1399.
His mutilated body was
buried by the Carmelite
friars and his monument
in Macclesfield
church records that
he was 'betrayed for
righteousness'.

failing in this objective, made their way to the Eastgate and removed the head of Peter Legh. They then roamed the streets seeking support, seized the keys to the gates, and issued a proclamation in Richard's name that all able-bodied men of the city and county should rally to his cause. A second assault was made on the castle and arrows were fired over the walls but the garrison of eight men-at-arms and 35 archers under the command of the constable Sir William Venables easily resisted the attack. The rebels received reinforcements the following day and the rising threatened to become dangerous but it then ended abruptly, presumably when it was learned that the earls' revolt had failed.[56]

The government was anxious to identify those involved and ordered searching enquiries. On 22 May 1400 a general pardon was granted to the people of Cheshire but 125 men were excluded and had to sue for individual pardons. A sizeable proportion came from the city and its environs, indicating that recruitment there had proved very successful, although it was noted that Robert Chamberlain had been forced to join the rising against his will. Property was confiscated from some townsmen, including their leader Thomas Cottingham, the mercer Richard del Halgh and the glover Thomas Banastre, one of the two men imprisoned in the abbey in 1394. Also named as rebels were Richard Warmingham plumber, John del Hey cutler, several glovers, tailors and weavers, a mercer, a mason, a shipman, a shoemaker, a skinner and a cook.[57] The insurrection was probably inspired by loyalty to Richard and by smouldering resentment of the 'havoc' wreaked by Bolingbroke's troops in August 1399, although one chronicler suggested that the tallage may have provided the motive. This was perhaps the sum of 3,000 marks due from the county when the king's son Henry was created prince of Wales and earl of Chester in October 1399.[58]

The rebellion of Owain Glyn Dŵr posed a far more serious threat to Henry IV and caused widespread destruction. The catalyst was the territorial dispute between Glyn Dŵr and his neighbour Lord Grey of Ruthin, but the political objective of ending English rule quickly emerged. The rebellion began on 16 September 1400 when Glyn Dŵr's supporters proclaimed him prince of Wales and the rebels' first target was Ruthin where they allegedly burned down most of the buildings.[59] The rebels moved on to ravage Denbigh, Rhuddlan, Flint, Hawarden and Holt, and the revolt spread to Anglesey. By January 1401 there was considerable alarm and parliament took measures to limit the freedom of Welsh men living in England and in the marches of Wales. In November the delivery of provisions into any part of Wales except for the use of English boroughs and castles was forbidden.[60]

Chester benefited once again from its role as a supply base, and barges laden with flour, wine, weapons and gunpowder were sent from the city to the Welsh castles. Provisions needed for the garrisons were obtained in the city and merchants like John Hatton and Richard of Hawarden supplied Spanish iron for castle repairs. A local nailer produced quantities of nails that were shipped to Caernarfon, and local boatmen and carters found regular employment. The city's portmote court was adjourned in February 1401 because the mayor and sheriffs were required to organize transport.[61] Chester's trade with the neighbouring parts of Wales was, however, adversely affected by the restrictions imposed by the authorities. In October 1401, a month before similar orders were made in parliament, the city's mayor, sheriffs and commonalty decreed that no-one was to provide arms or provisions to any in rebellion against the king or prince. People living in Flintshire had always purchased bread and ale at Chester, but when the situation deteriorated in the summer of 1402 licences had to be obtained and assurances given that the supplies would not be passed on to the rebels. Among those granted licences were the inhabitants of Hopedale, who claimed that they were in great need, ale sellers from Wrexham, Northop and Hawarden, and the abbot of Basingwerk. The cattle trade may also have been disrupted.[62]

The reactions of Chester's townspeople were doubtless mixed. From the early fourteenth century wealthy citizens had invested heavily in Welsh lands and many Welsh had migrated to the city and settled there. Large numbers of the inhabitants had Welsh kin and, inevitably, some townsmen continued to have Welsh loyalties. Geoffrey the tailor (whose name indicates Welsh origins) had lived in Chester since at least 1396 but in December 1401 he was accused of sending padded jackets to north Wales, where they were sold to the rebels.[63] A watch was kept on the city walls and in July 1402 panic swept through the city when it was rumoured that Glyn Dŵr and his adherents were at the gates. Four months later the mayor and sheriffs were ordered to array for the defence of the city all those with lands, tenements or rents worth £20 per annum, or with goods or merchandise valued at 100 marks.[64] By early 1403 English authority in the north and west of Wales was restricted to the castles of Beaumaris, Caernarfon and Harlech; in February the rebels penetrated Flintshire and burnt and destroyed the town of Hope.[65]

The king's troubles intensified when Henry Percy (Hotspur) arrived in Chester in early July and raised the standard of revolt in the name of Richard II. He was motivated by personal ambitions but was able to draw on the persisting support for Richard in Cheshire.[66] The former king had been dead since February 1400 but rumours that he was still alive persisted. In May 1402, for example, the piper John Lancaster told a crowd gathered at Winnington near Northwich that he had seen Richard at Berwick castle. According to the chroniclers Hotspur's party caused proclamations to be made in Chester and in every market town in the county that Richard was alive and might be seen in Chester castle. The promise that he would join former supporters at Sandiway in Delamere forest caused a 'multitude of imbeciles' to gather there and the numbers swelled as they marched to Shrewsbury.[67] Hotspur enjoyed great influence in the region; he had served as justice of Chester and north Wales since October 1399 and held other important offices and lordships in the Welsh Marches. His army came close to defeating the combined forces of the king and the young prince of Wales at the battle of Shrewsbury on 21 July 1403, in what was one of the great disasters in Cheshire history. The battle left 2,000 dead, including hundreds of the county's fighting men. After the defeat one quarter of Hotspur's body was sent to Chester for display at the Eastgate, together with the heads of Sir Richard Venables and Sir Richard Vernon, who had been executed after the battle. Hotspur's rebellion was essentially a Cheshire rebellion but the city was not heavily implicated and was pardoned in return for a payment of 300 marks, a payment later remitted in favour of ships and provisions for the garrison at Beaumaris. The constable of Chester castle and a former mayor were with the prince at Shrewsbury and only two townsmen were identified as rebels, at least one of them soon reconciled to the regime and serving as city sheriff in 1404–5.[68]

In August 1403 the Welsh of Flintshire joined Glyn Dŵr's rebellion. Flint was plundered, Rhuddlan burned, and Cheshire's borders threatened. William Venables, constable of Chester castle, rode out with an armed force to resist the insurgents and the city prepared for a state of siege.[69] On 4 September the mayor, sheriffs and aldermen were ordered to expel all Welsh residents from the city, both men and women. A curfew was imposed on Welsh visitors, who were obliged to leave their weapons outside the gates and forbidden from meeting in taverns and from assembling in groups of more than three. Gunpowder was purchased for the defence of Chester castle, and a spy was sent to Bala, Moldsdale, and Bromfield and Yale to discover the rebels' plans.[70] By the spring of 1404 Cheshire vills on the Welsh side of the Dee (Poulton, Pulford, Dodleston, Kinnerton, Marlston, Eccleston, Lache, Eaton and Claverton) and the town of Hawarden had been destroyed. Some rebels were within a mile or so of Chester itself and two were captured at Saltney just beyond the city liberties, one of them perhaps the brother of the spy. Their crimes were recited at a gaol delivery on 4 April 1404: they had participated in the burning of Rhuddlan and Hope and killed some Englishmen; they had stolen cattle at Lache and had abducted young women from Saltney, carrying them off to rebel hideouts. "Wharto shuld I nyk hyt?" ("Why should I deny it?") each answered when charged and they were sentenced to be dragged through the city to the gibbet at Boughton and hanged. In October 1404 a large group of rebels broke into the fulling mills at Handbridge and stole white woollen cloth; they also took livestock, including an ox and three cows belonging to William Venables. Those caught were hanged.[71]

In spite of repeated prohibitions trade continued. A watch was kept on the roads and over fords and ferries across the Dee, including the route through Pulford, Poulton, Eaton Boat and Eccleston, but it proved impossible to police all routes into Wales. In July 1404 the prince of Wales learned that large quantities of provisions and merchandise, including red pennons made in Lancashire, were sold to the rebels at Malpas and he ordered the seizure of such goods.[72] The same month three packs of woollen cloth *en route* to Ruthin were seized in Dodleston field. They belonged to Chester's mayor, Ralph of Hatton, and he and his servants immediately took them back and forwarded them to the rebels. A few months later a boat laden with cloth, knives and leather points destined for the insurgents was seized at Burton. On this occasion the arresting officer came to an agreement with those on board in return for a share of the merchandise. A Chester butcher was arrested in 1407 on suspicion of having purchased herring from the French, allies of Glyn Dŵr and in the region since March 1404 when they joined in the siege of Caernarfon.[73]

It also proved difficult to maintain a proper watch on the city walls. Townsmen absented themselves from 'le chekwache' and stole pole-axes and other weapons from those on guard. A Welshman was caught attempting to pass over the walls in February 1407.[74] The civic élite included men of Welsh descent and this caused particular difficulties. In January 1408 a bitter conflict erupted between the constable William Venables and the mayor John Ewloe and their respective followings, and although both sides were repeatedly bound over to keep the peace the quarrel persisted. In August 1409 the two men were suspended from office, Ewloe because he was 'tampering with the rebels' and his loyalty was suspect.[75] The sheriff of Cheshire was appointed 'keeper and governor' of the city and his deputy presided over the crownmote and portmote courts until August 1410 and possibly until the mayoral election in October.[76] Peace terms between Venables and the citizens were settled by arbitration in 1411 and reparations were paid the following year but the urban community remained divided.[77]

In October 1419 John Ewloe's son Edmund went with an armed group to the home of John Hope, elected mayor just a few days earlier. The plan was to murder Hope and his brother Robert, together with Robert's son and three other townsmen. When the case came to court in December it was alleged that since his election John Hope went through the city accompanied by a band of English and Welsh supporters wearing coats of mail and carrying swords and pole-axes. So too did his brother and Richard Mottram, elected murager and treasurer on the same day. The court hearing in December 1419 began with a reference to the parliamentary statute of January 1401, which prohibited Welshmen from holding property in English towns close to the Welsh borders. Yet John and Robert Hope and Richard Mottram had been born in Wales of Welsh parents and were 'wholly Welsh' (*meri Wallici*). The prohibition was quoted again in January 1420, when Edmund Ewloe was indicted for his role in the attack. The jury now learned that he and his father had also been born in Wales of Welsh parents, that they came from Cilcain in Dyffryn Clwyd and had been villein tenants of Reginald Grey, former lord of Ruthin.[78] Leading citizens of Welsh descent may well have had conflicting allegiances during Glyn Dŵr's rebellion.

Wheat harvests were bad throughout the country in 1416–17 and 1418–19 and, most unusually, the abbot of St Werburgh's purchased wheat from the Dee mills.[79] Successive years of exceptionally wet weather affected the harvests in 1437–40 and produced the last great famine of the medieval period. Much of northern Europe was affected and Chester suffered considerable hardship. According to the chronicler the city's poor were reduced to eating bread made from vetches, peas and fern roots. The disastrous crop yields were reflected in the accounts of the Dee mills: just over 30 quarters of wheat were sold in 1438–9, compared to some 112 quarters in 1434–5. In other parts of England the famine did not lead to a great increase in mortality, except when food shortages coincided with an outbreak of plague.[80] In 1445, when Cestrians claimed that the greater part of their city was desolate and sparsely inhabited, the reason given was that many inhabitants had moved elsewhere, not that they had died. Chester was poor because the Welsh insurrection had damaged trade and because the harbour had been destroyed by the 'wreck of sea sand'. Other towns were seeking fee-farm reductions at this time and also pleading poverty. Such claims, although doubtless exaggerated, sometimes contained an element of truth.[81]

John Rothley, sheriff of Chester in 1443–4 and 1444–5, was uncomfortably aware of the economic difficulties his city then faced. He had been unable to collect the revenues to pay the fee farm in full and was imprisoned for 36 weeks as a result. In 1445 the royal authorities reduced the farm from £100 to £50, possibly in acknowledgement of the validity of the city's claims. The reduction was threatened by the parliamentary act of resumption in 1450 but protests from Chester and from towns granted similar reductions induced parliament to agree that the act should not apply to towns.[82] This decision was not accepted by the palatinate authorities in Cheshire; arrears built up and legal action was threatened. A letter from the king to the chamberlain and auditors in November 1455 ordered them to withdraw the threats and to cancel the outstanding charges. The six pairs of sheriffs who had held office in the years from 1449–50 until 1454–5 were individually named in this concession, which perhaps resulted from Queen Margaret's visit to the city in 1455.[83]

The queen was anxious to win support for the court faction in its quarrel with the Yorkist lords. Henry VI had suffered a mental collapse in August 1453 and his failure to recover resulted in the government of the kingdom being placed in the hands of Richard duke of York in March 1454. Margaret was determined to secure the succession for her son, born in October 1453, and York's protectorate was ended in February 1455 when an improvement in Henry's health enabled him (theoretically) to resume his rule. Thereafter he remained under the control of his wife and she emerged as powerful leader of the court faction. Their infant son Edward had been created prince of Wales and earl of Chester in March 1454 and his lands and revenues, together with those of the duchy of Lancaster, provided a power base in the north-west for the court.

The queen again visited Chester in June and October 1456, on the second occasion perhaps accompanied by the king. Care was taken to reward Lancastrian supporters. The justice Thomas Stanley, although arriving too late to take part in the battle of St Albans in May 1455, was created 1st Lord Stanley in 1456; Sir Richard Tunstall was appointed chamberlain of Chester in 1457. After Stanley's death in 1459 the staunch Lancastrian John Talbot, 2nd earl of Shrewsbury, was appointed justice.[84] In the summer of 1459 the queen brought her son to Cheshire and repairs were carried out at the castle in anticipation of the royal visit; new beds, benches and trestles were purchased. The prince distributed the Lancastrian badge of the white swan to local knights and esquires, many of whom died at Blore Heath in Staffordshire on 23 September 1459. A tradition arose that Cheshire's loyalties were divided in this battle, with families fighting on opposing sides, although a recent study has found little supporting evidence.[85]

There are hints of Yorkist support within Chester in the months following Blore Heath.[86] The royalists, although defeated, captured the two younger sons of the Yorkist earl of Salisbury after the battle and sent them as prisoners to Chester castle, evidently expecting the city to remain loyal. Payments were made to six Cheshire esquires guarding these prisoners in December 1459, and in January and April 1460.[87] From November 1459 and throughout 1460, however, an exceptional number of peace bonds were issued, as the city authorities struggled to maintain law and order. Among those bound to keep the peace towards all the townspeople were William Venables of Golborne and his brother. They first appeared before the mayor John Southworth on Wednesday before the feast of St Alban (22 June), a unique reference to this festival in the city's records and perhaps deliberately chosen to commemorate the Yorkist victory at St Albans in 1455.[88] In July 1460, a few days after the battle of Northampton, the victorious Yorkists ordered that Thomas and John Neville, held prisoner in Chester castle since Blore Heath, be handed over to Thomas, 2nd Lord Stanley. Stanley had married their sister Eleanor, daughter of the earl of Salisbury and niece of Cecily, duchess of York.[89]

The duke of York had been governor of Ireland since 1447. Although he spent little time there he managed to establish a firm political base and it was to Ireland he fled after defeat at Ludford Bridge (Shropshire) in October 1459. By June 1460 he had licensed English merchants in Dublin to form a guild, some of whose members travelled regularly through Chester. York returned to England on or about 9 September 1460, landing at Redbank in Wirral. He spent a few days in Chester and entrusted the keeping of the castle to John Stanley. Food, wine and weapons were purchased for the garrison. On 13 September the duke rewarded the mayor John Southworth 'for past service and for service to be rendered' with a grant of a yearly rent of £10 from his lordship of Denbigh.[90] York was killed at Wakefield in December but soon after the total defeat of the Lancastrians at Towton (Yorkshire) in March 1461 his son became king. Edward IV renewed his father's grant to John Southworth in June 1461, probably in gratitude for continued service at a critical time, and Southworth received the annuity until his death in 1485. Southworth's son also served the Yorkist king, acting as clerk to the kitchen, and in 1489 he asked (somewhat ambitiously) to be buried in the college at Windsor, 'beside my old master King Edward.'[91] Chester benefited from Edward's gratitude and in September 1461 was granted a £50 remission of the fee farm for seven years, backdated to September 1460.[92]

Soon after his accession Edward embarked on a tour of northern England and of the north-west and the north midlands, regions which had been royalist strongholds. He was at Chester in May and June 1461 and wine and fuel were purchased for his household. There was still support for Henry VI in the area and in July the county sheriff was ordered to arrest and imprison twelve Cheshire men suspected of inciting rebellion. In August guns were dispatched from Chester to the castle at Chirk (Denbighshire) and ships were arrested in the Dee and paid for six weeks' service, presumably to supply the troops laying siege to Rhuddlan castle. John Tyle (or Gyle) 'wildfireshooter' and 464 soldiers were involved in the siege, which was over by November when the captured rebels were taken to London in the custody of the chamberlain William Stanley.[93] Around this time Chester's mayor and sheriffs sent letters to the king with details of rumours current in Wales and in February 1462 they supplied eleven horses for royal ambassadors riding to the Outer Isles. Scottish support for Henry VI was growing at this time and fighting in the border area was fairly constant. Chester contributed to Edward's northern campaign in the summer of 1463, paying for 24 soldiers and their jackets, and for a mustering arrow.[94]

A force under the command of the duke of Norfolk was based at Holt castle in Denbighshire from the end of 1462 until 1464, charged with subduing Lancastrian support in the region. Their difficulties intensified when the duke of Somerset deserted Edward and left Wales for Bamburgh (Northumberland) at the end of 1463. John Paston III wrote to his father from Holt in March 1464 with the news that 10,000 or more men from Cheshire and Lancashire had risen against the king but were 'down again', one or two of them having been beheaded at Chester.[95] City tradesmen profited from the presence of Norfolk and his entourage, supplying them with cloth, garments, bows and arrows, imported luxuries such as pepper and sugar, and vast quantities of horsebread. Innkeepers did good business, providing accommodation for the duke's servants and stabling for their horses.[96] The city's craftsmen and traders were continuing the long tradition of providing goods and services to soldiers.

Disturbances broke out in other parts of England in 1464. Trouble at Newcastle-upon-Tyne was quelled with the help of the great bombard (cannon) sent from Chester; all the gunpowder in store at Chester was used in the siege of the castle at Skipton (Yorkshire), evidently a protracted operation. The chamberlain Sir William Stanley incurred 'great and notable' expenses (amounting perhaps to £200) in repressing the rebels and predators who had assembled in Skipton castle, and he and his brother Thomas Lord Stanley, justice of Chester, received an additional £40 for the cost of the siege.[97] Lancastrian supporters in Wales continued to pose a threat and perhaps provoked the 'bloody fray' between the Welsh and a large group of Cestrians at Mold fair in 1465. Robert Bruyn, Chester's mayor in 1462–3 when the city paid for soldiers for Edward IV's northern campaign, was dragged from the fair and hanged by the Welshman who was to hold Harlech for Henry VI until 1468.[98] By 1467 rebels had congregated in the vicinity of Chester; extra grain was purchased for the castle garrison and the mayor was awarded ten marks in gratitude for his labours in keeping the city safe. In July 1468 Sir William Stanley rode out from Chester to Denbigh in order to resist Jasper Tudor who was preparing to land in Wales, sponsored by Louis XI of France. The authorities deemed it prudent to strengthen the castle garrison at this time.[99] The years 1469–71 saw renewed civil war and the brief resumption of the throne by Henry VI. The only serious disturbance recorded in Cheshire occurred at Nantwich in November 1470, when some 400 armed men attacked Sir William Stanley, shouting out 'King Henry, Prince Edward, a Warwick, a Warwick.' There was still support for the Lancastrian cause in Cheshire but it seems to have been easily contained.[100]

Edward IV was restored to the throne in April 1471 and he renewed the reduction of Chester's farm the following year. Archers for campaigns in Ireland were mustered close to the city in September 1474, in May 1475, and in June 1477. Ships were arrested at Chester, Conwy and Beaumaris to transport the troops for the 1475 campaign, and masters and mariners, bowyers and fletchers, and workmen for the artillery were pressed into service.[101] In the autumn of

1476 a committee of ten aldermen and ten councilmen prepared for a visit to Chester by the prince of Wales. This took place just before Christmas, and the prince was escorted to the castle 'with great triumph.'[102] In April 1483 the prince succeeded his father as king but within weeks he and his younger brother were murdered in the Tower of London and their uncle became king. Richard III needed to cultivate the widest possible support and in 1484 he readily agreed to Chester's request for a reduction of the fee farm, lowering it to £30 for ten years. The city's sympathies, however, may already have been with Henry Tudor, stepson of the justice Thomas Lord Stanley. Stanley's brother-in-law Sir John Savage was elected mayor of Chester in October 1484 and re-elected in 1485; eight of his nine sons became freemen of Chester in March 1485. The eldest son, also Sir John, was described as knight of the body of the king but he commanded the left wing of Henry Tudor's forces at Bosworth in August 1485 and was reportedly among his keenest supporters.[103] The battle swung Henry's way when Thomas Lord Stanley and his brother Sir William came over to him; Richard III was killed in the battle and Henry Tudor became king.

In March 1486 Henry VII rewarded the citizens for their 'good and laudable service' by reducing the farm to £20, and he visited the city with his queen and his mother in 1493 or 1495. If the visit was made in 1495, then it may have been linked to the execution for treason that year of Sir William Stanley, implicated in the plot of the pretender Perkin Warbeck.[104] In August 1499 Henry's son Prince Arthur visited Chester and was entertained by a performance of the Assumption of Our Lady at the abbey gate.[105] In 1506 came the award of the

FIGURE 2.6. The effigy of Sir John Savage junior in Macclesfield church. He was killed at the siege of Boulogne in 1492.

Great Charter, granted by Henry VII because of his great affection for the citizens, because of their good behaviour and great expenses, and because of the service they had rendered voluntarily against his adversaries and rebels. Chester was given county status and its constitution was formalized.[106]

In 1507 an outbreak of 'sweating sickness' caused the deaths of 91 house-holders in three days, only four of them women, and in 1517–18 a 'great plague' swept through the city and halted trade, resulting in grass growing a foot high at the Cross and elsewhere.[107] Chester in the 1520s was among 16 towns with perhaps 3,500–5,000 inhabitants and in terms of taxable wealth it may have ranked alongside Hereford and Lincoln.[108] The city was never again as important to English kings as it had been to Edward I during the Welsh wars but it continued to serve as a regional capital throughout the Middle Ages.

CHAPTER THREE

Topography

When Ranulph Higden, monk of St Werburgh's, wrote his *Polychronicon* in *c*.1340 most buildings of the legionary fortress of *Deva* had long since collapsed and the only recognisable survivals above ground were sections of the defences embedded in the north and east walls and two Roman arches incorporated in the medieval Eastgate. The Roman north gate may also have survived within its medieval successor.[1] Below ground, however, much Roman fabric remained. Higden described the underground passages, arched chambers and monumental inscribed stones and concluded that they would be seen as the work of giants or of Romans, and not of Britons.[2]

The layout of the Roman fortress profoundly influenced the medieval street plan. The four main gates and the four main thoroughfares within the walls had Roman origins. Bridge Street perpetuates the *via praetoria* and Eastgate Street and Upper Watergate Street correspond with the *via principalis*. The Roman *via decumana* ran south from the Northgate but then divided in order to pass to the east and west of the headquarters building (*principia*) and other large buildings immediately behind it. The line taken by Northgate Street since the early medieval period reflects these arrangements. The upper part of the street follows the line of the *via decumana* and the lower part of the street meets Eastgate Street slightly to the east of Bridge Street, having passed round the ruins of the eastern part of the *principia*. By 1200 a number of lesser streets skirted the Roman defences. Pepper Street, Cuppin Lane, St Nicholas Lane and Crofts Lane (Linenhall Street) lay outside the south and west walls; within those walls the line of the Roman *intervallum* road was followed by Whitefriars Lane, Berward Lane (Weaver Street) and Trinity Lane. Beyond the gates the medieval roads corresponded with their Roman predecessors, leading north into Wirral, east towards Northwich, and south across the Dee towards Whitchurch.

In the early medieval period one or two of the larger Roman buildings partially survived. The *principia* was sufficiently intact in the late tenth century to provide a base for the mint and secure storage facilities for the bullion, and the amphitheatre was robbed of stone in the twelfth century to build St John's church. The Dominicans and Franciscans took stone from Roman buildings standing outside the west wall of the fortress in the thirteenth century.[3] Other buildings collapsed and the accumulated debris obstructed later development. The remains of the legionary baths, for example, blocked the layout of streets from the east side of Bridge Street and the south side of Eastgate Street, and the

FIGURE 3.1. Braun and
Hogenberg's plan of
Chester dating from
c.1580 shows a city largely
unchanged from the
medieval period.

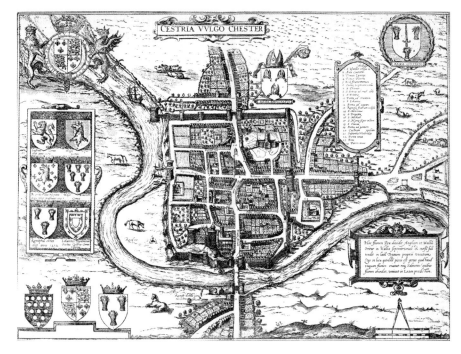

FIGURE 3.1. Braun and Hogenberg's plan of Chester dating from *c*.1580 shows a city largely unchanged from the medieval period.

curve of the amphitheatre dictated the shape of the street leading to St John's. The ruins of Roman buildings on either side of the four main streets created the differences in ground level which promoted the development of the Rows. Several of the parish churches were sited in relation to Roman structures. St Michael's and St Bridget's were built over the remains of the abutments on either side of the south gate of the fortress, Holy Trinity was built on or near the west gate, and St Martin's close to the south-west corner of the fortress. In the centre of the city stood St Peter's, several feet above street level on the foundations of the headquarters building and with its south door at Row level. It was described as *templum* in 1086, a term not used elsewhere in the Domesday Survey, which suggests that distinctive Roman fabric perhaps remained visible at that time. Almost 400,000 wagonloads of stone had been used when the Roman fortress was rebuilt in the early third century.[4] They left an enduring legacy.

The Normans made significant changes to Chester, the most dramatic of which was the construction of the castle to the south-west of the legionary fortress and the consequent expansion of the walled area. The Roman north and east walls had already been extended to the river in the early tenth century but it was the advent of the castle which led to the abandonment of the south and west walls of the fortress and the completion of the full medieval circuit. New streets emerged over the course of the twelfth century: Fleshmongers Lane, for example, ran south from Eastgate Street to Wolfeld Gate, later known as Newgate. The Shipgate had probably been built by the 1120s and was presumably already connected to Lower Bridge Street by Ship Lane.[5]

The local monk Lucian wrote his work in praise of Chester in about 1195, in the second earliest guide book to any English town.[6] Many of the features he described were recorded in the Assembly Book in *c.*1570, then said to have been copied from a survey made in the reign of Edward III. This suggests that the main elements of the medieval city were already in place at the close of the twelfth century. Lucian was much impressed by the religious symbolism of the urban layout, noting the 'two excellent straight streets in the form of the blessed Cross' which met and crossed in the centre of the city where [God] 'willed there to be a market for the sale of goods'. With a little poetic licence the monk listed the holy guardians who kept watch at the four gates: St John to the east, St Peter to the west, St Werburg to the north, and St Michael to the south. The civic authorities valued the cruciform layout for an entirely secular reason, seeing it as a convenient mechanism for governing their city. It seems certain that the four main streets already served as the administrative subdivisions of Chester in the thirteenth century and the four-fold division sufficed until the late 1480s when, perhaps as a result of increased bureaucracy, it became usual to list the suburbs separately. Administrative changes initiated by the charter of 1506 resulted in the division of the city into eight wards, each headed by an alderman.[7]

Records of the administrative business transacted by the city's mayors and sheriffs survive from 1392. All residents who attracted official attention, ranging from councilmen, jurors and constables to fine-payers and wrong-doers, were consistently listed under street headings. The civic records therefore provide a glimpse of the social and occupational topography of late medieval Chester and reveal a city which, although compact (for the area within the walls covered only some 126 acres), in fact comprised an assemblage of discrete neighbourhoods or urban villages.

The central market and High Cross

The central market place beside St Peter's noted by Lucian already existed in the later eleventh century, when the church was described as *de foro*.[8] Subsequent encroachments reduced the original market area. The surface of the early market place at the north-western corner of Eastgate Street was revealed by excavations in 1990–1 (see below). The Stone Seld at the corner of Bridge Street and Watergate Street, attested in 1425 and probably there by the 1270s, may be another example of infilling. An open area perhaps still remained at the corner of Bridge Street and Eastgate Street in the 1430s, when a shop adjoining the pillory was described as 'in the corner' (*in angulo*). The stone conduit house was built on this site in 1583.[9] The market place was the commercial heart of the medieval city and the focus of civic government. The Pentice, the city's administrative hub, abutted the southern side of St Peter's by 1288 and the High Cross stood next to the church entrance by the later fourteenth century.[10]

Eastgate Street

The broad thoroughfare of Eastgate Street extended from the central market at the Cross to the Eastgate, recorded as *porta Cestriae* in the late thirteenth century and evidently the city's principal gate. Eastgate Street, termed the city's principal street in 1463, was always listed first in the civic records and almost invariably produced the highest revenues from amercements and from licences to trade.[11] This was evidently a densely settled quarter, with houses crowded along the main frontages and in the adjoining lanes. Leen Lane, Godstall Lane and St Werburgh's Lane led off the north side of the street towards the abbey graveyard, and Fleshmongers Lane ran south to Wolfeld Gate. There were 127 taxpayers in 1463, among them several of the most prosperous craftsmen of the day. In the later fifteenth century more councilmen and constables were sworn in for Eastgate Street each year than for any other quarter.[12]

The commercial frontage of Eastgate Street began with the shops beneath the Pentice facing the market place. By the 1430s there were four or five shops in this prime location, commanding high rents and usually occupied by prominent hosiers, drapers and mercers. In 1472–3 one shop was occupied by a hardwareman, and at the end of the century an ironmonger rented the shop next to the High Cross.[13] On the opposite corner, at the junction of Northgate Street and Eastgate Street, were the Buttershops, premises where dairy produce was sold. In 1270, when the name was first recorded, these were permanent buildings but in earlier centuries this was open ground. Excavations on the site in 1990–1 revealed the surface of the late Saxon or early Norman market place and also the wall of a small cellar which represented encroachment onto the original market place, perhaps in the twelfth century. By the 1360s the Buttershops contained shops in multiple ownership, some with rooms above, and a Row ran through the complex.[14] Margery of the Buttershops was among a dozen women charged with forestalling cheese and butter in 1322–3 and in the following century various products were sold there. Joanna 'en le Buttershoppes' made candles in around 1415 and 20 years later meat was sold on the feast of St John the Baptist (24 June).[15]

It is possible that the highway (*alta via*) in the Buttershops was also known as Cooks' Row, first attested in *c.*1330 when John the saucemaker held land there. He had held this small piece of land (4¾ ells x 3¼ ells) since 1303–5 and saucemakers may have congregated in the area. Robert the saucer was churchwarden of St Peter's in 1319 and in 1393 a saucemaker plied his trade opposite the church. Cooks' Row was described in 1377–8 as 'against the Pentice' with buildings lying opposite St Peter's and fronting Eastgate Street.[16] In the fourteenth and early fifteenth century Chester's cooks were regularly fined for the hearths (*astra*) they set up on the 'common soil' of the city, which suggests that some open ground still remained at the junction of Eastgate Street and Northgate Street. By 1420 it seems that permanent buildings were beginning to replace the hearths and trestle tables. In that year one cook rented a shop on the common soil and the wife of another paid an annual rent of 18d for 'le cokery'.[17] In the early 1450s a cook rented the 'cokes kechyn' newly constructed in Eastgate Street and by 1468–9 this kitchen was one of five shops near the corner of the street, two of them occupied by cooks; the adjacent oven built in 1446 was rented by a third cook.[18] These premises lay to the south of the highway (*alta via*) in the Buttershops which by 1448 was also known as the 'Dark Lofts', perhaps because it was now overshadowed by the new buildings.[19] From the 1440s until redevelopment in the early 1990s, the Dark Row differed from Chester's other Rows: it lay behind buildings fronting the street and was not an elevated walkway above undercrofts but sloped down almost to street level.[20]

To the east of Cooks' Row lay Bakers' Row. It has been suggested that the two names may have designated the same thoroughfare but mention of both Rows in a property deed of 1330 indicates that they were distinct. The important bakehouse belonging to the hospital of St Giles lay behind the Row, close to Leen Lane, and other bakehouses were in the vicinity. Among the leading townsmen who invested in Bakers' Row in the late thirteenth century was the mayor Hugh of Brickhill, who held four vacant houses there in 1293 and obstructed the highway by building porches in front of them.[21] Bakers' Row was conveniently sited. Chester's corn market was in Eastgate Street by 1278–9, presumably, as in the mid fourteenth century, on the south side of the street. The market included a Row by 1303 and the houses had cellars in which grain was stored. The messuage and cellar known as 'le Melhous' recorded in 1354 perhaps stood near the western corner of Fleshmongers Lane. The corner property was leased to a descendant of the citizen licensed to import corn from Ireland in 1316 and from other parts of England in the 1320s. A corndealer occupied a house in the same area in the 1470s.[22]

Among the craftsmen who lived in the Eastgate Street quarter in the fifteenth century were shoemakers, fletchers, tailors and candlemakers. Goldsmiths congregated in the area, particularly in or near Fleshmongers Lane. Three were named among the taxpayers in 1463, including Roger Warmingham whose family already owned land in the lane in 1308.[23] Pewterers opted for this quarter of Chester, among them William Rawson who lived in St Werburgh Lane in the 1460s and was sheriff in 1466–7. He was accused of receiving prostitutes in his cellar in 1463, and a few years later two monks from the nearby abbey broke into his house and assaulted and raped his servant Elizabeth.[24] Glovers' Row was recorded on the south side of Eastgate Street close to the junction with Bridge Street in 1426, and glovers were still based in this location at the start of the seventeenth century.[25]

Residents included members of Chester's ruling élite. In 1411 the mayor Roger Potter lived close to the Eastgate in the third house east of Fleshmongers Lane, next door to the barber Richard Hankey who would be sheriff in 1430–1. William Hawkin, sheriff in 1455–6, was tenant of 'le Stonenhall' on the south side of Eastgate Street.[26] Henry Port mercer, William Heywood cook and the gentleman George Bulkeley, office-holders in the 1470s and 1480s, lived in Fleshmongers Lane, evidently a fashionable address. Gentry families owned property there, including the Duttons and the Savages, and the Norris family acquired three halls (*aulas*) in the lane in 1464.[27]

Bridge Street

Bridge Street ran south from the Cross as far as St Bridget's and St Michael's; below the two churches Lower Bridge Street continued the line to the Bridge-gate and the river. Several lanes led off westwards: Commonhall Lane, Pierpoint Lane and Whitefriars Lane above St Bridget's, Cuppin Lane and Castle Lane below. The remains of the Roman bathhouse prevented lanes developing east of Bridge Street but below St Michael's Pepper Street, St Olave's Lane and Claverton Lane extended eastwards. Pepper Street ran outside the south wall of the Roman fortress and possibly derived its name from the street surface, which perhaps consisted of gravel or small pebbles rather than large paving stones. Alternatively, the city's spicers may have congregated in this location. John Spycer of Pepper Street was mentioned in 1443.[28]

Bridge Street normally followed Eastgate Street in the administrative records; revenues were usually lower and fewer constables, councilmen and alewives were listed. It covered a more extensive area than the Eastgate Street quarter but contained the castle and the Gloverstone at its gate, outside the city's jurisdiction. The Carmelite precinct was also located in this quarter of Chester. Some streets and lanes were densely settled but other lanes contained large properties set in spacious grounds. Two lists of Bridge Street householders who paid tax in 1463 have survived and this perhaps explains why the number (152) exceeded the number recorded for Eastgate Street. The list of taxpayers began with householders living on the east side of Bridge Street at the junction with Eastgate Street and evidently proceeded south to the river diverting to include residents in the adjoining lanes, before returning along the west side of Bridge Street and the adjacent lanes. Properties close to the market place on the east side of Bridge Street were occupied by wealthy apothecaries and mercers; other mercers lived further from the Cross. Millers, fishers, skinners and a parchment-maker were based near the river; men involved with palatinate administration lived in or near Castle Lane. Cuppin Lane was home to a slater, a cooper, a wright and one or two glovers. Among the taxpayers were some who were not well-to-do, including a fiddler, a cardmaker and a number of single women.[29] As in all medieval towns, Chester's rich and poor lived in close proximity.

Other sources confirm the picture. Throughout the fifteenth century the higher end of Bridge Street was a prime location. The two cellars below the Stone Seld at the north-western corner were always leased to prominent citizens, men who were usually involved in the wine trade. Tenant in 1425 was the former mayor John Overton, a regular importer of Gascon wine since the 1390s and occasionally described as a vintner. The alderman Sir Thomas Smith, also a wine importer, occupied the premises in 1508.[30] The pillory stood at the north-eastern corner of Bridge Street, near the steps leading up to the Row. The mercer John

Cottingham leased the first shop in the Row on the east side of the street in the 1440s and his heirs did so in later years. The adjoining shop was occupied by a succession of glovers: Richard Coly, Henry Hatton and finally William Bushell.[31] A reference in 1363–4 to a cellar in 'le fishrowe' in Bridge Street suggests that the fishmarket may have been held below these shops in the mid fourteenth century, but this remains uncertain (see below).[32] New shops were built at Row level in front of house doors further down Bridge Street over the course of the fifteenth century. Nine had appeared by the late 1470s, two of them held by a London mercer who, with a later John Cottingham, supplied paper for use in the castle exchequer. By the late fifteenth century the Row on the eastern side of the street was known as Mercers' Row.[33] Bridge Street was a decidedly 'upmarket' retailing area, where customers could buy fine woollen cloth, squirrel skins and silver pendants.[34]

Among the craftsmen who lived and worked in cheaper premises away from the main thoroughfare were weavers, chaloners, fletchers, pinners and wiredrawers. Glovers, skinners and leather dressers congregated in Lower Bridge Street, already a focus of the light leather crafts in the eleventh century. A skinner occupied a garden on the south side of St Olave's Lane in the late 1420s and the three glovers who rented the shop in the Row in the fifteenth century also rented premises along the river bank.[35] Tailors gathered in Castle Lane, where they could display their wares to the gentlemen making their way to the exchequer and the shire court. Tailors at Westminster and Winchester also gained trade by exhibiting their products in the busiest areas. One of only two haberdashers recorded in Chester in the fifteenth century occupied premises in Castle Lane.[36]

Senior palatine officials naturally chose to live near the castle. Richard of Legh, master carpenter of the palatinate from 1326 until 1335, lived in Castle Lane and held land next to St Mary's churchyard. Hugh de Holes, justice of the King's Bench from 1389 and royal pleader in the county court from the mid 1390s, lived in a large residence in Ship Lane known as the Bulting House. William Troutbeck and his son John, chamberlains in succession from 1412 until 1457, lived in Ship Lane, as Philip the Clerk had done in the early thirteenth century. John Dedwood, who occasionally served as deputy chamberlain in the first half of the fifteenth century, lived close to the imposing stone mansion at the junction of Lower Bridge Street and Castle Lane built in the early thirteenth century by Peter the Clerk.[37] On the east side of Lower Bridge Street next to St Olave's church stood the grand residence of Richard the engineer, master mason from 1272 until his death in 1315. His son sold the property to the Praers/Pares family and it was from there that the chamberlain Robert Parys fled with the seals of the palatinate and the principality in August 1399, in an attempt to join Richard II in Wales.[38]

In Lucian's day the harbour lay to the south of the city, approached via Ship Lane and Shipgate.[39] Although the harbour later moved to the western side of Chester the river remained an influential feature, powering the corn and malt mills which stood just west of Dee Bridge, and attracting the glovers and other light leather workers. The postern in the city wall to the east of the Bridgegate known as Capelgate ('the horse gate') gave access to the river bank where horses were watered, where laundresses worked, and where waterleaders presumably drew buckets of water to supply the townspeople.

Watergate Street

FIGURE 3.2. Batenham's etching of the east side of Bridge Street in *c*.1818 indicates the infilling at the junction with Eastgate Street, site of the pillory in the 15th century, and at the corner of Eastgate Street and Northgate Street, focus of the cooks' trade in the later medieval period. Butchers occupy the shops at street level, possibly on the site of 'le fishrowe' recorded in 1363–4.

Watergate Street ran west from the Cross to the Watergate, crossing the line of the former Roman defences near Holy Trinity church. In the early thirteenth century the area west of the church remained underdeveloped and the Dominicans and the Franciscans were granted land within the walls in the late 1230s. Both friaries stood immediately within the gate, the Franciscan precinct on the north side of the street with the Crofts behind, and the Dominican precinct on the south side, with the Benedictine nunnery behind. Goss Lane, Gerards Lane, Trinity Lane and Crofts Lane led off the north side of Watergate Street, and Berward Lane and St Nicholas Lane led off to the south.

In the fifteenth century revenues from the Watergate Street quarter were always considerably lower than those from Eastgate Street and Bridge Street, although higher than those from Northgate Street. There were 60 taxpayers in 1463, among them a wealthy vintner, a prosperous ironmonger and David Ferror, an influential lawyer who served as one of three deputy chamberlains in the 1440s and 1450s and as mayor of Chester in 1461–2.[40] Other taxpayers included Alice Scott, Marion of Man and Geoffrey and Morris del Crofts, all immigrants living in poor quality housing in the back lanes.

Several butchers were named among the taxpayers. Fleshmongers' Row, first mentioned in the mid fourteenth century but probably in existence some 50 years earlier, extended from St Peter's church as far as Gerards Lane.[41] Butchers lived and traded here throughout the later medieval period. The butcher Thomas Kirby occupied the property adjoining St Peter's in 1374, paying 30s a year for the messuage and the shop below. In the fifteenth century a succession of leading butchers occupied this important tenement, including John Daa, imprisoned for buying herring from the French in 1407. Henry Procator and Nicholas Fitton, both butchers of some standing in the early fifteenth century, lived close by. When Fitton died Procator took over his chamber, shop and cellar but could not make immediate use of the cellar which was occupied by a third butcher.[42] Butchers regularly served as constables for Watergate Street in the second half of the fifteenth century; in 1503–4 they provided the majority of Passage court jurors from Watergate Street and on one occasion all nine jurors were butchers.[43]

By 1588 Chester's official fish market, the Fishboards, was on the south side of Watergate Street facing Fleshmongers' Row, but its location in the medieval period is uncertain. In 1356 the end of the Fishboards was said to be near the new stairs leading to Corvisers' Row and next to the pillory in the corner facing St Peter's church. The pillory stood at the junction of Eastgate Street and Bridge Street, and a reference to a cellar in 'le fishrowe' in Bridge Street in 1363–4 suggests that the fish market was then held on the east side of Bridge Street.[44] The date of its relocation is not recorded. Watergate Street was nevertheless closely associated with the fish trade. Large quantities of fish were unloaded at the harbour, particularly during Lent when demand was at its height. In the 1430s the Fishmongers' company rented a piece of land next to the gate of the Franciscan friary and throughout the century men involved in the trade lived in this quarter of the city. Residents in the 1460s and 1470s included Nicholas Netmaker and the shipman Richard Bold, the latter paying 2s a year for a licence to sell herrings.[45]

Prominent townsmen participated in the fish trade, among them William (III) of Doncaster whose successful career lasted from the 1290s until about 1330. He owned much property in Watergate Street, including the large house next to St Peter's and the house and shop on the corner of Berward Street opposite Holy Trinity church. The rector stole herring from this shop in 1293–4. In January 1318 herring and ling worth £6 were stolen from Doncaster's ship, the *Nicolas*, while it was in the port of Ravenglass in Cumberland.[46] John the armourer, mayor for seven terms between 1385 and 1395, was another successful Watergate Street merchant with trading interests around the Irish Sea. Originally from the Isle of Man, he requested burial in St Mary's chapel in Holy Trinity church and left a quarter share of his ship, the *Saint Mary bote*, to his apprentice David.[47] The draper John Hatton also lived in Watergate Street; in the early fifteenth century his ship regularly crossed to Ireland, returning with fish and animal hides, some in the hands of Dublin and Coventry traders. A shipman and a cook came to blows in the cellar beneath his home in 1415, possibly over supplies of fish.[48] The Corbets, a Manx family which began shipping herring to Chester in the late 1450s, had settled in Watergate Street by the end of the century. Occasional references in the 1490s to sales of salted salmon and to dealings with men from Carrickfergus in Ulster suggest they were already involved with the Bann salmon fishery, leased by Otiwell Corbet in 1519 for £60 a year. The family also imported wine and hides.[49] The house at 10 Watergate Street has a fireplace with a painted plaster chimney breast depicting the arms of the Corbet family and a frieze of sea monsters dating from the late sixteenth or early seventeenth century. The little evidence there is for the location of the Corbets' home in the early sixteenth century, however, suggests that it may have been on the south side of the street, adjoining a property with a stone-vaulted undercroft.[50]

Craftsmen living in and around Watergate Street in the fifteenth century included coopers, slaters, sawyers, bowyers, fletchers and one or two textile workers. Although there were brothels elsewhere in the city there seems to have been a particular concentration in the lanes skirting the friaries, close to the waterfront. John McCowle, Patrick McCally, Elizabeth Ireland and 'Gibon' from Blackfriars Lane were among 16 men and women accused of brothel-keeping in 1474; in 1506 Katherine Irishwoman was fined 12d for keeping a brothel in Greyfriars Lane.[51]

Greyfriars Lane led to the Crofts, an area with much open ground still remaining in the fifteenth century. Here the butchers rented small closes of land on which they pastured livestock prior to slaughter; leading townsmen held gardens, orchards and barns. St Werburgh's barn stood near the end of Barn Lane.[52] The area was home to a small community living in Crofts Lane and in cottages and shops adjoining St Chad's in Dog Lane. Among the prominent citizens who owned shops in Dog Lane was John Coly, who imported much Gascon wine in the 1390s and who was buried in Holy Trinity church in 1413.[53] The status of St Chad's is uncertain but it may once have been parochial, with a tiny parish later attached to St Martin's church.[54] It was not recorded before the early thirteenth century and it could be suggested (tentatively) that it was founded when the harbour was moved to the western side of the city. The population of the area perhaps increased as a result of this relocation, in part to cater for mariners and visiting traders. Witnesses at the inquest into the violent death of a shipman on the Crofts in January 1404 included John the smith of the Crofts, Thomas of Cornwall, Cona ap David, Nicholas of Trim and Stephen of London. These men, and others like them, formed part of an ever-shifting and undisciplined community.[55]

Excavations in 1998 on the site of the demolished Infirmary uncovered evidence of medieval occupation on the Crofts. A substantial medieval cobbled road ran north-south across the site, and a large sandstone structure was found on the southern part of the site, with a possible timber-framed building near by. Concentrated in one area were some roof slates and pieces from one or two louvers, perhaps from a single building. Ridge tiles covered with a pale green

FIGURE 3.3. The exceptionally well-preserved remains of a north-south road at the Royal Infirmary excavated in 1998. It originated in the medieval period and the photo shows a mainly cobbled surface with a clear central channel and sandstone blocks forming the right-hand kerb.

or yellow glaze were discovered in a large medieval pit on the northern part of the site, together with animal bone and pottery. Much of the pottery was from locally made jugs, jars and cooking vessels but there were some imported pots, including a few from south-western France. Gascon wine was regularly unloaded at the Watergate in the medieval period and many of the city's vintners lived in Watergate Street, among them Richard Massey, sheriff in 1451–2, who also rented a tenement on the Crofts for 20d a year.[56]

Northgate Street

Northgate Street extended from just east of the Cross to the Northgate. Narrow at its southern end, particularly so after the construction of the northern section of the Pentice against the east wall of St Peter's in the fifteenth century, the street broadened out in front of the gateway of St Werburgh's. This was the site of the fair granted to the abbey by Earl Hugh, probably in 1092, and of the city's second market place, established in the time of Earl Ranulph II (1129–53). This

FIGURE 3.4. The arches of the abbey gatehouse resemble those of the Welsh castles, particularly the Queen's Gate at Caernarfon. The gatehouse and precinct wall may have been built in the early 13th century, possibly under the supervision of Richard the engineer.

quarter of Chester was dominated by the abbey and its precinct, which occupied the north-east corner of the walled area. The eastern side of Northgate Street was followed for much of its length by the precinct wall of the abbey and only the lane which skirted the graveyard wall led off this side of the street. Houses lined the western side of the street, and Crook Lane, Parsons Lane and Barn Lane led off westwards. Behind the street frontages lay much open ground.

The abbot's manor of St Thomas included much property in Northgate Street, Parsons Lane and beyond the Northgate. The tenants owed suit of court to the manor court held in St Thomas's chapel outside the Northgate and not to the city's courts. This helps to explain why the Northgate Street quarter consistently produced the lowest civic revenues – £2 in 1409 compared to £15 from Eastgate Street for example – and why the constables and councilmen were relatively few in number.[57] Abbey tenants may have contributed to the tax levied in 1463. Among the 77 taxpayers were the mayor Robert Bruyn (a draper), the sheriff William Gough (an ironmonger), and householders who lived beyond the gate. Linen and woollen weavers and hosiers always congregated in this quarter of Chester.[58]

The south-western corner of Northgate Street was a prime commercial area. Four shops 'against' (*contra*) St Peter's church and towards the church of St Werburgh were recorded in *c*.1220.[59] Shops abutted the east wall of St

Peter's in the 1430s and by the 1460s there were four, the two nearest the Cross commanding rents of 30s a year and the two furthest away 13s 4d; these shops were usually occupied by drapers.[60] Ironmongers' Row lay immediately to the north and extended as far as the market place in front of the abbey gateway. It was first recorded in 1294 when a brass bowl stolen by the son and daughter of William Bruyn was sold there.[61] In 1416 a piece of land lying next to the steps at the end of Ironmongers' Row near St Peter's was granted to Thomas Cliff, who lived in the adjoining property and was probably an ironmonger. He built a small shop on this land and thereafter paid the civic authorities 6d a year in rent. His heirs paid the rent in the 1430s but by the 1460s the small shop was occupied by William Gough, who supplied Spanish iron to the chamberlain in 1461–2.[62]

North of the Buttershops on the east side of Northgate Street a Row extended to the market place, and there were more shops in Parsons Lane.[63] New shops were built in front of some houses in the second half of the fifteenth century: six were listed in 1467–8, two of them held by drapers.[64] Abbey tenants occupied small shops and cottages abutting the precinct wall.

Suburbs

Suburbs developed outside the gates of most walled towns. They were often inhabited by impoverished and marginalized social groups and were commonly the scene of unofficial marketing away from the watchful gaze of the civic authorities.[65] Large suburbs could acquire a bad reputation. Chaucer's canon's yeoman described the suburbs where he and his master lived as the haunt of thieves and robbers, where people lurked in hidden corners and blind alleys.[66] At Chester, suburban settlements were established to the north, east and south at an early date. To the west of the city the river ran close to the wall and prevented development; within the wall the area extending to the former western wall of the Roman fortress remained under-developed throughout the medieval period. It was occupied by religious communities, poor housing and small crofts and could perhaps be described as an 'intra-mural suburb'.

Chester's eastern suburb extended from the Eastgate as far as the hospital of St Giles at Boughton, the boundary of the city liberties. Settlement was dense along Foregate Street, lined with burgage plots as far as the Bars, the gate which closed the eastern end of the street by 1241 and which effectively marked a frontier between town and countryside.[67] Payns Lode led south from the Bars to the river and marked the boundary of the bishop's borough. Two lanes ran south from Foregate Street: Love Lane as far as Barkers Lane, and St John's Lane to the intersection with Little St John Lane. That lane led to St John's church and the line continued east along Vicars Lane to join Barkers Lane. Souters Lode (the shoemakers' lane) continued the line of St John's Lane to the river. Cow Lane ran north from Foregate Street to the common known as Henwald's

Lowe and beyond the common another lane, perhaps called the Greenway, meandered through the fields to the common pasture of Hoole heath. To the east of Cow Lane lay the town fields and they prevented the development of further lanes north from Foregate Street.

Travellers approaching Chester from the east entered the liberties at Boughton, location of the leper hospital and the gallows. It was common in all towns to site leper hospitals at a distance from the built-up areas and to set up gallows at the boundary of urban jurisdiction.[68] The road may have been lined by only a scatter of buildings until the Bars, where a smithy stood throughout the medieval period. In the fifteenth century it was owned by the Payns, presumably descendants of the family which held property there in the late thirteenth century. Ropers worked in the area, among them Richard Cook who rented land near the corner of Payns Lode in the 1420s. His neighbour was the carter John Byley, whose home was the venue for illicit trading in 1420, when a Lancashire man sold yarn to a local linen weaver without paying toll. Thatchers too were based near the Bars, where there was space to store their raw materials.[69]

Within the Bars houses became closely packed and an uninterrupted row of buildings faced onto Foregate Street. Love Lane evidently contained humble dwellings and workshops. Residents included Isabel the chider (scold) who kept a brothel there in 1417, and Gilbert Beggar who was fined in 1509 because he was deemed able-bodied and fit to work. A number of the city's heusters (dyers) may have been based in the lane, which was not far from the river, and Robert Belleyetter held a tenement there in the 1390s.[70] Cattle were led to pasture along Cow Lane but by the 1460s industrial activities were intruding on the rural scene. This was still an area of gardens and small crofts, some of them rented by butchers, but men were digging pits for clay near Henwald's Lowe and by the end of the century the Tile houses stood next to Cow Lane.[71] A wide variety of craftsmen lived and worked in Chester's eastern suburb: chaloners, heusters and fullers; tanners, saddlers and shoemakers; plumbers, potters and wrights; coopers, bowyers and fletchers. It was the main industrial area of late medieval Chester and 59 householders paid tax in 1463.

Foregate Street was the principal approach road to the city and contained a number of inns; space was available for stabling and grazing facilities.[72] Transport was a prime concern, serviced by wheelwrights, cartwrights and by the blacksmiths who worked near the gate, a favoured location for smiths in all walled towns.[73] Carters, carriers and porters were based in the eastern suburb and some engaged in illegal activities. On five occasions between April 1397 and April 1398, for example, a Coventry trader arrived with carts filled with merchandise and each time evaded tolls, with the connivance of local porter John Blount.[74] Foregate Street opened out like a market and there was much commercial activity, including forestalling and regrating. Forestallers intercepted goods coming to town and resold them at higher prices; regraters purchased goods legally early in the day and resold them later when shortages caused prices

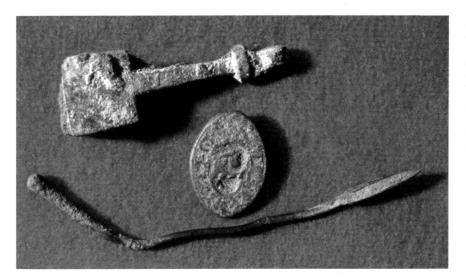

FIGURE 3.5. A parchment clip, seal matrix and unusual metal pen found during excavations at Chester Amphitheatre. The seal matrix is inscribed *S.ROBERTI. CAPLL'I* and displays the 'Pelican in her Piety' device.

to rise.[75] In 1405 a number of townsmen and women were in trouble with the authorities for purchasing foodstuffs and geese 'outside the market' in Foregate Street and in Cow Lane.[76] The suburb's bustling nature was reflected by the number of drinking places. In 1487 the constables listed five brewers and six ale sellers outside the Northgate, two brewers and 14 ale sellers in Handbridge, and 21 brewers and 33 ale sellers outside the Eastgate.[77]

St John's Lane led towards St John's church and was lined with houses along the whole of its length. The proximity of the important ecclesiastical precinct drew scriveners and barbers to the lane. Indeed, all the scriveners recorded in late medieval Chester lived in St John's Lane, close to the archdeacon's court which provided them with so much business. The medieval pen, seal matrix and parchment clip found during the amphitheatre excavations provide material evidence of their trade. The barbers perhaps supplied the dozens of candles always required for the altars in St John's and in the chapels in the precinct.[78] Tanners were recorded in St John's Lane and Little St John Lane from the late thirteenth century and Chester's tanneries were based in the eastern suburb throughout the medieval period.[79]

Behind the properties on the west side of St John's Lane lay the town ditch, constructed in 1264 to strengthen the north and east walls. Thirty years later its defensive role was forgotten and encroachments had begun. In 1294 seven men, two of them tanners, were indicted for making cess-pits in the ditch.[80] By the early fifteenth century sections of the ditch, together with the strip of land above it adjoining the city wall, were leased to individual townsmen, the authorities reserving the right of access should the walls need repair. In 1416 the strip of land and the section of ditch immediately south of the Eastgate were leased to the cutler John del Hey, tenant of the shop next to the gate. Six years later a barber occupied the house and cellar next to the gate and his strip of land extended 35 yards from the stones of the gate towards Wolfeld Gate; the

FIGURE 3.6. Aerial view of the Roman Gardens, St John's and Grosvenor Park. The strip of land outside the city wall was used for gardens in the later medieval period and the adjoining ditch (now gone) for industrial activities and cess-pits. Grosvenor Park was an area of arable and pasture known as the Headlands and tanners and dyers worked there by the 15th century.

neighbouring land was held by a skinner. The ditch contained water and in 1494, when a pewterer occupied the property, he agreed to clean the ditch at his own expense so that the water could flow as was customary. Three years later the smell from the ditch was so offensive that the rent was reduced.[81] It would have been simple to construct timber-lined pits below the permanent water level and the ditch was probably used for industrial or craft activities. The strip of land above the ditch and adjoining the walls was given over to gardens. Tenants in 1468–9 included Thomas Bellyetter and the goldsmiths Ralph Mutlow and Roger Warmingham. Warmingham held two gardens, one of them probably an orchard. At the end of the century the bellfounder Roger Tailor occupied the garden formerly held by Mutlow and blocked it and the adjacent highway near Wolfeld Gate with timber.[82]

A suburb developed at an early date south of the river in Handbridge, always considered part of Chester yet sufficiently distinct to have a separate name. In 1086 the place was known simply as 'Bridge', because of its location at the southern end of the bridge, but by c.1150 it was called Handbridge ('rock bridge'), the prefix denoting the rocky outcrop on which it stood. In the early fifteenth century the Welsh named it *Treboeth*, 'the burnt town', because of the destruction wrought during Glyn Dŵr's rebellion.[83] Roads from Hawarden to the west and Wrexham to the south converged on the suburb and the built-up area probably extended beyond the high street along both approach roads. Welsh migrants settled in the suburb and in 1463 a quarter of the 28 taxpayers had Welsh names.

The nuns were granted lands in Handbridge in the mid twelfth century and their holdings came to be regarded as a manor. The nuns' tenants held land in the open fields and had rights of common pasture in Saltney marsh. Other land was held by Chester's wealthiest inhabitants. In 1379, for example, the prioress granted Hugh de Holes a plot of land enclosed by hedges and ditches called Piecroft, and in 1484 a local fishmonger leased Martinhey in Handbridge field from Thomas Dedwood for four years, agreeing to plough and sow the land for two years and to lay it to grass in years three and four.[84] One or two hemp yards were recorded in the mid 1520s. The Earl's Eye, the great stretch of meadow to the east of the bridge and originally part of the castle demesne, contained pasture land in the later medieval period.[85]

Not all residents were agricultural workers. Quarries had been opened to either side of the bridge in the Roman period and a quarry east of the bridge was being worked by the mid fourteenth century. In 1441–2 the Dominicans owned a quarry at Hough Green to the west of Handbridge, perhaps located at the north-east corner of the green as it was in later centuries. Clay from the green was used to repair the walls of the great stable at the castle and to strengthen the causeway in the 1420s, and the area always remained an important source of clay. Carters could be certain of steady employment.[86] Mills stood at the Handbridge end of the causeway by the mid twelfth century and after their reconstruction in 1355 they were specifically described as fulling mills.[87] Textile workers congregated in the suburb and walkers and heusters prospered; hosiers, tailors and glovers also worked there. A glass-working enterprise was established in the later fifteenth century.

The hermitage of St James was built at the southern end of the bridge between the river and the quarry east of the bridge shortly before 1358. Five years later the hermit 'by the bridge' was commissioned to collect a grant of pavage and in 1367 licence for an oratory was granted; a chaplain was employed in the fifteenth century. The hermitage stood in a walled enclosure and the homeless and the destitute perhaps found shelter there.[88] In 1452 the civic authorities accused the hermit of St James of receiving robbers, sheltering malefactors, and keeping a brothel in his lodgings (*hospicio*). The transient population of poor and marginalized individuals evidently roused suspicions, some of them justified. Illegal trading certainly took place in Handbridge. In 1451, for example, one inhabitant forestalled the market by purchasing 79 cheeses from the Welshman bringing them to the city for sale.[89]

The northern suburb was Chester's smallest suburb and lay within the abbot's manor of St Thomas. The built-up area was confined to a ribbon development along the road leading from the Northgate to the chapel dedicated to St Thomas Becket which stood in the fork of two roads, one leading north-west towards the Wirral anchorages and the other leading north into Wirral and the ferry across the Mersey. The abbot held his manorial court in the chapel and the manorial mill lay on Bache brook to the north. Gardens lay behind the houses and fields approached close to the city walls to the north and east, at the end of Bag Lane. Abbey property in that lane was destroyed in 1264 when the town ditch was constructed at the suggestion of one of the city sheriffs, vilified by the monks as 'a certain cursed fellow called Robert the mercer'.[90] In the late 1450s the lane leading north from Bag Lane to the abbot's windmill was known as Raymond's Lane, named from the family which had held land in the vicinity for at least 130 years.[91] A lane ran west from the Northgate alongside the town ditch to the river and a lane branched off to Portpool, the anchorage established at the boundary of the liberties by the thirteenth century. The taxpayers outside the Northgate were not listed separately in 1463.

St John's hospital stood immediately to the west of the Northgate, occupying a narrow site extending 120 metres alongside the town ditch towards the Dee. There were quarries in the ditch near the New Tower and stone was used for civic building projects. In the 1460s and 1470s the authorities leased one quarry to a barber for 3s a year.[92] Sand for construction work at the castle came from a site beyond the New Tower in the mid fifteenth century.[93] To the east of the Northgate, between the city wall and Bag Lane, was another quarry; this was being worked by the 1290s and the stone used for castle repairs.[94] A smithy and its garden lay at the corner of Bag Lane diagonally opposite St John's hospital in 1270–1. The Blackburn family worked the smithy for much of the fifteenth century and in 1454–5 Thomas Blackburn added to his income by farming the Northgate as well. There was still a smithy on the site in the early seventeenth century.[95]

The northern suburb was home to men involved in maritime trade, including ropemakers, shipmen, mariners and carters. Hostelers provided food, stabling and accommodation for traders who needed to stay overnight.[96] When the tolls levied at Chester's four main gates were recorded in 1321, herring headed the list of commodities on which tolls were charged at the Northgate, followed by a variety of sea-fish and shell-fish. Unauthorized custom was taken from boats landing cargoes of herring and other fish between Bonewaldesthorne Tower and the Portpool. The Northgate was clearly a major entry point for fish and Chester's hostelers, like those at Exeter, became involved in the trade and held illegal fish markets on their premises. Complaints that foreign fishmongers sold fish outside Chester's market were voiced in the 1470s; the Great Charter of 1506 decreed that fish was only to be sold in the customary place and not in 'suburbs, hamlets, precinct or circuit.'[97]

There was no room for suburban development outside the Watergate but this was a busy area, its waterfront bustling with activity. Shifts in the river channel

affected access by the late thirteenth century and large sea-going vessels anchored downstream; their cargoes were brought up to the city in small boats.
Vessels involved in the coastal trade also sailed up to the Watergate. In 1322 the
New Tower was built to protect the harbour and a spur wall some 30 metres long
connected it to the main defences. It seems that the tower remained in or very
close to the river in 1391, when a small boat 'next' (*iuxta*) to it was stolen by a
shipman, but the water gradually receded and by 1506 the New Tower evidently
stood on dry ground. That year a close of pasture called the Roodee extending
from the New Tower on the north to the watch tower called the Lowse Tower
on the south was leased to two prominent citizens. Two closes near the walls
were excluded from the lease.[98]

Commodities subject to tolls at the Watergate in 1321 included dishes, cups,
knives, brushwood and coal, but the main emphasis was on sea-fish, shell-fish
and herring. The waterfront was particularly busy during Lent.[99] Casks of wine
from Gascony, millstones from Anglesey and slates from Wales were unloaded
there. In 1399 Edward the dosser, a carter's servant, was killed near the Watergate

FIGURE 3.7. The
New Tower, built in
1322–*c*.1326 at a cost
of £100, was linked to
Bonewaldesthorne Tower
by a spur wall, rebuilt
in 1730. It resembles the
water tower at Conwy
and although intended to
be 'in the water of Dee'
stood on dry land within
a century.

when he fell under the wheel of a cart loaded with slates. An inquest decided that his negligent driving was the cause of his death and that the seven horses pulling the cart were *in auxilio*.[100]

South of the Watergate lay the Roodee, a tidal area of salt marsh in the Roman period and still washed daily by the tides at the end of the twelfth century. A hundred years later it was normally dry and in 1288 the 'Eye' was the setting for archery practice. Between then and 1364 it became permanent grassland known as the Roodee, the 'meadow with a cross', named from the cross marking the boundary between the parishes of St Mary and Holy Trinity.[101] The Roodee belonged to the city and townsmen paid to graze horses, cows and sheep on the land. The authorities issued an annual ordinance which forbade the digging of pits and imposed a heavy fine on anyone who dug a pit and failed to fill it in within a fortnight.[102] The archery contest between the mayor, sheriffs and aldermen held on Easter Monday was staged on the Roodee in the early sixteenth century.[103]

The liberties of the late medieval city stretched beyond the suburbs and covered some 3,000 acres, much of it agricultural land. In 1354, when the boundary was defined formally for the first time, the liberties extended to Great Boughton to the east, to Saltney to the west, to Blacon, Bache, Newton and Hoole to the north, and encompassed part of Lache and part of Claverton to the south.[104] Some citizens invested in land in the liberties and their agricultural interests made a significant contribution to their income. Richard Holyns for example, a heuster living in Foregate Street in the 1390s, not only held several selions and butts in the town fields adjoining Henwald's Lowe but also 16 acres of arable land near Hoole heath and 6½ selions in the fields of Marlston, Lache and Claverton. He also received rental income from a messuage and 18 selions in Newton. The barker Thomas Stretton, another Foregate Street resident, evidently cultivated grain on a considerable scale. Failure to repair his barn in 1450 resulted in the loss of wheat, rye, barley and oats worth £6.[105] Other townsmen held small enclosed fields and kept a cow or two; they earned extra income by letting the grazing to men bringing cattle and horses to sell in the city. Short-term grazing facilities were always needed and demand peaked during the Midsummer and Michaelmas fairs.[106] Shared agricultural interests ensured that town and country were closely integrated and fostered the development of social networks.

CHAPTER FOUR

The Built Environment

Chester's status as a top-ranking town was reflected by its distinctive physical environment. All visitors to the medieval city would have recognised it instantly as a place of major importance, encircled as it was by massive stone walls and entered through imposing stone gates. The streets were paved, public spaces were reserved for markets, and there was commercial zoning in the Rows, the galleries at first-floor level which lined the four main thoroughfares. Impressive stone buildings lay within the walls, foremost among them the castle and the Benedictine abbey, but also including parish churches and private mansions, all built of the local red sandstone. The most ambitious building programmes on the walls, the castle, and all religious houses except the abbey had been carried out in the years before 1300. Major construction work continued at St Werburgh's until the Dissolution, albeit with lengthy interludes. Elsewhere building activity after 1350 was for the most part limited to smaller projects.[1] From the mid fifteenth century, like townsmen throughout England, Cestrians complained of decay. In 1445 they declared that the greater part of their city was ruinous and sparsely inhabited; in 1486 they claimed that a quarter of Chester was destroyed and that the walls had fallen into decay and ruin.[2]

City walls, gates and streets

The full medieval circuit of walls may have been completed in 1160–2. In its final form the two-mile circuit was embattled and included four main gates, at least six posterns, and eight or nine watch towers. In 1264, during the Baronial wars, the town ditch was constructed to strengthen the north and east walls. The intra-mural area covered some 126 acres, less than half the size of York (263 acres) and considerably smaller than Coventry (*c.*210 acres), but comparable with Gloucester (*c.*128 acres) and Bristol (*c.*136 acres).[3]

Town walls were costly to maintain and their upkeep was largely funded by royal grants of murage, an occasional tax on merchandise carried into and out of the city. Chester's first recorded murage was granted in 1249 and further grants were made until 1409, when the prince of Wales allowed the mayor and commonalty to take murages. This led to the appointment of two 'keepers of the walls and collectors of murage' who the same year reported a townsman for damaging the walls.[4] In 1440–1 the muragers' income, derived from tolls at the gates and from 78 foreign merchants, approached £15 and their expenditure slightly exceeded this sum. £10 went to the palatinate master mason John Asser for rebuilding the upper section of the wall between the tower on the Bridgegate and the old wall next to the bridge, and almost £5 was spent on repairs to the drawbridge at the Northgate and paving work in Eastgate Street. In 1453 some stretches of the walls were in such disrepair that townspeople were able to carry away stones. The citizens doubtless exaggerated when they claimed in 1486 that the walls had collapsed but there may have been justifiable cause for concern.[5]

The four main gates had been constructed by the time of Earl Ranulph III (1181–1232) and by the late thirteenth century they were held by hereditary keepers, charged with collecting tolls and organizing watches on the walls. The east gate had been the main entrance to the Roman fortress and the Eastgate was the principal gate of the medieval city. The keepers were responsible for inspecting the official weights and measures and it was at this gate that the heads and quartered remains of those who rebelled against the king were displayed, to serve as a grim warning to the populace. In the fourteenth century the east elevation took the form of a rather narrow archway flanked by two octagonal towers. The Bridgegate, a Gothic arch set between two round towers, guarded the approach from Wales and the keeper also had responsibility for the adjacent Shipgate and Capelgate. The Northgate comprised a narrow passage with square towers on either side, and was entered via a drawbridge over the town ditch.[6] In 1403, when fears of attack by Glyn Dŵr's adherents were at their height, the tenants of the plot of land to the west of the gate were obliged to rebuild the drawbridge and guard it night and day. The gaol buildings were incorporated within the Northgate, the dungeons below and the 'franchise house' where debtors were lodged, above.[7] The Watergate was the least impressive of Chester's gates, presumably because it merely gave access to the harbour and the Roodee and not to a major approach road. It may never have had towers and consisted of a single arch and a separate postern for pedestrians.

Some of Chester's streets were paved by the 1240s, the work financed by grants of pavage and the money collected by the overseers of pavage. A three-year pavage granted to the mayor and citizens in 1279 specified that the tax was to be levied on firewood and coals brought into the city, at the rate of a halfpenny a load. By the end of the thirteenth century pavage grants were regularly linked to murage grants and a hundred years later murage was used to fund both types of work. In 1395, when the city's walls and pavements were said to be in a very ruinous state, the mayor and commonalty claimed that both had been supported and repaired by murage from the earliest times.[8] The muragers regularly paid for paving work in the fifteenth century. In 1440–1 Miles Paver received 6s 8d for paving in Eastgate Street and outside the Bridgegate towards Handbridge, and some 40 years later John Paver repaired 12 feet of pavement in Cuppin Lane at the rate of a penny per foot.[9]

The cobbled surface of the medieval lane which ran alongside the city's north wall was found just to the south of Water Tower Street in 1972–3. It consisted of a single layer of sandstone cobbles and pebbles, up to 20cm deep, and was probably built in the early fourteenth century.[10] The medieval road excavated in the Crofts in 1998 was built partly of cobbles and partly of large chunks of sandstone; the surface sloped inwards from the sides to a central drainage channel. It may have been the surface of the *regia strata del Croftes* first attested in 1345 and seemingly on the same alignment. A plot of land 'lying between the stone wall of the Franciscans and the channel of the high street of the Crofts' was recorded in 1471.[11] There were drainage channels in other streets, placed centrally or to either side: some 4 yards from house frontages in Foregate Street in 1446, for example, and 2½ yards from the building at the north-western corner of Bridge Street and 2 yards from the building round the corner in Watergate Street in 1508.[12] A Roman roadside drain was discovered when Watergate Street was pedestrianized in 2000. The archaeologists have suggested that such drains still functioned in the medieval period. With the covering slabs removed they would have proved useful in carrying away rubbish.[13]

Dee Bridge

The Romans built their fortress at the lowest bridging point on the Dee and later bridges stood on or close to the site of their Roman predecessor.[14] In 1066 one man from each hide in the county was called up to repair the city wall and bridge, and repairs to the bridge remained the responsibility of the county until 1288, when it was agreed that the city should maintain the southern part of the bridge and the county the rest. As the bridge had reputedly been swept away by floods in 1279 or 1280 the agreement perhaps applied to a replacement, which evidently consisted of a wooden superstructure standing on stone piers.[15]

By 1346 the bridge was in poor condition and over the following two years the piers, arches and the tower at the southern end were repaired. Work was interrupted by the Black Death and from 1349 until 1354 the bridge was closed; crossings were made by the ford and ferry maintained by the keeper of the passage of Dee. The cost of a ferry crossing is not recorded but a Welshman and his men paid an annual sum of 3s 4d, as did Sir John Danyers and his entourage. Revenues ranged from about £11 to almost £15 a year.[16] When the bridge reopened in December 1354 the mayor and citizens had not completed the section for which they were responsible and three years later, having learned that they were delaying the work as long as possible, the Black Prince ordered them to complete it with all speed and in the same style as the rest.[17]

Floods had destroyed this bridge by 1383 and a three-year grant of murage was awarded for its repair. It remained broken in 1387 and many people were said to have drowned when attempting to make the crossing. Richard II may have seen the state of the bridge during his visit in July and this perhaps prompted his grant of the profits from the Dee passage and the murage for its reconstruction. In December 1388 came a three-year grant of pontage.[18] By February 1394 the bridge was again in use although the tower at the southern end was not completed until 1407. A civic ordinance prohibited carts with iron-bound wheels from using the bridge, under penalty of confiscation of the cart and 6s 8d to the king.[19] This prohibition was included among the ordinances throughout the fifteenth century but was largely ignored. In 1494 men from Handbridge and Saltneyside were fined for crossing with carts loaded with sea-coal, and the following year a Welshman drove his cart into an arch of the bridge tower and destroyed it, an accident which perhaps necessitated the rebuilding of the further end of the bridge in 1500.[20] The bridge was widened in 1826 by the addition of a footpath and railings but otherwise remains much as it was when rebuilt in the late 1380s: a sandstone structure with seven arches (reduced from eight) and a stone parapet.

Castle

The castle in the south-west corner of Chester was founded by William I in 1070 and passed from the Norman earls to the Crown in 1237. Royal ownership enhanced the castle's status and an ambitious building programme was undertaken to make the place fit for a king. An extensive outer bailey was added, enclosed by a stone wall from the late 1240s, and over the following decades the principal buildings were moved there.[21] The castle's military importance was at its height during Edward I's Welsh campaigns. The king stayed there in 1275 and 1277, and it again served as royal headquarters and military base in 1282–3 and 1294. New royal apartments, chapels and stables were built in the 1280s and 1290s, and an imposing gatehouse flanked by twin towers was constructed in the outer bailey. By 1300 the direction of the work was in the hands of Richard the engineer, who had gained his experience working on the Welsh castles and who remained royal engineer until his death in 1315.[22]

The castle then comprised an inner and outer bailey encircled by strong walls furnished with towers and entered via formidable gatehouses. The lodgings of the constable and other important officials were in the inner bailey, as too were the royal apartments, chapel and hall. The outer bailey contained further royal apartments and chapels, the shire hall until 1310, when it was relocated outside the castle gate, and the exchequer until 1401, when it too was moved outside the gate to a site adjoining the shire hall. Stables, kitchens and service buildings with cellars stood in the outer bailey, and here too was the great well. Conduits and gutters carried water to and from the various kitchens, halls and towers, and the main chambers were provided with latrines.[23] There were four gaols, including one in Gough's Tower and another in a tower in the outer gatehouse. New pairs of fetters and great locks for the doors were regularly purchased throughout the later medieval period. In 1457–8 a city locksmith was paid 5s for making three great bolts and a great chain to secure those incarcerated at the castle, and in 1470–1 a smith worked 60 lbs of iron for locks and chains for prisoners.[24]

The exquisite wall paintings in the inner gatehouse chapel commissioned by Henry III in the 1240s were covered with limewash when the chapel was converted into a treasury some 50 years later. Decorative schemes undertaken at the end of the thirteenth century included the colouring of ten ceiling corbels in the king's great chamber and, by command of the prince of Wales, the painting of images of Thomas Becket and the four knights who murdered him on a wall in the lesser chapel near the great hall.[25] Windows in the royal apartments and chapels were glazed. Strong winds in the winter of 1327–8 broke many of them, including eight in the queen's chamber, and all had to be replaced.[26] The damage done to the castle fabric that year was also made good but several decades of neglect followed and by the late 1340s many buildings, including the great chapel and the great hall, were in disrepair. Work was undertaken in the mid 1350s and in the 1390s Richard II ordered a considerable number of alterations, including the insertion of a heated bathhouse in the inner royal chamber. Expenditure on maintenance in Henry VI's reign averaged £25 a year and money was spent on improving the heating arrangements. In 1426 masons made a new fireplace in the justice's lodgings in the inner bailey complete with a 'mantilstone' brought from the quarry in Handbridge.[27] Work was underway on a fireplace in the chancellor's office in 1457–8, and sea-coal was regularly purchased for the royal auditors at this period.[28] The castle fabric was neglected during the reign of Edward IV and the office of master mason lapsed until 1495. Henry VII spent about £25 a year on maintenance, a not ungenerous sum but wholly inadequate. Although almost £300 was spent on repairs to the great hall, the shire hall and the gatehouses in 1511, twenty years later the great hall was in ruins.

Townsmen always profited by servicing the needs of the castle garrison and the palatinate administration. In the early fourteenth century William (III) of Doncaster received almost £15 for supplying lead to roof Gough's Tower and limestone tiles to mend fireplaces in chambers near the great hall; a local cooper was paid 4d for making a bucket for the well.[29] A century later Chester's merchants supplied Spanish iron for castle repairs, waxchandlers provided candles and torches for the royal chapel, and a spicer provided gunpowder for the defence of the castle.[30] In the later fifteenth century mercers supplied parchment, paper and sealing-wax, and a woman made candles to provide illumination when the justice, chamberlain and auditors worked long into the night.[31] Building projects provided employment for local carpenters, pavers, carters and waterleaders. Women gathered rushes to cover the floor of the exchequer, hemmed curtains for the window, and made canvas bags for the coins.[32] Those involved in the food and drink trades did well. During a seventeen-day visit in the 1390s members of the royal council spent almost £7 on spices, meat, fish, poultry and dairy produce, and 71s on ale and wine. While James Manley and his company of 20 men were on guard at the castle in 1469 their food cost more than £6.[33] Sir Thomas Manley, father of James, and his daughter Alice were also in Chester in April that year, he to serve as grand juror and she perhaps to mingle with high society.[34] Sessions of the county court were held every six weeks or so and lasted two or three days. Those attending patronized the city's shops and taverns and required accommodation for themselves and their horses. Local traders looked forward to this regular influx of wealthy customers with eager anticipation.

Causeway, mills and fisheries

Chester probably had corn mills from an early date but the first evidence for milling dates from the late eleventh century. By the 1190s a man-made causeway or weir had been constructed just above the bridge to enhance the flow of water to the mills, using a natural rocky feature on the river bed as the foundation.[35] The causeway was raised in 1355 to increase the power and care was always taken to keep it in good repair. In 1427–8, for example, the mason John Asser junior, assisted by two masons, a quarryman and seven labourers, packed 'pudelstone' (a mixture of clay and sand) around the large stones to make the causeway watertight. The 'pudelstone' was brought to the site from the New Tower and from Shotwick and more clay came from Hough Green. Three women carried 48 loads of moss from Eccleston wood to seal any remaining gaps.[36]

The corn mills were located beside the bridge at the Chester end of the causeway and the royal monopoly over milling within the city and its liberties ensured that they produced large revenues.[37] All the inhabitants were required to grind their corn in the mills and hand over a sixteenth of the grain as toll. The mills' profits came from the sales of this grain, which included wheat, maslin (mixed wheat and rye), and various types of flour and malt. Attracted by the potential profits, leading citizens leased the mills for long periods between

FIGURE 4.1. Dee Bridge and Bridgegate before 1784. This mid 17th-drawing shows the medieval Bridgegate, Shipgate and Capelgate. The tall turret over the Bridgegate was added in 1600–5 to act as an airpipe and improve the flow of water to the cistern at the Cross. The Dee corn mills evidently consisted of two buildings and the one that is shown housed three mill wheels under one roof. The mills built by Richard the engineer in the 1290s housed five mill wheels, three under one roof and two under the other.

1245 and 1377, among them Richard the engineer from the early 1270s until 1315. His lease in 1281 included the Dee fishery, a framework of hurdles under the bridge to which nets were attached, and thenceforth mills and fishery were almost invariably leased together. In 1377, perhaps in response to falling prices, the decision was taken to manage the mills and fishery directly and from then until 1503, apart from a brief period in the early 1390s, the mills were in the hands of keepers and administered by their deputies.

In the mid 1280s, while Richard the engineer was away on the king's service in Wales, floods caused much damage to the mills, sweeping away barns and weirs and preventing the fish-traps from being fixed under the bridge. The destruction of the causeway prevented the mills from grinding for almost three months and in 1290 Richard's rent was reduced to enable him to build two new mills on the site.[38] The new mills evidently housed five mill wheels and their machinery, three under one roof and two under another, the former perhaps used to grind corn and the latter to grind malt. In 1298 the mills were rebuilt on an adjoining site, perhaps because the causeway had been altered. The five stalls that held the nets of the fishery were weighted down by stones to prevent them from being swept away by floods. The stones were taken to the bridge on boats, and two quays were built on the far side of the Dee to facilitate the loading. In 1309 five carpenters carried out further work on the quay, assisted by 34 labourers who carried sand to dry the river bank and dragged and raised timbers with the help of ropes.[39]

For a few months in 1392 the mills and fishery were leased to John Walsh, although he had been accused of extortion, and he leased them again from July 1393 until January 1394, when he was indicted for the death of a man and fled. In August 1394 the two malt mills were burned to the ground, due to the carelessness of Walsh's wife who failed to extinguish the fire she had taken with her to provide light. It was claimed in court that the damage amounted to £200 but the mills were repaired for £50.[40] The walls of the malt mills were seriously damaged in 1406 by liquid filth flooding down Bridge Street and Lower Bridge Street after heavy rains.[41] The annual cost of maintenance of the mills and fishery in the fifteenth century ranged between £3 and £12 and expenditure on millstones was sometimes considerable. Millstones usually came from Anglesey, famous for their production in the medieval period, but supplies were interrupted during Glyn Dŵr's rebellion and in 1401–2 and again in 1404–5 millstones were obtained from quarries on Penket Cloud, a hill near Congleton in east Cheshire. They may have been a poor substitute; in 1405–6 a dozen arrived from Anglesey, each costing 30s.[42] Transport to Chester added significantly to the cost. In 1464–5 Jevan Milner travelled from Chester to the island to select the stones and purchased three for £3; it cost 23s to ship them to the Watergate and a further 2s to cart them to the mills.[43]

The royal fishery comprised the stalls attached to the bridge and the adjacent pool below the causeway, known as the King's Pool from 1445 when it was first leased to Sir Thomas Stanley and Thomas Pulford.[44] In the mid 1350s and from 1377 until 1445 the fishery was directly managed by keepers who received 26s 8d a year and a suit of clothes. The 'lord's fisherman' in 1354–5 was Robert Mustard, after whom the riverside buildings to the west of the corn mills were evidently named. Three messuages called Mustard Houses were listed in 1420 among property formerly held by Hugh de Holes.[45] They were perhaps used to store equipment, including canvas and thread to mend the nets; small boats used by the fishermen were probably moored nearby.[46] In the earlier 1380s the keepers accounted for salmon caught outside the pool in the *malagyn* in the Dee; this was destroyed in 1387–8 by men from Wales.[47] In 1402 local millers removed stones from the bridge and placed '*ingenia* called weles' in the pool, in order to catch lampreys, salmon and eels.[48] The fishery's main profits came from sales of salmon but lampreys were sold from time to time and, in the 1370s and 1380s, eels and sparling as well. The fishery could not function for seven weeks in 1470–1 while the quays were rebuilt, and it was blocked for three months in 1479–80 while the fulling mills were repaired. Three years later failure to repair the causeway led to the loss of profits from the fishery for five months.[49]

There were mills at the Handbridge end of the causeway by the mid twelfth century. Two quays were built beside them in 1298–9, to provide unloading facilities for timber brought down river by boat for the new corn mills.[50] In 1355 the Handbridge mills were specifically described as fulling mills. Two posts and other old timber from the fulling mills were sold in 1390–1 and a new fulling mill was built in 1392.[51] Tenter-frames stood near by.[52] Repairs to the fulling mills in 1426–7 cost almost £8 and the following year Thomas Potter supplied two dozen ridge tiles for the roof. Within the mills was a storehouse in which the castle masons kept their tools.[53] The fulling mills were neglected in later years and were in such a poor state by 1462–3 that they yielded no profits for nine months. They stood empty from Pentecost until Michaelmas in 1464–5 and were frequently unoccupied throughout the 1470s.[54] When members of the Goodman family and other citizens leased the mills in 1506–7, the lease specified that they were responsible for repairing the buildings and the iron machinery, and that the prince would supply the large timbers and three great iron 'cacchepynes'.[55]

Religious houses

Extensive archaeological investigations carried out in recent years on the sites of the lesser religious houses, and in the nave and south transept of the cathedral, have clarified our understanding of the building history of Chester's Benedictine abbey and nunnery, and of the Dominican, Franciscan and Carmelite friaries.[56] The publications of this research are essential reading and the following discussion seeks mainly to assess the impact of the religious houses on the lives of the townspeople.

The Anglo-Saxon minster dedicated to St Werburg was refounded as a Benedictine monastery in 1092. It was lavishly endowed from the start and all the Norman earls were buried there, with the exception of Richard who drowned in the *White Ship* in 1120. Its vast wealth enabled St Werburgh's to build on a grand scale and construction work on the abbey church continued intermittently throughout the medieval period. The monastic buildings lay to the north of the church, which separated them from the town and afforded privacy. The precinct was bounded by the city walls to the east and the north, and by the wall skirting Northgate Street to the west. South of the church, however, lay the graveyard of St Oswald's parish, regularly accessed by the parishioners. The south nave aisle of the abbey church served as the parish church and the congregation worshipped there until shortly after 1348, when building operations in the abbey church resulted in their removal to the newly-built chapel of St Nicholas in the south-west corner of the precinct.

Pilgrims entered the abbey church to visit the shrine of St Werburg. In the earlier medieval period the saint was greatly venerated but by the thirteenth century the cult was in decline. The shrine was rebuilt in *c.*1340 in the form of a miniature chapel with two storeys and the reliquary containing the saint's remains was housed in the richly decorated upper storey. The lower section was never completed and it seems that St Werburg did not command much devotion within the city. The saint's miraculous resurrection of a goose that had been cooked and eaten was carved on one of the misericords in the 1380s and John Southworth's son (in 1489) and son-in-law (in 1506) both left bequests to the saint. The latter asked to be buried in the abbey church beside his father-in-law.[57]

The mayor John Arneway requested burial in the abbey church in 1274–8 and left a considerable amount of property to endow a perpetual chantry at the altar of St Leonard. This became one of the abbey's most notable chantries and was remembered by other testators in later years.[58] The Virgin Mary was evidently regarded with especial veneration and seems to have been named in the dedication in the late twelfth century. The abbey church, like other large churches throughout England, acquired a Lady chapel in the later thirteenth century and held additional services in honour of the Virgin.[59] The east window of St Werburgh's contained scenes from her life; misericords depicted her holding the Child and her Coronation; the Assumption featured on the west front of the church, begun in the early sixteenth century. When the abbey was refounded as the cathedral church in 1541, the dedication was changed to Christ and the Blessed Virgin.[60]

Building programmes provided employment for Chester's craftsmen. The name of the carpenter Roger Burgess, sheriff in 1482–3, was included among the obits of the abbey and he perhaps supervised construction work at St Nicholas's chapel in the late 1480s, when the building was enlarged and given a new roof and doors. John Dean was retained to serve as abbey painter for a year from March 1485 but his salary was not paid in full and he was obliged to

FIGURE 4.2. The shrine of St Werburg was probably dismantled at the Dissolution. The current shrine was re-erected behind the altar in the 1880s and the statue is modern.

sue the abbot for the arrears three years later. In June 1491 the abbot attempted to recover 6s owed by a city glazier for two panes of glass.[61]

Relations between the monks and the townspeople were not always cordial. In the early fourteenth century the abbot was reported to the civic authorities for allowing effluent from the latrine to block the water course in the town ditch The huge drain 15 metres in length which carried effluent from the reredorter

FIGURE 4.3. The 13th-century drain for the reredorter (latrine) of St Werburgh's abbey. This fine masonry structure still survives in use, capped with brick, under the cathedral green. It evidently discharged into the town ditch outside the city wall.

(latrine) to the city wall has recently been discovered.[62] Another source of friction was the gate in the city wall which led to the Kaleyards, the monastic kitchen garden. The garden lay outside the east wall, beyond the town ditch, and in 1274–5 Edward I granted the monks permission to make a postern gate to give access. The citizens feared for the security of the city and in 1323 the monks agreed to make a drawbridge over the town ditch to protect the gate and to take measures for the safe custody of the keys. They also agreed to destroy the great gate in the garden wall bordering Cow Lane and replace it with a small postern that could be closed should the safety of the city require it. This access to the garden also caused difficulties.[63]

The Benedictine nunnery of St Mary was founded in the mid twelfth century by Earl Ranulph II on a site in the Crofts north-west of the castle.[64] The church and conventual buildings were centrally placed in a stone-walled precinct which extended from the castle ditch on the south to Arderne Lane on the north, and from the city wall on the west to Nuns Lane on the east. The east precinct wall contained the gate which gave access to the lane leading to the guest accommodation and service buildings in the outer courtyard, and a postern in the west wall led to a way across the Crofts. The church, 22 yards long and 15 yards broad, contained at least 13 altars by the early fifteenth century and there were many burials, one of them perhaps that of the nuns' steward who in 1526 asked to be interred in front of the image of Our Lady of Pity.[65] In the mid fourteenth century the prioress was said to keep ladies, damsels and children at her table, and there was evidently considerable contact between the nuns and the townspeople. John Hawarden in 1496, and the steward 30 years later, both left money in the keeping of the prioress and trusted her to distribute it according to their wishes.[66] Margaret Hawarden in 1520 left a coffer to the prioress for use in the nunnery, a painted coffer to the sub-prioress, and £10 towards the rebuilding of the cloisters.[67]

The Dominicans and Franciscans began to establish houses in England in the 1220s and the Carmelites and Augustinians arrived a few years later. Their mission was directed at towns and their presence reflected England's main urban centres in the thirteenth century.[68] Three orders of friars founded permanent houses at Chester, a clear indication of the city's high status. Friaries were typically located on the periphery of the built-up areas or in the suburbs and when the Dominicans arrived in 1237 or 1238 and the Franciscans a few months later, both were granted plots of undeveloped land immediately within the Watergate, the Franciscans on the north side of the street and the Dominicans on the south. The Carmelites were first recorded in Chester in 1277 and in 1290 were granted seven messuages near the Bars, but by the later 1290s they were established on a permanent site adjoining what became known as Whitefriars Lane.[69]

The Franciscans' precinct covered some seven acres, extending from Watergate Street on the south to Dog Lane on the north, and from Crofts Lane on the east to a wall skirting the city wall. A gatehouse opening onto Crofts Lane gave access to the friary church and public courtyards in the southern part of the precinct. The great cloister was sited to the north of the church and north of that was a second cloister which perhaps included the infirmary. Beyond were gardens, orchards and a walled area of pasture. The church was about 60 metres long and had a steeple with 'a sharpe spyar' and two bells. Its wide nave and aisles were designed to serve the friars' preaching mission but had fallen into disrepair by the early sixteenth century. Chester's merchants and sailors rebuilt them and in return were allowed to store sails and other nautical equipment in the church.[70]

The Dominican friary lay in a 5½-acre precinct bounded by a wall skirting the city wall to the west, St Nicholas Lane to the east, Arderne Lane to the south, and Watergate Street to the north. Orchards and gardens occupied the northern part of the precinct, separated from the church by a stone wall. The church possibly stood on the site of an earlier chapel dedicated to St Nicholas, and was accessed by a walled alley from St Nicholas Lane. The cloister lay on the south side of the church, a graveyard for the brethren to the east, and a graveyard for the laity to the south-west. A large preaching nave with two aisles was added to the single-celled church in the late thirteenth or early fourteenth century; subsequent work included a large crossing tower, removed in the later fifteenth century, and a prominent western tower was planned in the early sixteenth century, perhaps intended to rival the tower built by the Carmelites in 1495. The work was abandoned some ten years or so before the Dissolution.[71] The nave and aisles of the church were filled with interments, mostly males, and

FIGURE 4.4. This medieval grave slab found during excavations on the site of the nunnery in 2007 had been broken and re-used as building material in the wall of a late medieval or early post-medieval building.

prominent citizens were buried in the graveyard, including the former sheriff Thomas of Strangeways, who requested burial there in 1346 and left 20s a year for prayers for his soul.[72]

During the 1290s the Carmelites established their community on land adjoining the lane then known as Alexander Harre's Lane. Alexander Harre, an important citizen in the earlier thirteenth century and almost certainly son of Earl Ranulph III's nurse, owned a chapel to the north of the lane and the Carmelites perhaps took this over as the friary church. They acquired additional land in the mid fourteenth century and eventually their precinct extended from the lane on the south to Commonhall Lane on the north, and from Berward Lane on the west to the rear of houses on Bridge Street on the east. The friary church of St Mary stood in the southern part of the precinct and was accessed by the main gateway in Whitefriars Lane; there may have been a second gateway on Commonhall Lane. The cloisters lay north of the church and the precinct contained a barn, orchards, gardens, and a building where the Carpenters' company stored the equipment used in the Corpus Christi procession and pageant. The Carpenters also maintained a light in the friary church, to which Robert Scot, palatinate master carpenter, bequeathed a 'chyppynax' in 1408.[73] The Carmelite church became a popular place for burials. In 1439 John Hatton asked to be buried in front of Our Lady's altar near his father, mother and brothers; in 1496 John Hawarden requested burial within the church and left 40s towards the newly-built steeple, destined to become a valued landmark for sailors. His widow Margaret in 1520 asked to be buried on the north side of the church and left money and a lead furnace for her tomb and for repairs to the church.[74] In 1538 there were five altars in the chancel, two pairs of organs in the choir, and three bells in the steeple.[75]

Hundreds of hospitals had been established in England by 1300, the overwhelming majority of them in towns. Hospitals were primarily religious institutions and, like friaries, reflected urban status. Between a quarter and a fifth of hospitals were leper houses, usually sited some distance from the main area of settlement; the remainder cared for the elderly and infirm and they too were located in suburbs or on the town's boundary.[76] Chester's leper hospital of St Giles was probably founded in the mid twelfth century and the hospital 'for the sustentation of silly persons' in the early 1190s, acquiring its dedication to St John the Baptist within a few years. The hospital of St Ursula was established in the early sixteenth century.

The location of St Giles's hospital, on the boundary of the city liberties at Boughton, enabled inmates to seek alms from those travelling along a busy road. Nothing is known about the buildings but it seems that the care of the inmates was in line with current medical practice and focused on diet and cleanliness. Water for bathing came from the well within the precinct and Henry III granted money to buy clothes. The hospital's privileges included a toll on food brought to Chester for sale, fishing rights on the Dee, and an important bakehouse in Bakers' Row. Two lepers were admitted in the first decade of the fifteenth century but later the hospital, like leper hospitals elsewhere, became an almshouse and the inmates were elderly and infirm.[77]

FIGURE 4.5. The Dominican friary as it might have appeared in the 15th century.

St John's hospital, immediately outside the Northgate on a long narrow site running west alongside the town ditch, had a church and a burial ground by *c*.1200; a chapel was added in 1241. A century later church, chapel and hospital buildings needed re-roofing and money and timber were given for the work. At that date two chaplains celebrated daily mass in the church and a third chaplain celebrated mass in the hospital, presumably at an altar at the end of the long dormitory where the inmates slept. The hospital was required to accommodate as many poor and sick as possible but to keep 13 beds for poor townsmen and women. The hospital's chief priest and administrator lived in a chamber between the hall and the barns in the 1390s, and 20 years later he was given part of the garden at the end of the church for sowing seeds. He perhaps grew medicinal herbs.

The hospital of St Ursula developed indirectly from the will of former sheriff Roger Smith, who asked in 1508 that his house in Commonhall Lane be converted into almshouses for city aldermen or common councilmen who had fallen into need. His executors considered that the scheme was under-endowed and in 1510 obtained a royal licence to found instead a fraternity and hospital in honour of St Ursula. The almshouses were used as a hospital and the former common hall which lay behind them became the hospital chapel. The fraternity was never popular with the citizens and may have lapsed before 1547 when the chapel was sold to a townsman for £8.

Parish churches

Medieval Chester contained nine parish churches, dedicated to St John, St Oswald, St Mary, Holy Trinity, St Peter, St Michael, St Martin, St Bridget and St Olave. St Chad's church in the Crofts, in existence by *c*.1250 and housing an anchorite in 1300, may also have been parochial. It stood between houses and gardens in Dog Lane, known as St Chad's Street or Lane in the sixteenth century, and was said to be 'ruined and gone' in 1656.[78] The building history of the parish churches is described elsewhere and the following discussion attempts only to indicate how they differed one from another.[79]

St John's was founded in the Anglo-Saxon period and by 1086 was a collegiate foundation and the bishop's principal church in Chester. It was located in the bishop's manor of 'Redcliff' and served briefly as the cathedral of Lichfield diocese at the end of the eleventh century. A further indication of the church's importance was its possession of burial rights, originally shared only with St Oswald's, the other early minster church. By the mid thirteenth century St John's possessed the relic which became known as the Rood of Chester, a silver-gilt crucifix containing a piece of the True Cross. The Holy Rood became the city's most venerated relic and offerings to the Rood constituted a major source of the church's income. In the mid fourteenth century the east end of the church was reconstructed and a Lady chapel with flanking north and south chapels was inserted. By 1415 the church and college were 'ruinous' and the dean and chapter were licensed to collect alms for repairs. A new roof was in place by 1463 and the north-west tower was rebuilt between 1518 and 1523.

St John's stood in an important ecclesiastical precinct which included chapels of St Mary and St James, a hermitage and, from the late fourteenth century, the building which housed the fraternity of St Anne. St Mary's chapel, sometimes known as the White chapel, may have been the chapel of St Mary of Calvercroft in which the Tanners' company maintained a light by 1470.[80] The precinct also contained residences for the bishop and the archdeacon, whose court was held in St John's throughout the medieval period, and houses for canons, vicars and chantry priests. Other clergy houses lay outside the precinct in Vicars Lane.

The parish church of St Mary *de castro* had, as the name reveals, close links with the castle; Lucian noted that the earl and his court worshipped there in the late twelfth century. Parishioners in the fourteenth century included the palatinate master carpenter Richard of Legh and the lawyer Hugh de Holes, and in the fifteenth century the chamberlain William Troutbeck, who endowed the chantry chapel built on the south side of the chancel between 1433 and 1444.[81] The building agreement specified that there were to be five 'faire and clenely wroght wyndowes full of light' and that the chapel was to have battlements like the little closet at the castle. Troutbeck was buried in this chapel and the effigy on his tomb, probably erected by his grandson, showed him in rich armour, with a border of pearls, and a gold collar around his neck. This and other family monuments were destroyed when the chapel fell down in 1661. The former sheriff Matthew Johnson was buried in the church in the late 1490s and left his best gown to be sold for repairs to the church and a lead cistern for the bell tower.[82]

St Olave's church was very different. It may perhaps have originated as a private chapel for the owners of the adjoining mansion and their dependents. When responsibility for the maintenance of the chancel was disputed in the 1670s and 1680s, witnesses declared that the then owners of the house were considered to be the patrons and had been presented by the churchwardens for not repairing the chancel.[83] The adjoining house, then known as St Olave's Hall, had 'anciently' been called Pares Place or Hawarden Hall. In 1496 John Hawarden left 40s to the church and his best gown to make a cope or vestment; the bequests of his widow Margaret in 1520 included linen for altar cloths, a chalice and a missal.[84] The church in the 1680s was possibly much as it was in the medieval period: a single-celled building with chancel and nave of equal breadth, the chancel some 30 feet in length and the body of the church just over 33 feet in length.

St Peter's was closely associated with the civic authorities from the late thirteenth century, when the lean-to building which housed the Pentice was attached to the south wall of the church. Sessions of the piepowder court were held at the church door and oaths were sworn inside the church.[85] St George's guild, which enjoyed close links with the ruling élite, was housed in St Peter's, probably in the south aisle, and the guild chaplain rented the chamber over the church door by 1472–3.[86] The steeple was repaired in 1488–9 and the parson and others were said to have celebrated by eating a goose at the top. Two years later a 'principal' fell from the church during a great storm in Christmas week, killing one child and leaving another 'sore hurt'.[87] Thomas Runcorn requested burial in the church in 1511, asked for a priest to sing for his soul at St Stephen's altar, and left money to the high altar for the gilding of St Thomas. St Peter's also contained a statue of St Nicholas, before which Robert Coly asked to be buried in 1408.[88]

The medieval church of Holy Trinity was a two-aisled building. The south aisle contained St Mary's chapel, in which John the armourer asked to be buried in 1396. He left £60 to endow a chantry in the chapel and the best lead in his garden to the church fabric. John Whitmore, mayor in 1370–4, was buried in the chancel in 1374, beneath a marble effigy depicting him in armour. The vintner Thomas Wotton, mayor in 1433–4, was buried in the body of the church in 1451 and ten years later his widow Cecily was buried beside him. A marble gravestone, with a 'fair' picture of the couple and a brass border, marked their grave.[89] St Bridget's benefited from the generosity of John Arneway, mayor in 1268–78, who in 1274–8 left money for a priest to celebrate a daily mass of the Blessed Virgin. The Lady chapel in St Bridget's was recorded in 1527, when Elizabeth Hurleton requested burial there beside her husband, and early sketches of the church show two small windows below the east window, one perhaps lighting the Lady chapel.[90] Parishioners established chantries in St Michael's church in return for burial in the chancel or before the image of St Michael.[91] The chancel was rebuilt in the 1490s and the roof with its decorated panels was perhaps installed at that time. Nothing is known about St Martin's, and the only recorded bequest was made by Margaret Hawarden in 1520: a flaxen 'bord cloth' to be made into an altar cloth.[92]

Civic buildings

Chester's civic institutions were emerging by the 1230s and initially had no purpose-built premises. In the years before 1250 the guild merchant met in the selds, the long narrow market halls on the west side of Bridge Street owned by the élite citizens who dominated the association, and from whose ranks came the mayors who acted as president. The guild last met in the selds in 1250, by which date the first common hall had probably been built on a site to the rear, just south of the lane which became known as Commonhall or Moothall Lane. A 'common land-plot of the city' (*communem placeam terre civitatis Cestrie*) was recorded in the vicinity in *c.*1278; there was mention of land of the commonalty in 1314 and of a tenement of the commonalty in 1332–3. The common hall was specifically named in 1327–8.[93] Sessions of the portmote and crownmote courts were held in the hall and, in the later fifteenth century, judicial inquiries at which offences against the city's ordinances and breaches of the peace were presented. The charter of 1506 decreed that civic elections were to take place in the hall, in the presence of all citizens who chose to attend.[94] A few years later the common hall was converted into a chapel for the hospital of St Ursula and civic business was perhaps transferred to the Pentice.

The administrative hub of late medieval Chester was the Pentice, the lean-to structure abutting the south side of St Peter's church which housed the sheriffs' court by 1288. The city exchequer was also based there; its business included the registration of debts.[95] The Pentice was furnished with a cupboard and a bookcase, and in 1462–3 a new table to set before the mayor was purchased in London. The civic authorities were responsible for the clock in the tower of St Peter's, in place by the early fifteenth century. Maintenance cost 14s a year in the late 1420s and some 40 years later Christopher clockmaker was paid almost 8s for its repair.[96] A clock in the centre of Chester was more than a demonstration of civic pride. It regulated the working day and helped to ensure that those summoned to appear in the Pentice arrived on time.

The Pentice was built above a row of shops; by the 1430s there were at least seven shops, some of them perhaps beneath a northern extension of the building overlooking Northgate Street.[97] By the mid fifteenth century the Pentice almost certainly comprised two sections, a lesser northern section and a main southern section facing the market cross. In the spring of 1464 the southern section was demolished and work began on a replacement. The local tax levied in 1463 perhaps helped to fund the reconstruction, which may have been connected with the guild of St George, first recorded in 1462.[98] Timber from the old Pentice was re-used and new timbers were prepared in Delamere forest. The master carpenter and his men worked at Basingwerk and the timber was transported to Chester by raft. The new Pentice was ready in November 1464, the master carpenter and his five assistants having been paid 31s for 'labouring by candlelight'. The High Cross, which stood next the entrance of St Peter's by the later fourteenth century, was replaced in 1476 and a committee of aldermen and common councilmen was elected to collect the necessary funds. The new cross took the form of an octagonal pillar and head carved with images, topped by a crucifix.[99]

Commercial premises

Chester's streets and lanes were filled with shops, some of them retail outlets, some of them manufacturing workshops, and some combining both functions. The four main thoroughfares were lined on either side by the galleries known as the Rows, a distinctive system which allowed retailing at two levels and thus exploited the commercial frontage to the full.[100] The system comprised galleried walkways raised above undercrofts with shops on the inner side and display areas known as stallboards on the outer. Retailing on two levels was common in all medieval towns but particular circumstances at Chester allowed the split-level townhouses to be linked by a largely continuous gallery running through adjacent properties in different ownership.

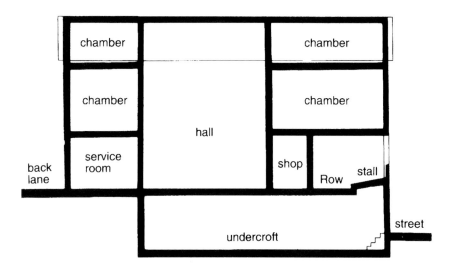

FIGURE 4.6. Section through a typical Rows building.

Recent research suggests that the Rows evolved gradually between 1200 and *c.*1350, as the split-level townhouse was adapted to suit the steeply rising ground on either side of the streets and the presence of bedrock close to the surface. The Row walkway allowed the number of stairways from the street to be limited, on average to every third plot. The late thirteenth-century arches spanning the walkway at 28–30 Watergate Street indicate that the walkway was planned from the outset, and the fact that the earliest Rows were associated with a particular trade suggests that they were intended for commercial use. Bakers' Row and Ironmongers' Row were recorded in 1293–4 and Saddlers' Row in 1303–4.[101] Row buildings differed in size but all were set relatively high above semi-subterranean undercrofts; the domestic accommodation lay behind the shops at Row level. A remarkable degree of co-operation from house owners was required to establish a system of public walkways running through the first floors of private properties and it is possible that the system was pioneered along one street frontage, perhaps in the area of the selds on the west side of Bridge Street. The selds were private market halls owned by the wealthy individuals who dominated the guild merchant and wielded huge influence in the city by the earlier thirteenth century. They may have readily agreed to lay out a Row through their commercial premises, fully appreciating the economic benefits that would result.

The selds, first recorded in about 1250 as the former meeting place of the guild merchant, were concentrated in Bridge Street and extended northwards from the area in front of the common hall to the junction with Watergate Street. These private 'bazaars' contained stalls perhaps ranged on either side of a central alleyway and traders dealing in particular merchandise may have congregated in separate selds, as they did in London's Cheapside.[102] Chester's selds were raised above undercrofts and fronted by shops and certainly contained a Row from an early date. The use of stallboards, the wide and gently sloping wooden boards on the street side of the Row walkway which increased the trading space, may have been pioneered here. Individual owners held a 'package' of retail premises, consisting of seld, shop, stallboard and undercroft.

Demand for stalls in the selds possibly peaked at fair-time, when non-citizen traders flocked to the city. The wall behind one seld was removed during the Michaelmas fair in *c*.1260, to provide additional space.[103] The selds remained in use until the late 1340s, offering gloves, girdles, veils, brooches, mercery wares, and woollen cloth from London and from Coggeshall in Essex.[104] In 1354, however, Henry Dunfoul's shop, stallboard, cellar and quarter seld were unoccupied and although a tenant was soon found for the stallboard and cellar, the seld and shop were not mentioned again, suggesting that redevelopment had taken place. The only seld to survive was the Stone or Staven Seld at the corner of Bridge Street and Watergate Street, possibly known as 'the seld of the city' in 1374.[105] Two cellars under a 'certain shop called stone seldes construction' were leased to a vintner in 1425 and the shop next to the stairs leading to the seld was rented out in the 1430s and 1440s. The alderman Thomas Smith rented the selds at the end of the century.[106]

The selds disappeared but the undercrofts, shops and stallboards continued in use. Undercrofts were found in many English towns but were exceptionally numerous in Chester, perhaps because of the absence of warehousing along the waterfront. Medieval stone party walls survive for 36 undercrofts in Watergate Street alone, and there would have been dozens more in the other main streets. There is occasional evidence for an internal staircase linking to the house above, indicating that the undercroft was used by the occupier of the house, but by the early fourteenth century it was increasingly common for undercrofts to be held separately.[107] Many were used for storage. Among the items stolen from undercrofts in the fourteenth century were malt, woollen cloth, herring, salmon and, on one occasion, six geese.[108] Massive floors dating from the thirteenth century and consisting of oak boards, layers of sand, rubble and stone flags survive above some undercrofts in Watergate Street. They date from a time when open fires burned in the centre of the halls and perhaps represented an attempt to fireproof the undercroft. As fish was commonly stored in undercrofts in Watergate Street they may also have served to prevent the smell of fish pervading the house above.[109] The problems this caused were recorded in 1585, when 'Mr Sheriff' and his guests were put off their food by the 'very stinking smell' coming from fish in a cellar in Trinity Lane.[110]

Some undercrofts functioned as alehouses. In 1393 William Hawarden's wife was in the cellar of their home when a disturbance broke out; bowls of ale were knocked to the ground and she was among those who were physically assaulted.[111] Other undercrofts were associated with the wine trade. Wine was subject to prise from the late thirteenth century and an elaborate procedure involved the unloading of the casks at the Watergate, their transport by cart

FIGURE 4.7. The stone arches spanning the walkway at 28–30 Watergate Street Row. This is the most complete 13th-century townhouse that survives and the stone arches demonstrate that the walkway existed from the outset. The arches are set within the side walls of the house, indicating that the adjacent properties also had walkways.

to the owners' cellars, their removal from the cellars by 'winedrawers', and carriage by cart to the cellars at the castle.[112] Chester's taverns were evidently held in undercrofts, as they were at Winchester, and both cities contained taverns named 'Helle', probably because they were underground and dark.[113] Taverns were nevertheless used for civic entertainment. Chester's stone-vaulted undercrofts may have been used for this purpose. Five survive, including the arcaded undercroft at 11 Watergate Street and the undercroft at 28 Eastgate Street with its elaborate frontage comprising an arched doorway and flanking windows. The only undercroft known to have had a rear window is at 12 Bridge Street. Was this the tavern of John Coly in the 1390s, scene of an ambush from which the victim escaped through the rear and took refuge in a house in Watergate Street?[114]

The shops at Row level were small, often measuring just 2m by 3m, and there could be as many as five fronting one house. Some perhaps functioned like booths, as did small shops in other English towns, the customers standing outside and the lowered window shutter serving as a counter. Occasionally there was a connected chamber above, used as storage space or as accommodation for the shopkeeper. Stallboards had appeared by the later thirteenth century, developing perhaps from the roofs of the porches erected in front of the undercrofts. Several townsmen were indicted in 1293 for building stallboards which encroached onto the street and a woman was indicted because her stallboard was wider than before. Their commercial value was appreciated. William (III) of Doncaster used the stallboard in front of his seld in Bridge Street to display cloth during the Midsummer fair in 1296.[115] Several butchers were charged in 1352 with obstructing the highway by hanging carcases from hooks, presumably on the underside of the stallboard.[116] The strip of ground below the stallboards belonged to the city. A tailor paid 4d a year in 1438–9 for the ground below another tailor's stallboard in Bridge Street, described a few years later as lying between undercrofts and extending from the house frontage to the street. Strips of land fronting the Staven Seld at the corner of Bridge Street and Watergate Street were leased to the alderman Thomas Smith in 1508; the dimensions matched those of the pre-nineteenth-century stallboards.[117]

Private houses and furnishings

The private houses of late medieval Chester ranged from the large residences of prosperous merchants and palatine officials to the modest dwellings of humble craftsmen and labourers. Outside the densely-settled areas important houses were built on a grand scale and set in spacious grounds. The principal residence of the Dunfoul family adjoined the city wall to the east of the Bridgegate and in 1380, when it was leased to the master mason William Helpston, it contained a kitchen, a hall, and chambers on two floors. A gatehouse gave access to the property and the grounds contained a dovecot, a barn and an orchard.[118] Tenants of St Werburgh's in the 1450s, in contrast, occupied tiny cottages or single rooms in larger houses and paid rent of just 2s or 3s a year.[119]

FIGURE 4.8. Cutaway reconstruction of the medieval form of 38–42 Watergate Street.

Domestic accommodation in the Rows lay behind the shops fronting the walkway. Houses constructed over one or two undercrofts with their halls lying at right angles to the street were most common. The halls of the larger houses lay parallel to the street and ran across as many as three undercrofts, with a screens passage at one end giving access to the service bay. These larger houses often occupied corner sites, enabling extra windows to be inserted and facilitating access to the stables and outbuildings to the rear. Repairs to the property near St Bridget's church in Bridge Street in 1356–7 involved re-tiling the roof and work on two chambers, the kitchen, the stable, the fence round the orchard and the door to the garden.[120] The continuous line of undercrofts and first-floor walkways precluded the courtyard plan and only one recorded building bore any resemblance to the courtyard houses found in other towns. This was the property at 14–16 Northgate Street, just south of the lane running east beside the graveyard wall of the abbey.[121] By the later fifteenth century an increasing demand for privacy resulted in the building of parlours. Rooms named by Margaret Hawarden in her will in 1520 included hall, parlour, study house and several chambers.[122]

In the period before about 1320 the most important houses were built of the local red sandstone. Among them were the house of Peter the clerk at the corner of Castle Lane and Lower Bridge Street and the major townhouse at the corner of Whitefriars Lane, the late twelfth- or thirteenth-century stone frontage of which survives. By the fifteenth century both were notable landmarks. In June 1424 rioters marched down Bridge Street from the 'Stone Place' near St Bridget's to 'le Stouneplace' at Castle Lane End, where they attacked two palatinate officials.[123] Most houses in the medieval city were timber-framed and the use of stone was restricted to the low walls on which they stood, the corbels which supported the timber floors, and the party walls of the undercrofts along the principal streets. Surviving structures within the undercrofts demonstrate how much timber was required: the product of seven or eight mature oak trees for the undercroft at 6 Lower Bridge Street for example. Some timbers in the arcade had come from an earlier roof and such recycling was common. When the Pentice was rebuilt in 1464, 44 cartloads of timber came from the old building.[124]

Domesday Book recorded the heavy fines imposed on Chester's burgesses for allowing fire to break out in their houses and *affraia ignis* remained a serious offence in the later medieval city. Only one example of regulations governing roofing materials has been found, in the lease of a house on the south side of Watergate Street in 1500. This specified that it was not to be roofed with thatch, shingles or boards, but with new Welsh slate or tiles.[125] Few thatchers worked in Chester in the fourteenth and fifteenth centuries and oak shingles were widely used, even on the great hall at the castle where the choice, as at Winchester, was determined by considerations of weight.[126] In 1354–5 shingles, shingle nails and 'thackboards' (which provided the firm base to which the shingles were nailed) were used to re-roof a malt kiln in a garden in Northgate

Street, and 'sclatstones' were used to re-roof the house.[127] Slaters were among
the occupational groups whose wages the civic authorities sought to control
in 1407, and they remained the most numerous of the city's roofing craftsmen
throughout the fifteenth century, working with slates shipped to the city from
Wales.[128] Clay floor tiles were manufactured on a site to the east of Cow Lane
in the thirteenth century and the Tile houses recorded in the vicinity in 1495
may have been workshops where tiles were made.[129] Few tilers were recorded in
the late medieval city and excavations consistently uncover a higher proportion
of ridge tiles (crests) than other types of tile. The crests provided a decorative
element along the ridge and cheaper materials may have been used for the roof
itself. The glazed ridge tiles and roof slates discovered on the Crofts in 1998 are
thought to have come from a single building.[130]

A fireplace was set against the wall of the hall at 17 Watergate Street (Leche
House) in the late fourteenth century but it seems that most houses in the
city made do with less sophisticated arrangements.[131] Chimneys were built
in increasing numbers in English towns in the fifteenth century but the iron
'chimneys' (*caminus ferri*) recorded in Chester from the 1380s had the meaning
of hearth not flue, and were iron grates or grids on which wood or coal were
placed. A *petit chymene de feir* in the kitchen of a London alderman in the early
1380s weighed over 4½ cwt and was valued at 34s. The 'chimney' in the home
of Chester's alderman Alexander Stanney in 1477 was worth only 8s, a sum that
included the fire-irons.[132] Fragments of pottery louvers were discovered on the
Crofts and two louver strings were stolen from a house in Fleshmonger Lane in
1497, but these louvers may have been used to provide ventilation rather than
to cover a smoke hole in the roof.[133] Brickmen were recorded from the 1460s
and brick chimney stacks may have been inserted in some houses. Roger Smith's
request in 1508 that his house 'be made up with chimnies and with drowghts'
for almshouses suggests, however, that chimney stacks were unusual even in
wealthy homes. The earliest bricks found by the archaeologists at Chester came
from a mid sixteenth-century garderobe.[134]

Chester was an important centre for window glass in the early fourteenth
century and evidence for glass-working in Handbridge by 1500 has recently
been discovered.[135] The glaziers who worked in the late medieval city were
employed by the religious houses and by the palatinate authorities at the
castle, and window glass has been found only on ecclesiastical sites.[136] The
grandest dwellings nevertheless offered well-furnished accommodation and
standards rose during the medieval period. Parlours appeared in the 1460s
and provided a private space for family life.[137] Painted chambers were replaced
by rooms adorned with fine textile hangings. In 1520 the hall in Margaret
Hawarden's home was furnished with cupboards, a counter board, a screen,
several forms and a great chair. The chambers contained brightly painted coffers
and tapestry cushions embroidered with harts, blue birds and gentlewomen.
The parlour with its fireplace and hanging 'chaundelor' decorated with flowers
was where Margaret slept, in a bed with a tapestry coverlet and with a carved

coffer standing at its head.[138] The richest townsmen displayed their wealth by purchasing silver plate. At the end of the fourteenth century John the armourer owned silver cups, beakers and a mazer with a silver-gilt cover, and in John Hatton's household silver vessels and spoons were in daily use. Forty years later John Hope's possessions included a silver bowl standing on three lions and a cup called a 'nut' with a gilt cover. David Ferror in 1505 owned silver cups and goblets worth more than £20, the most valuable of them a 'standing cup' with gilt cover weighing 48 ounces.[139]

Other homes were more modestly equipped. Alexander Stanney's furniture in 1477 consisted of several coffers, trestles, benches, two chairs and a form. A green cloth hanging embellished the walls of his hall and there were matching coverings and cushions on the benches. He owned a large quantity of bedding including a 'hanging bed of white', plus brewing and cooking equipment, treen ware, brass pots and a garnish of pewter. Among the goods found in a pewterer's household in 1503 were a folding table, a cupboard, three coffers, two mattresses, bedding, cooking pots, brass and pewter dishes, worth less than £2 in total.[140] Poor townsmen who lived in single-room dwellings or who rented a room in a larger house owned very little. The goods of a labourer in 1470 consisted of two sheets (one of canvas, the other of flax), two saucers, four plates and a dish, plus a cloth to hang over the window.[141]

FIGURE 4.9. The imposing mansion near St Olave's had frontages facing Lower Bridge Street and Claverton Lane in the medieval period. It was occupied by Richard the engineer in the early 14th century, by the chamberlain Robert Parys in the later 1390s, and by the Hawarden family in the late 15th century.

Water supply, sanitation and refuse disposal

In some large towns the authorities followed the lead set by the religious houses and provided piped water supplies from an early date; other towns relied on the friars for supplies.[142] Chester's Dominicans applied for permission to pipe water from Boughton in 1276 and two years later the monks of St Werburgh's were licensed to make a conduit from a well at Newton. This water supply was improved in 1282, when pipes were laid to bring water from a spring at Christleton through the city wall to a reservoir in the cloister garth.[143] None of these supplies were made available to the townspeople, nor did any wealthy citizen commission a public conduit. Throughout the medieval period the inhabitants obtained their water from wells, from rain-water cisterns in their gardens or from the river, and were not provided with piped water until after the Dissolution when the conduit begun by the Franciscans in 1537 was transferred to public use.

Medieval towns were packed with people living and working in close proximity and vast quantities of human, animal, household and trade waste accumulated. Chester's authorities were concerned about its efficient disposal and issued annual ordinances prohibiting refuse from being dumped in the street and instructing residents to clean the pavements before their doors. These regulations went largely unheeded. Householders filled the streets with rubbish and allowed their pigs to scavenge; butchers and fishmongers discarded entrails under their stalls; shoemakers and dyers threw old shoes and rotting woad into the highway; horses and livestock deposited heaps of manure. Problems arose even when waste disposal was organized. Women carried butchers' waste in uncovered baskets and emptied it near the city gates, a practice which could explain the 'disproportionate number of animal heads' discovered during excavations in the ditch outside the Eastgate in 1991.[144] The only drainage was provided by the open channels in the streets and these were often choked with garbage. It was reported in 1406 that all householders living between St Peter's and the Dee mills habitually raked dung into the gutters and that heavy rain had carried this unpleasant waste down to the malt mills where it had seriously weakened the walls.[145]

The castle was well furnished with latrines and there was an impressive sewerage system at the abbey, where a drain carried effluent through the city wall and discharged into the town ditch. Townspeople also used the ditch for sewage disposal and were regularly indicted for the nuisance caused by their cess-pits. Souters Lode was blocked in 1352 when a cess-pit in a nearby garden overflowed, and in 1474 a latrine obstructed the flow of water in the ditch near the Eastgate.[146] Medieval pits containing sewage have been found throughout the city, some of them stone-lined. Two rock-cut pits found in the yard behind 12 Watergate Street in 1985 were covered by flimsy wooden superstructures in the mid thirteenth century and had evidently functioned as privies.[147] There is no documentary evidence for public latrines at Chester in the late medieval period.

Gardens, orchards and backyards

Although much of the intra-mural area was densely settled space remained for gardens, orchards and crofts, and land immediately beyond the walls was also put to productive use. The abbey's walled vegetable garden occupied an extensive area between the town ditch and Cow Lane, and the friary precincts contained orchards and areas of pasture.[148] There was a garden in the castle ditch by 1150, in the keeping of the official who probably also held the serjeanty of the Bridgegate, as in the later medieval period. According to ancient custom the castle gardener claimed the fruit from the 'restyng tree' and the fruit remaining on other trees after the first shaking, in return for supplying 'caules' (kale or coleworts) from Michaelmas to Lent and leeks during Lent. The 'restyng tree' was the stock tree from which grafts were taken and was evidently replaced from time to time. Two hundred young apple and pear trees were purchased in 1287.[149] Revenues from the garden were always small and in some years nothing was received: in 1275–6 because the king and his household had eaten all the fruit during their visit, and in 1353–4 because the fruit had been eaten by the masons and labourers rebuilding the wall between the inner bailey and the garden.[150] A little extra income was received in 1358–9 when the masons' lodge in the garden was sold for 3s 4d, and in 1395–6 when a filbert tree was cut down and sold to a local dyer for 13s 4d.[151]

Gardens were also designed for pleasure. A bridge was constructed from the castle into the orchard in 1245, to enable the king and queen to stroll at leisure, and in 1292 a more private garden was created beside the new chapel. Two doors gave entry to this garden, which was carpeted with turf and contained a covered cloister. Green turf was laid in three gardens newly made in 1303 in preparation for the arrival of the prince of Wales.[152] These gardens were called *herbaria*, a term explained in Bartholomew's encyclopaedia as 'a green place and merry with green trees and herbs', and were perhaps inspired by gardens designed for Eleanor of Castile, wife of Edward I. She was a keen gardener and brought gardeners from Aragon to plant vines and fruit trees in her garden at King's Langley in Hertfordshire in the late 1270s. A herber was made for her at Conwy in 1284 and carpeted with two cartloads of green turves. The only other *herbarium* recorded in late medieval Chester was the one adjoining the chapel once owned by Alexander Harre and granted to John Arneway's widow in 1278. When the Carmelites established their community in the area in the 1290s chapel and herber may have been enclosed within their precinct.[153]

Townspeople's gardens were put to practical use. Eleven kerchiefs stolen from one garden in 1450 had presumably been laundered and put out to dry. Cabbages, onions, parsnips and garlic were grown, and a variety of herbs including parsley, sage, savory and thyme.[154] Apple, pear and plum trees were plentiful and fruit trees were planted on the bank outside the city wall.[155] Remains of the fruit and vegetables recorded in the documents are found in archaeological contexts: brassica seeds, onion skins, plum stones, and apple and pear pips at 12 Watergate Street for example.[156] In the late fourteenth century there was a garden known as the Vineyard near Foregate Street, but the vines were probably grown for decorative effect rather than for fruit.[157] In the late 1480s saffron growing in a saddler's garden and in a garden in the castle ward was eaten by pigs.[158] Many gardens contained privies, pigsties, poultry pens, and outbuildings used as fuel stores. The more spacious plots contained stables, dovecots, malt kilns and barns.

Decay and recovery

Cestrians claimed in 1445 that the greater part of their city was in ruins and some 40 years later declared that the walls had fallen into decay and that almost a quarter of Chester was destroyed and desolate. Rentals of civic property in the early 1480s listed many arrears and described several shops in Watergate Street as *ruinosa et prostrata*.[159] In 1484, however, ten townspeople presented for obstructing the streets with posts and building timber were pardoned because they were building with it, and a thatcher was accused of taking excessive wages.[160] These may be signs that reconstruction work was in progress. The undercroft at 17 Watergate Street (Leche House) was extended in the late fifteenth century and a new timber framework erected above. Nearby stood the house with vaulted undercroft leased to a prominent citizen in 1500 with the proviso that it was to be roofed only with tiles or new Welsh slate. Twenty years later he added an extra bay to the rear.[161]

The parish churches launched building campaigns in the late 1480s and 1490s. St Nicholas's chapel was extended and St Peter's steeple repaired; work was underway on the tower of St Mary's and the chancel of St Michael's. The religious houses were also building. The Dominicans appear to have rebuilt their choir in the late fifteenth century and the Carmelites constructed a handsome tower on their church in 1495. Construction work at the abbey, the nunnery and the Franciscan friary continued in the early sixteenth century.

CHAPTER FIVE

A Hierarchical Society

Although Chester's population in the later medieval period remains a matter of conjecture it is clear that it was small for a regional capital. No attempt has been made to estimate the number of inhabitants before the Black Death and the total of 4,600 for 1377 is the highest suggested for the period between the mid fourteenth and early sixteenth centuries. The townspeople probably recognised one and another as they passed through the streets even if they were not personally acquainted; this was a 'face to face' society. Numbers swelled as visitors flocked in and out: to attend the county court, to buy and sell at the Midsummer and Michaelmas fairs, and to embark at the port. At busy times the city was perhaps filled to bursting point.

The resident community was far from homogeneous. A fundamental division separated those who were freemen from those who were not. The citizens bore the burden of local taxation and office-holding and in return enjoyed various privileges, including the right to buy and sell in the market without paying tolls and to keep retail shops. Only citizens could become members of craft organizations. The unenfranchised were outsiders (foreigners) and their legal status was inferior but there was no clear economic distinction between them and the citizens. Wage-earners were found in both groups and, as the unenfranchised could purchase a licence allowing them to sell retail, so too were independent shopkeepers. Highly visible disparities of wealth and degree separated the successful merchants from the middling craftsmen, who were themselves set apart from the poorer townsmen who worked for wages.

Immigration

Medieval towns were unhealthy places and the rate of mortality was high. All depended upon a constant flow of immigrants to maintain their populations. Throughout the medieval period men and women, often young, were drawn to Chester in search of new opportunities. The streets were not paved with gold but people believed that the city offered brighter prospects than other places. Among the newcomers were economic migrants like the slater from Kirby-in-Kendal (Westmorland) who, when hauled up before the city sheriffs in 1415, declared that he had come solely to practice his trade. Others were 'betterment' migrants. Elys ap Gruff arrived from Wales in the late 1430s, evidently intending

TABLE 5.1. Locative surnames of Chester residents before 1350.

Aldford, Ches	Carrington, Ches	Handley, Ches	Middleton, Lancs	Stanlow, Ches
Audlem, Ches	Caverswall, Staffs	Hargrave, Ches	Mobberley, Ches	Stanney, Ches
Allerton Lancs	Chesterfield, Derbys	Harrington, Lancs	Monnington, Heref'd	Stapleford, Ches
Alvanley, Ches	Christleton, Ches	Hawarden, Flints	Morley, Ches	Stirchley, Shrops
Appleby, Leics	Church Leigh, Staffs	Helsby, Ches	Mouldsworth, Ches	Stoke, Ches
Arderne, Ches	Churton, Ches	Hemington, Leics	Ness, Ches	Stone, Staffs
Arrowe, Ches	Claverton, Ches	Hockenhull, Ches	Newcastle, Staffs	Strangeways, Lancs
Ashbourne, Derbys	Coddington, Ches	Hodnet, Shrops	Newland, ?	Sutton, Ches
Bache, Ches	Coleshill, Warws	Holt, Denbighs	Newport, Shrops?	Swettenham, Ches
Backford, Ches	Conwy, Caern	Holywell, Flints	Newton, Ches	Tamworth, Staffs
Bakewell, Derbys	Cotes, Staffs	Hoole, Ches	Norley, Ches	Tarvin, Ches
Barrow, Ches	Coupland, Westmld	Hope, Flints	Northenden, Lancs	Tattenhall, Ches
Basingwerk, Flints	Coventry, Warws	Hull, Yorks	Nottingham, Notts	Thelwall, Ches
Bebington, Ches	Crompton, Lancs	Huntington, Ches	Oscroft, Ches	Thornhill, Staffs
Bedford, Beds	Croxton, Ches	Huxley, Ches	Oswestry, Shrops	Thornton, Ches
Betley, Staffs	Cuerdley, Lancs	Huyton, Lancs	Packington, Leics	Tilston, Ches
Beverley, Yorks	Daresbury, Ches	Iddinshall, Ches	Peckforton, Ches	Toft, Ches
Bickerton, Ches	Derby, Derbys	Kegworth, Leics	Pedley, Ches	Tottenham, Mx
Birmingham, Warws	Didsbury, Lancs	Kelsall, Ches	Pontefract, Yorks	Towcester, N'hants
Blackrod, Lancs	Ditton, Lancs	Kendal, Westmld	Poulton, Ches	Trafford, Ches
Blacon, Ches	Doncaster, Yorks	Kingsley, Ches	Prestatyn, Flints	Tutbury, Staffs
Blurton, Staffs	Dounes, Ches	Kirby, Ches	Preston, Lancs	Tytherington, Ches
Bostock, Ches	Dudley, Worcs	Knaresborough, Y'ks	Pulford, Ches	Vale Royal, Ches
Boughton, Ches	Dunham, Ches	Knutsford, Ches	Raby, Ches	Wainfleet, Lincs
Boulton, Derbys	Dunston, Staffs	Lancaster, Lancs	Repton, Derbys	Wakefield, Yorks
Brackley, N'hants	Dutton, Ches	Lawton, Ches	Ridley, Ches	Walsall, Staffs
Bradbourne, Derbys	Eastham, Ches	Ledsham, Ches	Rudheath, Ches	Warmingham, Ches
Bradford, Yorks	Eaton, Ches	Leen, H'fords	Rycroft, Staffs	Warwick, Warws
Bradwell, Ches	Eccleshall, Staffs	Legh, Ches	Salesbury, Lancs	Waterfall, Staffs
Bramhall, Ches	Eccleston, Ches	Leicester, Leics	Sandbach, Ches	Weaverham, Ches
Breadsall, Derbys	Egerton, Ches	Leigh, Ches	Sandon, Staffs	Werrington, Staffs
Brereton, Ches	Ellenhall, Staffs	Lichfield, Staffs	Saughall, Ches	Weston, Ches
Bretton, Flints	Elworth, Ches	Lincoln, Lincs	Seacombe, Ches	Wheatley, Lancs
Brickhill, Bucks	Evesham, Worcs	Lostock, Ches	Shavington, Ches	Whitmore, Staffs
Brinnington, Ches	Exeter, Devon	Ludlow, Shrops	Shipbrook, Ches	Wich, Ches
Bromborough, Ches	Flint, Flints	Lynn, Staffs?	Shottle, Derbys	Wigan, Lancs
Bromley, Lancs	Frodsham, Ches	Macclesfield, Ches	Shotwick, Ches	Wincham, Ches
Broxton, Ches	Galway, Ireland	Manchester, Lancs	Shrewsbury, Shrops	Winchester, Hants
Burton, Ches	Gloucester, Glos	Marbury, Ches	Sound, Ches	Wirksworth, Derbys
Bury, Lancs	Golbourne, Ches	Markington, Yorks	Stafford, Staffs	Witton, Ches
Capenhurst, Ches	Greasby, Ches	Marthall, Ches	Stamford, Ches	Wootton, Staffs
Cardiff, Glam	Gresford, Denbighs	Marton, Ches	Stanbridge, Beds	Wybunbury, Ches
Carlisle, Cumbld	Hadley, Shrops	Melbourne, Derbys	Standish, Lancs	York, Yorks
Carrickfergus, Ulster	Hales, Staffs	Meols, Ches	Standon, Staffs	

Unidentified: Aspenewell, Boteby, Burg', Chatfield, Chirdelhous, Cloudesdale, Dartsett/Dersett, Derwaldshaw, Godinchester, Guldenlak, Heginton, Holcroft, Holfeld, Horsale, Kervenet, Mulneton, P'stlan', Sallowe, Temeston/Tomeston, Thornihurst, Tin'ersholt, Twynam, Wylme.

to improve his education, but he soon moved on, leaving behind debts to a scrivener for instruction and to a townsman for his board.[1]

We can learn something about the origin of Chester's population by studying the locative surnames of the inhabitants in the period before 1350. Surnames had not yet become hereditary and the locative names probably indicated the places from which individuals or their fathers or grandfathers had come. Some 45 per cent of the places from which the names were taken lay within a 20–mile radius of Chester (compared with just over half at York, Nottingham and Exeter) and 20 per cent lay between 21 and 40 miles from the city.[2] Immigrants came from settlements along the major transport routes. The Brickhill family, for example, originated in the Buckinghamshire township astride Watling Street regularly used as a stopover by those travelling to and from London. The relocation proved a good move. The Brickhills played a prominent role in Chester from the 1280s until the 1330s, and at least four family members served as mayor. Employment opportunities brought the master masons John and Robert of Helpston to Chester, probably from the village of that name close to Barnack in Lincolnshire, an important quarrying centre from the pre-Conquest period.[3] John built the New Tower in 1322 and both men worked on the castles at Chester, Shotwick and Flint in the later 1320s. Robert became palatinate master mason a decade later and William of Helpston held that post by 1359.[4]

Non-citizens

The most fortunate newcomers were engaged as servants and lived in the household. The poll-tax records for other towns reveal that in the late fourteenth century 20 to 30 per cent of the tax payers were servants, a high proportion unlikely to have differed a century earlier.[5] Servants at Chester perhaps accounted for a similar proportion of the population. The less successful migrants found only casual work and were never certain of full employment. Short-term contracts were particularly common in the building trade. In 1460 a slater was employed for 14 weeks, at the end of which he owed 13s 4d for food, drink and accommodation. A shilling a week seems to have been the going rate for board and lodging in Chester throughout the fifteenth century and many townspeople added to household income by renting out rooms, sometimes for just a few weeks or months at a time.[6] Lodgers formed an unstable group in the lower reaches of the social hierarchy.

Among the immigrants were craftsmen who hoped to work as independent artisans from the outset. This was possible on payment of an annual fine, provided that the craft was not subject to strict guild control. Ropers and netmakers were able to pursue their occupations without interference, and it seems that linen weavers escaped regulation in the first half of the fifteenth century. Many non-citizens paid an annual fine for a licence to sell retail, as they did in other towns.[7] In the later fifteenth century between 75 and 100 men and women were licensed each year to sell retail and a few paid to practice their craft. The size of the fine varied: 8d for a licence to weave linen in 1451–2, for example, and 8s to sell retail.[8] Some traders lived and worked in the city for many years. John Roper of Northgate Street was listed from 1451–2 until 1473–4, and William Wright of Eastgate Street from 1451–2 until 1468, paying 12d at the start, 2s from the mid 1450s, and just 8d in 1466–7 when his wife was also named. Possibly his health was failing.[9] The vast majority of fine-payers were named only once, indicating that this section of the urban community was in a constant state of flux. An alternative explanation for the massive turnover is that only those who were caught paid the fine, but those who paid only once were not named in other records so this seems unlikely. Some may have died and some women may have married, but many must have quickly moved elsewhere.

Citizens

There were three ways of gaining Chester's franchise in the later medieval period: by inheritance, by redemption (purchase) and by gift of the Assembly. Sons whose fathers had been free at the time of their birth paid 10½d, and after 1452 they also offered a gift of wine and the 'accustomed fee' to the mayor. The entry fine for those who purchased the franchise was 26s 8d but could be higher, perhaps if the new freeman was not well-known in the city. A man from Speke (Lancashire) paid 33s 4d in 1393, and in 1420 David Dewe of Nantwich paid 66s 8d and agreed to take up residence in Chester within a year and a day. Admissions may always have involved a residential qualification and there was a new emphasis on the requirement to live in the city after 1452, perhaps aimed to stem the flow of citizens moving away to escape the 'insupportable burdens' of the fee farm.[10] The payment of entry fines was made easier at that time by allowing new freemen to pay in three annual instalments. New entrants always needed to find three or four citizen sureties.[11] In 1401 one man was excused payment because of his 'good service' and a few men were awarded the freedom by gift of the Assembly in the 1480s and early sixteenth century, all of them esquires or gentlemen who had served the city in some legal capacity or who had given 'good counsel'. Among them were the eldest son of Sir John Savage who helped Chester obtain a reduction of the fee farm in 1484, and John Tatton who gave advice concerning the city's liberties in 1501.[12]

In some towns apprenticeship was a normal method of acquiring the franchise but there is no explicit evidence for this at Chester. Men who worked in the same craft or trade commonly sponsored a new entrant but he still paid the entry fine and had clearly not earned the freedom via a lengthy and arduous apprenticeship. Apprentices rarely feature in the sources but many master craftsmen doubtless had one or two such youngsters living in their households. The boys usually began their training at the age of twelve and were provided with food, drink, clothing and instruction over a period which normally lasted for seven years but which could be as long as nine. It cannot have taken

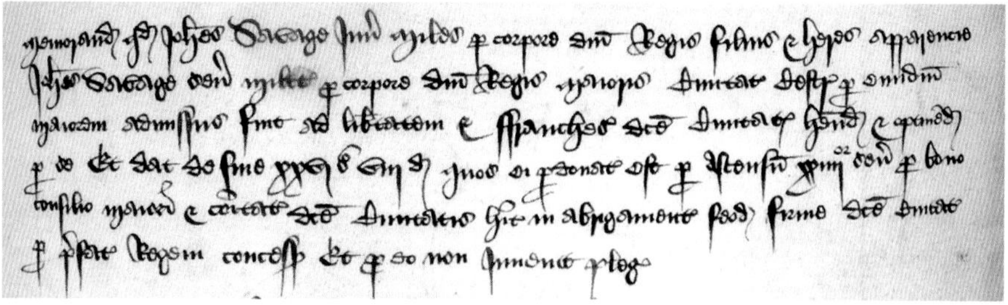

FIGURE 5.1. An entry in the Mayor's Book on 5 July 1485 recorded that John Savage knight of the body of the king was admitted to the franchise and that his entry fine of 26s 8d was pardoned because he had helped to secure a reduction of the fee farm. His eight younger brothers had become freemen on 14 March 1485.

so long to learn a craft and it seems likely that apprentices were commonly exploited and used as cheap labour. Some were dismissed without cause after working for several years; others left because they were not given the promised training.[13] In the early 1420s, when the sheriffs reprimanded a citizen who beat his apprentice for playing dice for money, the citizen complained to the mayor, asserting that there was no law to punish a man for beating his apprentice (or his wife) and that it was reasonable to chastise the boy for disobedience. Other youngsters were more fortunate. David, apprenticed to John the armourer, in 1396 received a generous bequest of money, clothing, weapons and a share in *St Mary's bote*.[14]

Records of freemen admissions survive for 50 or so years between 1392–3 and 1520–1, many of them incomplete. Full entry details survive for some 400 men admitted before 1500, an unknown fraction of the original total but perhaps a representative sample. One in six inherited the freedom, indicating that Chester, like London and York, depended on newcomers to maintain its population.[15] Some families were recorded over three generations. The butcher John Fenton arrived in the 1440s and set up a successful business. He was followed by his three sons, one of whom served as sheriff, and his grandson carried the business forward into the sixteenth century.[16] The Monksfields originated in Dodleston and derived their name from land in the parish held by Dieulacres abbey (Staffordshire). The family was recorded in Chester from the 1440s until the 1510s, each generation including an apothecary. The first two generations were wealthy and provided two sheriffs in the 1450s and another in 1478–9. The third generation included a skinner who served as common councilman and one family member named as a common gambler.[17] The Warmingham family provides an exceptional example of longevity. Richard and William Warmingham were influential men at the start of the fourteenth century and held property in Fleshmongers Lane. There may have been more than one branch of the family and they lived in the area for generations, working as goldsmiths and naming their sons Richard, William and Roger. In the early seventeenth century Richard Warmingham, aged 93, made a silver badge for the mayor; in 1722 Thomas Warmingham paid rent for an enclosure in Fleshmongers Lane.[18]

The fragmentary state of Chester's admission records, combined with the uncertainties of the population figures, makes it impossible to estimate the size of the citizen body. Possibly it compared with London, where one in four adult males may have enjoyed the franchise in the late fourteenth century, or Winchester in the early fifteenth century, where the figure was perhaps one in five.[19] Official documents described citizens in moral terms. All were upright, law-worthy and trustworthy (*probos*, *legales*, *fidedignos*), but the wealthy men who held high office were 'better people' (*meliores*). Sheriffs were selected from the 'more sufficient, discreet, and honourable' persons (*de magis sufficientibus discretioribus et honorabilibus personis*).[20] The terminology emphasized the hierarchical nature of the citizen body. The 'more sufficient' were the rich merchants who dominated town government and influenced all aspects of the urban economy. These powerful men towered above the leading master craftsmen and traders who, in turn, were far removed from the small shopkeepers and independent artisans. Those who worked piece-rate for others were at the bottom of the social hierarchy.

A man's status was highly visible. Wealthy men were distinguished by the number of their attendants, by the quality of their horses and accoutrements and, most conspicuously, by their dress. Aldermen were handsomely attired, in scarlet robes on ceremonial occasions and in gowns furred with beaver, marten and fox. They wore silk tippets and caps of tawny velvet, silver belts and gold chains, and rings set with diamonds or sapphires.[21] Prosperous citizens were less grand but aimed to dress as richly as possible. Red and green were favourite colours and violet gowns and girdles of purple silk became fashionable from the late 1480s.[22] Their gowns were trimmed with squirrel fur or lambskin, their soft leather belts were ornamented with silver buckles and silver studs, and they sported silver daggers and silver rings. The bequests of the feltcapper Nicholas Deykin in 1518 included five high-quality woollen gowns, three of them furred, and a chamlet doublet. A few years earlier a testator asked his executors to choose from among his gowns the one most suitable for his servant, who was evidently not to dress above his station.[23] Sumptuary legislation intended to restrict what people wore according to their rank was first introduced in 1363 and repeated from time to time but always proved ineffectual.[24] Price was doubtless a more influential factor. In Chester in the 1480s a scarlet gown edged with squirrel fur cost eight times as much as a gown of russet.[25] The everyday wear of most townsmen was rather drab, often made of grey russet cloth, but brightly-coloured garments could be purchased second-hand for holidays.[26]

Women

In late medieval Chester, as in other urban communities, the female inhabitants perhaps outnumbered the males, although the disparity may not have been large. Towns offered more economic opportunities than did country villages. Girls were employed as servants, wives worked alongside their husbands, widows continued running the family business, and single women traded on their own account, usually selling foodstuffs and ale. Females were routinely described in Chester's civic records in terms of their relationships with men: as daughter, sister, wife or widow of X; as servant, tenant or concubine of Y.[27] The emphasis on the familial relationships from which a female derived her social status underlined the importance of the household in the medieval economy. The female hierarchy mirrored the male, with aldermanic wives at the apex and lone immigrant women at the base.

There was considerable demand for female servants in Chester. Middling townsmen usually employed one such woman and wealthy households employed two or more. Four female servants received monetary bequests from John the armourer in 1396, the amount evidently depending on the length of time they had spent in his service. Margaret Hurleton in 1527 named six, including Ellyn of the kitchen.[28] Girls usually entered domestic service in their mid to late teens and their surnames suggest that many came from nearby villages; others had migrated to the city from Wales and the Isle of Man. They commonly agreed to serve for a year, receiving between 7s and 12s in wages. In 1436 one young woman agreed to serve a local weaver 'well and faithfully' for twelve months in return for a salary of 8s, a *bolet*, a pair of shoes and two weeks' holiday.[29] Some servants broke the agreement and left; others remained in the same household for a number of years. They never received any formal craft training but their role was not restricted to sweeping away the rubbish and delivering laundry. They presumably cooked, sewed and cared for the children, and many learned to brew and to sell ale. Seventeen of the 30 individuals licensed to sell ale in *c*.1408 were female servants.[30]

Young female immigrants who failed to find employment as household servants were in a vulnerable position. Those who arrived with little money and without relatives or contacts in Chester may quickly have fallen into debt. Single women were regularly taken to court because they owed money for rent, ale, and locks and keys for the door of their chamber. A tailor claimed in 1443 that Joanna Wyot owed him 10d for rent, 3d for shears, 2d for cheese, 2d for a lock, and 1d for a loan. She was evidently attempting to earn her living as a seamstress and we can imagine her problems if this venture failed.[31] Single women purchased an annual licence to carry out their trade, which usually involved selling food and drink. Some managed to eke out a livelihood, and in 1463 a dozen or so had prospered sufficiently to become independent householders and thus liable to local taxation. Among them were several brothel-keepers, and their 'employees' may well have included women who had been reduced to a life of petty crime and prostitution.

Female employment prospects improved after the Black Death but most women nevertheless hoped to find a husband, well aware that marriage provided greater security. Once married, a woman lost her separate legal identity but many worked in partnership with their husbands, the couple operating as an economic unit based in the family home. Weavers' wives prepared yarn and worked at the loom; fishmongers' wives sold and delivered fish; tailors' wives hemmed garments. Merchants' wives negotiated credit, transacted loans, and supervised the household's brewing activities without any loss of dignity. Margery Kempe of Norwich, daughter of a former mayor, became a brewer because she wished to 'maynten hir pride' and acquire fine clothes.[32]

In the early fourteenth century a number of Chester's élite wives were styled *mercatrix*, a title which enabled them to plead under merchant law. They were evidently self-confident women fully capable of holding their own in court. One wife, confronted by a Northampton merchant who swore on oath that she had made the tally recording a debt, snatched his hand from the holy book and declared that his claim was false.[33] Borough custom allowed married women the right to trade separately from their husbands as *femmes soles* but it seems that such women were formally registered only in London. It was not until *c.*1460 that *femmes soles* were recorded in Chester, perhaps as a result of increased bureaucracy, and over 50 wives opted to trade in this way in the closing decades of the fifteenth century. Their independence, however, was restricted to selling bread and ale.[34]

For some women widowhood resulted in poverty and they depended on family and charity for support. Widows of craftsmen and traders were more fortunate and were often able to carry on the business, having learned the skills and gained the expertise during their married life. Some handed over when the son came of age; others remarried, commonly finding a second husband among the fellow craftsmen or traders of the first.[35] Wealthy widows pursued the mercantile interests of their late husbands, importing wine and iron, for example, and selling spices and gunpowder. After John the armourer's death in 1396 his widow remained involved in business for 20 years; she was a member of Coventry's Trinity Guild and pursued debt claims in the hundred court at Macclesfield.[36] In the late 1470s John Cottingham's widow took over his shop in Bridge Street and continued to supply paper and wax for use in the castle exchequer.[37]

Chester's Worshipful Wives, responsible for staging the Assumption of Our Lady by the 1490s, were perhaps members of the prestigious fraternity of St Anne and shared their husbands' status. Only three women were entitled Mistress (*Domina*) in the surviving sources, all of them widows: Alice, widow of John the armourer; Cecily, widow of Thomas Wotton; and Katherine, widow of John Hope.[38] This was evidently not a courtesy title bestowed on all élite widows and as none of the three seems to have remarried it is possible that they had taken vows as a vowess. Alice Armourer's continued involvement in business argues against this explanation, so perhaps the title indicated that they were gentle-born. Chaucer mocked the burgess wives who aspired to be called *madame* and have their mantles carried like royalty when they attended vigils but many wives in Chester would have relished being set apart in such a manner.[39]

A woman's status, like a man's, was revealed by her dress. Little is known about the gowns, kirtles, smocks, aprons, hose and linen garments worn by the townswomen but prices indicate that the material, styling and workmanship varied enormously, and this would have been very obvious to the female eye. Wives of the most prosperous citizens wore gowns with collars of velvet or fur, and set them off with silk kerchiefs and silk girdles with silver or silver-gilt decorations.[40] There was an element of 'keeping up with the neighbours'. One goldsmith in 1491 was asked to make a girdle in the same design and style as that worn by a wealthy saddler's wife and was taken to court when his copy proved inexact.[41] Élite wives outshone the rest. Among Margaret Hawarden's bequests in 1520 were black and tawny gowns furred with grey and black, a worsted kirtle, her best hood and frontlet, and a sarsenet tippet. She owned a velvet girdle, a second adorned with pearls, and a third embroidered with gold thread. Her jewellery included a number of gold rings, one of them set with a ruby and one set with images.[42] Margaret Hawarden was an elderly widow and her clothing was rather sombre in colour. Most townswomen, whatever their status, preferred red.

Urban gentry

A parliamentary statute of 1413 required a man's status to be added to court records and the palatinate authorities quickly complied. Within a few years the citizens John and Edmund Ewloe, Robert Chamberlain, and John and Robert Hope were styled gentlemen in the indictment rolls of the county court.[43] Citizens of gentry status were recorded in Chester in later years, although they were never numerous. Some owed their gentility to ownership of land; others achieved gentility by service, either to the crown, or to powerful individuals, or to the city itself. Lawyers were regarded as gentlemen because of their profession and it was normal to accord the mayor's serjeant and swordbearer the title. By the end of the century a town's mayor was usually knighted on the occasion of a royal visit. During his visit to Chester in 1499 Prince Arthur made the mayor Richard Goodman an esquire.[44]

It is often assumed that townsmen who acquired large estates moved out of town to become country gentlemen but this was not always so. Richard the engineer invested heavily in land in Eccleston, Pulford and Eaton yet remained resident in Chester, farming the mills and serving as mayor, until his death in 1315. The Whitmore family owned vast acreages in Wirral, including the manor of Thurstaston, by the mid fourteenth century.[45] John Whitmore also chose to remain in Chester, living in Watergate Street and serving as mayor from 1370 until 1374. He was buried in Holy Trinity church, his tomb marked by a marble effigy depicting him in armour with a heraldic shield at his side. His son John was mayor in the years 1412–15, and his great-grandson William in 1450–1 and again in 1473–4. William was described as esquire in 1459 and in the late 1470s.[46] In the early sixteenth century a descendant married into the Hurleton family.

The Hurletons achieved gentility by serving a powerful individual and later by serving the palatinate. Henry Hurleton was appointed justice's clerk in 1441 by the justice William de la Pole, earl of Suffolk, in return for his service in

FIGURE 5.2. This medieval gold ring set with a garnet was found during excavations on the site of the nunnery in 2007. It was recovered from the back-fill of a late medieval or early post-medieval cellar and is paralleled by an example from London dated *c*.1350–1400.

the earl's retinue in the French wars without fee or reward.[47] Hugh Hurleton, appointed janitor of the outer gate of the castle in 1461, and his son Hugh, appointed janitor in 1485 and mayor of Chester in 1487–8, were both described as gentlemen, as too were Thomas Hurleton, sheriff in 1477–8, and Roger Hurleton, mayor in 1481–3 and 1492–3.[48] Roger Hurleton lived in the house at the junction of Bridge Street and Cuppin Lane once the home of John Ewloe, and was buried in the Lady chapel in St Bridget's. John Southworth owed his gentry status to service to Richard duke of York, father of Edward IV. He was mayor when York returned from Ireland in September 1460 and the duke granted him an annuity of £10 'for past service and for service to be rendered'. This grant was confirmed by Edward IV in July 1461 and Southworth received it until his death in 1485. He was described as gentleman in 1463 and as esquire in the 1470s, when he again served as mayor.[49]

John Hawarden 'man of law' and his brother William, clerk of the Pentice, were both described as gentlemen in the early fifteenth century.[50] Their mother was the daughter of Robert of Eaton and it was at Eaton in February 1427 that John Hawarden gentleman handed out livery (green suits of clothes decorated with silver) to a baker, a cutler and three weavers from Chester. The previous November the mayor John Hope gentleman distributed livery (black and red woollen garments) to three townsmen in the city itself. Two city bailiffs were among the recipients of red gowns distributed by John Whitmore at Thurstaston in 1423. Two years later they joined a group led by George Whitmore which ambushed John Savage at Tarvin Park.[51]

Country gentlemen were drawn to Chester by the demands of palatinate administration and many invested in residential and commercial property. In 1445–6 the Egertons, assiduous jurors at the county court throughout the century, owned a shop in Castle Lane, a messuage, four shops and gardens near St Olave's, and 15 other shops and gardens in Foregate Street. The Duttons of

FIGURE 5.3. The effigy of John Whitmore (d.1374) in Holy Trinity.

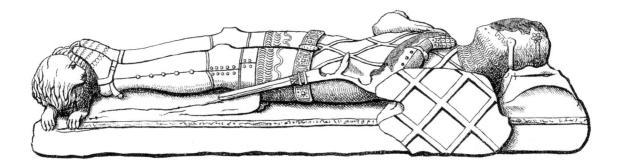

Dutton held property in Northgate Street, Bridge Street, Castle Lane, and a messuage in Fleshmongers Lane known as Bartholomew's Inn.[52] Some country gentlemen and esquires developed close ties with the urban élite and became members of the fashionable fraternity of St Anne. Others entered the franchise. William Stanley of Hooton and Thomas Pool of Pool were made free in the late 1460s and each paid 10½d because their fathers had been free at the time of their birth.[53] In the second half of the fifteenth century, as happened in many towns, some local gentlemen began to take an interest in urban politics. John Dutton of Hatton esquire was mayor in 1451–2 and Sir Piers Dutton on three occasions in the early sixteenth century, although he was removed from office in 1515 when it was declared that he had not been properly elected.

The urban gentry ranked high in Chester's social hierarchy and were linked to the local gentry by ties of marriage and shared values. Country gentlemen were not permanently resident yet their impact on the community was considerable. Townspeople doubtless enjoyed the excitement generated by the periodic gatherings of high society and certainly benefited from the increased trade. The disturbances that could erupt when feuding gentlemen were in town were an acceptable downside.

The clergy

The clergy perhaps constituted 5 per cent of the population in medieval towns and the percentage was certainly higher in Chester, an important ecclesiastical centre throughout the Middle Ages. The regular clergy, who belonged to religious orders and followed a religious rule, declined in numbers over the years and by the later medieval period most clergy were seculars, men who lived 'in the world'.[54] The church was closely integrated into the community, and its functions were social as well as spiritual. Churches were places where loans were agreed and repaid, where disputes were settled by arbitration, where oaths were sworn, and where inquiries known as proofs of age were held. The widespread use of saints' days as the normal method of dating reveals how deeply religion permeated daily life. When a loan was arranged before the altar of St Paul in St John's in 1303, the borrowers promised to repay at the feast of St John the Baptist. In September 1428 St Mary's was the setting for the proof of age of Katherine, daughter of Richard Hatton and relative and heir of Edmund son of John Ewloe. Witnesses attested on oath that she was born in Chester on the feast of St Giles (1 September) in 1414 and baptised in St Peter's.[55]

Regular clergy

The abbot of St Werburgh's was the wealthiest churchman in the archdeaconry and in the clerical poll tax of 1379 was assessed to pay £4, the statutory rate for peers of the realm. Each of his 26 monks paid 3s 4d, a higher sum than that paid by many beneficed clergy.[56] The number of monks had fallen from the 40 recorded in the thirteenth century, and 28 monks remained at the Dissolution. Surnames suggest that fourteenth-century recruits came mainly from the abbey's manors in Cheshire and from Shropshire, Staffordshire and Lancashire.[57] Many were of humble birth and some were illegitimate. This did not bar their progress. The monk Hamo Bostock, son of unmarried parents, served as abbey steward in 1416 and three years later a papal dispensation granted him eligibility for all monastic offices 'below the dignity of abbot.'[58]

It is difficult to assess the abbey's intellectual achievements but the surviving books, manuscripts and archives indicate that there was an active scriptorium and a substantial collection of written material housed in a library with a minimum of 18 shelves or cupboards. The librarian and head of the scriptorium in the mid fourteenth century may have been Ranulph Higden, an outstanding scholar and author of the *Polychronicon*, the most popular universal history of the later medieval period. He was summoned to Westminster by Edward III in 1352 and ordered to bring his chronicles with him. Higden had an encyclopaedic knowledge of classical writers and early medieval authorities and perhaps had access to many of these works in his own library.[59] Some classical authors he knew only through intermediate sources, including the compilation *De Proprietatibus Rerum* (*Concerning the Properties of Things*) by the Dominican Bartholomew Anglicus. This book was stolen from the abbey in the early fifteenth century, as too was a work by Avicenna, the foremost philosopher and physician of the Muslim world in the eleventh century.[60]

No monastic accounts survive and it is impossible to evaluate the contribution made by St Werburgh's to the urban economy. Chester's own records indicate that the monks rarely purchased foodstuffs in the city, suggesting that the abbey's manors produced sufficient grain and livestock for its needs, at least in normal years. Only in 1416–17, a year of bad wheat harvests everywhere, was the abbot recorded buying wheat at the Dee mills.[61] Occasionally the abbot purchased wine and herring from townsmen, or woollen cloth and cushion cloths.[62] There is no evidence for large-scale production for the market, just a few isolated references to sales of wool, peas, hay and tallow.[63] St Werburgh's possibly became involved in the trade in animal hides in the later fifteenth century, perhaps after the abbot became bishop of Man in 1478. Hides were sold in the 1480s and 1490s, and one or two monks travelled to the island and to Ireland. In 1508–9 a city tanner purchased 100 dozen sheepskins from the abbot.[64]

A number of issues led to friction between St Werburgh's and the urban community in the later medieval period, foremost among them the abbot's exclusive jurisdiction over all pleas except manslaughter during the Midsummer fair. Individual monks provoked hostility by roaming the streets at night and visiting prostitutes. Brawls between monks and townsmen often resulted in serious injuries and deaths.[65] The abbey's relationships with its own tenants were not always harmonious. In 1460 the abbot accused a city tailor and other townsmen of abducting Elena of Newton from his manor of Upton and preventing him from chastising her as a fugitive villein, as was his right.

Thirty years later the abbot and a fellow monk allegedly carried off a man from Boughton to Huntington where they burned his feet with fire.[66]

The Benedictine nunnery of St Mary's was a small and poorly endowed house, often in financial difficulties. In 1331 the income was deemed barely sufficient to support the inmates and the bishop forbade further admissions without his permission. The prioress was assessed to pay 13s 4d in the clerical poll tax in 1379 and each of the 12 nuns paid a shilling.[67] In the years 1496–1540 there were between 12 and 14 nuns, and at the Dissolution 11 nuns and three novices remained, an indication that the house was still attracting new recruits. Some came from citizen families. Alice of Doncaster entered the convent in the late 1360s, bringing with her an annual rent of 20s from a messuage in Bridge Street; she became prioress in 1386.[68] Alice Leyot, prioress in the 1440s, was presumably related to John Leyot, sheriff of Chester in 1436–7. Other nuns came from gentry families, including the Duttons, the Vernons and the Grosvenors. A similar mixture of daughters of wealthy burgesses and of country gentlemen was typically found in convents in all large towns. The widespread practice of demanding a dowry on entry, although strictly forbidden by canon law, ruled out girls from poor families.[69]

Nuns regularly increased their income by providing accommodation for lay women and children, a practice frowned upon by the church authorities since it disturbed the peace and quiet of the cloister. Chester's prioress kept 'ladies, damsels and children' at her table in 1358, among them young women like Katherine daughter of Philip of Raby, who was abducted from the nunnery in 1363 by Robert of Carrington with the aid of her former nurse.[70] The nuns' financial problems were compounded by incompetence. In the mid fifteenth century they proved unable to conduct elections properly and could not afford legal advice; the church and other buildings needed repair; the prioress had pawned the ornaments and mortgaged three pastures. Money was owed to a number of townsmen: 2s for meat, 23s 4d for grain, £ 4 10s for cattle, and almost £10 for ale.[71] The priest engaged to celebrate mass for a year from Michaelmas 1458, for a stipend of 46s 8d plus food and drink, was not paid in full. The nuns' credit rating was low and when the prioress was sued for money owed for wax in 1459, the convent cart had to be offered as surety; during these difficult years a man broke into the precinct and stole a brass bowl, a basin and ten towels. This was a time for prayer. Several private prayers dating from the fifteenth century survive in a book owned by the nun Dame Margery Byrkenhed, including 'A prayer to the Good Angel' which asks the angel to watch over her 'in this worlde of wyckednesse'.[72] The nuns' poverty may have endeared them to the townspeople and bequests in the later fifteenth and early sixteenth century suggest that they remained popular up to the Dissolution.

Very little is known about the size of Chester's three friaries. At the surrender in 1538 ten Carmelites, seven Franciscans and five Dominicans were named as witnesses.[73] Each house had more members in earlier centuries. There were 14 Carmelites in 1367 and their friary may always have been the largest. Among the friars were some whose surnames suggest Cheshire origins: the Carmelites John Somerford and Richard Bowdon, the Dominicans Richard Runcorn and John Dunham, and the Franciscan Robert Thornton.[74] Other names indicate links with city families, including Coly, Launcelyn, Danyell, Hawarden and Hurleton.[75] In the early fifteenth century one of Glyn Dŵr's adherents mocked Chester's Franciscans for their denunciations of immorality, poor clothing and bare feet, but the description suggests that they remained true to their vows of poverty.[76] The wide nave and aisles of their church, and the large nave and aisles added to the Dominican church in the late thirteenth or early fourteenth century, indicate the importance of the preaching mission. Small bequests to the friars were the most popular form of pious bequest in the years 1400–1540, with testators usually making a donation to each order.[77]

The friars came into contact with the townspeople on a daily basis. The Dominicans were recorded buying meat, arranging for a delivery of wheat, organizing supplies of coal for the winter months, and purchasing goods from the mercer John Cottingham.[78] They owned a quarry on Hough Green in Handbridge and sold stone for civic building projects. Their church occasionally served as the venue for arbitration when protracted disputes were settled.[79] The friary contained a library soon after its foundation and in the thirteenth century two of the brothers were notable scholars. The Dominicans possibly retained a reputation for learning. The son of William Hope was sent to board with them in the 1440s, and it was to the Black Friars that the rector of Holy Trinity bequeathed his book *Summa Confessorum* in 1506.[80]

The Franciscans, living close to the Watergate, inevitably developed links with men involved in maritime trade. The Fishmongers' company rented a small piece of land close to the friary gate in 1435–6, and the Franciscans were in regular contact with fishermen from the Isle of Man and with traders from inland towns who came to Chester to buy fish. In 1480, when a Stafford trader attempted to recover white fish detained by one of his fellow townsmen, the warden acted as pledge for both parties.[81] The church was easily accessible to the townspeople, through the gatehouse at the southern end of Crofts Lane, and in the fifteenth century three or four friars were licensed to hear confessions. The nave had fallen into disrepair by the start of the following century and the city's merchants and sailors carried out repairs. In return they were granted unrestricted use of the nave and aisles for the storage of their sails and tools.

The Carmelites had regular dealings with the urban community and the priors were recorded lending money, purchasing coal, and renting out property in Whitefriars Lane.[82] The Carpenters' light burned on an altar in their church and the prior frequently acted as pledge for building craftsmen. In October 1401 a carpenter was among the group of armed men who broke into the friary at 11 o'clock at night, causing such a disturbance that the great bell was rung and the hue and cry raised.[83] A townsman asked to be interred in the Carmelite church in 1348 and the church later became a fashionable place for burial. Bequests made to the Carmelites in the years 1500–40 almost equalled the combined total of those made to the Franciscans and Dominicans.[84]

Secular clergy

By the later fourteenth century the secular clergy outnumbered the religious. They included the archdeacon's representatives, the vicars choral of St John's, the incumbents and chaplains of the parish churches, the chaplains to the castle, hospitals and fraternities, and an ever-growing number of chaplains serving chantries and private individuals. The richest benefices were the deanery of St John's and the rectory of St Mary's; the other livings, with the exception of Holy Trinity, were poor. In the clerical poll tax of 1379 the dean of St John's and the rector of St Mary's were each assessed to pay 13s 4d; the vicar of St Oswald's and the rector of St Olave's each paid 2s.[85] Some rectors of St Mary's were absentees but many resided, including Richard Pensell, kinsman of William Troutbeck and rector from 1430 until 1458. He rented a plot of city ground lying between the rectory and the churchyard and had a privy built on the land; his successors continued to pay 4d a year for this 'jakes' or 'house of easement' in the early seventeenth century.[86] Pensell loaned money to townsmen, arbitrated in disputes, and in 1449 acted as executor for Hugh Woodcock, mayor in 1441–2. An inscription formerly in the window near the vestry door requested prayers for Pensell's soul.[87]

Occupants of other benefices included kin of city families. Alexander le Bel, rector of Holy Trinity in the early fourteenth century, was connected by marriage to the Arneways; Henry del Hey, rector of St Peter's from *c.*1430 until *c.*1444, was related to the cutler John del Hey, for whom he acted as pledge in the Pentice court.[88] John Mynns, rector of Holy Trinity from 1427 until his death in 1450, probably grew up in the city. He and his brother entered the franchise together in March 1432, each paying 10½d as sons of a freeman. John's brother, a tailor like the father, was not recorded again but John remained in Chester for the rest of his life.[89] A family link with John Mynns, chaplain of St Bridget's from the 1420s until 1450s, remains uncertain. The chaplain was first recorded in 1424, when he allegedly stole a silver rosary and crucifix from one of his parishioners, and in later years he was often in debt: to a shoemaker in 1434 for example, for a pair of shoes and a pair of galoshes.[90] Chester's more affluent clerics, like parish clergy elsewhere, acted as money-lenders. Henry Rainford, son or grandson of a former mayor of Chester and rector of Holy Trinity from 1482 until 1506, loaned money to a butcher's widow in 1487. Parishioners supported their priests. A butcher acted as pledge for the chaplain of St Peter's in 1497, when the cleric was pursued for a debt of 6s for horse hire.[91]

Minor posts as chantry chaplains proliferated in the later medieval period and many wealthy testators left money to endow masses for their souls. Thomas del Fere's bequest of £10 13s 4d in 1384 was to pay for a chaplain to celebrate mass for two years in St Michael's for himself and his wife. John the armourer in 1396 left £60 for a chaplain to sing in St Mary's chapel in Holy Trinity church for the souls of himself, his wife and all the faithful departed. In 1518 the feltcapper Nicholas Deykin asked to be buried beside his wife in St Catherine's aisle in St John's; he left £25 for a priest to sing at St Catherine's altar for five years and the profits from his dwelling house for a priest to sing at the altar of the Holy Rood each Sunday, Wednesday and Friday for eight years, and thereafter at St Catherine's altar. A collegiate vicar was probably employed as cantarist.[92]

Chester's wealthiest citizens had oratories in their homes and some maintained private chaplains. Twenty or more prominent townsmen and women were licensed to have an oratory in the years 1361–81, including several mayors and sheriffs. A few widows continued to maintain oratories granted to their husbands and evidently valued the opportunity for private prayer, although they would have continued to attend their parish church.[93] Among the private chaplains recorded in the fifteenth century were Nicholas chaplain of Robert Hope in 1424, and Master William former chaplain of John Flint in 1431. The chaplain who agreed in 1453 to serve Thomas Wainfleet in the office of priest for a year left because he did not receive his full salary. John Hawarden in 1496 asked the priest appointed to his chantry to attend his wife and be at table with her.[94] There are examples of chaplains serving a townsman for a few days at a time, among them one employed for three days by a tailor in 1420, at the rate of 4d a day. Their role may not have been spiritual. Chaplains acted as attorneys, wrote wills and undertook secretarial work; some were described as scriveners. Master John Paule 'chaplain and physician' was taken to court in 1491 for failing to cure a townswoman as he had promised. He rented a room in Bridge Street and was perhaps not a permanent resident. The chaplain who owed a glover for food, drink and a tippet in 1488 may also have been in the city on a temporary basis.[95] Some minor clerics, like the building workers, moved in and out.

Welsh, Irish and Manx residents

Chester's location ensured close and enduring links with settlements around the Irish Sea from early times. A flourishing trade with Ireland resulted in the establishment of a Hiberno-Norse community south of the Roman fortress in the tenth century, and archaeological evidence reveals contacts with the Isle of Man.[96] North-eastern Wales was locked into Chester's economic hinterland by the eleventh century; the Welsh frequented the city's markets and fairs and became familiar figures on the streets. They were unfairly treated when their goods were stolen and in Lucian's day relationships between Cestrians and their Welsh neighbours were far from cordial.[97] In later years the Welsh accounted for a significant proportion of the population. Irish and Manx settlers were less numerous but formed distinctive groups within the urban community.

Links with Wales were disrupted during Edward I's campaigns but once peace was established many Welshmen moved to Chester. Some found only labouring

jobs but others were more successful. William of Flint was named among
Chester's bakers in 1306 and in *c.*1315 a member of the prominent Hurrell family
engaged Eynon Walens and entrusted him with £14 to buy woollen cloth.[98] Ties
were strengthened as leading citizens acquired land and offices in Wales and
as prosperous Welshmen acquired property in Chester. Madoc of Capenhurst,
whose forename suggests Welsh links and whose family owned property in
Flint, was sheriff of Chester nine times between 1329–30 and 1345–6. John of
Stoke of Rhuddlan held much property in Chester in these years, including a
tenement in Watergate Street adjoining one owned by the Doncaster family
and a plot of land in Pepper Street between plots owned by the Brickhills and
the Doncasters. He served as sheriff in 1338–9.[99]

There was much migration from Wales throughout the later medieval period,
in particular from Flintshire and the surrounding areas. The newcomers met
with varying success. Some found only menial employment and were always
poor; others prospered, particularly as weavers, tailors and butchers, and became
freemen; the most successful grew very wealthy and joined the ruling élite. This
caused difficulties during Glyn Dŵr's rebellion in the early fifteenth century but
the Welsh continued to arrive and to settle. In 1463 the tenth most common
forename among the city's taxpayers was David.

The Welsh lived in all quarters of the city but there was a particular
concentration in Handbridge, in the nuns' manor on the south side of the
Dee. Both the brewers and six of the 14 ale sellers recorded in Handbridge
in 1487 were Welsh.[100] The clerks occasionally struggled with the spelling of
Welsh names and wrote them phonetically: 'Thlannelwey' and 'Dulgethle' for
example.[101] The Anglicization of some Welsh names hints at a process of accultura-
tion. Madok the wright thatcher, attested in Chester in 1398, had changed his
name to Matthew the thatcher by 1402; the butcher John ap Wyllym, active in
the city in the 1450s, was also known as John William; the chaloner David ap
Howell, living in Handbridge at the end of the century, was sometimes named
David Powell.[102] Welsh words were occasionally used. In 1499 John Gruff sold
'godartes', described by Ranulph Higden as pots of white and red clay made in
north Wales. Drinking cups known as 'goddards' were still used in north Wales,
and especially in Anglesey, at the end of the nineteenth century.[103]

Contacts with Ireland, the main focus of Chester's overseas trade throughout
the medieval period, were always close. John Hatton, sheriff in 1380–1, was
given lands and tenements in Ireland by his first wife and he bequeathed this
property to his nephew John. The younger man lived in Watergate Street
and his ships regularly crossed to Ireland, carrying woollen cloth and salt. He
served as pledge for a Drogheda man who entered the franchise in 1419, had
business dealings with a merchant from Malahide, and was mayor of Chester
in 1423–4.[104] Robert Nottervill, twice mayor of Drogheda, was admitted to
Chester's franchise in 1460, served as sheriff in 1468–9 and as mayor ten years
later. He was a prosperous mercer and remained closely involved in trade with

FIGURE 5.4. The church of St Cynfarch and St Cyngar at Hope. John Hope, mayor seven times in the years 1419–28, left 6s 8d to works at St Kyngar's church in 1439. A new nave had been added to the church by the early 16th century. Hope was 'wholly Welsh', having been born in Wales of Welsh parents, and his name suggests that he originated in the town. His migration to Chester proved an outstanding success.

FIGURE 5.5. St Laurence's Gate at Drogheda dates back to the 13th century and derived its name from the friary to the east of the town. This outer defence gate still survives and is regarded as one of the finest of its type in Europe.

Ireland, handling merchandise imported by Dubliners and trading in grey yarn and 'narrow Irish cloth'.[105]

Official concern about the large numbers of 'artificers and labourers' who were choosing to leave Ireland and settle in England in the early fifteenth century led to royal proclamations ordering their return. The unruly behaviour of Irish immigrants in some towns resulted in a parliamentary decree in 1422 ordering their mass expulsion from the realm; these ordinances were repeated in the early 1430s. Permission to stay was granted in return for a monetary payment. In May 1439 Henry Waterleder of Chester and his wife were among 42 Irish nationals who paid to remain in England.[106] Katherine of Trim, who paid for a licence to sell retail in Chester in 1419 and again in 1431–2, apparently managed to avoid expulsion. Among the many Irish immigrants who struggled to make a living were John le Iryshe workman, accused of theft in 1415, and Emmota Trim and Agnes Irish, fined for brothel-keeping in 1463.[107]

Chester developed strong trading links with the Isle of Man in the later medieval period. The island's exports probably included hides, sheepskins and herring, as in the seventeenth century.[108] One prominent citizen with relatives on the island was John the armourer, who died in 1396. He owned a ship called 'St Mary's bote of Pull', a probable reference to Wallasey Pool on the north-western corner of Wirral, which became involved in trade with the Isle of Man in the later fifteenth century.[109] Manx migrants formed a distinct group within the urban community, congregating in the Watergate Street area and working mainly in the fish trade. They were a close-knit, if not always harmonious, community and provided board and lodgings for new arrivals, loaned one another money, and acted as pledges when required.[110] They could be recognised by their names. Men were commonly called Patrick, Donald or Gilbert (Gybon), and surnames often began with the patronymic 'Mac': Maccally, Maccoryn, Macroke, Maccandell, Maccavell, Maccane, Macrowle and Macknevy were among those recorded in the 1480s and 1490s.[111] One or two changed their names. Thomas Croke and Gilbert Kelly, close associates in the 1490s, came from families called Macroke and Mackelly.[112] The shipmaster Patrick Man *alias* Black Patrick, the brothel-keeper Black Meg, and John Davy *alias* 'Blakjohn of the Isle of Man' were recorded in Chester in the later fifteenth century.[113] Did a swarthy complexion distinguish these islanders from other members of the urban community?

The Corbets migrated to Chester from the Isle of Man and acquired considerable wealth. The foundations of the family fortunes were laid by David Corbet, master of the *George of Man* and the *Longebote of Man* in the 1450s and 1460s.[114] Thirty years later Thomas and Robert Corbet were Manx shipmasters and Otiwell Corbet was regularly named among the merchants with goods on board. The family dealt mainly in fish, particularly in herring and salmon. They had trading links with Carrickfergus in Ulster by 1494 and with the Bann salmon fishery by 1505.[115] All three became freemen of Chester: Robert in 1494–5, and Thomas and Otiwell in 1500–1. When Otiwell was attacked in Watergate Street in January 1501 he defended himself with a 'skeyne', a type of knife or dagger used by Irish foot soldiers as one of their chief weapons. Its appearance in Chester in the hands of a citizen of Manx origin indicates the cross-cultural linkages at play within the urban community.[116]

The poor

At Chester, as elsewhere, the poor went largely unrecorded. Considerable numbers of the destitute probably congregated in the city, as they did in all large towns, in the hope of receiving charitable assistance. In London in 1322 the crowd gathered at the gate of the Black Friars when alms were handed out was so large that over 50 people were trampled to death.[117] A fifth of Coventry's population may have been in dire need in the crisis years of 1520–3 but in normal times the city's poor were less numerous.[118] Testamentary bequests suggest that the poor were familiar figures in Chester, to be found lying in the shops (*in skopis*) and in the cottages (*in casis*) without shoes or money to pay rent.[119] The resident wage-earners experienced periodic bouts of poverty. An accident at work or a downturn in trade resulted in unemployment, and old age ushered in hard times for many.

Religious houses were charitable institutions and monastic accounts indicate that 2 per cent of a monastery's income was typically given to charity.[120] The annual income of St Werburgh's was just over £1,000, which would have yielded a charitable fund of some £20 a year. Additional grants provided money for alms on the anniversaries of the deaths of a Norman earl and a former abbot, and each Maundy Thursday £14 was handed out for the souls of the kings of England. The monks were expected to distribute left-over food on a daily basis but sometimes gave it to the greyhounds and other hunting dogs instead. The nuns distributed a tenth of their income (which was just below £100) in alms on Maundy Thursday, a large sum for a poor house. In the early years of its foundation St John's hospital was expected to take in as many poor and sick as possible but by the later medieval period the number of inmates was perhaps limited to 13, the number symbolising those present at the Last Supper. The six almshouses endowed by Roger Smith in 1508 were intended for 'decayed' aldermen or councilmen; only if there were no such candidates could places be offered to the poorest inhabitants of the city, including widows. The daily fare in these institutions was adequate but not over-generous. In the earlier fourteenth century each inmate at St John's hospital received a loaf of bread, a dish of pottage, half a gallon of ale, and a piece of fish or meat. The number of recipients was, however, always very small.[121]

The parish clergy were obliged by canon law to assign a quarter or a third of their revenues to the poor but rarely seem to have given more than a few shillings.[122] There is no evidence that Chester's parish clergy were more generous. Parish charity could take the form of a church ale, a convivial gathering which enabled parishioners to help those in need, and Chester's congregations may have organized such events. A civic ordinance of 1486 forbade attendance at common ales outside the liberties.[123] The city's craft companies probably supported members who were suffering hardship and the fashionable fraternity of St Anne, whose own members were too wealthy to need assistance, may have offered financial help to their tenants on occasion. In 1404–5 the fraternity gave 6s 8d in alms to one woman, perhaps recently widowed.[124] Wealthy visitors handed out small sums. The expenses of a member of John Howard's retinue in January 1464 included 3d for alms, a quarter of the sum spent on ale.[125]

Leading townspeople remembered the poor in their wills. In February 1398 John Hatton asked that all his linen and woollen garments and furs be given to the poor within three days of his death. Margaret Hawarden was mindful of the cold weather when she drew up her will in December 1520; she requested that her flax and yarn be made into cloth for poor men and women and that her wood and coal be distributed to the poor.[126] Many testators limited their charitable bequests to the white garments given to the dozen paupers who carried torches at their funeral and to doles of bread to those attending the service. In 1506 Henry Rainford, wealthy rector of Holy Trinity, left 10s to be distributed to the poor at the rate of 1d each. This would have provided 120 people with one meal of bread, ale and a piece of meat or fish.[127] Had 100 similar bequests been made in any one year they would have provided temporary relief for only a tiny fraction of the city's poor.

Beggars were viewed with increasing alarm after 1349 and laws were passed controlling their movements. Among Chester's first surviving by-laws in 1393 was one prohibiting men from roaming the streets without sufficient means on which to live; the prohibition was repeated in 1404. These by-laws were perhaps prompted by legislation of 1391 and 1403 which re-iterated the principle that the poor should be relieved by the local community.[128] In the mid fifteenth century the city's tapsters were accused of sheltering vagabonds and keeping their doors open at night, and the hermit of St James in Handbridge was accused of harbouring thieves and malefactors. Vagrants perhaps found shelter in the hermitage. Harsh measures were taken by the authorities in the 1490s and early sixteenth century; beggars were ordered to take up employment or face imprisonment and townsmen were fined for providing them with accommodation.[129]

Late medieval Chester was a rigidly hierarchical society, with a small group of wealthy merchants at the summit and the poor and disadvantaged at the base. The inequalities were clearly visible. The leading citizens strutted the urban stage in furred gowns, with silver daggers at their belts and gold rings on their fingers. The poorest inhabitants went barefoot and were unable to pay for a roof over their heads.

CHAPTER SIX

Urban Government

The beginnings of self-government at Chester can be traced back to the late twelfth century when the citizens became responsible for paying part of the city farm and were granted the right to hold a guild merchant, enabling them to determine who could trade in the city without paying tolls.[1] Initially the guild warden or alderman perhaps served as the head of the citizen body, as local tradition later alleged, but the mayor emerged as the chief representative in the 1240s. Sheriffs with responsibility to the citizens rather than to the earl were recorded in the 1230s and by 1244 two were appointed each year. The mayor was often named in the court records in association with the 'good men' (*probi* or *boni homines*) of the commonalty. The collective duties of the 'men of Chester' included the maintenance of the city's streets, walls and bridge, and the management of the town fields.

The mayor's role gradually expanded during the later thirteenth century. He, as senior civic official, was given the responsibility of keeping the larger portion of the seal of Statute Merchant when Chester was authorized to act as a centre for the registration of debts. The smaller portion of the seal was kept by a new official, the clerk for the recognizance of debt, first recorded in 1291. The citizens' rights were formally defined in the new charter granted to Chester by Edward I in 1300. The charter recognised the office of mayor and granted the mayor and sheriffs the right to hold the pleas of the Crown, at that time a unique privilege. It confirmed that the farm was in the hands of the citizens and fixed the figure at £100, only half the sum demanded in the 1230s. The citizens were also granted the right to build on vacant plots of land within the liberties and to take revenues from other plots to pay the fee farm.[2]

By the mid fourteenth century the mayor's dominant position was firmly established. He presided over inquests at which market offences were presented, dealt with fair-time pleas, and acted as escheator. He and the sheriffs headed a new civic institution, the Assembly, which had emerged by the early 1390s. This new organization included a body of aldermen known as the Twenty-Four and a group vaguely described as 'many other citizens' or as 'the whole community' who gave their assent to decisions taken *in plena congregatione*, regularly agreeing *viva voce*.[3] Most aldermen were former mayors and sheriffs and their number always exceeded 24. In 1398, for example, 26 were named, among them several who had held office in the early 1380s and one who had been sheriff in 1379–80.[4] Their accumulated wisdom and experience was considerable and the mayor constantly looked to them for advice, enabling them to influence key decisions. Their routine duties included attendance at the portmote court where they witnessed property transactions, and service as jurors at the assize of wine. Failure to attend when summoned risked the imposition of a hefty fine.[5]

From the 1390s a written record of Assembly orders and much other administrative business was kept in the Mayor's Book. The early ordinances were endlessly repeated throughout the later medieval period: pavements were to be kept clean, pigs were not to roam the streets, butchers were not to kill animals in their shops, and carts with iron-bound wheels were not to cross the Dee bridge.[6] The Assembly was served by a growing number of officers. By the 1390s the custodian of the seal of Statute Merchant had been replaced by a common clerk who dealt with legal matters, soon known as the clerk of the Pentice, and a treasurer accounted for the city rents. By 1416 two treasurers were appointed each year and those then in office, both former sheriffs, witnessed the grant of a plot of city land at the end of Ironmongers' Row and saw the document sealed with the common seal of the city.[7] Responsibility for the upkeep of the walls had devolved upon the city authorities by the early fifteenth century. From *c.*1407 two muragers were appointed annually and charged with collecting money to maintain the defences and presenting those who damaged the walls. They derived their income from customs levied at the gates and from goods entering and leaving the city.[8]

The old guild merchant, so powerful before the Black Death, had lost its supremacy by the end of the fourteenth century but remained closely linked to the new civic institutions. From the 1390s until at least 1420 membership of the guild equated with the freedom of the city but after 1430–1 new freemen entered the 'liberty and franchise', not the guild.[9] The role of the guild merchant evidently changed during this period. In 1437 two former wardens (*custodes*) attempted to recover money owing for custom, with a shipman acting as their pledge, and two 'leavelookers of the city of Chester' named in 1439 were almost certainly their successors. Both men were involved in long-distance trade and it seems that the guild merchant had already become an association of non-resident traders, as it was in the second half of the fifteenth century.[10] Leavelookers were responsible for collecting the entry subscriptions from the members and for levying a tax on their merchandise. The money was used to pay for the hospitality offered to distinguished visitors.

From 1452 admissions to the freedom were made on condition that the new freemen reside in the city.[11] A body of common councilmen known as the Forty-Eight appeared at this time. They represented the four quarters of the city and, like the Twenty-Four, always had more members than the designation implied. In 1476–7, for example, 65 potential councilmen were named: 32 from Eastgate Street, 13 from Bridge Street, and 10 each from Watergate Street and Northgate Street. Of these, 57 were 'sworn'.[12] The councilmen's duties included the supervision of civic finances. In the 1450s, for instance, the treasurers' and leavelookers' accounts were audited by four aldermen and by four or eight councilmen, chosen from the four main streets. In 1475–6 ten members of the Twenty-Four and ten members of the Forty-Eight were asked to settle the differences which had arisen between the craft guilds. The following year a similar committee prepared for the visit of the prince of Wales, and a smaller committee of four aldermen and four common councilmen supervised the construction of a new cross and chose men to collect the funds.[13]

The Forty-Eight were not artisans and small-scale traders but established craftsmen and young mercers and drapers at the outset of their civic career, and were perhaps selected from the 'saddist and most substanciall comynors of the citie' as they were in the sixteenth century.[14] They were expected to give money as well as time. In 1462–3 they contributed £4 10s to the special levy imposed by the mayor, half the amount given by the Twenty-Four, and when the city rented two new pieces of pasture in 1496–7 the councilmen gave between 20d and 6s 8d each, the aldermen between 6s 8d and 20s, and the mayor gave 40s.[15]

The charter of 1506 confirmed the existing constitution and gave the city county status. Minor alterations were made to the size of the governing body, which had possibly grown somewhat unwieldy: 31 aldermen and 56 common councilmen were 'sworn' in 1500–1.[16] The charter fixed the number of aldermen at 24 and of councilmen at 40 (although 35 aldermen were listed in 1507–8 and 27 were 'sworn'). The freemen, now acknowledged as part of the corporation, selected two aldermen as candidates for mayor. One was appointed mayor by the aldermen, who also nominated one of the two sheriffs; the second sheriff was elected by the whole Assembly.

By the 1430s the mayor received a fee of £10 and was attended by a swordbearer and a serjeant-at-mace, each of whom received a fee. Salaried officials in the later fifteenth century included the recorder and three or four men who gave legal counsel, and expenditure on fees approached £20.[17] The Assembly depended upon rents from city property for most of its income but more came from freemen admissions, from writs of error, and from leasing the pasture on the Roodee. The city already owned a considerable amount of property in the 1430s, including shops below the Pentice and near the pillory which commanded high rents. Rental income approached £13 in 1441–2 and increased to £16 in the later fifteenth century as new rents were added. Total income barely reached £21, sufficient for the officers' fees but with little to spare for contingencies.[18] The accounts were in serious arrears in the early 1460s, partly because of the rebuilding of the Pentice and partly because of the troubled political situation. The cost of equipping 24 soldiers and sending them to the north in 1462–3 exceeded £16, and more was spent on the constant stream of messengers dispatched to London, York and other places. These extraordinary commitments were financed by the special tax levied by the mayor. A similar tax perhaps funded the reconstruction of the Pentice in 1463–4.[19]

Policing the city

By the 1290s Chester was divided into four quarters based on the four main streets for administrative purposes and these subdivisions formed the basis of administration until the early sixteenth century. The serjeants of the gates were responsible for policing the city, supervising the watch, and collecting tolls at the gates. Although the citizens never received a formal grant of the right to keep a gaol the serjeant of the Northgate had charge of the prison by 1294. The charter of 1300 contained a clause which authorized the imprisonment in the Northgate of all those arrested within the liberties and awaiting gaol delivery according to the law and custom of the city.[20] By 1321 the duties of the keepers of the Northgate included sounding the horn for the portmote, holding the keys of the gallows, taking charge of the pillory, and supervising prisoners.[21]

By the late fourteenth century policing activities had been removed from the ancient serjeanties and had become the responsibility of a group of 16 leading property holders drawn from the four main streets: five each from Eastgate Street and Bridge Street, four from Watergate Street, and two from Northgate Street. Two properties lay between Fleshmongers Lane and the Eastgate, one at the junction of Bridge Street and Watergate Street, and others between St Peter's church and Goss Lane. Property holders in the years 1385–1410 included

FIGURE 6.1. A replica version of the Great Charter was presented to the mayor at the Cross on 6 April 2006, five centuries after the original grant.

FIGURE 6.2. The city sword is believed to be of 15th-century manufacture. A swordbearer attended the mayor by the 1430s and received a fee of 40s. Hugh Dutton held the office intermittently from the late 1450s until the 1480s and probably longer. In 1494, at the especial request of the earl of Derby, he was awarded an annuity for his long service. The charter of 1506 gave the mayor the right to have the sword carried before him point upright, in the absence of the king or his heirs.

Sir Hugh de Holes (Eastgate Street), Robert Chamberlain (Bridge Street), the abbot of St Werburgh's and Laurence of Doncaster (Watergate Street), and John Whitmore (Northgate Street). Their duties, performed by deputies, included keeping the Christmas watch, guarding condemned felons and taking them to the gallows.[22] Four bailiffs assisted the sheriffs in running the Pentice court; they summoned defendants, assembled jurors, distrained goods, collected fines, and also acted as attorneys for litigants unable to attend in person.

Constables were recorded from *c.*1450 and, like the common councilmen, were listed under the headings of the four main streets with those representing Eastgate Street and Bridge Street always the most numerous. Their numbers varied from year to year: Eastgate Street appointed ten in 1474–5 and four in 1476–7, and Bridge Street eleven and five respectively.[23] Service as constable may have been a stage in a man's civic career and many constables became councilmen within a year or two. Young men from wealthy mercantile families did not hold this office. Constables regularly served as jurors at the portmote and may well have represented their particular subdivision, presenting offenders who lived in their quarter of the city.[24] The first reference to 'wards' was in 1487 when the constables were ordered to summon the city's brewers and ale sellers to bring their measures to be stamped. In 1507–8 the constables were listed in eight wards, each of which was under the supervision of an alderman.[25]

The gallows were sited at the boundary of the city liberties in Boughton, the gaol was within the Northgate, and the pillory stood in the market place in front of St Peter's church. In an undated petition the abbot of Vale Royal complained about the pillory recently erected by the mayor and commonalty in front of the abbey's tenements 'where none was used to be'. The property stood unlet as a result and he requested the pillory's removal.[26] A city rental of 1554–5 recorded two shops formerly owned by Vale Royal near the new steps at the north-eastern corner of Bridge Street. These new steps were recorded in 1356 and led to Corvisers' Row near the pillory.[27] The pillory remained in the angle at the junction of Bridge Street and Eastgate Street throughout the fifteenth century and was leased by the city to various townsmen, including the fishmonger Robert Dewe in the 1430s and 1440s.[28] A new pillory costing almost 16s was made in 1461–2 and the following year a new shop was erected next to it. The city soon recovered its outlay. The pillory was rented for 8s a year in the 1460s and 1470s, and two shops below the pillory were rented for 5s each.[29] A link with the fish trade continued. One shop was rented by a fishmonger's widow in the late 1460s and then taken over by Alice wife of William Dewe, fined for throwing fish entrails under her market stall in 1474. It seems that the pillory was raised high above street level, a tradition which may have persisted. In the seventeenth century a scaffold was made at the High Cross 'for the cheats to stand on'.[30]

Craft guilds

Closely associated with Chester's Assembly in the later medieval period were the craft guilds, which staged civic pageants and helped to regulate urban manufacturing and retailing.[31] They were always subordinate to the governing body, which kept a watchful eye on their internal affairs and stepped in to settle disputes and determine the level of entry fines.

Separate associations of shoemakers and tailors existed by the early fourteenth century, although the unitary guild merchant in theory still represented all the city's trades. The Shoemakers claimed in 1499 that they had been established as the guild of St Martin before 1285–6 (and later asserted that their guild had originated in the twelfth century).[32] The Tailors claimed in the early fifteenth century that their guild had existed since ancient times (*ab antiquo*) and a collective body of tailors evidently existed by 1302, when they paid 2s a year to the chamberlain to ensure that no-one 'communed' with them on 3 September.[33] A tailor accused that year of making the sleeves of a doublet so badly that another tailor had to remake them with new material, asked for the support of his fellow craftsmen, further evidence for an association. The Tailors' guild was sometimes styled the guild or fraternity of St Mary in the late fourteenth and early fifteenth century.[34] The Tailors and Shoemakers may have originated as religious guilds and this perhaps explains why they were the only craft companies to be called guilds in the fifteenth century.[35] The standard terms for other companies were art (*ars*), craft (*artificium*), or the occupational name alone. In the 1420s the term fraternity was sometimes used, perhaps when the emphasis was on their religious role.[36]

The Tanners were recorded in the 1360s when they squabbled with the Shoemakers over the right to produce leather.[37] A cluster of references to other craft fellowships appeared in the 1420s, prompted perhaps by the elaboration of the Corpus Christi festival and possibly also by a contemporary reorganization of the admission to the freedom. The Carpenters, Ironmongers, Fletchers, Bowyers, Stringers, Coopers, Turners, Bakers, Glovers, Weavers, Barbers, Goldsmiths and Smiths existed by the 1420s, as did journeymen organizations of Bakers, Shoemakers and Tailors.[38] The Walkers, Drapers, Mercers, Fishmongers and Masons were named in the 1430s;[39] the Drawers of Dee (fishermen), Saddlers, Skinners and a journeyman organization of Weavers in the 1440s;[40] the Butchers in the 1450s, the Cooks in the 1460s, the Heusters (Dyers) in the 1470s, and the Painters in the 1480s.[41] The journeymen Glovers were recorded in 1492, an indication perhaps of the growth of that trade, and the Vintners, Tapsters and Hostelers were named in *c*.1500.[42] Some companies comprised a number of related crafts. The walkers, chaloners (blanket weavers) and shearmen belonged to the Weavers' company, and the Smiths' company in 1501 included cutlers, pewterers, founders, cardmakers, girdlers, pinners, wiredrawers and spurriers.[43] The feltcappers, newly established in Chester in the 1460s, never formed a company of their own and were part of the Skinners' company by 1489; the name of their craft was added to the title when one served as steward.

The glaziers belonged to the Painters' company by 1482 and the name of their craft was added when a glazier held company office.[44]

Twenty-five craft guilds existed in 1475–6 and at the start of the sixteenth century probably 26 companies staged the Corpus Christi play. There is a little evidence for the size of individual companies. Sixteen tailors and their servants were accused of confederacy in 1392, when they swore on oath to support one another in court. Fourteen men witnessed the Bakers' charter in 1463, including the company alderman and the two stewards, and 19 men witnessed the Fletchers and Bowyers' charter in 1468.[45] The Butchers and the Bakers each had a membership of about 17 in the 1490s and the numbers increased in the early sixteenth century.[46]

The Bakers and the Fletchers and Bowyers were the only companies chartered by the city in the fifteenth century. The Bakers' charter in 1463 stipulated that only those who had joined the company and deposited their mark in wax before the mayor could carry out the craft, and ruled that members were to pay for the Corpus Christi play and light when required.[47] The Fletchers and Bowyers' charter in 1468 recorded a similar mixture of religious and economic regulations. All members were to contribute to the Corpus Christi pageant and light; apprentices were to train for seven years; master craftsmen were not to take work from their fellows; the length of the working day was determined; the entry fee was fixed at 26s 8d.[48] The entry fees fixed by the mayor and aldermen for 19 of the city's companies in 1475–6 were lower. Fourteen companies agreed that apprentices should pay 6s 8d and strangers 13s 4d; the Butchers, Fishmongers and Cooks agreed on fees of 6s 8d and 10s, and the Drawers of Dee on fees of 3s 4d and 6s 8d; no figures were recorded for the Bakers. The ruling clearly demonstrated the subordinate role of the craft guilds, which accepted that the fees should be 'as the mayor and his brethren will'.[49]

The companies were always anxious to preserve their monopoly and initiated legal proceedings in the Pentice court against those who 'occupied' a craft without belonging to the relevant guild.[50] Guild stewards also took action against members who failed to pay their dues or who infringed the company's ordinances. In the early 1450s the weaver Richard Dodd incurred the wrath of his company by refusing to contribute the customary 12d to St Mary's light and by employing a non-freeman. The stewards responded by breaking into his house and destroying the reeds of his loom.[51]

The guilds were religious organizations. The Tailors were dedicated to the Virgin Mary and the Shoemakers to St Martin, on whose festival (11 November) their stewards were elected. St Eligius (St Loy) was the patron saint of Chester's smiths.[52] The Carpenters maintained a light on an altar in the Carmelite church and the Tanners maintained a light on the altar of St Mary Calvercroft at St John's. The church which housed the Weavers' light of St Mary was never named in the records.[53] Each guild carried large candles or torches, perhaps six in number, as they processed through the city on the feast of Corpus Christi.[54] The guilds played a crucial role in the procession and plays, and in the Whitsun plays which succeeded them in the early sixteenth century. No guild halls were recorded in Chester in the late medieval period but the companies did rent plots of city land where they stored equipment used in the plays. In the 1430s the Fishmongers rented a plot next to the gate of the Franciscan friary and the Mercers rented the Shipgate.[55] By the 1480s the Saddlers were storing their carriage in a garden next to Truants Hole (a drain-hole in the city wall east of the Wishing Steps), the shearmen were storing their carriage somewhere in the Northgate Street quarter, and the Mercers and Drapers had carriage houses at the end of Greyfriars Lane.[56]

Religious fraternities

The guild of St Mary was probably founded long before the earliest documented reference in 1330–1. That year the guild met several times in the house of former mayor John of Brickhill in Bridge Street (perhaps near the common hall); 49 new entrants accepted the guild 'wands' (*virgas Gilde Beate Marie*) and 40 existing members acted as their pledges, including three of the four *seniores*. Most men were members of the leading city families which dominated the guild merchant but one came from Denbigh and another from Thornton; four clerics were named, including the vicar of Frodsham.[57] St Mary's guild evidently served as a social and religious association for the civic élite, its activities centred on fellowship and conviviality. Many of the same men assembled as the guild merchant to control urban government and economic affairs.

If the two guilds were related in this way, then they may have developed side by side in the second half of the thirteenth century, a period that witnessed especial veneration of the Virgin Mary. The abbey church, like large churches throughout England, acquired a Lady chapel, and John Arneway, mayor from 1268–78, left money in 1274–8 for a chaplain to celebrate a daily mass in honour of St Mary in St Bridget's, close to the common hall where the guild merchant met.[58] The tailors' fraternity of St Mary may have originated in the later thirteenth century. Was it linked in some way to the guild merchant? The tailors' guild at Winchester was one of that city's most popular fraternities in the fourteenth century, its membership coextensive with that of the merchant guild although still serving the particular needs of the tailors.[59]

St Mary's guild was recorded for the second and final time in July 1348 when the steward, former sheriff Roger the harper whose son headed the list of new entrants in 1330–1, sued two coopers for debt.[60] It may have been a casualty of the Black Death and was possibly replaced by the fraternity of the Blessed Trinity, the Assumption of Our Lady and St Anne, whose members were licensed in 1361 to acquire property to maintain a newly ordained chantry and two chaplains in St John's church.[61] The fraternity flourished after its refoundation in 1393 as a fraternity in honour of God, the Virgin and St Anne, later known as the fraternity of St Anne. The dean of St John's and twelve leading citizens were named as founders and the foundation document allowed for the election of

FIGURE 6.3. Seventeenth-century plan of St John's church and precinct.

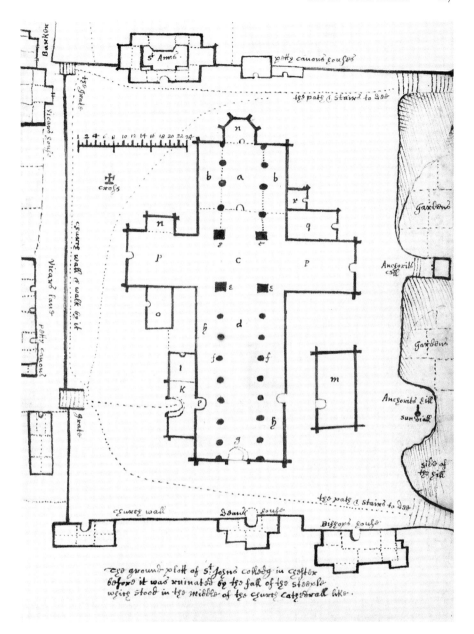

two wardens or masters and for the employment of two chantry priests to pray for the souls of the royal family and fraternity members. Initial endowments were worth almost £20 a year and annual income had doubled by the later fifteenth century.[62]

The fraternity of St Anne was open to men and women and it became an exclusive 'top people's club' with a membership dominated by leading townsmen and their wives. Only the wealthy could afford to join. The wife of William Venables, constable of the castle, paid an entry fee of 20s in 1404–5.

Prominent local gentlemen and clergymen became members and sometimes took a leading role: the masters in 1424 were John Bruyn of Tarvin and Henry Waterford, rector of Tilston.[63] The membership of St Mary's guild in 1330–1 was similar, and perhaps included women, although no evidence survives. Successive guilds with similar names and purposes were not necessarily connected but the original location of the chantry of St Anne and the dates chosen for important meetings hint at links with the Virgin Mary. Before the fraternity acquired its own premises in the precinct of St John's it seems to have been housed in a chapel of St Mary, either in the church or in the precinct. Founder member John Hatton requested burial in the chapel of St Mary in 1398; ten years later the palatinate master mason Robert Scot bequeathed a torch and candle to the chapel of St Mary and his property to the fraternity of St Anne.[64] In 1404 the annual accounts were presented a few days after the feast of the Assumption (15 August), and the masters and brethren met again to issue various ordinances just before the feast of the Virgin's Nativity (8 September).[65]

Although a chaplain of St George was named in 1436 the religious guild of St George was not recorded until 1462.[66] The guild was open to men and women and was housed in St Peter's church, probably in the south aisle, where two chaplains prayed for the souls of benefactors at the altar of St George. By 1472–3 the guild chaplain Ralph Manley was renting the chamber over the Pentice door, presumably the chamber 'over the door' of St Peter's occupied by the guild's chaplain in the 1530s and which was known as the rectory house of St Peter's by 1555.[67] In 1476 Ralph Manley and Ralph Davenport were named as rent collectors and guild property included three shops adjoining the church.[68] Generous bequests were made in the late fifteenth and early sixteenth century and at the Dissolution rental income amounted to about £12 a year.[69] St Peter's was the civic church and the guild had close links with the governing body. In the early sixteenth century the names of the guild stewards were recorded in the Mayor's Books immediately after the city officers.[70]

The *cursus honorum*

In the later thirteenth and early fourteenth century the élite citizens who participated in urban government progressed through a *cursus honorum* which began with service as doomsman in the portmote and continued with the shrievalty; the most successful men eventually became mayor. Hugh of Meols, for example, served five times as sheriff between 1270–1 and 1284–5 and as mayor in 1285–6. John Blund, granted the serjeanty of the Northgate in the early fourteenth century, was sheriff in 1311–12, mayor in 1316–17, and died during his second term of office in 1317–18.[71] Richard the engineer and William (III) of Doncaster were figures of national importance and both served as mayor without first serving as sheriff.

The *cursus honorum* grew more complex as new civic institutions emerged and new officers were appointed to serve the Assembly. By the 1390s the body of

	John Cottingham mercer	John Barrow ironmonger	William Sneyd draper	Ralph Davenport merchant
Offices				
Freedom	-	1453 (10½d)	1462	1475 (macebearer)
48	-	listed for WS 1459–63: not sworn	1466–70 (NS)	never listed
Sheriff	1435–6	1473–4	1473–4	1480–1
Mayor	1455–6 1456–7	1490–1	1479–80	1489–90 1493–4 1501–2
Other offices	Treasurer 1440–1	Treasurer 1480–1	Treasurer 1475–6	-
Guild office	-	Alderman of Ironmongers 1476–7	-	Alderman of St George's Guild 1493–4
24	listed 1454–75 (esquire in 1475)	listed 1474–93	listed 1474–1508 ward alderman 1507–8	listed 1484–1505 (not sworn in 1504–5)
Property				
Dwelling house	Bridge Street	Watergate Street (possibly corner of Trinity Lane)	Northgate Street	Bridge Street
Commercial property	Shop at north west corner of Bridge Street	Shop below Pentice	Rents shop outside his house 1469–73	
Other property	Foregate Street, next to Northgate (outside gate) and Crofts			Watergate Street and adjoining St Peter's in Northgate Street
Family	Elizabeth (wife) Christian (daughter and heiress, wife of Sir Hugh Calveley)	Ellen (wife) Thomas (son) mercer, mayor 1496–7, 1506–7 Robert (grandson) ironmonger, m 1526–7)	William (son), draper freeman 1497 and mayor 1516–17 (another WS mayor 1531–2)	Christian (wife, d'ter of John Southworth); 2 of 3 sons import wine in early 1500s; 2 daughters

TABLE 6.1. Examples of *the cursus honorum.*

aldermen known as the Twenty-Four was in place and a treasurer kept accounts of city rents. Two muragers were appointed each year from *c*.1407, two treasurers by 1416, and two leavelookers by the late 1430s. In the later fourteenth and earlier fifteenth century many mayors held office repeatedly. Alan of Wheatley was mayor from 1360 until 1364, John of Capenhurst from 1395 until 1400, and John Hope for seven terms between 1419 and 1428. From the 1430s the office usually changed hands each year. It may have seemed a less attractive proposition as duties and responsibilities multiplied, although the mayor's powers also increased. The emergence of the common councilmen and the constables in the early 1450s marked the completion of the city's governmental structures and all stages of the *cursus honorum* were in place.

A man's civic career began with his admission to the franchise, perhaps when he was in his early to mid-twenties. Young men from prosperous families occasionally became councilmen soon after they entered the freedom but most citizens waited several years before serving as a member of the Forty-Eight, which suggests that some qualification of wealth or property-holding applied. From the early 1450s membership of the Forty-Eight was a normal stage in the *cursus honorum*, although one that was routinely bypassed by the most influential men. Lists of councilmen always exceeded 48 and perhaps represented the 'pool' of qualified candidates. The 57 who took the oath in 1476–7 were a typically diverse group, including new recruits and experienced 'old hands'. Nineteen were in their first or second year and eleven had served intermittently since 1462.[72] They included men from most occupational groupings and two currently serving as guild stewards; four would hold guild office in the future. Among the councilmen were the current leavelookers and the leavelookers of 1474–5.

Fourteen of the 57 councilmen of 1476–7 (including all four leavelookers) went on to serve as sheriff: three mercers, two drapers and a merchant; a butcher, a cook and a fishmonger; a heuster, a saddler, a carpenter, a locksmith and an apothecary. The sheriffs had numerous judicial, administrative and financial duties. They assisted the mayor in the portmote, presided over their own Pentice court (which sat three times a week) and over the Passage court, at which a jury determined cases that had not previously been settled. The sheriffs officiated at the appointment of attorneys, the registration of debts, and the valuations of distrained goods and chattels. Their most onerous responsibility was the payment of Chester's fee farm, set at £100 in 1300, reduced to £50 in 1445, to £30 in 1484, and to £20 in perpetuity in 1486. Each sheriff was evidently responsible for half the farm and failure to pay in full had serious consequences. At least two sheriffs were imprisoned and had their possessions confiscated and sold.[73] No medieval sheriff is known to have evaded the office but many probably shared the reluctance of Daniel Peck, elected sheriff in 1704, who complained bitterly about being 'extreamly hindred by an unprofitable office' that he had been forced to enter.[74]

Until 1506 former sheriffs automatically became members of the Twenty-Four, an extremely powerful body composed almost exclusively of men who had held high office. The 35 aldermen listed in 1476–7 were named in chronological order of their tenure of office, the seven ex-mayors followed by 27 ex-sheriffs. Only the gentleman George Bulkeley, whose name was inserted between the sheriffs of 1468–9 and 1470–1, had not held high office. He became sheriff in 1477–8 and went on to serve twice as mayor. Nine of the aldermen of 1476–7 had experience of civic government going back to the 1450s and the only new members were Bulkeley and the sheriffs of the preceding year, who were not political novices. This group of aldermen was typical and included men whose ages perhaps ranged from the mid-thirties to the late sixties or seventies. The old had status in medieval society, being seen as repositories of custom and precedent, and Chester's mayor turned regularly to his 'breder and lerned counsell' for advice.[75]

Each year one of the Twenty-Four was chosen to serve as mayor. Money and time were needed to fulfil the duties and responsibilities of the office. The mayor acted in a judicial capacity between 35 and 40 times a year, presiding over the portmote, the crownmote and piepowder courts. He admitted freemen, served as escheator, controlled the markets, and oversaw the registration of debts. There are instances of the mayor admitting freemen on a Sunday, and carrying out official business on the Saturday in Easter week and on Christmas Day.[76] Duties took the mayor out of the city: to Northwich with several aldermen on Ascension Day in 1411 for a day of reconciliation with William Venables of Kinderton and his supporters; to Hawarden and Swanlow sourcing timber for the new Pentice in 1464.[77]

Chester's mayors had to give generously of their money as well as of their time. In 1497, for example, the contribution made by the mayor towards the rent of two fields was double the amount given by any of the aldermen.[78] The mayor received an annual fee, which increased from £10 to £11 6s 8d in the later fifteenth century. Perhaps, like the fee given to the mayor in 1539–40, it was 'towards his kitchen'.[79] They may have received other rewards and privileges, like their counterparts in other towns. Mayors and aldermen in London got their water supply free and were able to enrol their apprentices without charge. London's mayor was also allowed to admit six men to the citizenship until 1434, when the privilege was converted into a gift of wine.[80] It was noted in Chester's Assembly Book in 1539–40 that 'of old time' the mayor had made a freeman 'at his pleasure'.[81] The opportunity to operate 'at his pleasure' was doubtless a major attraction of the mayoralty in the medieval period. The office brought rich returns in the form of legal influence, lucrative contracts and powers of patronage. Chester's mayors almost certainly used their public position for personal gain and, with their wives, relished their enhanced status and *dignitas*. Scarlet gowns 'of the city's livery' were prized possessions and were passed on with pride to a man's heirs.[82]

Aldermanic status gave access to other influential positions. The treasurers were always members of the Twenty-Four and many progressed to the mayoralty. Some pairs of treasurers served for two or three years in succession and acquired considerable expertise. Alternatively, one treasurer remained in office for a second year and was joined by a new colleague, who himself stayed on the following year to guide a new appointee in his turn. A similar pattern was followed in the eighteenth century, with the man appointed junior treasurer one year becoming senior treasurer the next, and almost invariably elected mayor two or three years later.[83] The system reduced the opportunities to hold office but helped to ensure that civic finances were in capable hands. In the later fifteenth century it seems that the muragers were chosen from among the aldermen. All 13 known to have held the office had already served as sheriff and four had been mayor. By 1506 the muragers' status may have declined and aldermen perhaps considered the office beneath their dignity. The charter stipulated only that the muragers were to be citizens; muragers were selected from the councilmen in the early modern period.[84] The leavelookers, first recorded in 1438–9, were evidently chosen from the common councilmen but there is no indication that they acted as leaders of the Forty-Eight in the fifteenth century. Seven of the eight men known to have served as leavelooker in the 1470s and 1480s became sheriff within a few years but none became mayor.[85]

A privileged élite monopolized political power in later medieval Chester. Middling craftsmen and traders served as constables and sometimes as councilmen but were unable to make further progress. There were two routes to the shrievalty and mayoralty, one taken by the most successful citizens and the other taken by those whose social standing and wealth enabled them to bypass the onerous offices *en route* to the top.

Matthew Johnson may be taken as an example. He became a freeman in 1471 and pursued a successful career as a heuster in Handbridge for a quarter of a century. He served as constable and councilman for Bridge Street in 1476–7, as sheriff in 1479–80, was named among the aldermen until 1496–7 and was always 'sworn'; in 1493 he was one of his company's stewards. In his will in February 1497 he requested burial in St Mary's church and named his wife as his executrix. The couple had no children. The saddler Edmund Farrington followed a similar path. He entered the franchise in 1474, served as constable and councilman for Eastgate Street from 1475 until his election as sheriff in October 1491, and took the oath as a member of the 24 until at least 1507–8, when he also served as alderman of the Saddlers' company. He too left no heirs.[86] Through a combination of commercial acumen and good fortune Johnson and Farrington succeeded in gaining entry to the upper echelons of power but neither man was chosen to serve as mayor. That office was the preserve of the merchants, mercers and drapers, and of the influential men whose privileged family background, inherited wealth and high status marked them out as political high-flyers.

An example is William Massey of Coddington, a country gentleman whose estates adjoined lands in Edgerley held by Adam Wotton, mayor in 1434–5. He invested in commercial property in Chester and held two adjoining messuages in Fleshmonger Row by 1431–2, the year he became a freeman. He married Wotton's daughter, served as sheriff in 1440–1, as mayor in 1449–50, and was named among the aldermen until his death in 1462–3. He never abandoned his landed interests and was one of the mize collectors for Broxton hundred in 1442. He and his father-in-law sold wool to a city weaver in the late 1440s and Massey sold livestock to city butchers until the early 1450s.[87] Wotton became assimilated to the local gentry through his daughter's marriage to Massey and his two grandsons chose to live as country gentlemen, the elder at Edgerley and the younger at Coddington.[88]

Chester's urban patriciate was small but it was by no means closed and new members were regularly recruited to fill the gaps left by families which had moved away or died out. Failure to produce heirs brought urban dynasties to an abrupt end in all medieval towns, and Chester was no exception.[89] The families so prominent in the early fourteenth century, among them the Brickhills, the Wheatleys and the Blunds, had disappeared by the 1360s. Families which produced mayors and sheriffs in the fifteenth century, including the Hopes, the Cottinghams, the Whitmores and the Hurletons, did not feature among the office-holders of the early modern period. Infant mortality doubtless took its toll and other men had no sons, or sons who preferred life on the family's country estates.

An early example is Richard the engineer, mayor in 1305–6 and a significant figure in Chester until his death in 1315. Two sons were established at Belgrave and elsewhere during his lifetime but his son Amaury lived in the city, acting as his father's bailiff and supervising building work at the castle. In 1321, however, he sold the family home in Lower Bridge Street and moved away.[90] Among the heirs of John Blund in 1368 was Elizabeth, also heir of Robert Strangeways. She married John Ewloe and their son Richard, contracted in marriage to the daughter of John Donne of Utkinton in 1397, was never named in the civic records and either left the city or died. John Ewloe's son Edmund, named as his heir in 1418, died two years later; the younger son James was named only once, as grantor of a property in Bridge Street in 1426.[91] John Hope, mayor in seven years between 1419–20 and 1427–8, had one son, Oliver, who continued to live in Chester for at least 30 years after his father's death but played no part in civic life.[92]

This suggests that public service may not have been compulsory and that, as in fourteenth-century Colchester, it could be viewed as a choice rather than a duty.[93] Brothers of office-holders were perhaps able to concentrate on generating the wealth required for political success. The Warmingham family possibly chose this option. Roger Warmingham, sheriff in 1460–1, had three sons, the eldest of whom served as sheriff in 1476–7 and as alderman until his death in early 1485. The two younger sons became councilmen but did not progress further in the *cursus honorum*. Christopher, a member of the next generation, did pursue a civic career, entering the freedom in 1501, serving as constable later in the decade, and as sheriff in 1520–1.[94] Other prominent families, among them the Ledshams, the Sneyds and the Lightfoots, similarly included men who played a major role in urban government and men who did not.

A well-ordered city

A primary concern of Chester's governors was the maintenance of peace and order. They issued annual ordinances designed to control economic activity and social behaviour, and used the city courts to enforce their legislation and to punish offenders.[95] The principal city court in the later medieval period was the portmote, first recorded in the early thirteenth century. By the 1290s the portmote met every second or third Monday under the presidency of the mayor, with lengthy recesses at Christmas, Easter and Midsummer. Although pleas of real estate formed the bulk of its business the portmote dealt with all types of pleas except those of the Crown. The charter of 1300 granted Crown pleas to the citizens and initially these pleas may have been heard at sessions of the portmote. A separate crownmote court emerged in the later fourteenth century, holding its sessions at six-weekly intervals and its business including coroners' inquests into violent deaths. The crownmote dealt with infringements of civic ordinances and indictments for trading offences until the 1450s when the business was transferred to judicial inquiries in 'full' portmote, held four times a year and quarter sessions in all but name.

The sheriffs' Pentice court, named from the lean-to building attached to St Peter's in which it was held, was well established by 1288. By the 1390s it met three times a week, on Tuesdays, Thursdays and Fridays, including fair time, and dealt with all categories of personal pleas except those concerning real estate. These fell into the familiar categories of debt, trespass, detinue and broken contract, with pleas of debt always the most numerous. The piepowder court offered speedy justice to non-Cestrian merchants and the amount of business in the early fourteenth century may have warranted the keeping of separate records. Only a handful of sessions were recorded in the fifteenth century, two of them held at the door of St Peter's in the 1470s, and the court ceased to meet in the early sixteenth century.[96] City officials had no part to play in operating the court established in 1353–4 to deal with trespasses at the Dee mills and fishery, although townspeople served as jurors and presented offences committed by the millers, who in turn presented offences committed by the townspeople against them. Sessions were held intermittently until the mid fifteenth century. The archdeacon's court, held in St John's church, dealt with marriage, divorce and testamentary affairs.

FIGURE 6.4. St Peter's church and the Pentice in the 17th century. The medieval Pentice was less grand but the form of the building remained the same: a chamber used as a court house set above a row of shops and fronting the market place and Cross.

Civic ordinances

The first recorded ordinances date from 1392–3. They were intended to control the markets and the food trade, to promote public hygiene and to prevent disturbances, and were constantly re-issued throughout the later medieval period. Foremost among the rules was one which forbade the purchase of all types of grain and malt *en route* to the market for resale elsewhere; other regulations ordered householders to clean the pavements before their doors and prevent their pigs from roaming the streets.[97] The fines paid in 1392–3 by the city's butchers and cooks for a licence to trade were also listed in the early pages of the first Mayor's Book, as too were records of the assize of bread. Three sessions were held, in November and December 1392 and in August 1393, on either a Saturday or a Wednesday, the city's market days. At each session four jurors, two of them bakers, reported the market price of wheat to the mayor and sheriffs. The price (4s a quarter in November, 3s 6d in December and 3s 4d in August) was used to fix the weight of a loaf of bread. Bakers whose bread was underweight were fined and the dozen or so named each time always included the jurors.[98] There was no mention of the assize of ale but the authorities would have fixed the price of ale in line with the cost of barley. In 1306 a dozen men were fined for underweight bread and twelve men and one woman were fined for defective ale measures, among them William (III) of Doncaster.[99]

Many civic ordinances were routinely ignored and official attempts to control prostitutes, brothel-keepers, gamblers and night walkers were no more successful. The same offenders were fined year after year. Emmota Trim was named between 1454 and 1463, initially for roaming the streets after curfew without carrying a light and later for keeping a brothel, always in the Watergate Street quarter of the city. The 'careers' of her contemporaries Cecily Abraham and Emma Bulhalgh lasted for a dozen years, from 1455 until 1467, and Agnes Englefield kept a brothel in the Bridge Street area from 1465 until her death in 1484. Husbands of prostitutes regularly played dice, gambled and frequented taverns after hours.[100]

In some years the ruling élite had particular concerns. In the late thirteenth century, when Chester was at the height of its prosperity and evidently in the midst of a building boom, they attempted to control encroachments. Men were indicted in 1293–4 for building porches and adding stallboards; Robert the mercer was in trouble because he had erected stone steps near the Northgate.[101] In 1381 the authorities sought to control rates of pay, which had risen after the Black Death because of the shortage of labour. Among those presented for taking salaries in excess of the statute were all the leather-dressers, smiths, coopers, cartwrights, carpenters, and male and female linen weavers. In 1407 the smiths, cutlers, goldsmiths, coopers, cartwrights and slaters were named.[102] Vagrants were always viewed with suspicion but increasing concern can be detected from the late 1480s when an ordinance forbade the harbouring of foreigners; in 1509 came the first mention of an able-bodied beggar who was fit to work.[103] The governing body also showed increased concern for public morality, in 1503 ordering all wine taverns and ale cellars to be closed at nine o'clock. Householders who allowed card-playing for money on their premises were to be fined and the players imprisoned. In 1510 six women were imprisoned for adultery and for receiving other people's servants in their homes.[104]

The standard punishment for infringements of civic ordinances was a monetary fine. The authorities built a new pillory in *c.*1461 and spent money on its repair in the early 1480s but there is no record of it ever being used. Bakers were liable by law to the pillory for selling loaves of short weight or poor quality but Chester's bakers, like those in London, were fined for breaches of the assize of bread.[105] Those with money and influence were presumably able to avoid this humiliating form of punishment by paying a fine. The poorest members of the community, and perhaps women in particular, were most likely to be put in the pillory, women like the common scold and 'chider' Katherine Walsh who was sentenced to the 'cokstole' in 1506.[106]

Breaches of the peace and disorderly behaviour

Lucian considered that the one grave fault of his fellow Cestrians was their hot temper, and in later years they and the men of Cheshire gained a reputation for unruly behaviour. The Black Prince claimed in 1354 that the city contained more lawbreakers than the entire county and in 1449 the bishop of Coventry and Lichfield wrote despairingly of the many adulterers, fornicators and other evil-doers in both city and shire whom his officers dared not correct, some because of the men themselves, others because of the maintenance they had of powerful men.[107] Such contemporary evidence led earlier historians to portray the region as notoriously turbulent, even by the standards of late medieval England, but it is now accepted that although Cheshire had distinctive characteristics, including a population accustomed to war and a location on the border with Wales, lawlessness was no worse than elsewhere.[108] The city's governing body dealt with breaches of the peace, thefts and assaults identical to those perpetrated in other towns, although the presence of the castle and the port doubtless heightened the potential for disorder.

Arbitration

Arbitration was in widespread use in late medieval England and most city and borough courts promoted its use, both in disputes between private litigants and between craft organizations.[109] This alternative system of settlement often proved more effective than the antagonistic process of the law and Chester's ruling body incorporated it in the civic ordinances, assigning to four or five neighbours the initial role of attempting conciliation in the hope that social pressures would produce an acceptable solution. In the event of failure the mayor attempted to mediate and if he did not succeed, then the matter could be taken to court. The Smiths' company in 1501 ruled that the aldermen and stewards were to arbitrate when 'variance' arose between brethren and if they could not agree, then the parties had leave to complain further.[110] A rare record of neighbourly intervention dates from 1497 when the neighbours of a Boughton resident ordered the Cestrian who had committed various offences against him to make amends by giving him 1½ bushels of wheat.[111]

Chester's authorities routinely appointed arbitrators to settle disputes, three or four men 'indifferently elected' from the leading craftsmen, aldermen and city clergymen.[112] When Richard Warmingham and Jonet Acton disputed the rightful ownership of two tenements in St John's Lane in 1474, three arbitrators met them at the Dominican friary to hear their challenges and replies. Their judgement was conciliatory. Warmingham was to relinquish his claim but was to continue to receive the chief rent, and both parties were ordered to 'be fully accordet and frendes'. Details of the award were reported to the portmote and enrolled in the court records. A dispute between private litigants over the unlawful detention of a fletcher's tools in 1489 was settled by four arbitrators, two of them saddlers.[113]

Peace bonds

Peace bonds were widely used as a method of maintaining law and order. Mainprizes, legal instruments that bound individuals or groups to keep the peace, were issued by the mayor in the portmote court. They were evidently considered an effective method of controlling disruptive behaviour and were issued in considerable numbers in the later fifteenth century: over 300 in 1487–8 and again in 1490–1 for example.[114] Many were issued at the final session of the mayoral year, suggesting that the outgoing mayor was endeavouring to leave an orderly city for his successor.[115]

Men and women were named as subjects of mainprizes and were bound over to keep the peace towards one individual or towards several: a man and his wife or servants, a group of craftsmen, all the people of Chester, all royal officers, or all the king's lieges. Opposing parties could be bound over, each side agreeing to keep the peace towards the other. Subjects were normally bound over until a later session of the portmote, when they either found further sureties or were dismissed by proclamation, presumably because the authorities considered that the threat to public order had receded. The laconic court entries hint at tensions in the urban community: a breakdown in the marriage of a potter and his wife; a trading dispute souring relationships between two carters; a local minstrel's prejudice against merchants from Spain.[116] In 1477 the shoemakers and their journeymen were evidently at loggerheads with the barkers; the bakers were squabbling among themselves in the late 1480s and 1490s.[117] In early July 1477 'variaunce and discorde' developed between the aldermen Alexander Stanney and Henry Port over possession of a parcel of land and both were bound over to keep the peace until October. The mayor consulted his brethren and learned counsel and at the end of July ordered both parties to gather written evidence. Stanney's death in September brought the dispute to an end.[118]

Violence and unrest

Violence was endemic in urban society and Chester's rulers were unable to maintain peace and order all of the time, in spite of their best endeavours. Throughout the later medieval period hundreds of presentations were made in the city court concerning breaches of the peace and hue and cry. Assaults reported to the sheriffs in the 1290s and early fourteenth century involved assailants wielding sticks, stones, knives and bows and arrows, but injuries were rarely life-threatening and damage was often restricted to torn clothing. Townsmen sought compensation because they had been called 'robber', 'thief', 'son of a hangman' or 'serf' (*rusticum*).[119] Name-calling disappeared from the records in later years but little else changed. The city perhaps witnessed increased disorder in the 1390s and early 1400s but the familiar offences continued to be brought before the courts. Townsmen and visitors routinely carried knives and some were armed with pole-axes, swords or bows and arrows. In November 1450 a local goldsmith wounded his victim with an arrow fired from a gun. Women used sticks, stones and pewter pots as weapons, often inflicting serious wounds. Tavern brawls, street scuffles and hotheaded exchanges were part of daily life; blood flowed, heads were broken, but victims recovered. Higher fines were imposed as penalties if blood was drawn, or if the assault was carried out on the day of a major festival or during the hours of darkness.[120]

As an important trading centre and port Chester attracted large numbers of strangers, whose presence inevitably provoked friction. The city was perhaps especially unruly during fair time, when the population was swelled by itinerant traders, the taverns and ale cellars well patronized, and tempting merchandise on display. Items worth stealing were always available, however, and theft was common. Many of those caught and imprisoned until brought to trial at the crownmote were outsiders; most were poor. In September 1460 the labourer Margery Scot, accused of stealing six yards of woollen cloth, and a stringer from Caernarfon accused of stealing money and a silver ring, were both sentenced to be hanged. Neither of the accused had any goods or chattels. Other men and women who went to the gallows were also poor and we may suspect that their lack of money and influential contacts helped to determine their fate.[121] Townsmen who enjoyed higher standing in the community usually escaped prison and the gallows. Some got away with murder. On Trinity Sunday 1487 the fletcher Robert Warburton made an (allegedly) unprovoked attack on the draper Henry Wiksted in Fleshmonger Lane, striking him such a violent blow on the head with a 'hanger' (short sword) that he died a few days later. The case was heard at the crownmote in April 1489 and the jurors, Warburton's fellow townsmen and neighbours, found him not guilty.[122]

The tailor John Man tried the patience of the civic authorities for 16 years, from 1474 when he was presented for assaulting an Irishman until 1490 when he was hanged for theft.[123] In the intervening years he caused continual nuisance with his pigs, breaking down hedges to give the animals access to his neighbours' crofts and allowing them to roam the streets and to forage on the Roodee and Henwald's Lowe for months at a time. In 1485 Man broke into a carter's house and stole money and a girdle with silver-gilt decorations, a theft for which he was temporarily imprisoned in the Northgate gaol. Unrepentant, he resumed his anti-social behaviour on release. As the carter's house lay outside the city liberties the theft was dealt with in the county court. The authorities there proved less tolerant than those in the city and John Man went to the gallows in December 1490.[124]

Bad relations within and between crafts could provoke major disturbances. On 29 May 1399, the feast of Corpus Christi, more than 80 clothworkers were involved in a great affray in front of St Peter's church, a confrontation that saw master craftsmen armed with pole-axes, daggers and iron-pointed staves attack their own journeymen.[125] In the early fifteenth century feuding among the civic élite regularly led to violence on the streets. One night in June 1416 John Ewloe and his son Edmund, accompanied by their Welsh servants and several city craftsmen, attempted to kill John Bruyn in Eastgate Street, an assault perhaps linked to the murder of two of Ewloe's servants at Ewloe earlier in the day. The perpetrators of that crime celebrated by parading through Hawarden to Chester chanting and boasting of their misdeeds, and by marching round the city brandishing weapons for three days in diverse 'routs'. In September 1419 Edmund Ewloe and several accomplices, incited by the wife of former mayor John Overton, broke into the home of John Hope with the intention of killing him and his brother Robert, an attack which caused John's wife to miscarry. A few days later John was elected mayor and Robert murager and in the ensuing weeks the two allegedly went round the city wearing armour and carrying weapons, surrounded by an armed group of Welsh and English supporters.[126]

Sessions of the county court could lead to outbreaks of violence. Should feuding gentlemen meet face to face then the threat to social harmony was grave and efforts were made to keep them apart. In September 1426, when Sir John Stanley arbitrated to settle the 'vareance, hevynes and debate' between Sir Edward Weaver of Weaver and Richard Bulkeley of Cheadle, he ordered them to come to Chester on separate days to make their recognizances. Each man was to come 'in esy wysse' and accompanied by no more than twelve supporters.[127] Three years earlier the rival affinities of Sir John Savage and John Kingsley of Nantwich had terrorized the townspeople. Sir John Savage had summoned his adherents to join him in Chester at dawn on 31 May and Kingsley and 300 of his men arrived the following day. Contrary to the statute, all the men were armed and they created such a disturbance that the county court session was adjourned until July. On that day Savage and Kingsley and their armed supporters returned and caused such a great breach of the peace that the court had to be suspended yet again.[128]

Townsmen who accepted the livery of local gentlemen were drawn into their disputes. Former mayor John Whitmore distributed red gowns at Thurstaston in 1423 to a number of men, including two city bailiffs. The following year four leading craftsmen joined Whitmore in an armed attack on a man from Picton, and in December 1425 George Whitmore assembled 20 townsmen at Tarvin Park to ambush John Savage junior. Six men from Chester were among a group who accepted the livery of John Hawarden, son of former mayor William Hawarden, at Eaton in 1427. All six joined him in an attack on William Venables in 1432.[129]

Challenges to urban government

The abbot of St Werburgh's and the prioress of St Mary's had the right to hold manorial courts for their tenants, and these jurisdictional privileges were resented by the civic authorities, as too was the tenants' exemption from tolls and other local levies. The prioress's court aroused less hostility. Her tenants were few in number and mostly poor, but their privileges nevertheless caused some jealousy and were challenged by the civic authorities from time to time. The prioress's agreement in 1391–2 that her tenants would appear in the city courts and pay dues like other citizens proved short-lived. Entries in the fifteenth-century Pentice court rolls occasionally noted that a defendant could not be fined because he was a tenant of St Mary's; nor could the sheriffs arrest people on the nuns' land. In 1492–3 their attempt to make such an arrest resulted in their indictment in the county court on a charge of breaking and entering.[130]

The jurisdiction of the Benedictine abbey posed a more serious threat to social harmony. St Werburgh's manor of St Thomas was the most important manor within the liberties, with many tenants in Parsons Lane, Northgate Street, and beyond the gate in the northern suburb. At the end of the eleventh century the abbot had also been granted jurisdiction over the three-day fair of St Werburg 'in the summer' (21 June). All pleas which arose during fair time (20–22 June) were dealt with in his court, and the abbot retained the right to hold all pleas arising during those three days in the mid fourteenth century when the fair lasted for four weeks and centred on Midsummer Day (24 June).[131]

In 1354 the mayor and sheriffs allegedly took advantage of the abbot's absence in Rome to seize some of his demesne lands, and other men initiated pleas against him in the mayors' courts. In 1359 they challenged his view of frankpledge in Northgate Street and in 1360 the abbot complained that he, his fellow monks and servants were often indicted by malicious persons living in the city.[132] The city's rulers were perhaps deliberately provoking conflict in order to obtain a new *modus vivendi*, just as the citizens of Hereford provoked conflict with the bishop in order to consolidate and define the powers of their franchise *vis-à-vis* the immune franchise of the cathedral.[133] In 1379–80 Chester's mayor and commonalty were bound over in a sum of £3,000 not to do any harm or violence to the abbot and his monastery. On 22 June 1406 the mayor, sheriffs and other leading citizens, each carrying a bundle of wood, gathered at the gates of the abbey with the intention of burning the buildings down to the ground.[134] The attack took place on 22 June, as the abbot's fair-time jurisdiction was ending, and almost certainly represented a challenge to his franchise.

The city's challenges grew ever bolder. In the 1420s the sheriffs demanded payments from abbey tenants, only small sums but demanded on several occasions and representing an attempt by the civic authorities to establish their right to such payments. In the late 1470s the sheriffs broke into the homes of abbey tenants in Northgate Street and freed a man imprisoned in the home of the abbot's bailiff. On 24 June 1482 they seized metal bowls and other items from five men living beyond the Northgate.[135] On 22 June 1485 they arrested

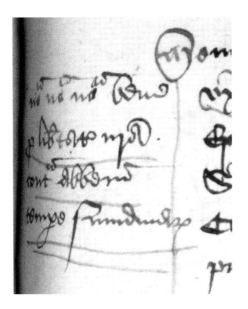

FIGURE 6.5. The sheriffs successfully challenged the abbot's fair-time jurisdiction in June 1485 and this marginal entry in the Mayor's Book records the city's delight: *Nota nota nota bene! Pro libertate nostra contra abbatem tempore nundinarum* (on behalf of our liberty against the abbot at fair time).

two women involved in a scuffle in Northgate Street and handed them over into the custody of the city gaoler. A marginal entry in the Mayor's Book encapsulated the city's triumphal reaction to this curtailment of the abbot's fair-time jurisdiction. In 1506 all jurisdiction within the liberties was assigned to the mayor and sheriffs but the abbot apparently violated this grant the following year and it was only in 1509 that arbitrators declared that the abbot should no longer keep a court during the fair.[136]

Official attempts to control the city were sometimes frustrated by the townspeople's lack of due deference towards those in authority. A sheriff who tried to break up a street brawl in 1398 met with a torrent of abuse; in 1420 the sheriffs attempting to execute a writ had the house door slammed in their faces; in 1432 a sheriff was attacked in the city exchequer by a man wielding a dagger.[137] Time and again the city bailiffs met with a violent response when they attempted to carry out court orders: people broke arrest, took back goods seized in distraint, and forced open tavern doors sealed on the mayor's instructions. Women were not as respectful towards their 'betters' as might have been expected. One November night in 1454, for example, Katherine Horne of Watergate Street cursed and attacked the gentleman John Trafford, sheriff the preceding year.[138]

Citizens performed civic duties with reluctance and this caused further problems. Four men were fined in 1306 for failing to attend the crownmote when summoned and William (III) of Doncaster was among several doomsmen fined for non-attendance at the portmote. Two men appointed to assess the fines imposed on bakers whose bread was underweight also failed to appear.[139] In the fifteenth century, although citizens were liable to jury service until they reached the age of 70, the bailiffs often struggled to assemble twelve *probos et legales homines* to serve.[140] The jury's impartiality was sometimes questioned. One defendant in 1456–7 was so concerned that he would not receive a fair hearing in the sheriffs' court that he wrote to the mayor asking for his case to be transferred to the portmote, claiming that the plaintiff enjoyed 'divers affinities and aliaunce' with the sheriffs, and that eminent individuals were seeking to influence the verdict on his (the plaintiff's) behalf.[141]

Those in positions of authority regularly abused their office and corruption was common. In 1293–4 the serjeant of the Northgate demanded excessive tolls from men and women bringing fish to the city for sale, and the serjeant of the Watergate seized fish arriving by sea. The mayor was charged with sentencing several men to be drawn on hurdles although he had no right to inflict this punishment.[142] In the early 1380s the city gaoler extorted money from prisoners in the Northgate and at the start of the fifteenth century the sheriffs conspired with the city's butchers to set the fines payable for regrating and forestalling.[143]

Palatinate and ecclesiastical officials also proved corrupt. In the early fifteenth century the chief clerk of the justice, responsible for the court records, allegedly erased names and accepted money for entering fines. In 1437 the former dean of Chester was accused of extorting 4d from a city saddler for proving his wife's will and 3s from a weaver for proving the will of a female relative.[144]

Dissatisfaction with the judicial system may explain the institutionalized outbreak of violence in Chester on 22 June 1424, the feast of Corpus Christi. The mayor, sheriffs and some 200 armed men assembled near the townhouse of the archdeacon of Chester in St John's precinct and swore to support one another in all plaints (*querelas*), declaring that the plaint of one was the plaint of all. Their numbers grew as they made their way to the stone house near St Bridget's and the group, now 300 strong, then advanced to the 'Stoune Place' at the end of Castle Lane, close to the home of the deputy chamberlain John Dedwood. In the ensuing assault Dedwood and the justice's clerk were badly wounded, money and a ring were stolen, as too was the key to the chest in which the exchequer seal was kept.[145] Grievances connected with jurisdiction perhaps lay at the root of the trouble. The disturbance began in the vicinity of St John's church, where the archdeacon of Chester held his court, and it ended with an attack on palatinate officials in the vicinity of the castle. It broke out on the date that marked the end of the abbot's fair-time jurisdiction, which in 1424 coincided with the feast of Corpus Christi, recently reorganized and towards which guild members contributed with considerable resentment.

FIGURE 6.6. The stone façade of 48 Bridge Street (the Three Old Arches) dates from the late 12th to the mid, or even late, 13th century and fronted a townhouse orientated at right angles to the street. The building was combined with properties to the south in the early 14th century and a major town house was built with a hall parallel to the street. It belonged to Roger Derby in 1424 and was known as the 'Stone Place'.

CHAPTER SEVEN

Making a Living

Most of Chester's permanent residents were involved in crafts and commerce and the range of occupations was wide. About 170 different occupations were recorded in the years 1275–1520, similar to Winchester (163) and London (over 180).[1] Some were mentioned only once or twice – spoonmakers, paniermakers and treaclers for example – and others changed over time. Lorimers, who made metal horse-trappings, and parmenters, who dealt in furs or fur-trimmed garments, were not named after the fourteenth century. A clockmaker was at work in the city in *c.*1410 and a century later bookbinders and organ-players had appeared. The total number of occupations practised in Chester at any one time was about 70, comparable with Leicester and Northampton.[2]

In the thirteenth-century list which characterised English towns according to a typical feature or trade, Chester was noted for fur. In 1066 the city rendered 120 marten pelts as part of its farm and the fur trade played a significant role in the city's commerce in the early Middle Ages.[3] In the later medieval period no single trade or craft predominated. Many inhabitants earned their living providing food, drink and clothing for the townspeople; others worked in the leather, building and metalworking trades. Chester's role as a garrison town and its involvement in military campaigns provided work for an above-average number of bowyers, fletchers and furbishers. As a high-ranking centre the city was able to support merchants who traded in luxury products. It was common for individuals to combine their main occupation with one or more sidelines. Butchers sold wool and cloth, tailors baked bread, glovers wove cloth, and the treacler skinned cats and sold the fur.[4] In the 1420s and 1430s the cooper John Carrock gained extra income by keeping the clock at St Peter's church and taking in a lodger. Twenty years later two coopers were named 'Blodletter' and evidently carried out basic medical treatment.[5]

The workshop based on the household was the main unit of production and the workforce was small, often consisting of the craftsman, his wife and any children who were old enough to work. Master craftsmen were assisted by one or two apprentices and employed a maximum of three journeymen. Large gangs of building craftsmen and labourers worked on major projects and a sizeable staff was employed at the Dee mills. In the mid fourteenth century the master supervised three journeymen, three servants and six apprentices, two in the corn mills and four in the malt mills.[6]

Food and drink

In *c.*1125 William of Malmesbury described Chester's hinterland as barren and unproductive of cereals, especially corn, but noted that the inhabitants much enjoyed bread made from barley and wheat.[7] Local supplies of grain were always inadequate and in the fifteenth century the city's bakers obtained much corn from neighbouring parts of Wales, occasionally travelling to Bromfield to buy wheat.[8] They purchased supplies at the Dee mills and were recorded in the accounts for 1485–6 buying a quarter of wheat at a time, enough to bake 250 loaves weighing about 2 lbs each.[9] The bakers also brought grain to be ground at the mills and regularly accused the millers of extortion, of stealing their flour, and allowing it to fall into the river. The millers complained that the bakers refused to pay toll and came to the mills armed in order to evade payment. The two groups frequently came to blows.[10] The bakers sometimes took their grain to the abbot's mill at Bache or to his windmill, or to the mills at Trafford and Eccleston.[11]

About 16 bakers worked in the city in 1297–8 and a century later the number had fallen to a dozen or so. The Bakers' company contained 17 members in 1493–4 and 20 in 1507–8.[12] They were recorded in many parts of the city but the focus of the trade was Bakers' Row, close to St Giles's bakehouse and other important bakehouses. The baker Richard Hockenhull, sheriff in 1491–2, occupied a house and land in Bakers' Row abutting the west side of Godstall Lane. The contents of his bakehouse in 1528 included 'boards, troghes, sacks, arckes, pannes … and other stuffe belonging to the occupation of bakers'.[13] The large stacks of gorse used as fuel posed a fire hazard and by the end of the fifteenth century were forbidden within the walls. By 1535 part of the common at the end of Cow Lane was designated as a storage place, later known as the Gorse Stacks.[14]

Loaves of bread were sold at standard prices of ¼d, ½d or 1d. The assize of bread held before the mayor calculated the weight of the loaf according to the current price of wheat. Bakers stamped their loaves to enable the identification of substandard products and deposited a wax copy of their stamps with the authorities; those whose products were underweight or badly baked were fined. Bread was made from wheat, barley and rye flour, and white bread became increasingly popular over the course of the fifteenth century. The finest quality white bread was *wastel* and other products included 'cokett ferlyng', 'parombred ferlyng', tarts and Chester cakes.[15] The bakers also produced horsebread, made

FIGURE 7.1. An extract from the assize of bread held on Saturday 23 August 1393. The bakers Richard Brou' and Thomas Soule served as jurors and both were named among those whose bread was underweight. Thomas Soule was tenant of St Giles's bakehouse.

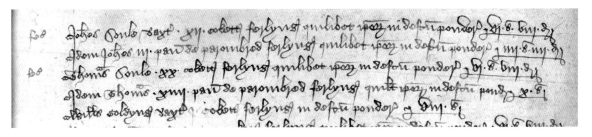

from bran, peas and beans.[16] In 1518 the abbot agreed to supply four white loaves and three rye loaves called *paynquartons* each week to the wife of the music teacher.[17] The bakers' customers included the city's *femmes soles*, recorded in the 1480s and 1490s buying several dozen loaves at a time, presumably to sell from baskets in the streets.[18]

William of Malmesbury noted that Chester's region was rich in beasts and fish and that the wealthier inhabitants lived on meat. More people ate meat after the Black Death, when labour shortages resulted in a new emphasis on pastoral agriculture and an improvement in real wages.[19] The number of butchers accused of marketing offences rose from twelve at the start of the fourteenth century to sixteen at the close.[20] The number remained fairly constant throughout the fifteenth century, although falling to nine in *c.*1409–10 and in 1449; nineteen were listed in 1513.[21] A few widows were named among the members of the Butchers' company in the years 1487–1511 and had perhaps taken over the business until their sons came of age.[22] There is no evidence for wives' participation in this physically demanding trade and the only females involved were those who carried away entrails for disposal beyond the city walls.[23]

Chester's butchers purchased beasts from country gentlemen and from fellow townsmen like the barker Thomas Stretton, who in the mid fifteenth century evidently fattened animals on his lands near the Bars.[24] Most livestock was obtained from drovers who had purchased the animals in the countryside and driven them to the cattle market, perhaps held in Bridge Street and Lower Bridge Street in the medieval period. Many animals came from Wales and the fathers or grandfathers of butchers surnamed Mancot, Hawarden and Hope had presumably made the same journey. One drover became a freeman in 1415 and 50 years later the drover Edward Walsheman paid to sell retail in Watergate Street.[25]

The main focus of the butchers' retail trade was Fleshmongers' Row on the north side of Watergate Street. Many butchers held property along this stretch of commercial frontage, both at Row level and in the cellars below.[26] They grazed and slaughtered animals on the land they rented in the Crofts and they also killed animals in their shops, discarding the unwanted entrails in the street. Official tipping places where offal could be carried away by running water were not recorded in medieval Chester and much of the butchers' refuse removed from the street was dumped near the gates.[27] Butchers also kept livestock in crofts adjoining Cow Lane.[28]

The butchers sold beef, veal, mutton, lamb and pork. Although craftsmen could afford to buy meat on a regular basis the best customers were the city's cooks.[29] There is no evidence for official inspection of carcases but very few references to substandard meat have been found. Butchers occasionally sold measly pork or beef from cattle that had died of murrain. Two villagers from Clutton returned home with rotten beef on Christmas Eve in 1426.[30] Butchers grew wealthy by selling the by-products of their trade, including tallow used to make candles. Nine were accused in 1448 of charging 10s for a 'wegh' of tallow, instead of the 7s or 8s considered reasonable.[31] Sales of animal hides and skins were a major source of income. Butchers sold untreated hides to local barkers and tanned hides to shoemakers and saddlers.[32] They sold skins to pointers and parchment-makers, and sheepskins to the glovers. In 1459 Thomas Waltham, then occupying the house adjoining St Peter's, agreed to supply one glover with the skins of all the sheep he slaughtered over the following twelve months.[33]

The Church decreed that fish replace meat on almost 150 days of the year, including Fridays, Saturdays, the vigils of major feasts, and the six weeks of Lent.[34] Fish was therefore a vital component of medieval diet and Chester was well-placed to meet the demand. Flooker's brook ('the fluke-catcher's brook') formed the northern boundary of the liberties and Crabwall ('cray-fish stream') lay just beyond the boundary. An important salmon fishery on the Dee at Eaton in Eccleston was recorded in Domesday Book and Lucian described his city's river as abounding with fish.[35] Chester also enjoyed easy access to the fishing grounds of the Irish Sea.

By 1358 the banks of the Dee were lined with fish-stalls and their nets and 'devices' obstructed the passage of boats to the bridge. Fish-stalls were valuable assets, owned in the fifteenth century by Hugh de Holes, John Ewloe, William Troutbeck and other prominent individuals.[36] The royal fishery at Dee Bridge, known from 1445–6 as the King's Pool, was a significant commercial enterprise. Fully grown salmon, young salmon and breeding salmon (kippers) were the prime catch, and the number of *mortes* (dead salmon?) was sometimes considerable: 395 in 1389–90 for example.[37] Sales of eels and sprats were recorded in the 1370s and 1380s, and a few lampreys from the late 1370s until the mid 1430s. Prices naturally varied according to the size and type of fish, and to the season.[38]

In the 1320s tolls were taken at the city gates on a dozen or more varieties of fish and shell-fish.[39] Herring was of prime importance. It was a relatively cheap fish that the poorer townspeople could afford and large quantities were imported from Ireland and the Isle of Man. As it deteriorated quickly it was preserved either by salting (white herring) or smoking (red herring). The former was attested most often in Chester. Salmon too was salted and in the early fifteenth century many Irish traders who arrived with herring and salmon returned home with hogsheads and crannocks of salt.[40] There was particular demand for fish during Lent and in 1476–7 tolls were taken at the Watergate only during that period.[41] Other fish sold in the city included mackerel, haddock, milwell, ling and stockfish.

The city's fish market may have been located at the north-eastern corner of Bridge Street in the mid fourteenth century but before 1588 it was moved to the south side of Watergate Street, opposite the butchers' shops.[42] The fishmongers' wives participated in the trade, routinely throwing entrails under their stalls.[43] They habitually intercepted supplies of fresh and salted fish *en route* to the city and bought it cheaply to resell at higher prices. In the 1490s Joanna Fraunces continued to regrate and forestall the market after her husband's death and her name also appeared in the customs records, indicating that she had taken over the business and was importing fish.[44]

Six or seven fishmongers were active in the city at any one time, some handling a range of merchandise and becoming very wealthy. In a career spanning the years 1406–47 Richard Smith, himself the son of a fisher (the usual term for these merchants), owned a ship, imported herring, and dealt regularly with men from Carrickfergus and Drogheda. He purchased salt (and was perhaps involved in the preservation of herring) and traded in wine, cloth, iron and pitch. One of his daughters married a man from Beaumaris, a link which may explain his trade in whetstones, a characteristic product of Anglesey. His cellar and shop in Eastgate Street were leased after his death to a local cook. It was common for the trades of cook and fishmonger to be combined.[45]

A fishmonger's cellar in 1473 contained half a butt of salmon, ten mease of 'stik eles', four mease of 'midlyng eles', and three dozen 'cane eles', worth in total more than £6. Eels were nutritious yet relatively inexpensive and cooks put them in pies. Cooks also used stockfish (dried cod), paying 10s for five dozen in 1488.[46] Herring dominated the market and wealthy merchants like William (III) of Doncaster participated in the trade, aware that good profits could be made.[47] Herring was often purchased by the barrel and was evidently kept in store. In early Lent 1480 one man's stock of herring (worth more than £7) proved to have been insufficiently salted and quickly went rotten.[48]

Fish was bought and sold by non-residents. Those who came to Chester with fish for sale were accused in 1475–6 of failing to take it to the market and of selling it instead in private houses. Much illegal trading took place in the northern suburb. Horses and carts carrying fish from Wirral approached the city from the north and cargoes of herring were unloaded on the river bank between Bonewaldesthorne Tower and Portpool. Fish was sold illegally in houses and inns, with local hostelers playing a significant role, as they did in Exeter and Winchester. In the mid fifteenth century the hosteler Thomas Wainfleet held illegal fish markets in his house several days each week and had regular dealings with foreign traders.[49] Men who came to buy fish could pay a fine for a licence to trade within the liberties and were then exempted from tolls at the gates.[50]

The focus of the cooks' trade was at the corner of Eastgate Street and Northgate Street, facing St Peter's. Until the early fifteenth century food was evidently cooked on hearths set up on the pavement. In *c.*1308–9 a number of cooks were in trouble with the authorities because their hearths (and each cook had two) had burned the street surface, and cooks paid rent to the city for hearths set up on the common soil until about 1410.[51] A decade later they were paying rent to the city for shops on the common soil and a cluster of cooks' shops had been built by the late 1460s, their tenants including John Dedwood and William Troutbeck esquire.[52] A cook's equipment in *c.*1430 consisted of little more than a 'molding' board worth 20d, a skimmer and a rolling pin. The two stools outside his door were worth 10d and, like those placed in the street by Westminster's cooks for their customers, would have been considered a nuisance by the authorities.[53]

The cooks purchased meat from the butchers and salmon, ling, stockfish and herring from the fishmongers. One cook rented a dovehouse.[54] They regularly purchased capons, chickens, geese, pigeons, goats and oysters *en route* to the city's market. In *c*.1308–9 five were presented for selling pies that were not properly cooked and food that was not well seasoned.[55] Food waste from their activities was discovered during excavations at 3–15 Eastgate Street in 1990–1: meat-bearing bones of cattle, sheep/goat and pig, and perhaps a few oyster shells. Two shells found in a mid seventeenth-century context were burnt and had perhaps been roasted in an open fire. Oysters were cooked in this way in the medieval period.[56]

In the fourteenth and early fifteenth century Chester's cooks, saucemakers and piemakers included non-citizens who paid for a licence to carry out their trade and who rarely stayed in the city for long.[57] The cooks became more prosperous when the open-air hearths were replaced by permanent premises. John Chivaler cook (often named John Cook chivaler) worked in the city from 1447 until the early 1480s. He rented a cook shop, purchased currants from the mercer John Cottingham, and served as councilman and company steward.[58] The cook William Heywood was first recorded in 1459 when he was taken to court by the company stewards for cooking geese and fish without licence, and he lived in Eastgate Street until his death in 1486 or 1487. He became wealthy and served as sheriff in 1480–1 but in the last years of his life he was often in debt, owing money for salted herring, ling and beef.[59]

The brewers of Chester were mentioned in Domesday Book and brewing remained an important activity throughout the later medieval period. The city was also a centre for the production and sale of malt. Ale, with its cereal base, formed a staple of medieval diet and was a vital source of nutrition for young and old, rich and poor. Each 'feeble and infirm' inmate of St John's hospital received a daily allowance of half a gallon and in 1518 the wife of the abbey's music teacher was given seven gallons a week – four gallons of convent ale and three gallons of second ale called servants' ale.[60] Most ale in Chester was brewed from barley malt, although there was occasional mention of the inferior oat-based brew. A civic ordinance prohibited the production of wheat malt, a practice considered harmful to the city.[61] Beer brewed from hops was introduced into southern England by Flemings and Dutchmen in the early fifteenth century and was first recorded in Chester in 1477, when a 'beerman' paid for permission to trade in the city.

Brewing was a domestic activity. In modest households wives did the brewing, often on an occasional basis, and in wealthy homes it took place on a large scale, the mistress supervising three or more female servants.[62] The wealthiest citizens invested in the trade, producing the malt that was needed, some of it from grain grown on their lands and dried in the malt-kilns in their gardens. The equipment needed in a large establishment was expensive. Robert Hope in 1423 claimed ownership of two furnaces, three ale leads, a brew lead and a vat, with a total value of £20. The bailiff employed to take charge of a smaller enterprise in 1451 had at his disposal a brew lead, a 'mash comb' (brewing tub), a trough and six shallow tubs worth just under £5.

Ale was sold not only by the brewers but also by townspeople who did not brew, many of them women. The tapsters who kept alehouses were heavily outnumbered by those who sold ale as a sideline, including non-citizens who paid for a licence to sell ale.[63] The authorities regulated the trade, ordering ale to be sold in measures that had been sealed by the mayor and at prices set by the assize of ale. It is difficult to establish how many people sold ale in the city in the fifteenth century. Some 60 individuals brought their measures to be sealed in 1407 and an incomplete list dating from 1487 named 158 individuals. Ten years later 94 townspeople were presented for using false measures.[64] The price of best ale may have been 1½d a gallon; prices of 2d or 2½d a gallon were considered excessive.[65]

FIGURE 7.2. A late medieval/post-medieval cistern, probably used for brewing; it is unusual for having two bungholes. It was made in Flintshire and found during excavations of part of the medieval city ditch to the north of Foregate Street.

Wine was among the expensive commodities handled by Chester's wealthiest merchants, men who also traded in iron, spices and fine woollens. The term vintner was first recorded in the city in the 1390s and one of five vintners named in that decade was Innocent of Chesterfield, previously described as a taverner. He spent time in Gascony in 1388 and regularly shipped wine from Bordeaux and La Rochelle to Chester in the 1390s. He may have been a specialist wine merchant and was appointed to select wine within the city for the household of the prince of Wales in April 1404.[66] The taverners named in the fifteenth-century records were not wealthy and were perhaps employed as tavern-keepers. Until the 1490s only two or three merchants imported wine at any one time but numbers then increased to half a dozen or so. The amounts of wine shipped

to Chester were small, ranging from some 2,000 tuns (504,000 gallons) in the second decade of the fifteenth century to less than 600 tuns in the 1470s, and although 2,500 tuns were shipped in the period 1510–20 this was a small total compared to the trade of Bristol and Southampton.[67]

Most of the wine sold in Chester was red Gascon wine; the white wines described as *Rochel* wine, *rupelle* wine and Rhenish wine were less expensive. The assize of wine in 1393 set the prices at 6d a gallon for red Gascon wine and 4d a gallon for white *rupelle* wine, and the prices remained the same in 1415. Like ale, wine was to be sold in sealed measures.[68] In *c.*1413 a Coventry merchant arrived with three barrels of malmsey, one of the sweet Mediterranean

FIGURE 7.3. The under-
croft at 11 Watergate
Street has the best stone
vault in Chester. It has
traditionally been dated
to *c.*1250–*c.*1290 but the
capitals of the central
arcade may date from
the 15th century. The rear
wall contains a cupboard
and an original doorway
leading into an extension
of the undercroft with
stone rubble walls. The
stone-vaulted undercrofts
perhaps functioned as
wine taverns.

wines which became increasingly popular in England in the fifteenth century. This wine, and the butts of malmsey found in a local porter's house in 1419, were perhaps destined for Ireland but rumney and malmsey wines were sold in Chester and sweet wines from Spain and Portugal were imported from the mid 1480s.[69]

Wine was purchased by the abbot of St Werburgh's, the prior of Birkenhead and local knights. In the mid 1440s the vintner William Stanmere regularly dispatched casks of wine to the Stafford household at Macclesfield.[70] Townsmen bought a gallon or two at a time. A carpenter owed a taverner 4½d for wine in 1399 and the members of the Fraternity of St Anne spent 4d on wine when they met in the master's house in September 1404.[71] John Coly, a leading wine importer in the late fourteenth and early fifteenth century, had a tavern in Bridge Street later occupied by his nephew Robert, who also imported wine. In 1474–5 the city's leavelookers spent 2s 8d on wine in Roger Hurleton's cellar at Christmas and almost as much at Easter.[72]

Textiles and Clothing

Cloth was produced in the city but the quality was poor and although small amounts of 'Chester cloth' were exported to Ireland in the mid fifteenth century most was destined for the home market.[73] Local demand was considerable and as the city served as a centre to which cloth was brought to be finished, the city's textile workers always comprised a significant percentage of the work force.

Chester's region was not noted for wool production. Sacks of wool were sold at the city's fairs in the 1350s and one or two woolmen from Coventry and Derbyshire were recorded in the city in the early fifteenth century. A local woolman also organized supplies in those years.[74] Some wool and woollen yarn may have been imported from Ireland.[75] Women carried out the primary processing of wool before weaving, by combing until the 1390s and by carding thereafter. Christiana la Irysshe was the last kempster recorded in Chester, in 1395, and William Wells, the first cardmaker, appeared in the city the same year. This move to carding was paralleled elsewhere.[76] Spanish iron was particularly suitable for making cards and was readily available.[77] Spinning too was a traditional female activity, enabling wives to add to household income and widows to earn a livelihood. The clothworkers put out work to the spinners and perhaps provided the wheels, which cost between 8½d and 20d in the 1440s.[78]

The clothworkers distributed the yarn to the poorer craftsmen to be woven and may have also provided the looms. These were expensive, their cost varying from 5s in 1409 to 20s in 1460 and 1490.[79] More affluent weavers worked piece-rate for others on their own looms, and the most successful men employed two or three journeymen and became considerable entrepreneurs. The only types of woollen cloth specifically described as having been woven in Chester were russets and says.[80] Chaloners produced bed coverings on vertical chalon looms.

In the years 1390–1430 six or seven worked in the city at any one time, some of them wealthy men who employed servants and sold wool and who perhaps congregated in St Johns Lane.[81] By the end of the century the number had fallen to four or five, all based in Handbridge and all of them Welsh.[82]

Woollen cloth required several finishing processes, of which dyeing was the most expensive. Chester's dyers, termed heusters in the sources, occasionally dyed raw wool and yarn but the bulk of their work consisted of dyeing cloth.[83] They were the wealthiest of the city's textile craftsmen. Dyehouses contained expensive equipment, including the vessels needed to heat large quantities of water. One dyehouse in 1475 contained a lead furnace valued at 15s, a timber vat, 'lethy' pipes, and a wooden frame on which to hang cloth.[84] Dyestuffs too were costly, as was alum, used to fix dyes on to the fibre. The most commonly used dyes were madder and woad, usually supplied by London merchants, and orchil, a reddish-purple dye prepared from lichens and often referred to as 'cork'. Wood-ashes were needed to make woad soluble.[85]

Heusters required vast quantities of firewood, a good water supply, and a place to dump the waste from their dye-vats. From the 1340s until *c.*1460 many lived in the vicinity of Foregate Street and St John's Lane. They had links with residents of Love Lane and in 1428 one heuster was granted three plots of land, two of them near Love Lane, and a third near land of the dean and chapter of St John's and the Dee.[86] This area may have been the focus of the dyeing industry. There was a spring of clear water near the river (later the water fountain in Grosvenor Park) and the river perhaps served as a place to dump waste.[87] In the later fifteenth century the tanners may have taken over the area and by the 1480s Chester's leading heusters worked in Handbridge.

A dozen or so heusters were active at any one time in the fifteenth century, many of them assisted by two servants and John Pomfret in the early 1430s by three. In 1452 they were presented for throwing 'corrupt woad' into the street in front of their doors and for overcharging their customers by refusing to dye five yards for the price of four, as was customary.[88] Debts in the court rolls indicate that much cloth was dyed red (*rubius* or *blodius*) and madder is the dye most commonly found in medieval textiles. Violet became popular in the later fifteenth century.[89] Weavers from Ruthin and Cilcain (Flintshire) brought cloth to Chester to be dyed in the 1430s and Welsh merchants purchased dyestuffs in the city. William Spicer of Caernarvon bought 250 quarters of madder from a London grocer in 1488 and later discovered that it had been mixed with red ochre.[90]

The finishing processes of fulling and shearing were carried out by walkers and shearmen. The former were more prosperous, often employing the latter and providing their tools. Shears were expensive, costing between 10s and 30s in the later fifteenth and early sixteenth century. Tools and equipment stolen from a shearman's shop in 1507 included shears, a bag of teasels, a table called 'thrumbulbordes', and a table called 'burellbordes'.[91] The shearman Richard Greteby of Northgate Street, active in the city from 1430 until at least 1465, was unusually successful. He purchased wool, bought cloth and commissioned its dyeing, and had close links with the hosiers and drapers. He employed others to shear the cloth, among them the man who made an agreement during the Midsummer fair in 1446 to 'frise' (raise the nap) ten pieces of russet for 6s 8d.[92]

The quantities of cloth processed in the fulling mills were recorded in the mid 1390s, when the mills were managed directly by the Crown. 13,500 ells of cloth were fulled in 1394–5, at the rate of 20d per hundred, and 3,700 ells the following year. In 1394–5 1,200 ells were stretched on the tenter-frames, at the rate of ten for a penny, and 310 ells in 1395–6.[93] The walkers who leased the mills in the fifteenth century for £10 or £11 a year needed at the very least to match the figures for 1394–5 to cover their costs, especially as they were responsible for maintenance and repairs. A slump in trade in the mid fifteenth century followed by years of inadequate maintenance resulted in the mills standing empty for long periods. The lessees were granted a rent reduction and may have diversified their interests.[94] Several walkers became involved in the fish trade.[95]

Linen was needed for tablecloths, towels, sheets, shirts and underwear. Chester's mercers imported fine linens from Holland, Flanders and Brabant, and skilled craftsmen from the southern Netherlands may have migrated to the city to find work. John *le Braban* was named first among the linen weavers presented for taking excessive wages in 1381. In the early fifteenth century eight or nine linen weavers paid an annual fine to carry out their craft, paying 6d per loom. Some paid for two looms and worked with a wife or a servant. By the 1430s the number of linen weavers had fallen to five and in 1451–2 just one was named.[96] The Weavers' company may have put pressure on outsiders and forced them to join the guild.[97]

Flax was occasionally sold in the city and Flanders flax was recorded in 1502 but Irish yarn was more common. An Irish trader paid for a licence to sell two

FIGURE 7.4. Galfridus Prestaton linen weaver of Northgate Street heads the list of those who paid to carry out their 'artifice' in 1410. The following four individuals also came from Northgate Street and included a second linen weaver and two weavers. Next came a hosier from Bridge Street and a cardmaker from Watergate Street. A smith and a farrier from Northgate Street paid for their 'artifice' and for permission to sell ale; the farrier also paid for permission to sell bread.

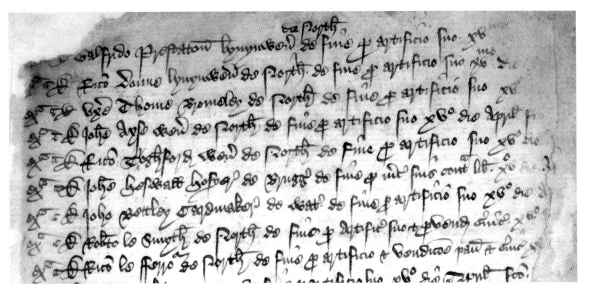

bundles of yarn in Chester in 1410 and prices in the later fifteenth century ranged between 3d and 8d a pound.[98] A newcomer to the craft in 1483 purchased a linen reed (used to separate the threads of the warp and beat up the weft) costing 6½d, a canvas reed costing 5d, and he gave 2d to the experienced linen weaver who warped his loom.[99] After it was taken from the loom linen had only to be washed and laid out in the sunshine to bleach.

The tailors were the largest occupational group in late medieval Chester, as they were in most English towns. Theirs was a labour-intensive craft, particularly after 1350 when tightly fitting garments became fashionable. They made new garments and also repaired and altered old ones which had been handed down from one person to another, a common practice in the medieval period. The leading tailors commissioned the dyeing of cloth and were actively involved in the cloth trade. Their customers included wealthy men like Sir John Savage and country esquires.[100] Most of the city's tailors operated on a modest scale and purchased fustian, kendal and linen cloth as it was needed, or used cloth provided by the customer.[101] The poorest tailors, many of them Welsh immigrants, worked for the more prosperous men and needed only pins, needles, thread, and a pair of scissors costing just a few pence.

Chester's tailors profited from military campaigns, making short jackets for horsemen and foot soldiers in 1328 and green and white coats for the Black Prince's Cheshire archers in 1350, but their routine business consisted of making clothes for the townspeople.[102] In the earlier fifteenth century they charged 18d for making a woman's garment, 20d for making a worsted gown, and 22d for making a doublet and cap. Each item evidently involved several days' work.[103] More time was required to make lined garments and to trim them with squirrel fur or lambskin.[104] By the late 1470s the city's mercers stocked velvet, damask and green silk, and tailors were among the purchasers, perhaps using the material to make collars, tippets and girdles for the wealthy élite.[105]

In the second half of the fourteenth century, as male tunics became shorter, the demand for hose increased. Although one or two specialist hosiers worked in Chester many tailors made hose, perhaps with an accompanying doublet. Tailors also made caps. The green lined cap made by Geoffrey the tailor for Thomas Cottingham in 1410 was probably worn for the first time on St George's Day.[106] Felt caps became fashionable in the mid fourteenth century and were imported to England from Spain and Flanders; some may have been produced in London. Felt was made of compacted wool fibres, to which fur or animal hair could be added, and the fabric was shaped over a mould. Felt caps were first recorded in Chester in the 1450s, and feltcappers appeared in the 1460s and 1470s, working in Foregate Street and Handbridge. The tools of one felt-capper in 1489 included three 'beame' knives, four other knives, and two moulds.[107] These craftsmen were not always popular with the city's weavers. In 1495 the felt-capper Nicholas Deykin was accused of receiving stolen wool, a charge dismissed when it was learned that it was based on 'malicious' information from the weavers. Deykin went on to enjoy a successful career, serving as company steward, becoming wealthy, and establishing chantries in St John's where he was buried in 1518.[108]

Leather and animal skins

Large numbers of townsmen were involved in the manufacture of leather and leather goods. Tanners, curriers and tawyers prepared the raw material; leather workers used it to make clothing, containers, animal harness, saddles and military equipment. Lower Bridge Street was the focus of the light leather trades and many tawyers and glovers were based there. Chester's tanneries were located outside the Eastgate and shoemakers and saddlers congregated in Foregate Street.

A tanner held land in Little St John Lane in the 1270s; a second tanner was granted land opposite Wolfeld Gate in the 1280s; in the following decade two tanners were presented for making cess-pits in the town ditch.[109] This suggests that the tanneries were then in the vicinity of St John's Lane and Little St John Lane. The industry subsequently moved further east. In a survey supposedly made during the reign of Edward III and transcribed into the city's Assembly Book in *c*.1570 the lane leading east into the fields was called Barkers Lane. A

FIGURE 7.5. Conjectural reconstruction of the Western Tannery at The Green, Northampton. The tanning complex dates from the late 15th to the 17th century.

large pit for tanning hides dating from the late medieval period was discovered in the western part of Grosvenor Park during excavations in the summer of 2007 and excavations carried out in the 1990s indicate that the area in the vicinity of the Bars was a focus of the trade.[110] The written sources provide supporting evidence. A barker (the term used at Chester) worked near the Bars in 1448 and another was presented in 1476–7 for failing to clean his ditches in Chester Lane.[111]

Tanning was a lengthy process. Hides were washed and the hair and flesh removed, soaked for one to two months in pits or tubs containing weak tanning liquor, then transferred to other pits and laid out flat between layers of oak bark and water in a fresh tan solution. After nine to twelve months the hides were removed from the pits, rinsed, smoothed and hung up to dry slowly in a dark shed away from direct sunlight.[112] In the 1350s and 1360s Chester's shoemakers challenged the tanners' monopoly and in 1370 they were granted the right to tan leather.[113] Sixty years later William Calthorne, described as barker and shoemaker, operated on a large scale, purchasing up to 2,000 ox and cow hides at a time and employing a man to govern his barkhouse. In 1443 he claimed (falsely) that the man's negligence had caused the loss of 250 hides and 120 calf-skins worth £40.[114] A barker occupied a messuage near the Eastgate on the north side of Foregate Street in 1511, close to the town ditch. In the garden stood a kitchen, a stable and a two-bay barkhouse. Evidence for tanning was found in the medieval ditch during excavations at 5–7 Foregate Street in 1991, including a large quantity of oak bark, wooden staves perhaps used to line the pits, and cattle horn.[115]

Chester's barkers obtained hides from local butchers.[116] Other suppliers included a local heuster and the abbot of St Werburgh's. In 1457 one barker employed a man to buy hides for him in Ireland.[117] Bark was subject to toll at the Eastgate and the Bridgegate and came from the estates of local gentlemen and from the royal forests. The bark of all oaks felled in Delamere forest for the king's use in 1399 was sold to a barker and a shoemaker at the rate of 2s 6d per oak.[118] The Tanners' company claimed in 1797 that they were permitted to convey hides down Dee Lane and wash them in the river 'according to [their] ancient and undoubted right and privilege'.[119] Barkers probably washed hides there in the later medieval period. In earlier years, when the tanneries were located near St John's Lane, hides were perhaps taken to the river bank at the end of Souters Lane.

The shoemakers, always among the most numerous craftsmen in late medieval Chester, were described as *sutores* when named as a group but as corvisers when named individually.[120] In other towns *sutores* were cobblers, men who remade old shoes for sale or mended them. Three cobblers were named in Chester in the earlier fifteenth century, all relatively humble men.[121] Eleven souters' shops (*seldae*) were located in Bridge Street in the 1350s but in the fifteenth century the corvisers congregated in the Eastgate Street quarter and especially in Foregate Street. All seven presented in 1477 for throwing old shoes into the

FIGURE 7.6. A late 14th-century front-lacing ankle-shoe found during the excavation of part of the medieval city ditch to the north of Foregate Street.

street lived there, including one who occupied a tenement next to the Eastgate. Remains of shoes dating from the thirteenth and fourteenth centuries were found in the ditch outside the Eastgate, together with shoemaking waste.[122] The butchers occasionally supplied untreated hides but most shoemakers preferred to purchase leather from the barkers and prominent citizens.[123] Supplies came from monastic tanneries: from Vale Royal in 1450 and from Dieulacres in Staffordshire in 1492.[124]

Sixteen corvisers were embroiled in a dispute with nine barkers in 1477 and another six or seven corvisers were not involved, bringing the number then at work in Chester to about 22, which may have been typical. One corviser in 1497 worked with a 'drawyng-iron', a 'spoke sha', and a 'turning staf', the last perhaps used to turn the shoes inside out during the construction process.[125] Customers included local townspeople, chaplains and country folk from neighbouring villages.[126] Shoes cost between 5d and 7d a pair in the earlier fifteenth century; a pair of slippers cost 12d in 1502.[127]

Chester's saddlers were a sizeable group, numbering a dozen or so at any one time in the earlier fifteenth century and about 15 from the 1480s. Their main work consisted of covering wooden saddle-frames (trees) with leather or cloth. Saddle-trees were produced by fusters, possibly in Fustard's Lane (later Whitefriars Lane) in the earlier medieval period, but as only one fuster was recorded in later years frames were presumably made elsewhere. Those sold by a palatinate carpenter to a saddler in 1396 had perhaps been made in Delamere forest.[128] The saddlers obtained leather from the barkers; when the type was specified it was calf-skin.[129] They purchased nails, and wool on occasion, possibly using it to stuff the side panels.[130] In the earlier fifteenth century saddles cost between 3s and 12s and the quality evidently varied a great deal.[131] Saddlers also made bridles, halters and stirrup leathers and, like saddlers in other towns, became involved in the sale of metal horse-trappings. One saddler in 1501 owed a city merchant 48s for 40 bridle bits, 100 buckles and 20 pairs of stirrups.[132] Saddlers' Row was on the west side of Bridge Street near the common hall at the end of the thirteenth century and saddlers' shops were recorded there in 1342.[133] Later, possibly when the selds fell out of use, the saddlers congregated in Eastgate Street and Foregate Street.[134]

Six or seven parchment-makers were recorded in the fourteenth and early fifteenth century, perhaps based in or near St John's Lane where scriveners were to be found. After 1450 John Strongbow of Handbridge appears to have been the sole representative of the craft.[135] Parchment-makers used sheepskins and calf-skins, occasionally from animals that had died naturally but usually supplied by local butchers. The skins, which cost 4s each in the early 1430s, were washed, scraped and stretched on frames. A 'shavyng iron' used to scrape the skins cost 3s in 1445.[136] Chester's sheriffs purchased a dozen pieces of parchment in 1437–8; the muragers paid 2d for a cover for their account book in 1478.[137] Fifty dozen parchment skins were required to record business handled by the justice and chamberlain in 1458–9 and this was not unusual. They cost 2½d or 3d each and Strongbow was often the sole supplier, although he sometimes shared the business with a local mercer.[138] An impressive book was made to record the exchequer receipts in 1397–8. It was the work of Henry the clerk stationer (a very early example of this occupation), who was paid 12d for making and binding a quartern of parchment and 3d for the white leather sheepskin used for the cover.[139]

Glovers were a relatively large group and their numbers increased from the 1420s. They worked with sheep, deer and rabbit skins, purchasing white leather that was ready for use and skins that required preparation.[140] They obtained sheepskins from local butchers, occasionally contracting to buy the skins of all animals slaughtered during the year, and bought the alum needed for the tawing process.[141] Leading glovers had sizeable quantities of wool to sell as a result of their involvement in leather preparation.[142] Many were based in Bridge Street and in the second half of the fifteenth century several rented land along the river bank to the west of the corn mills. Some became very wealthy, including Richard Wirral and Nicholas Newhouse, mayor and sheriff in 1495–6. Newhouse, who lived in Fleshmongers Lane, rented the adjacent tower on the walls called 'wolfegate' and a plot of land next to the Dee measuring 26 yards by 8 yards.[143]

Gloves were offered for sale in the selds in Bridge Street during the Midsummer fair in 1340. In later years Eastgate Street may have been the focus of the retail trade. Glovers' Row was located there by 1426, on the south side and close to the junction with Bridge Street. Three shops known as the

'Glovers' Shops' still occupied the site in 1606.[144] One glover's shop was located just round the corner in Bridge Street by the late 1460s. Described as the shop 'next to the new stairs' it was held by three glovers in succession, each of whom also leased land near the river.[145] Among the goods found in a glover's shop in 1474 were two dozen unfinished gloves (12d), four dozen finished gloves (3s), a pair of scissors/shears (12d), 12 skins (2s), three woolfells (6½d) and one kid-skin (2d). Glovers also made purses, including one of white leather made for the great seal of the new principality in 1397–8. Two glovers supplied 15 white leather bags for use in the castle in 1477–8: large ones for the account rolls and memoranda, and small ones for the prince's coins.[146]

When Earl Ranulph II (1129–53) restricted trading during the June fair to the stalls before the abbey gate, his charter singled out parmenters and shoemakers for particular mention. It seems probable that the parmenters traded in furs, as they did in twelfth-century Winchester, and that their trade was of considerable importance. In the mid thirteenth century furs were regarded as the characteristic feature of Chester but in the following century, as at Winchester, the trade evidently declined. Two parmenters were recorded in 1342 and a third in 1397 but none thereafter, although garments trimmed with miniver, beaver and snow weasel were occasionally mentioned.[147] In the fifteenth century Chester's skinners (*pelliparii*) traded in the skins of lambs, squirrels and rabbits. Tawyers, who prepared skins by scraping, treading and stretching them, were rarely attested, suggesting that the skinners controlled the process. Some skinners became wealthy men. Roger the harper, sheriff in 1328–9 and steward of St Mary's guild in 1348, was among the most influential citizens of his day.[148] In the 1440s two skinners served as sheriff and Edward Skinner was mayor two years in succession.

Marten furs were imported from Dublin in the tenth century and Ireland remained the major source of furs and animal pelts throughout the later medieval period. In the early fourteenth century Cestrians were recorded buying 500 black and white lambskins at Carrickfergus fair and rabbit-skins at Drogheda. In 1424 a local skinner served as pledge for a Dublin skinner, and in 1443 a Dublin trader claimed that a Cestrian owed him a considerable sum for sheepskins.[149] The skinner William Hawkin, sheriff in 1455–6, regularly shipped goods across the Irish Sea. The brothers John and David White, leading skinners in the city from the early 1420s until the mid 1440s, were almost certainly related to Richard White of Ireland, exporter of animal pelts.[150]

The processes involved in dressing skins produced offensive smells and were carried out beyond the walls. In the earlier fifteenth century one skinner rented land in and above the town ditch near the Eastgate and another rented a garden next to the quarry outside the Northgate.[151] Skinners gravitated towards the river. One held land near St Olave's church in *c.*1268, possibly close to the garden granted to a skinner in 1429–30. Hugh de Holes leased part of his house in St Mary Lane to a skinner in 1390. By 1545 the lane running west from the Dee mills along the river bank was known as Skinners Lane.[152] Rabbit-skins cost 1d each in the 1390s and squirrel-skins stolen from a skinner's shop in Bridge Street during the Midsummer fair in 1407, some of them the summer fur known as *pople*, were worth 3d each.[153] At the end of the century the price of lambskins was 3d (white) and 2d (black). Many townspeople could afford garments lined with lambskins or trimmed with squirrel fur and wealthy citizens and gentlemen distanced themselves by wearing more expensive furs, like the grey fur worth 40s delivered to a tailor by Sir John Savage in 1425.[154]

Building trades

The majority of houses in late medieval Chester were timber-framed and the carpenters were the most numerous of the building workers. Skilled carpenters employed by the civic authorities in the early 1440s, and those working at the castle in the late 1450s, were paid 2s 6d a week.[155] The sawyers, many of them immigrants, were usually paid piece-rate.[156] Many carpenters were based in Foregate Street and outside the Northgate, where there was space for a saw-pit. Tools included broad axes, framing axes, chipping axes, adzes, saws, chisels and augurs, and there was mention of a 'Chester axe' in 1505, when axes and saws cost 12d each and a chisel cost 3d.[157] Building timber came from a variety of sources. Five prominent citizens supplied the timber for the new Northgate bridge in 1440–1, and city officials rode to Hawarden and to Swanlow to procure timber for the new Pentice in 1464. The master carpenter and his servants worked at Basingwerk and at Darnhall and wood from the demolished structure was re-used.[158] Chester's carpenters were not recorded selling timber although some occasionally added to their income by selling nails and boards.[159] Very little of their work survives above the level of the undercrofts. The best examples include a thirteenth-century doorway to the open hall at 28–34 Watergate Street, a mid fifteenth-century roof at 63 Northgate Street, and the elevation of the rear wing of 48–50 Lower Bridge Street (*Old King's Head*) which perhaps dates from the fifteenth century.[160]

Imposing houses with external walls of stone were built in Chester in the twelfth and earlier thirteenth century but in later years the use of stone was largely restricted to the low walls which supported the timber-framed superstructure and to the walls of certain undercrofts. Masons were always outnumbered by carpenters. Two were recorded in the city in the years 1298–1312, for example, compared to twelve carpenters. The new Pentice in 1464 was a timber-framed building and a mason worked for only two weeks, setting 13 corbels in place.[161] Three or four masons worked in Chester in the 1460s and 1470s and their numbers increased in the 1480s and 1490s, perhaps because of building projects at the parish churches and the Carmelite friary. Building programmes were underway at St Werburgh's throughout the later medieval period but the abbey workforce possibly had little contact with the townspeople. Palatinate masons were more visible. Thomas Bates, who agreed in 1433 to build the Troutbeck chapel in St Mary's, was to work under the supervision of master mason John Asser. William Troutbeck agreed to supply the free stone, lime, sand, windlass and 'stuff for to scaffalde with'. John Asser was steward of the Masons' company in 1437 and he rebuilt the upper section of the city wall near the Bridgegate in 1440–1.[162]

Only eight thatchers were recorded in Chester in the fourteenth and fifteenth centuries, at least three of them based in Foregate Street and one living close to the Bars. John Wright, active from the early 1480s until 1496 and whose wages of 4d a day plus a meal were said to be excessive, was the only thatcher who worked in the city for any length of time. He also bought and sold grain, malt and building timber.[163] The slaters were the most numerous of the roofing craftsmen. The price of 'sclattestones' was 3s 8d per 1,000 in 1328 and 3s 4d per 1,000 in 1425–6.[164] Oak shingles were widely used as a roofing material, even though they were laborious to produce and lasted for only 20 to 30 years. They were ideal for large buildings when the weight of the roof was an issue and cost 3s 4d per 1,000 in 1304, much the same as slates.[165] The task of nailing the shingles to the 'thackbordes' which served as the base was often carried out by carpenters, who were sometimes described as shinglers for this reason. Two shinglers worked in Chester in the late 1480s and 1490s and collaborated closely with other roofing craftsmen. One married a slater's widow.[166]

There is evidence for the manufacture of floor tiles on a site north of Foregate Street and east of Cow Lane in the late thirteenth century; the Tile houses recorded in 1495 were probably in the same area. Manufacturing tile waste has been found near the Gorse Stacks.[167] References to plain clay tiles (*tegulas*) increased in the 1480s and 1490s; slaters were paid for tiling and kept stocks of tiles, costing 8s 4d per 1,000 in 1489.[168] The first brickman was recorded in Chester in 1459 and another five appeared between then and the early sixteenth century. The earliest archaeological evidence for bricks dates from the time of the Dissolution.[169]

Among the plumbers who found regular employment at the castle was the monk from Combermere abbey who worked on the roof of the great tower in the inner bailey in 1303–4. A plumber supplied lead and repaired the gutter at the Pentice in *c*.1460 and private houses also had gutters. The theft of lead from the gutters of Richard Wirral's house in Bridge Street in 1501 resulted in serious damage to the walls.[170] Plumbers frequently worked in association with glaziers. Chester was an important centre for window glass from the thirteenth century. Brother Robert of Chester glazed windows in the Dublin Exchequer in 1282 and John of Chester headed the list of six master glaziers working at St Stephen's Chapel, Westminster, in 1351.[171] A glass-making site possibly dating from the fifteenth century has been found in Delamere forest and may have been connected with the abbey of Vale Royal, known to have been concerned in the manufacture of glass in earlier years.[172]

There is no evidence for glazed windows in domestic buildings and the dozen or so glaziers recorded in Chester in the later medieval period worked either at the castle or on religious buildings. Among the most successful was

William Thurkyll, who began his working life mending windows in the king's chambers and chapel in 1426 and ended it in *c.*1460 glazing the window in the exchequer.[173] There was mention of a glazier's 'instruments' in 1391, and the book stolen by a glazier in 1439 may have been a sketchbook containing stock designs.[174] Archaeological evidence for glass-working has recently been discovered in Handbridge. Glass-working began on the site before 1500 and the same family continued the business in the sixteenth and seventeenth centuries.[175]

The glaziers were frequently named together with painters and stainers and belonged to the same guild. This close association suggests that the production of church windows was the most important part of their work. The painters and stainers purchased their colours from local merchants.[176] The principal residence of the Doncasters in Watergate Street contained rooms decorated with paintings in 1297, and there were painted chambers in the Black Hall in Pepper Street in 1369.[177] Stainers painted on cloth. The new altar hangings provided for the castle chapel in 1454–5 were made of fine linen cloth painted by William Stainer.[178]

Metal trades

Some 15 metal-working crafts and trades were recorded in late medieval Chester. In 1407 seven smiths, four farriers, a locker, a cutler, a sheather and a wirecapper were indicted for taking excessive wages; five goldsmiths were named separately.[179] They presumably represented the most important metal-working occupations in the city at that time and the numbers perhaps indicated the relative size of each group. Small metal objects are among the most common finds in urban excavations and sites in Chester have produced considerable numbers of medieval buckle frames, hinged rings, spurs, horseshoes, knife blades, padlock keys, and chest or casket keys.[180]

Iron-working was of crucial importance, because all other craftsmen depended on the smiths for their tools. In the late medieval period Chester's smiths worked mainly with Spanish iron, probably imported long before the first specific reference in 1377–8. They purchased supplies from local ironmongers and from other merchants.[181] The smiths were often based near the city gates, busy locations with much passing trade. William the smith occupied a smithy and garden at the corner of Bag Lane outside the Northgate before 1270–1; William the smith 'next to the Northgate' was at work in 1311. Smiths were recorded next to the Bridgegate, next to the Bars, in Foregate Street and in Handbridge.[182] The smiths' forges posed a fire risk and the coal used as fuel produced unhealthy fumes; town authorities everywhere sought to keep them outside the walls.[183]

The smith's anvil was his main piece of equipment and other tools included hammers, chisels, punches, files and tongs.[184] Smiths made shears, scythes, augers, spits, andirons and iron chimneys; they purchased wooden harrows and cart wheels and added the iron fittings; they sharpened the pickaxes and wedges used by men paving the city streets.[185] Much of the smiths' business consisted of shoeing horses and in this the trade overlapped with that of the marshals. The marshals, however, were more concerned with horse-doctoring. In 1313, when the health of a horse handed over to Thomas the marshal became worse not better, the owner demanded 20s in compensation. Marshals inevitably became involved in the buying and selling of horses.[186]

Lorimers made bits and other metalwork for horses and a tradition, perhaps dating from the fourteenth century, maintained that they had their own Row 'against' the abbey in 1155. Five lorimers were recorded in Chester in the fourteenth century but in later years it seems that metal horse-trappings were produced elsewhere and the saddlers controlled the trade. The spurriers succeeded in maintaining their independence but were never numerous. They purchased iron from local merchants, associated with the saddlers, and occasionally acted as pledges for country gentlemen.[187] The cutlers too were few in number although there would have been considerable demand in an age when men routinely carried knives. The miller in Chaucer's *Reeve's Tale* had a short blade at his belt, a dagger in his pouch, and a Sheffield knife in his hose.[188] The cutlery trade comprised several sections, including bladesmith, hafter, sheather and cutler; the last-named perhaps assembled the parts and sold the finished article. One of Chester's most successful cutlers was John del Hey, attested from 1398 and particularly active in the 1410s and 1420s. He lived in St John's Lane and rented a shop near the Eastgate and adjacent land in and above the town ditch. His business contacts included one or two sheathers and a cutler who made sheaths for daggers and knives.[189] Bladesmiths and hafters were not recorded in Chester suggesting that, as at Winchester, knives were manufactured elsewhere. Cutlers from Shrewsbury sold knives in Chester in the 1430s.[190]

The few recorded cardmakers and wiredrawers regularly combined both crafts and some had additional interests. William and Robert Leche, for example, participated in the fish trade in the 1490s.[191] The first pinner was mentioned in 1451 and three others were named in the following decades. One man established a sizeable business, which provided work for his wife and several servants.[192] Locksmiths found steady employment throughout the later medieval period. All townspeople needed locks and keys to protect their homes from intruders and to safeguard the chests and coffers in which documents, money and other valuables were kept. Servants who absconded by night leaving the door open behind them were heavily fined; those who unlocked the door and admitted thieves were gaoled.[193] Lodgers were expected to provide a lock and key for the door to their chamber.[194] Hundreds of locks and keys were manufactured for the castle, ranging from large ones for the outer gate to small ones for the wicket gate leading to the garden. The door of the great treasury where the rolls and memoranda were stored had three locks and three keys, as did the great chest which held the rolls in daily use. The chamberlain kept one key, the justice or his deputy the second, and the controller the third.[195]

FIGURE 7.7. Late medieval key from a contemporary rubbish pit at Newgate Row, Grosvenor Precinct, in 2004.

Chester's wealthiest men owned coats of mail, skull caps, and gorgets of steel and were perhaps able to purchase these items in the city. Two or three armourers were recorded in the fourteenth and fifteenth centuries, and two brigandmakers in the 1470s and 1480s.[196] Many citizens owned swords, which were not very expensive. The mercer John Cottingham sold six for 15s in 1430.[197] The furbishers, who repaired and polished weapons, were busy men. From the 1430s onwards four or five were always at work in the city and seven were recorded in the 1480s. Much of their trade consisted of mending swords and hangers (short swords hung from the belt), and they also repaired and polished hauberks, steel caps, thigh armour, gorgets and pairs of gleaves.[198] One furbisher purchased hilts and pommels from a Shrewsbury smith in 1443, further proof of that town's involvement in the trade in blades.[199] Chester's furbishers do not appear to have sold weapons.

Precise distinctions between the potters, brasiers, belyetters and founders who worked copper alloys remain unclear. In the 1430s David Potter was also known as David Belleyetter potter and the brasier John Bullock was paid 7s 5d for making a bell.[200] This suggests that these metal-workers were not specialists but made a variety of copper-alloy objects. Archaeological evidence supports this suggestion. A dump of fragments of clay moulds used in the casting of cauldrons and small bells was discovered near the junction of City Road and Foregate Street in 2003.[201] At least three potters lived in or near Foregate Street in the fifteenth century and three others caused a nuisance in 1452 when they dug pits next to Henwald's Lowe, presumably for clay for their moulds.[202] David Belleyetter purchased metal and copper from two city merchants in 1424 and 'ponne brasse' (costing 2s) from a city mercer in 1436; he also paid 12d for coal.[203] Only Roger Tailor, sheriff in 1481–2, was described as a founder. He purchased charcoal, sold iron, associated with pewterers and brasiers, and kept timber in the ditch and highway near Truants Hole. He also imported Gascon wine.[204]

Brass pots, pans, posnets, basins, dishes, cans and candlesticks were in widespread use in the later medieval city, and many townspeople owned basins made of the alloys maslin and latten. In 1477 Alexander Stanney owned 1 cwt of brass and maslin worth 20s.[205] Prices of individual vessels varied according to size and quality; in 1432 one brass posnet was valued at 3s 4d and another at 2s 6d. Such items were worth repairing, a task carried out by tinkers, some of whom settled in Chester. One lived in Fleshmongers Lane in the 1440s and purchased 'ponnebrasse' and other metal from a brasier.[206] Pewter vessels were in use in well-to-do households by the end of the fourteenth century and one or two pewterers were recorded in the city in the 1420s. Their numbers increased in the later fifteenth century and many were based in Eastgate Street.[207] There is only one reference to the metal itself, in 1492, and Chester's pewterers were perhaps dealers rather than manufacturers. William Rawson, sheriff in 1466–7, was once described as a draper and also purchased wine, and the only indication that he actually carried out metal-working was in 1463–4 when he mended the inkpot in the castle exchequer.[208]

Chester's goldsmiths prospered in the later thirteenth and early fourteenth century and regularly served as doomsmen in the portmote court. At least seven worked in the city in the years 1292–1302, congregating in Eastgate Street and Foregate Street.[209] That area remained the focus of the trade throughout the later medieval period. Leading goldsmiths lived in or near Fleshmongers Lane in the 1460s and 1470s, one renting the tower on the adjacent wall and the garden next to Truants Hole later held by the founder Roger Tailor. In the early sixteenth century a goldsmith occupied a house and garden near Godstall Lane.[210]

From the 1420s between ten and twelve goldsmiths may be identified in each decade. They worked mainly in silver, often using old plate or coins provided by the customer; one was given 7½ ounces of broken silver in 1424 and in 1500 another received coins worth 4s 5d from which to make spoons.[211] Spoons were perhaps their staple product. Most prosperous townsmen owned half a dozen or more and their increased spending power produced a growing demand for silver rings, silver crosses for rosaries, and silver fittings for girdles and scabbards.[212] Girdles with silver-gilt decorations became fashionable at the end of the fifteenth century.[213] A goldsmith's widow attempted in 1424 to recover money owed for 'bedes and glasses', the latter possibly tiny white glass beads used as imitation pearls.[214]

At the start of the fourteenth century Thomas the goldsmith made a copper seal for use until the palatinate seal arrived; in 1457–8 a local goldsmith provided the silver for a new seal for the chamberlain and made and engraved it, for which he was paid 46s 8d.[215] Ownership of seals spread during the late medieval period and they came to be used by many sections of society. In 1439 a corviser put his seal to the document which recorded the lease of a garden and in 1463 all the city's bakers added their seals to the company charter. Wealthy citizens owned silver seals attached to silver chains.[216] A copper-alloy seal matrix showing a stylised pelican with her young in the nest was found at the amphitheatre in 2004.

Valuable items, charters and money were entrusted to goldsmiths for safe custody, and perhaps deposited in stone cupboards like those which survive in one or two vaulted undercrofts.[217] Goldsmiths occasionally betrayed the customer's trust and refused to return the articles. One goldsmith in 1393 committed a more serious offence, conspiring with two accomplices to mix silver with copper, lead and 'alkemany', and then use the false metal to make coins, girdles, trimmings for knife scabbards and 'lokets'.[218]

TABLE 7.1 The leading occupational groupings

1297–1349	%	1350–1399	%	1400–1449	%	1450–1499	%	1500–1520	%
tailors	8.0	tailors	8.0	tailors	8.2	weavers	7.2	tailors	7.1
carpenters	6.3	corvisers	7.5	weavers	6.6	tailors	6.2	butchers	7.0
bakers	4.7	weavers	6.6	butchers	6.4	corvisers	5.3	weavers	6.3
shearmen	3.9	bakers	6.0	corvisers	5.6	glovers	5.3	bakers	5.8
glovers	3.8	butchers	5.6	carpenters	4.9	butchers	4.8	shearmen	5.6
barkers	3.6	carpenters	4.8	bakers	4.3	bakers	4.4	drapers	5.2
corvisers	3.6	glovers	4.1	glovers	3.7	carpenters	4.3	carpenters	5.2
butchers	3	skinners	3.9	skinners	3.4	shearmen	3.7	glovers	5.1
cooks	3	walkers	3.3	fishers	2.7	heusters	3.5	smiths	4.5
taverners	3	fishers	2.9	heusters	2.6	barkers	3.3	corvisers	3.8
				saddlers	2.6				
individuals	559		663		1330		1442		574

Other trades

Chester's bowyers, fletchers and stringers were relatively numerous, a result perhaps of the city's role as a garrison town and important military base, particularly in the late thirteenth century. Records of disturbances on the city streets indicate that many townsmen and visitors carried bows and arrows. Men purchased arrows more frequently than bows and the fletchers always outnumbered the bowyers. Three fletchers and two bowyers worked in the city in the first decade of the fourteenth century and eleven fletchers and four bowyers were recorded in the 1480s and 1490s.[219] The fletchers were also more prosperous. Robert Elswick, who occupied a messuage and cellar on the south side of Watergate Street, was sheriff in 1478–9.[220]

York was renowned for the manufacture of bows in the late medieval period and in 1420 a bowyer from that city became a freeman of Chester.[221] The type of wood used by Chester's bowyers is not known. In 1465–6 the chamberlain purchased 13 made of elm, considered to be second only to yew in quality and much used by the Welsh.[222] Bows purchased by townsmen cost between 12d and 14d in the 1330s and between 16d and 18d in the fifteenth century; high-quality bows cost twice as much.[223] Bows purchased in Chester for members of the duke of Norfolk's household in 1463 cost 2s or 3s, and the bowyer received an additional 21d for 'pesynge', 'ovyrdrawynge' and 'pykynge' them. These processes required considerable skill. When John Bower sold a bow to a city painter for 18d in 1461 he charged an extra 4d for 'pesyng' it.[224]

Fletchers sometimes traded in bows but the bulk of their work consisted of making arrows. Their tools were inexpensive. The saws, knives, 'shavers' and file owned by one fletcher in 1490 were worth just over 3s.[225] Most arrows were fitted with goose feathers and cost 1d or 1½d each in the fifteenth century.[226] Peacock-feathered arrows, like those hanging at the belt of Chaucer's yeoman, were more expensive. A dozen stolen in Chester in 1449 were said to be worth 3d each.[227] In the years 1401–5 all the arrowheads used in the campaigns against Glyn Dŵr were made in Sheffield and cost 1s per 100; in 1431 the arrowhead-maker John Elcock of Sheffield paid for a licence to sell his wares in Chester.[228] In 1490 one of the city's fletchers purchased 200 arrowheads from a local hardwareman at the rate of five for a penny.[229]

Demand for barrels was always high in a city with a busy harbour and which served as a distributive centre for fish. The household books of John Howard reveal how difficult it was to obtain enough pipes and barrels to store supplies for a naval expedition, and recorded payments to coopers for making tubs and packing barrels with herring.[230] Chester's coopers found steady employment, both in the city and at the castle. Eight were accused of taking excessive wages in 1407, including one who lived outside the Northgate and another who lived beyond the Bars.[231] Successful coopers employed servants and a seven-year apprenticeship was required to learn the trade. Grou the cooper produced butts to store salt for the castle garrison in 1398–9, assisted by his servant Richard Culmer. Culmer worked in the city for a further 35 years, becoming a freeman and eventually a prosperous master craftsman with servants of his own.[232] The cooper Hugh Lake shipped goods from Ireland in the late 1490s and his bequests to St Peter's in 1503 included a pair of gimlets called a 'brest wymble'. A fellow cooper was employed for one voyage to Ireland in 1502, perhaps to make barrels for herring.[233] Specialist hoopers also worked in the city. One struck a cooper on the finger with a mallet in 1430, an injury which perhaps threatened the victim's livelihood and for which he claimed £10 in damages.[234]

There was much work for Chester's cartwrights and wheelwrights, many of whom were based in Foregate Street, a busy approach road thronged with long-distance and local traffic. These craftsmen needed land where they could work and store raw materials, like the garden and two plots of ground in Cow Lane occupied by a wheelwright in the 1350s. Pairs of wheels cost 2s or 3s in the mid fifteenth century; a cart with iron-bound wheels cost 16s in 1479.[235] Carts frequently needed repair after long journeys and Chester's cartwrights probably spent more time mending carts than making them.

The numerous carters and carriers formed two distinct groups: one group undertook long journeys which could take a week or more and the other group carried goods short distances and returned home each evening. They all needed yards and sheds to store their carts and stable their horses and accordingly lived in the suburbs and in the adjoining settlements of Boughton, Blacon and Saltney. Carts loaded with wine, millstones, fuel, building materials and rubbish lumbered through the city streets, some pulled by as many as seven horses.[236] In the mid fifteenth century it cost 1d to transport a load of gravel from beyond the New Tower to the Northgate and 2d for a load of sand. Timber was carted from Shotwick to the castle in 1471–2, in large carts at the rate of 13d a load and in smaller carts at the rate of 12d a load. The cost of transporting shingles and boards from Delamere forest was 10d a load.[237]

One of the city's most successful carters was Henry Kettle, who originated in Hawarden and began his career in the early 1430s carrying coal to Chester. He soon moved to the city, perhaps to premises outside the Northgate, and for ten years or so carted dung, fuel, stones, salt, salmon and wine.[238] By 1450 his business was well established; he employed another carter, sold horses and hay, and was in contact with prominent merchants including one from London. Kettle's carts now made longer journeys and, anticipating time away, he appointed an attorney to represent him in the city courts. He was last recorded in 1460.[239]

Merchants

The merchants were Chester's wealthiest men. Those who lived there at the height of its medieval prosperity, in the late thirteenth and early fourteenth century, were able to amass great fortunes. The Doncasters, recorded from *c.*1250–1350, enjoyed spectacular success, largely due to the activities of William (III) who began his career in the 1290s provisioning the royal army and garrisons in north Wales. He had links with Ireland, Gascony and Antwerp, and traded in wine, corn and fish. He had influential contacts at court and was appointed collector of customs and searcher of money in the ports of Chester, Conwy, Beaumaris and Caernarfon. In a letter written in 1305 the prince of Wales asked him to take a royal valet into his service.[240] Doncaster's contemporaries, including the Brickhills, the Hurrells, the Russells and the Dunfouls, also traded over long distances and acquired considerable wealth.

Opportunities dwindled from the 1320s onwards and the closure of Chester's port to the export of wool in 1347 made it difficult for its merchants to handle England's most valuable export. They continued to diversify their trading interests and to combine these activities with investment in land and money-lending, thereby spreading the risk. They played a dominant role in the life of the community, monopolized high civic office, and were often interrelated. Adam Wotton, active in the city from *c.*1418 until the 1450s and mayor in 1434–5, may be taken as an example. He dealt in fish, cloth, wax, copper, woolfells, leather and metal bowls, and had business links with merchants from Coventry. His second wife was the widow of a prominent fishmonger and former sheriff who had traded in spices. Wotton purchased land at Edgerley six miles south of Chester and raised livestock which he sold in the city. His daughter married William Massey, a prosperous gentleman from neighbouring Coddington, whose sister married into the Cottingham family.[241]

Few fortunes were made in the fifteenth century. The number of merchants who imported wine and Spanish iron was always very small and there was a limited market for the fine continental linens sold by the city's mercers. No specialist spicers or grocers were recorded and the commodities they handled were sold by mercers like Alexander Stanney, whose trading stock in 1477 included pepper, saffron, cloves, mace and aniseed. The total value of his goods barely reached £50, an indication of the straitened economic circumstances of those years. In the 1490s and the early sixteenth century Chester's merchants began to prosper once again. Among those who imported wine and iron were Ralph Davenport, Thomas Barrow, Hamo Goodman, and Thomas and Roger Smith, all of whom served as mayor or sheriff.[242]

Women

There were good economic opportunities for women in Chester, as in all medieval towns. Perhaps as many as one in three households employed a female servant and prosperous citizens employed two or more. Daughters sometimes worked as servants in the family home but most servants appear to have been young women from nearby villages and more distant places who moved to Chester to find work. Service agreements indicate that they often arrived in the city during the Midsummer or Michaelmas fairs.[243] Some moved on at the end of the year but others chose to stay with their employers, sometimes for many years. Their long and faithful service was rewarded by generous bequests.[244]

Female servants undertook domestic tasks, spun yarn and delivered goods to customers.[245] Under the guidance of the mistress of the household many became accomplished brewsters and acquired skills which enabled them to achieve independence. In later medieval Chester brewing was largely in female hands, as it was in rural and urban communities throughout the country.[246] Élite households brewed on a large scale and the wives were actively involved. Victims of the millers' extortions in the malt mills were usually female and the plaintiffs named in the court records were typically the wives of the serving sheriffs and of aldermen. Alice Dewe worked as a servant in a wealthy household in the early 1430s. She was first recorded in 1428 owing 2s for red cloth and by 1436 she had branched out on her own and was thereafter described as a tapster. She pursued this trade for some 20 years, buying ale in small quantities from leading townsmen and operating from a cellar for at least some of the time. She never married and was often in debt but nevertheless succeeded in earning a living for two decades.[247]

Married women enjoyed greater security and status but did not lead a life of leisure. In addition to their household tasks and looking after the children they brewed on an occasional basis and sold the surplus, purchased and delivered goods, wove woollen and linen cloth, and made garlands, candles and pins.[248] They worked as kempsters, spinsters, threadmakers, seamstresses, laundresses, midwives and nurses, typical female activities also carried out by single women and widows.[249] Matilda nurse of Richard Erneys was recorded in 1335, five years after he had last held the mayoralty, and perhaps cared for him in his old age. Infants also required care. In 1486 one wife agreed to act as wet nurse to the infant son of the goldsmith Stephen Warmingham for a year, for which she was to be paid 16s.[250] Generations of laundresses washed clothes in the river. Alice the launder was attacked 'at Dee' by a millward's son on Whitsunday 1306; in 1486 a civic ordinance forbade the washing of clothes from Dee bridge to the 'hyngyng stones'.[251] Some women carried out labouring tasks in a man's world. Among the workforce repairing castle buildings and the causeway in the 1420s were husband and wife Nicholas and Alice Gifford. He quarried stone and daubed walls for 3d a day and she carried water, sand and straw for 2d or 3d a day. With two other married women she carried moss from Eccleston wood, a round trip of some four miles for which she was paid a 1d per load.[252]

Some women earned money by keeping a brothel or working as prostitutes. Although the authorities strongly disapproved of these activities they did not banish prostitutes from the city but instead imposed fines on the offenders. All 25 brothel-keepers named in November 1457 were female and included 20 single women, four wives and a servant. In January 1463 again all 13 brothel-keepers were female, three of them wives and the rest single women.[253] From the later 1460s townsmen were presented for keeping brothels, including parchment-maker John Strongbow. Among those who received immoral women in their homes and cellars in 1474 was the alderman John Cottingham.[254] Brothels were run by husband and wife, by a man and his concubine, by mother and daughter, by sisters, and by widows.[255] Some brothel-keepers remained in business for several years. Cecily Abraham, a Bridge Street householder who paid the local tax in 1463, was recorded from 1455 until 1467, as was Emma Bulhalgh.

Cecily Abraham and Emma Bulhalgh were each fined 3s 4d for brothel-keeping in 1463 and Marion of Man was fined 6s 8d, perhaps a reflection of the scale of their activities. In later years fines ranged from 4d to 6s 8d and most offenders paid 1s or 2s.[256] As the same names appeared year after year it seems that the authorities were in effect licensing brothel-keepers to operate. Among them were women who also sold bread and ale, and for them prostitution and brothel-keeping may have been a means of supplementing their income. A list of brothel-keepers in 1476 named two in Eastgate Street, two in Northgate Street, nine in Bridge Street, and 18 in Watergate Street.[257] Prostitution was evidently a characteristic feature of the Watergate Street area, where prostitutes could be found in small cottages tucked away in the side streets, especially in Greyfriars Lane, Blackfriars Lane and Nuns Lane. Among them were many immigrants, including Agnes Irish, Emmota Trim, the wife of Candy Morris, and the daughters of Gruff Truthyn and Hoell ap Res.[258] The city authorities perhaps tolerated the activities of prostitutes in marginal areas until the 1490s, when attitudes evidently hardened. Brothel-keepers were now accused of receiving the servants and apprentices of 'upright' townsmen and encouraging them to amuse themselves both night and day. In the early sixteenth century fines of 6s 8d became standard and some women were imprisoned until they found sufficient security.[259]

CHAPTER EIGHT

The Wider World

....

In the later medieval period Chester's economy depended not only on its position as a centre of craft manufacture but also on its position as a market with an extensive hinterland, a trading centre which attracted merchants from other English regions, and a port with contacts around the Irish Sea.

Chester had been at the hub of important routeways since the Roman period and the Gough map of *c.*1360 depicted major roads converging on the city from Caernarfon to the west and from Bristol to the south, the latter continuing to Liverpool via the ferry at Birkenhead.[1] By the fourteenth century the building of bridges on the sites of fords had improved road travel and the road from Chester to London went east over Stamford Bridge via Nantwich and Stone (Staffordshire) to join the major thoroughfare running south from Carlisle. A stretch of road some five miles north-west of Nantwich evidently ran through boggy ground (the site of a ford) and before 1363 had been improved by a stone causeway known as the Wetfield pavement. In 1396 John the armourer left 20s for its repair and 6s 8d for the repair of the bridge at Bridge Trafford on the road to Manchester. Other leading merchants also left money for bridge and road repairs. These bequests counted as acts of charity and were popular with testators, who saw the opportunity to benefit in both this world and the next.[2] Broken bridges added considerably to the cost of journeys, in time and money. In 1372–3, when the bridge over the Weaver at Frodsham was broken for several months, travellers were obliged to cross the river by ferry. A York mercer left £2 for work on Frodsham bridge in 1482, perhaps because he passed that way on business and possibly because of family links with Ince, the nearby village from which he may well have derived his surname.[3]

Road transport was slow but reliable. Main roads did not become impassable in the winter months and heavily laden carts continued to make long journeys. In late November 1394 a local carter agreed to transport merchandise from Chester to London and deliver it by Christmas. This was a journey of some 180 miles, a distance which could be covered in ten days or so and for which he was to be paid 20s, half of it in advance. The six pack-horses hired by the mercer Thomas Cottingham to carry his goods from London to Chester in November 1453 travelled more quickly.[4] Men travelling on horseback averaged between 25 and 35 miles a day and those riding fast on good horses could travel between 35 and 40 miles a day. When Chester's chamberlain William Troutbeck and his entourage rode to London to attend a meeting of the king's council in January

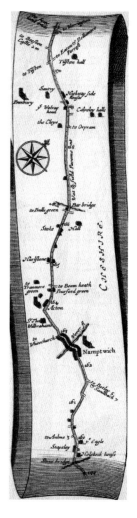

1427 their journey took six days, with overnight stays at Newcastle-under-Lyme, Lichfield, Coventry, Towcester and Dunstable, and breaks for food at Stone, Coleshill, Daventry, Brickhill and St Albans. In March 1426 Troutbeck and his party travelled *c*.85 miles from Chester to Leicester, setting out early on Friday and completing the journey by Sunday evening, with stopovers at Newcastle-under-Lyme and at Burton-upon-Trent and meals at Uttoxeter and Ashby-de-la-Zouch.[5]

It cost about 5d a mile to transport malt from Lichfield to Chester in 1447–8 and 5s 4d to cart two barrels of herring to Coventry in 1489.[6] Packs of merchandise were perhaps charged according to weight and as the carrier was liable for their safe delivery he may have added a sum for 'insurance'. Carts regularly carried four or five packs at a time, each containing goods worth £5 or more. Merchants depended upon carriers and considered them trustworthy, although goods were listed and casks were sealed to prevent interference.[7] Carriers were entrusted with money, and women sometimes travelled as passengers. One townsman paid 2s 6d for his wife's journey from London to Chester in 1434.[8]

Markets and Fairs

In the late medieval period Chester's markets were unrivalled and the city served as the marketing centre for a hinterland which extended well beyond the usual six-mile radius to encompass settlements in north-east Wales. Wednesdays and Saturdays were the market days and country dwellers came with grain, livestock, poultry and dairy produce, returning home with meat, fish, malt and manufactured goods such as metal bowls, pack thread and items of clothing.[9] Shops stocked with high-quality merchandise and imported luxuries were open throughout the week and wealthy consumers came to buy fur-lined gowns and costly silk girdles.[10]

Chester's Midsummer and Michaelmas fairs attracted visitors from further afield. By the 1280s the Midsummer fair extended beyond the original three-day fair centred on the feast of St Werburg's translation (21 June) granted to the abbey in the late eleventh century and lasted a month, focusing on Midsummer Day (24 June), the feast of St John the Baptist.[11] The Michaelmas fair was first recorded in the early thirteenth century but may have been much older. It lasted a fortnight and never matched the Midsummer fair in importance. The arrangements made in 1260–1 to enlarge the trading space in a seld during the Michaelmas fair suggest that these bazaars were in particular demand during fair time.[12] Among the items offered for sale in the late thirteenth and early fourteenth century were woollen cloth, gloves and girdles.[13] Cloth featured prominently among the commodities traded at the Midsummer fair in the fifteenth century: Kendal cloth purchased by a Coventry merchant in 1416 for example, and fine lawns and green, blue and black buckram sold by a Londoner in 1445. Livestock, horses, tanned leather, grain, metal, dyestuffs and spices

FIGURE 8.1. Part of the Cheshire section of the road from London to Holyhead drawn by John Ogilby in 1675. It shows Watfield Pavement between Barbridge and Calveley. Chester's mayor was appointed overseer of repairs to the Watfield Pavement in 1594. Today the Shropshire Union Canal runs alongside this section of the A 51.

were also traded.[14] Merchants from London, Coventry and Yorkshire expected to meet at Chester's Midsummer fair and people from rural communities came to consult skilled medical practitioners. One Brombororough resident left the fair in 1450 owing 10s for 'lechecraft' and a Welshman arrived at the fair in 1463 seeking a cure for his sick wife.[15]

Commodities available at the Michaelmas fair included lambskins, metal, firkins of soap and hedging bills.[16] In the mid 1490s two Welshmen purchased dozens of loaves of bread and another returned home with Holland cloth, linen thread and 120 pairs of hose.[17] September fairs offered the opportunity to buy livestock, including oxen which had come to the end of their lives as plough animals. In 1346 the Black Prince ordered 100 'great fat beasts' to be purchased for his larder at Chester's Michaelmas fair and in 1493 an Aldford man bought bullocks and heifers, paying a Handbridge resident 8d for grazing until he returned home.[18] The great concentration of livestock in the environs of the city attracted cattle thieves. Over 100 animals were taken from Eccleston by men from Whitchurch during the Michaelmas fair in 1458, and 30 oxen from Salghton by two Wrexham men during the fair in 1462.[19]

Hinterland

In *c.*1125 William of Malmesbury described Chester's hinterland as rich in beasts and fish but unproductive of cereals, which had to be imported from Ireland. Ranulph Higden, writing in *c.*1342, declared that the city had abundant supplies of corn, flesh and fish, especially salmon, and that it lay close to sources of salt and metals.[20] Citizens grew corn in the town fields and peasants living in mixed-farming communities in Wirral and in the Dee and Gowy valleys cultivated wheat, barley, oats and rye. These local supplies were always inadequate.[21] There may have been a greater emphasis on animal husbandry after the Black Death and Chester's butchers purchased livestock reared in the hinterland and sheep from the marshland pastures and hill-grazing areas of the Mersey estuary.[22]

Thatching material from the lower Gowy and Ince marshes was used to cover the fair booths at the gate of St Werburgh's abbey in the early thirteenth century and to thatch other buildings in the city in the 1430s.[23] The hinterland was well supplied with brushwood, kindling and gorse, and firewood was carted to Chester from Stapleford, Tattenhall and Tarvin. In 1397 a city baker purchased firewood from a villager living in the appropriately named Gorstylowe ('mound at a gorse-hill').[24] Local woodland was plentiful and Delamere forest was an important source of building timber, used not only for works at the castle and mills but also granted, as a sign of royal favour, to repair the city's churches and religious houses. When the Pentice was rebuilt in 1464 a number of carpenters and sawyers spent several weeks working in the forest at Darnhall and the mayor rode out to organize transport from there and from Kelsall. The bark of oaks felled in the forest was sold to the city's tanners and corvisers.[25]

Timber and brushwood also came from the royal park at Shotwick, some four miles north-west of Chester on the banks of the Dee. Dry wood and the crop and lop of trees could be sold, with the agreement of the master carpenter, as too could turf and gorse from the heath. The park-keeper complained in 1408 that a baker from Foregate Street had 'hewyn and away led' six cartloads of gorse without payment.[26] A townsman purchased all the underwood and crop from Libb wood next to Shotwick church in 1454–5, agreeing to 'hewe to earth all the cokyn stubbs' growing there for three years. Three citizens paid over £3 in 1457–8 for the crop, lop and stubs of trees cut down that year in Shotwick park and Saughall wood.[27] Other profits came from the 'cokshotes', places in woodland across which nets could be stretched and into which wild fowl could be driven. Seventeen 'cokshotes' were leased in 1407–8, for 6d apiece. Further revenues came from the sale of licences to fish from the shore and from the fish-yards and flood-yards, including one next to the castle.[28] Fisheries lined the Wirral shoreline. Those at Blacon and Saughall were among several recorded in Domesday Book; John Whitmore's property in 1437–8 included six fisheries at Caldy and a fishery at Ness in 1479–80 was called 'Friday'.[29] There were more fisheries along the northern and eastern shorelines.[30]

Chester's economic hinterland encompassed part of north-east Wales, extending as far as Denbigh to the west and Wrexham to the south-west. Although those towns had markets, as did smaller places like Flint, Holywell, Hope and Overton, the Welsh regularly travelled to Chester to buy ale, wine, fish, iron, shearing shears, woollen cloth and dyestuffs.[31] Wales had long been a major source of livestock and the names of fifteenth-century butchers, including Flint, Northop, Hawarden, Mancot and Hope, suggest that these men had Welsh roots.[32] Aldford and Pulford were regularly mentioned in connection with livestock and some drovers evidently approached Chester from the south, possibly heading towards grazing land in Christleton and Eccleston.[33] Cattle at Christleton (some belonging to William Troutbeck) were stolen by Yorkshire and Nottinghamshire butchers in 1431, and an ox and five cows belonging to Elias ap Dio were taken from a field in Eccleston by a city butcher in 1474.[34] Welsh villagers also supplied Chester's bakers with the 'meately good corne' of Flintshire and Denbighshire.[35]

In the late thirteenth and early fourteenth century timbers, planks and shingles for castle repairs were prepared in the woods at Hope and at Lightwood in Overton close to the Dee and taken to Chester by boat.[36] Welshmen purchased licences to bring timber to the city to sell.[37] Coal was mined at Ewloe and Buckley in Flintshire by the early fourteenth century and the mines were farmed by prominent citizens, including David of Ewloe in 1378–9 and his son John in 1396–7.[38] Coal was carted to Chester by men living in settlements along the route, including Hawarden, Saltneyside and Handbridge, and the iron-bound cartwheels posed an on-going threat to Dee bridge.[39] Purchasers included the city's smiths, bellmakers, heusters and saddlers, who required it for industrial rather than domestic use.[40] Coal was used in the castle and the

FIGURE 8.2. Ridge and furrow at Saughall, Wirral. In the medieval period Saughall was a manor of St Werburgh's abbey.

friaries, and in 1474–5 the leavelookers' purchased several sacks of coal, costing 5d a sack. They also purchased six sacks of charcoal, costing 6d a sack. Wood charcoal was used for braziers in rooms without fireplaces and for cooking.[41] In 1487 the founder Roger Tailor accused a carter of failing to deliver 80 quarters of charcoal, priced at 16d a quarter. Coal cost 2s a cartload in 1503, double the cost of a cartload of firewood.[42]

Iron was mined at Ewloe and smelted at Hopedale in the medieval period. In 1301–2 a carter was paid 3d for bringing 21 pieces of iron from Ewloe to Chester castle; iron from the forest of Rusty was used at the castle in 1378–9. The iron used by the city's smiths, when specified, was always Spanish iron.[43] Lead had been mined at Halkyn (Flintshire) in the Roman period and there was an active lead-mining industry in north-east Wales from the time of the Edwardian conquest. The miners at Holywell made an annual payment of 20s for their privileges, which they claimed dated back to that conquest. Numerous shafts survive to the south and south-west of the town.[44] William (III) of Doncaster purchased lead from the mines of Englefield in the first decade of the fourteenth century, paying 3s per load of lead and 4d per dish. By 1311 he was leasing the mines and selling lead for roofing work at Chester castle.[45] The mines were leased by the vintner John Hall in 1402–3 but were in rebel hands in the years 1403–5. Hall leased them again in 1406, evidently considering them a profitable investment.[46] In 1302–3 an attempt was made to mine copper at Dyserth in Englefield and experienced miners were brought over from Germany and from Ashbourne in Derbyshire. As the value of the ore failed to cover the cost of their wages the men were quickly dismissed.[47]

Salt was a vital commodity, needed to flavour food, make cheese, preserve fish and meat, and prepare animal hides. The Cheshire salt towns lay within easy distance of Chester and the list of tolls taken at the Eastgate in 1321 began with those levied on cartloads of salt. Two official measurers of salt were appointed in 1398–9 (one of them John Hall) and this may have been standard practice.[48] Two salters paid for permission to trade in Eastgate Street in 1410, one of them becoming a freeman a few years later. His kinsman David Dewe of Nantwich became a freeman in 1420.[49] Dewe owned a ship and regularly crossed to Ireland, returning with animal hides and herring. Other Nantwich traders exported salt and imported fish and hides at that time.[50] Men from Northwich were less active but one sold salt to a city fishmonger in 1420 and another was named in 1490.[51]

There was considerable demand for salt in the city, especially from local tanners, fishmongers and cooks. One townsman purchased three barrels and a pipe of salt costing 20s at Martinmas 1490, and 13 non-citizens were presented for selling salt in the market in November 1497. That month may have seen particular demand because the feast of St Martin (11 November) was the traditional date for slaughtering animals that were not to be kept over the winter. The Shoemakers claimed that only guild members could purchase fresh skins from then until the feast of St Andrew (30 November).[52]

FIGURE 8.3. The Nantwich 'salt ship'. This medieval cistern for storing brine was excavated in 2003. Analysis of the wood has revealed that the tree from which the 'ship' was hollowed out was felled between 1246 and 1282. The 'ship' has been conserved and is now on display in Nantwich Museum.

Contacts with English regions

Large numbers of merchants from other parts of England travelled to Chester in the later medieval period, many of them *en route* for Ireland. They came from as far away as Kendal to the north, York and Hull to the east, Worcester and Bristol to the south and, in particular, from Coventry and London.

Chester had close links with neighbouring Lancashire, and surnames reveal that many city families originated in towns and villages north of the Mersey, including Hale, Rainford, Blackrod, Strangeways, Eccles, Rochdale and Northenden. Newcomers from Lancashire became freemen in 1393 and 1410.[53] In the fifteenth century the Lancastrian traders recorded in Chester were almost invariably on their way to Ireland. A few came from Preston and Salford but most were from Manchester. The commodities they exported were rarely described but certainly included woollen cloth.[54] A Lancashire man sold russet cloth in Chester in October 1432, possibly during the Michaelmas fair.[55] The ferry at Birkenhead, perhaps already in existence when the priory was founded in the later twelfth century, linked Chester and Liverpool, and facilities improved in the early fourteenth century when the monks were granted leave to build lodgings to accommodate travellers and to sell food.[56] Merchants established business contacts and families intermarried.[57] Liverpool's emergence as a serious rival to Chester in the Anglo-Irish trade was already apparent by the later fifteenth century. In the 1460s one or two merchants disembarked from Ireland at Liverpool and by the 1490s many Irish goods were shipped through the port.[58]

In the late ninth century Chester had benefited from its location near a direct route linking Dublin and York and the city served as a staging post for men travelling from Yorkshire to Ireland in the later medieval period. Having crossed the Pennines Yorkshire traders journeyed to Chester either via Manchester, Salford, Warrington and Frodsham, or followed a more southerly route through Tintwistle, Stockport, Northwich and Stamford Bridge. In the early fifteenth century the majority came from York or Sheffield. York had a reputation for bows and Sheffield already specialized in the manufacture of edged tools, including arrowheads. Demand for weapons was high, in Chester because of Glyn Dŵr's rebellion and in Ireland because of the serious threat to the English colony there.[59] Bowyers from York supplied the castle garrisons at Chester and north Wales with bows, charging 6s a dozen in 1401–2 and 7s a dozen in 1403–4; John del Smythy of Sheffield supplied all the arrowheads, charging 1s per hundred.[60] York bowyers continued to embark for Ireland in the following decades; seven set sail together in *c*.1420, accompanied by a bowyer from Hull. One York bowyer became a freeman of Chester in 1420 and a maker of arrowheads from Sheffield paid for permission to trade in the city in 1431–2. Yorkshire bowyers were recorded in Chester until the mid fifteenth century.[61]

In 1406 a York mercer sold madder and grain to a Chester heuster and four years later a York merchant sailed to Ireland with a quantity of woad.[62] In later years the trade in dyestuffs was replaced by the trade in fine woollens from the West Riding, already a centre of cloth manufacture in 1379. Merchants from Pontefract, Halifax and Bradford regularly passed through Chester in the later fifteenth century, sometimes without paying custom or tolls. Brian Wilkinson of Bradford, for example, arrived in the city on 30 October 1476 with four packs of coloured woollen cloth worth £60 and sailed to Ireland on the *Trinity of Dublin* two weeks later, having failed to pay custom.[63] Chester's drapers developed trading links with Yorkshire merchants. One employed a fellow townsman to act for him in York in 1451 and another served as pledge for a Halifax clothman in 1503. The draper Thomas Hurleton junior set out on a journey to Yorkshire in the early 1480s but was murdered at Lostock Gralam just beyond Northwich.[64] Yorkshire traders perhaps obtained animal skins in Ireland. When two were wrongfully imprisoned by Chester's sheriffs in 1445 a local barker acted as their pledge; Robert Skinner of York was named the same year in a court case involving furs and skins.[65]

Traders from Shropshire, Herefordshire, north Worcestershire, Warwickshire and Staffordshire came to Chester primarily to buy fish. Regular traders paid an annual fine for exemption from tolls and were listed in the official records under the heading *piscatores de patria*. As many as 18 or 19 were named each year in the earlier fifteenth century and a dozen or so towards its close.[66] They came from Evesham, Pershore and Worcester; from Ludlow, Shrewsbury and Wellington; from Stafford, Walsall and Wolverhampton.[67] Carts laden with barrels of herring and eels regularly travelled to Lichfield, Stafford and Coventry.[68]

These traders brought specialities of their own region to sell: knives, hilts and pommels from Shrewsbury; metal horse-trappings from Walsall and Newcastle-under-Lyme; fruit and wood-ash from Worcestershire.[69] Many roads near Walsall and Wolverhampton were named Chester Road, indicating the importance of the trading route. A plum stone found in a pit at the rear of 12 Watergate Street in 1985 resembled a semi-wild plum grown from suckers in an old orchard in Worcestershire and may be a relic of medieval trade.[70]

Coventry was the regional capital of the Midlands in the late medieval period and ranked second only to London in the urban hierarchy of the north-western plain. It lay at the hub of the regional communications network some 90 miles from Chester and the roads between the two cities were busy with traffic throughout the year. Coventry merchants did considerable business in Chester. They came with cloth, dyestuffs, spices and sweet Mediterranean wines; they purchased horses and kendal cloth.[71] They loaned money, pursued debtors, and established strong trading links with the wealthiest Cestrians. When a Coventry mercer became a freeman of Chester in 1418 Thomas Cottingham was one of two mercers who acted as pledges.[72] Chester's élite citizens and their wives joined Coventry's Trinity Guild.[73]

Many Coventry traders carried their cloth and dyestuffs through Chester and embarked for Ireland. Some made regular journeys. William Fifield passed through the city five times between March 1397 and April 1398, with one, two or three carts of merchandise, failing to pay custom and tolls on each occasion.[74] In the early fifteenth century Coventry traders formed a sizeable percentage of those who travelled to and from Ireland and among them were men who were prominent in their native city, serving as bailiff or mayor.[75] Coventry merchants continued to ship woollens and dyestuffs to Ireland in later decades, their return cargoes consisting of salmon, eels, herring, sheepskins and hides. Several became freemen of Dublin and some married and settled there. Their numbers dwindled towards the end of the century and fell away in the early sixteenth century, a reflection perhaps of economic difficulties in their own city.[76]

By the later medieval period London's commercial dominance over the provinces was firmly established and the city was the primary distributive centre for inland trade. The communications system centred on the capital and its merchants developed trading contacts with towns and cities throughout the land.[77] Londoners who travelled to Chester were often *en route* for Ireland to buy raw materials, especially animal skins.[78] Some traded over long periods. The grocer Robert Smithfield was recorded in Chester in 1457, when he failed to pay customs and tolls on Mediterranean wines and dyestuffs, and in 1465 when he was assaulted by four local merchants and thrown out of the city.[79] James Wells was named in the customs records from 1462 until 1485, and in some years ships carrying his merchandise entered port every four to six weeks.[80] In 1474–5 he became a member of Chester's guild merchant, by then a body of non-resident traders, and in 1480–1 he was master of the guild of English merchants based in Dublin. He was possibly a descendant of London grocer John Wells.[81]

London grocers sold dyestuffs, paper, figs and raisins in Chester, and its mercers supplied fine linens and costly silks.[82] London mercer Hugh Wych, recorded in Chester in 1448 attempting to recover money owed for lawn, fustian and buckram, did so much business in the city that he appointed an attorney to represent him in the local courts. In 1455, with two Cestrian mercers, he rented a property with a cellar and two shops in Bridge Street.[83] Wych was born in Nantwich and had relatives there and it may well have been these links which brought him to Chester on such a regular basis. London grocer William Wettenhall and the mercer Ralph Verney, both of whom traded in Chester in the 1450s, also had Cheshire connections.[84] A London merchant occupied a house in Bridge Street in the 1470s, paying 16d a year for two shops newly-built at the door.[85] London merchandise was evidently considered superior. The mayor's new table was made there in 1463, as was the silk cope of tawny velvet bequeathed to St Peter's in 1506. Alexander Stanney stocked London pins (valued at 10s per 1,000) in the 1470s. The capital had its own attractions. When a Chester slater sent a man to London to bring his daughter back home the girl refused to come.[86]

It was common practice for ambitious merchants from provincial towns to establish branches of their business in London and the Cottinghams were perhaps among them. Thomas Cottingham, recorded in Chester in the late fourteenth century and sheriff in 1406–7, traded in mercery wares and animal hides.[87] His descendants John, mayor in 1455–7, and Thomas, mayor in 1470–1, were wealthy mercers. Members of the London branch of the family, also named John and Thomas, travelled to and from Ireland in the years 1420–*c.*1448.[88] A younger Thomas Cottingham was making similar journeys by the 1450s.[89] John Cottingham of Chester wrote to his namesake and 'well bylovet cosyn' in London in that decade, informing him that he had heard from the last vessel that Thomas fared well and that 'great gentleness' was being shown to the Londoner in the matter of murage.[90] Influential contacts were highly advantageous.

The port and overseas trade

The importance of sea-borne trade to Chester's economy in the eleventh century is revealed by the entry in Domesday Book, with its unusual details of ships entering and leaving the port and of the tolls levied on their loads. In *c.*1195 Lucian noted that ships from Aquitaine, Spain, Ireland and Germany unloaded their cargoes at the harbour on the south side of Chester, and he praised the merchants whose labour and skill brought plentiful supplies of wine and other goods to the city.[91] Later in the medieval period the harbour shifted to the western side of the city and the waterfront extended north from the Watergate. In 1322 the New Tower was built to protect the harbour and the great rings of iron fastened to the walls which served to attach vessels 'of great burden' remained in place in the later sixteenth century.[92] By then, however, the river had long since receded and the tower stood on dry land.

It seems that the Dee was particularly prone to silting at what had once been the head of the estuary, a process to which the construction of the weir in the Norman period perhaps contributed. Before 1296 a second anchorage was established a short way downstream, on the north-western boundary of the city's liberties. Known as the Portpool, it was described by Leland in the late 1530s as a dock within two bowshots of the northern suburb where a ship could lie at spring tide.[93] Chester's control of the whole of the estuary enabled the city to establish additional anchorages beyond the liberties. The citizens' rights and privileges were first recorded in the charter of 1354 and confirmed in the charter of 1506: they were allowed to levy tolls, customs and dues on imports and make attachments for offences committed in ships in the Water of Dee between Heronbridge (on the boundary of the liberties upstream from the city) and Arnold's Eye near Hilbre at the north-west tip of Wirral.[94] The additional anchorages were at Shotwick, Burton and Denhall (probably two ends of the same anchorage), Neston, Gayton, Heswall and Redbank in Thurstaston. The Portpool Way, which led from the northern suburb to the anchorages, became increasingly important in the later medieval period.

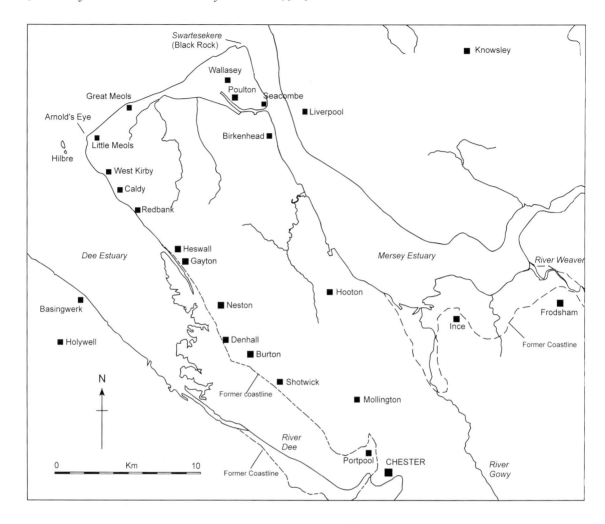

FIGURE 8.4. Map showing the former coastline and the medieval outports.

In 1361 the citizens claimed that they lived by trade, sometimes in foreign parts, and when they petitioned for a reduction of their fee-farm payment in the later fifteenth century they put forward the decay of the harbour as a prime cause of their poverty. They described how in the past Chester derived much of its prosperity from the crowds of foreign traders who landed with their merchandise at the Watergate, and how the river channel had subsequently been blocked by the influx of gravel and sand, preventing merchant ships from approaching within twelve miles of the city. They were uncertain how long ago this destruction had occurred, citing 40 years in 1445, 60 years in 1484, and 200 years in 1486 when they also claimed that traders were using other ports and places in the same district (*patria*) where they could unload and reload their goods more easily.[95] The third statement was the most accurate. Ships carrying wine were already using anchorages some twelve miles down the estuary in the early fourteenth century. A Dartmouth vessel anchored at Heswall in November

1302 and William (III) of Doncaster's ship, the *Holirode Cog*, anchored at Redbank in July 1319. Both places were equipped with windlasses. The cost of 'wyndage' in 1302 was 2d per cask and the cost of transport by boat from the park near Heswall to the city was 8d per cask.[96] In the years 1353–1492 ships carrying wine and iron almost invariably anchored at Redbank, and from the mid 1490s at Burton and Denhall.[97] The shift was perhaps due to the growing involvement of Chester's merchants in overseas trade and their preference for anchorages closer to the city. An alternative explanation is that Redbank, in a more exposed position near the mouth of the estuary, had been affected by the 'vehement inflow' of the sea mentioned in the petition of 1486. The choice of outports depended upon the 'skittering' sands of the Dee, an unpredictable river with a constantly shifting channel.[98]

The trade with Ireland and the coastal trade were the mainstays of Chester's port. Receipts from 'small tolls and custom of ships and boats' were listed among the city's revenues in 1274–80 and by 1319 included payments by alien merchants for herring, salmon and eels. In *c*.1400 the city claimed custom of every ship entering the liberties loaded with wine, herrings, fish, salmon, corn or any other merchandise at the rate of 4d per tun of wine or cartload of merchandise and 1d per horseload.[99] The surviving customs accounts, the earliest dating from 1398–9, are fragmentary but indicate that until the 1480s it was unusual for more than 40 vessels to arrive in any one year. Numbers then increased; 48 were recorded in 1497–8, 60 in 1500–1, and 56 in 1525–6.[100] Some of the vessels were very small. A 'letell bote of Man' entered port in 1451–2 carrying the goods of just one individual; the 'skaf' and the 'spinas' of Man arrived a few years later. The *Andrew* in contrast, commandeered at Redbank in August 1460, was crewed by a master and 37 mariners. In 1467 the master and twelve mariners of the *Margaret of Chester* swore on oath in St Peter's that the goods on board their ship had not been damaged by a leak or by their negligence but by the grace of God.[101]

Ships involved in the Irish and coastal trade routinely anchored at Denhall and Burton. A series of what were thought to be medieval quays across the mouth of the inlet, presumably used for offloading goods, were revealed during a survey at the site of the medieval hospital at Denhall in 1999.[102] Customs officers were based at Denhall in the early fourteenth century and in 1406 the bailiff-errant confronted two Conwy chapmen at Burton and arrested their boat, together with the leather points, knives, cards and yarn found on board. A large group of merchants from Dublin, Trim, Drogheda, Bradford, Manchester, Wigan and Stockport plotted a currency fraud at Burton in October 1475.[103] The cost of shipping nine barrels of fish from Drogheda to Burton in 1485 was 9d per barrel; carriage from Burton to Chester was 2d per barrel, and 9d was charged for watching over the barrels for three nights.[104]

In 1493 a ship-owner claimed that a city baker owed him £2 for freighting herring from the Isle of Man to Chester. A decade later the cost of freighting a ship from Beaumaris to the Isle of Man was 13s 4d, and from Chester to Conwy and back again cost double that amount. Two anchors detained by a mariner at Portpool in 1506 were valued at £3 6s 8d and two cable ropes 18 fathoms in length were worth ten marks.[105] Crews included pursers, pilots and 'berthmen'.[106] One man agreed in 1451 to serve as a boatman for a year for 13s 4d but many men were engaged on a one-voyage basis: from Chester to Mathafarn and the Isle of Man in 1456, from Chester with wine to Penwortham near Preston in 1493, and from Chester to Bordeaux and back in 1505.[107] The cooper Hugh Lake who made at least four journeys to Ireland in 1500–1, and the cooper who agreed to serve on a voyage to Ireland in 1502, were perhaps employed to make the barrels of herring tight.[108]

Sea voyages were always hazardous. Welsh rebels posed a particular threat in 1402–3 and when the *Mary of Malahide* was commandeered to take victuals from Caernarfon to Harlech a 'lodesman' (guide) was hired because the passage was dangerous and the master a foreigner. Voyages along the coast and across the Irish Sea were also perilous in peacetime. A ship's equipment in 1490 included a compass, a 'loterope', oars, resin, oakum, caulking irons and 4 lbs of gunpowder. The archbishop of Armagh wrote to Wolsey in June 1514 informing him that the Chester ship he had hired with ordnance and men of war to keep the coast safe had a fight with two Breton pirate ships near Dublin.[109]

Ireland

Early writers emphasized the significance of Chester's connections with Ireland. In *c.*1125 William of Malmesbury noted that goods were exchanged between the two places and that the cereals which could not be grown locally were supplied by the toil of the merchants. At the end of the twelfth century Lucian described Chester's harbours as holding the key of Ireland and Robert of Gloucester in *c.*1300 considered the city's location 'against Ireland' a distinctive feature.[110] Ireland remained Chester's principal overseas trading partner throughout the later medieval period. The ports named most often in the customs records were Dublin, Howth, Malahide, Rush and Drogheda within the Pale, and Carrickfergus in Ulster.

Corn was imported from Ireland in the twelfth century and the island remained a major source of grain until the 1320s.[111] Some Irish corn was shipped to Chester in the later fourteenth and early fifteenth century; Irish traders continued to arrive with crannocks and 'weys' of wheat until the 1420s.[112] Bristol was shipping corn to Ireland by 1437 and the island's supplies were perhaps running short. Exports were banned in 1472.[113]

Animal pelts, and marten in particular, were imported from Ireland in the eleventh century and remained among the island's chief products throughout the later medieval period. The list of Irish products included in a poem written in 1436 began with hides and continued with skins of marten, deer, otter, fox, squirrel, hare, rabbit, sheep and lamb, all said to be plentiful.[114] Cestrians purchased lambskins at Carrickfergus fair and rabbit-skins at Drogheda in the early fourteenth century. Dublin skinners supplied Chester's skinners in the fifteenth century.[115] Irish hides, although not considered to be of the highest quality, were nevertheless in demand. Regular shipments reached Chester in the fifteenth century, some to be sold in the city and some destined for Coventry and other inland markets.

It has been suggested that fish had perhaps become the major Irish export by the late fourteenth century.[116] Salmon, hake and herring were listed immediately after animal skins in the poem of 1436. The Irish Sea fishery was closely linked to Dublin and the Pale and large quantities of white (salted) herring and red (smoked) herring were shipped to Chester from ports along that stretch of coastline, mainly between September and March and peaking during the six weeks of Lent.[117] The salmon trade was well established by the late fourteenth century.[118] Some of it was in the hands of Drogheda merchants, among them one who in 1477 described his role in the bitter dispute involving five butts of salmon delivered to William Stanmere at Chester and subsequently sold in Shrewsbury.[119] Traders from Carrickfergus were also involved in the salmon trade, perhaps handling supplies from the Bann fisheries and preserving some salmon by salting it.[120] The Corbet family, who leased the Bann fishery in the early sixteenth century, already dealt with men from Carrickfergus in the mid 1490s.[121]

Chester obtained cloth from Ireland in the late thirteenth and early fourteenth century, much of it coarse woollens such as friezes and serges. Irish cloth was sold at Chester's Michaelmas fair in 1297 and in 1335.[122] Woollen and linen cloth and falding were listed among the island's chief products in 1436. Heavy woollen mantles were also produced, allegedly so voluminous that they could be used as a bed or even a tent.[123] In 1475 the prior of Dublin's Black Friars and a Chester saddler disputed the ownership of a pack containing 250 yards of black and white Irish frieze wrapped in two Irish blankets. Many packs and bundles shipped from Ireland to Chester would have contained similar merchandise.[124] A flourishing linen industry developed in Ireland during the fifteenth century and Irish linen was brought to Chester. Some must have been sold in the city although no direct evidence has been found.[125]

Ireland lacked the salt needed for the trade in hides and fish and may have imported this vital commodity from Chester as early as the mid tenth century. Traders from Drogheda, Malahide and Rush regularly crossed the Irish Sea in the early fifteenth century bringing red herring, white fish and salmon to Chester and returning to Ireland with considerable quantities of salt.[126] Nantwich residents participated in the trade, among them Thomas Wervin and David Dewe who both became freemen of Chester.[127] David Dewe was first recorded in *c*.1410 and soon had a ship of his own; he regularly exported salt to Ireland and brought back herring, hides and wine. His widow married a Malahide merchant with whom he had trading links.[128] Cheshire salt was shipped to the east coast of Ireland until *c*.1450 when it was replaced by salt from the continent, in particular from the bay of Bourgneuf in Brittany.[129]

Merchants from London, York, Coventry, Shrewsbury and other midland towns regularly passed through Chester with fine woollen cloth, Mediterranean wines, dyestuffs, haberdashery, bows, knives, cards and combs destined for Ireland.[130] Irish merchants also traded through Chester, some of them making such frequent visits that they found it advantageous to join the city's guild merchant, perhaps already an organization of non-resident traders by the 1430s. At least six of the 17 new entrants in 1474 came from Dublin and a seventh came from Drogheda. Each paid 18d for 'chapman's guild' and the goods they brought from Ireland included herring, hides and linen cloth.[131] Links with Drogheda were particularly strong. When William Preston of Drogheda became a freeman of Chester in 1419 his pledge was John Hatton of Watergate Street, whose ship regularly crossed the Irish Sea and whom he doubtless knew through trade. John Symcock of Drogheda, participant in an infamous journey to Iceland in 1457 which left a colleague stranded, was described as 'formerly of Chester' when indicted in the county court in 1461.[132] Robert Nottervill, Chester's mayor in 1478–9, had twice served as mayor of the Irish town.[133]

Anglesey, the Isle of Man and northern England

Among the 26 'havens, bays, creeks and rodes' of Anglesey recorded in the seventeenth century were the haven of Beaumaris and the 'creek of Dulas and the enterynge there'.[134] Vessels from the two ports regularly sailed to Chester in the later medieval period. Beaumaris became the principal port not only of the island but also of Gwynedd by the end of the thirteenth century, within a few years of the town's foundation. Welsh frieze, cloth and wool were exported from Anglesey to Chester and imports included iron, steel, hardware, felt caps and almonds.[135] The herring fishery at nearby Llanfaes and the one at Ynys Dulas probably accounted for much trade with Chester, although the most profitable fisheries were on the north-west coast around the Skerries.[136] Thomas Overton of Beaumaris married a daughter of one of Chester's leading fishmongers before 1453–4 and other city fishmongers had trading links with men from Anglesey.[137] Thomas Sherwin, employed to manage a small brewing enterprise in Chester in 1445 but failing to account for his administration, had moved to Beaumaris by 1448 and leased the fishery near Llanfaes friary for 20 years at 6d per annum. *Sherwins bote* entered Chester's port in 1450–1 and the following year he was named as master of the *Michael of Beaumaris*. He was described as a boatman in 1455–6 when he was paid 16s 8d for shipping four pairs of millstones to the Watergate.[138]

Millstones were Anglesey's most important product and the best came from the limestone quarries at Mathafarn and Penmon in the east. They were routinely purchased for the Dee mills and shipped to Chester at considerable expense. In 1350–1 three pairs of millstones cost 26s 9d and their carriage by sea cost 22s. In 1384–5 the cost of six pairs of millstones produced in the quarry of 'castelbulghwyn', their transport overland to the port of Mathafarn, and their shipment to Chester exceeded £10.[139] A Welshman agreed to carry a pipe of herring from Mathafarn to Chester in September 1454 (but destroyed it through negligence); in September 1457 Patrick Helsby agreed to serve Richard MacCally on a voyage from Chester to Mathafarn and Man (but left without permission).[140]

The Isle of Man occupied a strategic location in the Irish Sea region and finds of jewellery and pins at Chester indicate contact between the city and the island in the tenth century.[141] By the later medieval period a regular trading route evidently ran from Chester to Conwy and along the eastern coast of Anglesey to the island. In 1502 the *Michael* of Dulas was freighted to sail from the port of Chester to Conwy (55s), from Conwy to Chester (26s), and from Beaumaris to the Isle of Man (13s 4d).[142] Fish was imported from the island and Manxmen settled in the city. John the armourer, seven times mayor in the 1380s and 1390s, had kin living in Man and perhaps originated there. His ship was named *St Mary bote de Pull*, probably Wallasey Pool near the north-eastern tip of Wirral, a place linked with the herring trade and destined to become a significant centre for fishing.[143] Sir John Stanley of Lathom (Lancashire) was granted the lordship of Man with its crown in 1406 and this perhaps encouraged the development of trade. Both he and his son had trading interests and in April 1414 the *Mary of Man*, owned by the younger Sir John, entered Chester's port.[144] Relatively few Manx ships visited Chester in the early fifteenth century but they were arriving on a regular basis by the 1450s and activity increased in the following decades. The home port, when specified, was usually Castletown but ships from Douglas, Ronaldsway, Holmeton and Rushen were also named. The Stanley involvement continued. The *Mary* of Stanley was recorded in the 1460s and in 1492–3 Lord Stanley, created earl of Derby in 1485, sailed to Chester on the *Mary of Castletown*. Robert Corbet was master of the vessel.[145]

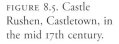

FIGURE 8.5. Castle Rushen, Castletown, in the mid 17th century.

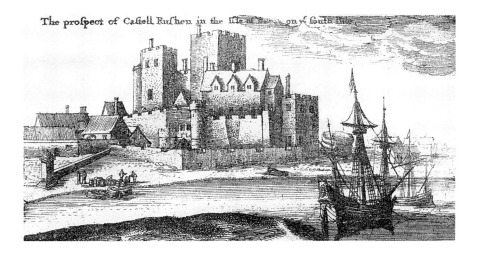

Chester's fishmongers had links with Manx traders by the 1490s and in 1501 the customs entries recorded the arrival of barrels of herring and salmon from the island. Manx herring sold in Chester was invariably white and had been prepared by salting, by this date with salt from Brittany. The 'black' cloth of Man sold in Chester in 1460 was perhaps typical of the coarse woollen cloth exported from the island.[146] There is no direct evidence for exports from Chester to the Isle of Man but the occasional references to city mercers, drapers, tailors, glovers and locksmiths trading with the island in the later fifteenth century suggest that woollen and linen cloth and other manufactured goods were in demand.[147]

From the 1490s ships based in ports as far north as Furness, St Bees and Harrington in Cumberland were named in Chester's customs records. Among them was the *St Bees* which arrived with a cargo of 800 mudfish in 1501.[148] The *Antony de Ayer de Partibus Scotie* (Ayr in Scotland) entered Chester's port on 17 February and 12 March 1499. The master was Laurence Dalrimple/de le Rumpe, possibly kin to John de Rumpyll who preyed on ships venturing to Ulster in the 1480s. John commanded two Scottish ships which captured a vessel from Minehead in Somerset in 1482 and demanded ransom for its release.[149]

Continental trade

Gascon wine was shipped from Bordeaux to Chester in the later thirteenth and early fourteenth century, some of it in ships owned by prominent citizens, and green-glazed Saintonge pottery formed part of the cargoes. International trade was disrupted by the outbreak of the Hundred Years' War in 1337 and by the Black Death in 1348–9 but a number of city merchants were shipping wine in the 1380s, albeit in ships from other ports. The vintner Innocent of Chesterfield imported wine from Bordeaux and Rochelle throughout the 1390s, in ships based at Bristol, Newcastle and Tenby. When the *Magdelene of Tenby* was driven 'by stress of weather' into the port of 'Crowpoll' in Milford in 1395–6, prise was levied on his wine there.[150] Only small quantities of wine were shipped to Chester in the earlier fifteenth century, usually in vessels based in the West Country. Among the wealthy merchants who traded in wine were some who also traded in Spanish iron, shipped to Chester long before the custom of iron

FIGURE 8.6. A Saintonge mottled green-glazed jug dated *c.*1250–1350. It is an import from south-west France and was found during excavations at the Old Market Hall site in Chester.

was imposed in 1464–5. Almost 500 lbs of Spanish iron 'in pieces' was purchased for work on the castles at Chester and Flint in 1377–8, and in the 1390s and early fifteenth century John of Preston and John Hatton, both of whom became mayor, supplied Spanish iron for work at the castle.[151]

The wine trade remained depressed throughout the earlier fifteenth century and was disrupted by the loss of Gascony in 1453. The truce with France ten years later helped to restore trade and a few vessels from Brittany began to arrive. They brought goods such as saffron in addition to wine and their return cargoes included hides and tallow.[152] One or two Spanish ships were recorded in the early 1470s and more came in the 1480s, bringing wine and iron. In 1484 Spanish merchants returned to their home ports on the Bay of Biscay with friezes, kerseys and goat-skins; in May 1494 they left with coloured woollen cloth and calf-skins.[153] The detailed description of imports recorded in the local customs accounts for 1525–6 reveal that in addition to wine and iron Spanish ships carried woad, tar, resin, chamlets, train, wax, cork, cloves, Cordovan skins, sugar, raisins and comfits. French ships brought cargoes of salt, linen cloth, oil, tar, resin, pitch, brasil and paper.[154] Chester-owned ships were always few in number and in 1484 the citizens claimed that for many years their city had no merchant ships of its own. The situation began to change in the late 1490s: three Chester ships were recorded in 1497–8, five in 1503–4, and seven in 1511–12.[155] Many Cestrians nevertheless opted to venture their cargoes in ships based in other ports.

Among the handful of aliens recorded in Chester in the fifteenth century were the shoemaker Janyn frensheman who lived in Foregate Street in the late 1440s and Johanna frenshwoman, perhaps his wife, who was victim of an assault in 1451.[156] Guillaume of Orléans was then languishing as prisoner of Elias Longworth and was subsequently abducted by another man.[157] Several Flemings and men from Brabant were named and one or two Dutchmen, including Godfrey 'upon the North' who passed through Chester *en route* for Ireland three times in 1476–7.[158] The treaty of Medina del Campo in 1489 facilitated trade with the Iberian peninsula and the arrival of these foreign traders produced tensions in the city. A local minstrel was bound over in 1493 to keep the peace towards all the merchants from Spain; a townsman struck a Spanish merchant on the face in 1498; four years later a physician was taken to court for failing to cure someone afflicted with *le Spanyssh pokkes*.[159]

CHAPTER NINE

Education, Medicine and Leisure

Little is known of schooling in medieval Chester. Lucian received his early education at St John's and noted that it was customary for the clergy and choir to visit the adjacent church of St Mary on Sundays and Holy Days. The custom evidently persisted. In 1353 the master and boys of the music and grammar schools at St John's attended services in the chapel dedicated to the Virgin which stood in the churchyard, commonly known as the White chapel. The music school, probably a song school, was not recorded again and the grammar school only once more, in 1368.[1] The prioress kept children at her table in 1358 and this has led to the suggestion that the nuns ran a school. If so, nothing further is heard of it.[2] Larger monasteries admitted secular pupils to be taught in the outer precincts but there is no certain evidence for a school at St Werburgh's before *c.*1530. The nearby abbey at Basingwerk provided schooling for between 30 and 40 local boys in the mid fifteenth century and it would seem likely that Chester abbey also accepted lay pupils. Evidence from other monasteries indicates that they came from wealthy families and lived in the household of the abbot or prior.[3] When Chester's Dominican prior agreed in 1448 to take care of William Hope's young son and provide him with food and clothing, one of his friars perhaps educated the boy.[4]

Levels of literacy in towns were relatively high. In London in the 1460s and 1470s perhaps 50 per cent of laymen could read English and 40 per cent could read Latin. Traders living in smaller towns certainly appreciated the value of literacy and left instructions in their wills for their sons to be kept at school until they could read and write.[5] The master of Ruthin's grammar school was in Chester on the feast of Corpus Christi in 1378. A schoolmaster was recorded at Malpas in 1426 but the town's grammar school was not founded until 1528. Stockport's grammar school was founded in 1488 and those at Macclesfield and Northenden in the early sixteenth century.[6]

The schoolmasters and schoolmistresses recorded in Chester in the fifteenth century probably ran small private schools that offered a mixed elementary education. These schools were sometimes run by scriveners like Bartholomew Norwich, who claimed in 1439 that a Welshman owed him 3s 4d for instruction.[7] Norwich was never named again at Chester and presumably moved on. Henry Mikulhalgh, in contrast, managed to make a living as a schoolmaster for a dozen years or so and served as councilman for Watergate Street from 1475 until 1485.[8] He was perhaps succeeded by Thomas Stafford, first named in 1486 and who was still running a school in 1493, when his wife was fined for running a brothel.[9] The 'skolesmastresse' accused of trespass in *c.*1418 and Isabel scolemaistr[ ] named as a Welshwoman's pledge in 1430 probably taught reading and song to girls and small boys.[10]

In the fifteenth century school fees were about 2d a week in London and 1d a week at Basingwerk.[11] Ralph Peacock charged 20d in 1428 for the schooling of one boy for three quarters of a year at Chester, and a chaplain pursued a debt of 3s for teaching two boys for an unspecified period in 1452. Some 30 years later a young townsman claimed that Margery Patrick owed him 8d for the schooling of her son William. She was not wealthy but evidently hoped that money spent on the child's education would prove a sound investment.[12] School fees were beyond the means of poorer families, many of whom in any case saw no practical benefit in literacy and needed the money their children could earn.

No sources survive which allow us to estimate the levels of literacy in Chester. Proclamations by the town crier brought important matters to public attention but occasionally a written notice was posted, as in 1387 when the charge against Robert de Vere was nailed to the door of St Peter's.[13] The assumption was that people could either read the notice themselves or be standing next to someone who could. Townspeople were well aware of the importance of written records, textual evidence to which reference could be made in the event of a dispute, and the fact that tallies were sometimes used to record debts does not mean that the parties involved were unable to read. Much written evidence was produced in the city's courts and many townspeople used seals in the later medieval period. A triple-towered castle was depicted on the seal of William (III) of Doncaster, and a flower on that of his granddaughter Cecily.[14] A considerable number of townsmen were truly literate, in the sense that they could both read and write. Among them were not only the merchants and the bailiffs who managed the business affairs of leading citizens, but also lesser tradesmen like Richard Bithewall who in 1481 wrote 39 letters of pardon for the warden of the Franciscan friary, charging 1½d for each one.[15]

Townspeople owned devotional books, including psalters, breviaries and missals, and educational books like the grammar book stolen from a mattress-maker in 1487. Other books were read solely for pleasure. One city butcher in 1439 owned a book written in English entitled *Sydrak*, a well-known work that was also available in French.[16] Among Henry Hurleton's collection in 1469 were a mass book, a book of sermons, an English book and a book called *Manavyle*, presumably the *Travels of Sir John Mandeville* written in about 1356 and which remained a bestseller for centuries.[17] The value of a book depended on the binding and the quality of lettering and illumination. Books stolen from St Werburgh's in the early fifteenth century included a medical treatise by Avicenna worth £20, and a bible and a copy of Bartholomew's encyclopedia *De Proprietatibus Rerum* worth £10 apiece.[18] Devotional books owned by townspeople in the fourteenth and fifteenth centuries ranged in value from 6s

8d up to 40s. A book dealing with the glazier's craft and a grammar book were each worth 6s 8d.[19] A Ruthin bookbinder was recorded in Chester in 1493 and a bookbinder lived in the city in 1503. A few years later another bookbinder was in trouble with the authorities for selling books in the city although he was not a freeman.[20] Printed books began to appear in Chester at this time; a 'masse booke of prynt' was bequeathed to the high altar in St Peter's in 1511.[21]

Medicine

The monks who tended their sick brethren in the infirmary at St Werburgh's were probably more skilful than the medical practitioners who worked in the city. Those men were usually styled *medicus* in the earlier fourteenth century and 'leche' from the 1360s onwards.[22] They were able to charge high fees: 10s to cure wounds suffered by the rector of Plemstall and two companions in 1319, and 25s for saving a patient's leg in 1505. They faced legal action if they failed to effect a cure.[23] In a letter from Helsby to his cousin in *c*.1459 Ralph Helsby expressed his dissatisfaction with the medical men who had come to treat an elderly widow. 'I have sente the Chestre leches awaye', he wrote, 'Noe gode could thaie doe butt mayde her sykenesse growe gratelie', and he asked that a message be sent to brother Peter or some other good leche in all haste.[24]

The physicians, usually styled 'Master', were more distinguished. One was recorded in Chester in 1427, a second in 1453, and seven were established there in the 1480s and 1490s, including Master Paules and Master Jakes whose names suggest continental origins.[25] Master Jakes was described as surgeon and physician when he sought payment for treating an injured hand in 1490, and the surgeon Thomas Syndelton was charged with trespass by the Barbers' company in 1506. The only other recorded surgeon was John Leche 'surgeon of the king' who lived in Bridge Street in 1397, with a barber as a near neighbour.[26] Barbers everywhere provided a variety of medical services: they practised blood-letting and dentistry, set fractured bones, and applied plasters and leeches. One Chester barber treated a serious head wound in 1432 and other barbers had close links with the city's leches.[27] John Leche and Robert Barber were named several times as joint plaintiffs in the early 1450s, suggesting that they shared a guild. In *c*.1480 the leche Thomas Chaloner was indebted to the stewards of the Barbers' guild.[28]

Apothecaries worked on the fringes of the medical professions, their trade resembling that of the modern pharmacist. Chaucer noted the close collaboration between the doctors and the apothecaries who supplied drugs and electuaries, and the money they made from their collusion.[29] One or two apothecaries worked in Chester in the later fifteenth century. Nicholas Monksfield, recorded selling spices in Chester in 1456, was described as an apothecary in 1487 when his two sons entered the franchise. The younger son followed his father's trade and in the early sixteenth century was named in association with the apothecary Thomas Monksfield, perhaps his son.[30] The apothecary Gervase of 'Vulder' became a freeman in 1484.[31]

Leisure

Before we consider the pursuit of leisure we must say something about attitudes to work. In late medieval towns the working day was long. The day-bell in each of Coventry's two parish churches was rung at 4 am and an hour later unemployed building workers were required to gather at the central crossroads in the hope of work. Many wage-earners started work at 6 am and were expected to work until 6 pm, with breaks for meals (often provided by the employers) at breakfast, noon and dinner.[32] A twelve-hour working day was perhaps specified at Chester although, as elsewhere, it may not always have been strictly observed. Work evidently stopped earlier on Saturdays. In 1468 the ordinances of the city's Fletchers and Bowyers stipulated that master craftsmen should stop work at the third peal of evensong (which began at 3 pm) on that day and apprentices should stop after the Anthem bell.[33] The clock in St Peter's church tower may have been used to measure the working day, just as it was used to ensure timely arrival at the Pentice, to which people were summoned to appear between 8 am and 4 pm.[34] Winter, with its shorter hours of daylight, lasted from All Saints (1 November) until the Purification of the Virgin (2 February) and the working day was naturally curtailed during those months.

The day ended early and the hour of curfew was 9 pm in both winter and summer. This was closing time for wine taverns, ale cellars and ale boards. City custom demanded that all those who walked the streets after 9 pm should carry a light but this ordinance was routinely disregarded and night walkers, both male and female, were regularly hauled up before the authorities.[35] The fear that night walking could provoke disorder was justified. In December 1418 a weaver and his wife caused such an affray in the street between 11 pm and midnight that the hue and cry was raised, and in July 1452 two men terrorized the populace by repeatedly roaming the streets after 9 pm carrying weapons.[36] At the start of the sixteenth century a seemingly new civic ordinance required former mayors and sheriffs and all innkeepers, both those who had signs and those who did not, to hang lighted lanterns at their doors until 9 pm during the winter months.[37]

The working week lasted from Monday until Saturday, although important religious festivals were holidays which had to be observed by cessation of work. The labourers who worked for five weeks in the summer of 1299 on a site near the fulling mills gained three additional (unpaid) holidays because the vigils of the feasts of St James, St Peter *ad vincula* and the Assumption of the Blessed Virgin fell within the period. The carpenters, slaters, sawyers and labourers repairing the castle in the spring of 1472 did not work on Good Friday and so received only five days' pay for the week before Easter.[38] Some employers complained when their servants took time off on such occasions. In 1449 one city tailor demanded damages of 20s from the servant who had allegedly broken his contract by leaving work on Whit Monday and other feast days.[39] Such contemporary evidence has led modern historians to conclude that workers in the period 1375–1520 readily stopped work once they had earned enough money to buy the necessities of daily life, and that this could be earned in just a few days thanks to the combination of rising wages and of falling and then steady grain prices after 1375. Their increased spending power, so the argument goes, enabled wage-earners to stop work after a few days and resort to the alehouse. The belief that there was a less developed work ethic in the late medieval period has recently been questioned and good evidence put forward to show that households worked hard to maximize their incomes.[40]

Wage-earners in the period 1375–1520 were relatively fortunate. Reduced grain prices enabled labourers in fifteenth-century Chester, as in other towns, to buy bread made from wheat and ale brewed from barley malt. They could afford more meat and fish. A family could enjoy this superior diet at the cost of about 3d per day.[41] Wage rates had risen considerably. An unskilled labourer was paid 1½d per day at the end of thirteenth century, 3d per day in the mid 1420s, and 4d per day in the late fifteenth century. Carpenters employed at the castle obtained 3d per day in 1298, 4½d per day in the mid 1420s, and 6d per day in the 1450s. Winter wages were of course slightly lower.[42] Wives made a significant contribution to household income: working beside their husbands at the loom, manufacturing candles, making canvas bags, sweeping floors in public buildings, and laying new rushes.[43] Healthy young women humped salt into the castle cellars and carried water and raw materials to the building workers, sometimes earning as much as their husbands.[44]

Work was gruelling and depressingly tedious and we can be sure that leisure time was eagerly anticipated. This was limited to a few hours after work on week-days and to the weekend, which began after work on Saturday, pay-day for many, and included the whole of Sunday.[45] Wage-earners probably spent more time in public places than did the wealthier townspeople. Their homes were not so well-heated or illuminated and outside space was often restricted to an unsavoury backyard. The poorer inhabitants featured prominently among those presented for playing illegal games such as dice and cards in the city's alehouses, and for gambling after hours. In the later fifteenth century the civic authorities linked alehouses with prostitution, which they believed fostered other criminal activity. Alewives and their young female servants became associated with the seduction of married men, thus posing a threat to the patriarchal order of society and undermining its traditional values. Ale cellars acquired an unsavoury reputation and alewives encountered a public antipathy which became immortalized in the depiction of the alewife in the Cooks' play in the city's Whitsun cycle.

Townspeople rich and poor enjoyed a variety of outdoor pursuits. At the end of the twelfth century Lucian mentioned a place beyond the walls which had been the site of a recent tournament, possibly the croft in the city's north field known as 'Justynge Haddelond' in 1450.[46] Practice at archery butts was encouraged and several men were shooting on the Roodee in December 1288 when one was wounded in the thigh by an arrow.[47] Archery contests were held in the city in the early 1460s. Members of John Howard's household spent almost £2 on meat and drink during four days' shooting in November 1463; they purchased expensive bows and gave money for drink to three shooters from Nantwich.[48] There was mention of shooting on the Monday following *Clausum Pasche* (the Sunday after Easter) in 1497, an event perhaps replaced by the archery contest between the sheriffs, mayor and aldermen held on Easter Monday on the Roodee in the sixteenth century and allegedly begun in 1511.[49] Youngsters at a loose end inevitably got into trouble. The authorities banned the use of catapults but a boy was accused in *c.*1296 of stoning ships and boats coming up the channel to the city, and a century later a young servant fired a stone from a 'stonebow' (catapult) and seriously wounded a little girl.[50]

Lucian noted that bears and bulls were baited in Chester at the end of the twelfth century and Berward Lane ('the bear-keeper's lane') ran south from Watergate Street by *c.*1240.[51] There is no evidence for these sports in the later medieval period and the only hint that bulls were baited before they were slaughtered dates from 1494, when a butcher broke the city's ordinances by killing a bull without first obtaining licence from the mayor and then sold the meat 'fraudulently' to the townspeople. The bull bait at the Cross which marked the end of the mayor's year of office in later years was said in 1619 to be an ancient custom.[52] John Grimsditch, sheriff in 1497–8, kept a bowling alley in his garden which the authorities evidently viewed with disfavour and which was the scene of an assault in 1503. It was claimed in 1540 that the Shrove Tuesday football game played by the Shoemakers, Drapers and Saddlers from the cross on the Roodee to the common hall was a long-standing tradition but football was not recorded in the medieval period.[53]

Some outdoor sports enjoyed by townsmen in the fifteenth century were illegal. The royal park at Shotwick and the forest of Delamere lay close enough to the city to make a day's (or night's) hunting a tempting proposition. Local shoemakers and saddlers joined clerks and gentlemen to chase and kill the king's deer, often on Fridays and Saturdays. Some of the meat was distributed in the city.[54] The smith who took hares, rabbits and pheasants from the abbot's warren in 1464, the two glovers who killed five cygnets in the abbot's close at Bache on Trinity Sunday 1477, and the bailiff who killed 24 rabbits with ferrets and nets in the abbot's warren at Great Boughton on a Sunday in November 1486, were perhaps motivated as much by monetary gain as by the sport.[55]

Music was an important component of medieval culture and was enjoyed in both ecclesiastical and secular settings. John Arneway left money in *c.*1274–78 for two chaplains to celebrate for the souls of himself and his family, with music on Mondays, Wednesdays and Saturdays, and without music on the other days of the week.[56] The words and music were written down. Chaplains were named in a dispute involving two song books valued at 40s each in 1445 and in the theft of a book of prick-song worth 40s in 1503.[57] Organ building developed rapidly in the late fifteenth century and in 1503–4 three organ-players were attested in

FIGURE 9.1. The first verses of a carol included in the *Processional of the Nuns of Chester*. The simple melody and refrain indicate its popular character.

Chester. In 1518 the abbot employed a secular clerk to arrange music for services at St Werburgh's. A Lady mass with prick-song and organs was to be celebrated daily and on Fridays a Jesus mass with prick-song and organs was staged. The clerk was to instruct six boy choristers and to teach the monks to sing 'playn songe, fafurden, prykksong and descant'.[58] At the Dissolution the Franciscans and the Dominicans had pairs of organs in the choir, and the Carmelites had two pairs, including a 'great pair' over the choir door.[59]

The words and music of the anthems and hymns sung at St Mary's priory in the fifteenth century survive.[60] The nun who owned the book now known as the *Processional of the Nuns of Chester* carefully noted at the end: 'This booke longeth to Dame Margery Byrkenhed of Chestre'. Written in red and black, with decorated initials, the manuscript allows us to follow the liturgical year and indicates the more important festivals, prominent among them the Purification of the Virgin on 2 February. This was Candlemas Day 'when candles byn halowed' and after the priest had sung the first anthem the nuns processed from the choir stalls to the church door. Further anthems were sung as the procession left the church, at the frater door, and at the parlour door. On Palm Sunday the procession began with the blessing of the palms and progressed from the choir to the church door, from the door to the 'city of Jerusalem', from there to the high cross in the churchyard, and finally back into the choir. Anthems were sung at each stage. The carol celebrating the Nativity was written in plainsong notation, with simple words and refrain.[61]

Music was also part of everyday life. Among Chaucer's pilgrims were several talented musicians, including the squire who composed songs and sang and fluted all day and the miller who brought the group out of town playing his bagpipes.[62] Chester's townspeople certainly heard and made a great deal of music. Minstrels were regularly named as were singers and pipers, and men who played the fiddle, the lute, the harp and the psaltery.[63] Their association with taverners and hostelers suggests that they provided entertainment in the city's drinking houses and this could explain their regular involvement in disorderly behaviour.[64] Minstrels were sometimes pardoned for these breaches of the peace,

FIGURE 9.2. An angel musician playing a stringed instrument carved on a misericord in Chester Cathedral. The misericords date from the 1380s or perhaps a little later and the quality of the carving is high. The king's master carver William of Newhall was palatinate master carpenter from 1377 until the late 1390s and perhaps supervised the team which carried out the work.

presumably because they were dealt with by the minstrelsy court, held by the Dutton family in the later medieval period.[65]

For some townsmen music-making was a part-time occupation. In the 1470s the piper John Drake also worked as a barker (known as John Piper), and in the years 1492–1506 the minstrel William Wells and his wife sold bread and ale and kept a brothel.[66] Harps were popular. The smith Thomas Blackburn owed 3d for harp strings in 1436 and a few years later a local butcher paid for his wife to be taught how to make harp strings, evidently considering this a likely source of additional income.[67] A lute-maker and an organ-maker were named in the late 1480s, the latter also working as a painter. The gentleman Richard Sneyd owned a pair of virginals in 1513.[68]

Many urban authorities employed a small group of wind instrumentalists known as waits to perform at official functions and entertain visitors. Official musicians were evidently employed at Chester by the 1450s, when a trumpeter and two men surnamed Wayt were mentioned.[69] Their duties in 1540 included playing 'as accustomed' five mornings a week (every day except Wednesday and Friday) and in the evenings on Mondays, Thursdays and Saturdays. In the fifteenth century the town's governors occasionally employed visiting performers to entertain important dignitaries. When Lord Stanley dined in the Pentice in 1474–5 the city's leavelookers gave 5s to 'my lord of Clarence's minstrels' and 20d to some tumblers.[70]

Important religious festivals were celebrated with public ceremonial. In 1451–2 a local painter agreed with the city paver to produce paintings of St Katherine, whose feast day was 25 November, and of the Virgin Mary for the feast of the Purification on 2 February. The painter also agreed to collect the money to pay for them.[71] The Invention of the Holy Cross (3 May) was the most important festival of the year at St John's which housed the Holy Rood, a silver-gilt crucifix containing wood from the True Cross, in front of which stood a tablet inscribed with the history of the church. Although the cult may have enjoyed its greatest popularity before the mid fourteenth century the feast day remained a major celebration. On 3 May in *c.*1420 two chaplains from St John's assaulted two city barbers in the street and threw to the ground the wax candles shaped into images they were carrying. On the Sunday preceding the festival a few years later one of the chaplains, now sacrist, accused all the city's barbers of extortion, perhaps because they had seized the opportunity to increase the price of candles.[72] Pilgrims came to venerate the Rood throughout the year and their offerings made a significant contribution to the church's income. A city plumber in 1492 agreed to make a mould depicting an image of St John; this would have been used to make the lead pilgrim badges which were such popular keepsakes. A few years later a Dublin merchant broke into the church and stole 10s in gold which had been fixed to the relic.[73]

By the fifteenth century the major event in Chester's civic year was the feast of Corpus Christi, the date of which was determined by that of Easter Sunday and which fell between 23 May and 24 June. The first known celebration in England was at Ipswich in 1325 and observance of Corpus Christi spread widely during the later medieval period. The cult became especially popular in towns and in some large towns it developed into a visual representation of urban unity.[74] This demonstration of harmony often provoked conflict and the 'horrible affray' between the masters and journeymen of Chester's textile crafts in front of St Peter's on Corpus Christi day in 1399 was perhaps related to the festival.[75] In the fifteenth century the celebrations at Chester became very elaborate and involved plays as well as a procession.

The festival began with a celebration of mass in the church of St Mary on the Hill, after which the consecrated Host was carried through the streets to St John's church, escorted by a procession of guildsmen and, presumably, civic officials. In other towns the guilds processed in strict order of precedence, the humbler crafts first and the wealthiest and most influential behind them, followed by the councilmen, aldermen and sheriffs. Last of all came the mayor, walking beside the Host and the clergymen.[76] The participation of Chester's governing body is not documented but could have been expected in a procession intended to represent the whole membership of the urban social body. The order of the procession at Chester in the fifteenth century is also uncertain. The list of 19 companies which accepted the mayor's ruling on entry fines in 1475–6 began with the Mercers and Drapers, undoubtedly the most prestigious organizations, but named other companies in an order that did not reflect their standing. It appears, however, that there was a set order and that the companies were concerned to safeguard their rightful position. The city's Fletchers and Coopers squabbled over their place in the procession in 1476 and the mayor decreed that the Coopers should go before the Fletchers, carrying three lights on one side of the pavement and three on the other.[77]

The earliest reference to a play at the festival dates from 1422, when the Ironmongers and the Carpenters each claimed the support of the Fletchers, Bowyers, Stringers, Coopers and Turners in putting on their pageant. The mayor's ruling made it clear that the plays were not being performed for the first time and it seems that problems had arisen because of a recent reorganization and elaboration.[78] A rash of litigation between company officials and their members in *c.*1422–6 (which provides the earliest evidence for the Bakers, Goldsmiths, Glovers, Weavers and Barbers, and for journeymen organizations of Bakers, Shoemakers and Tailors) involved guildsmen in debt to their company. When the reason was specified, the debt concerned the company light and play.[79] Possibly the reorganization had increased the cost of staging the procession and plays and members were reluctant to contribute. Perhaps it had been decided to hold the procession and plays on succeeding days in order to avoid a clash, as happened in York in 1426 when the commonalty decreed that the Corpus Christi procession should take place on the feast day itself and the plays on the following day. The sequence was reversed a few years later.[80] The plays contained coarse humour and this sat uneasily with the liturgical aspects of the celebration.

FIGURE 9.3. Painting of St John the Baptist in St John's church.

The Corpus Christi plays were performed at the conclusion of the procession, probably in St John's churchyard. The mayor's ruling in 1422 made reference to plays assigned to companies in what was termed 'the original', indicating that a written text existed.[81] The plays evidently included demanding roles that required considerable talent. In 1436, for example, a man sued the Ironmongers for 20d owing to him for performing in the Corpus Christi play, and in 1448 a baker claimed that he was owed 2s 6d for playing the demon in his company's play.[82] Several of the plays staged in the earlier fifteenth century can be linked to the Whitsun plays that replaced them before 1521. The Fletchers staged the Flagellation and the Ironmongers the Crucifixion in 1422, and they continued to perform the same plays in the following century. The Goldsmiths and Masons, who staged the Massacre of the Innocents in the Whitsun cycle, apparently already did so by 1435. In January 1436 the goldsmith Roger Warmingham accused the mason John Asser of failing to return two torches, a bag and a sumptuous play garment worth 13s 4d (equivalent to a year's rent of a small property) which must surely have been worn by Herod.[83]

Guild members again proved reluctant to contribute to the Corpus Christi plays in the late 1430s and 1440s.[84] By then some companies were renting small parcels of public land: the Mercers at the Shipgate, for example, and the Fishmongers adjoining the gateway of the Franciscan friary.[85] From the late 1460s city rentals specified that the land was used to store the company carriages, the painted and gaily decorated 'pageants' that carried the actors and scenery.

FIGURE 9.4. The demon also had a starring role in the Corpus Christi pageants. In 1486 the weaver John Jankynson performed the role in the Cooks' play, perhaps because none of the company members could act.

FIGURE 9.5. Crowds watching a parade in Bridge Street.

The shearmen stored their carriage somewhere in the Northgate Street quarter of the city, the Saddlers on land next to Truants Hole, the Mercers and Drapers at the end of Greyfriars Lane.[86] The Saddlers complained in 1472 that strangers and 'persons of incurably obstinate disposition' were practising the craft in the city yet refusing to support the play and pageant, and claimed that they could no longer bear the expense without help.[87]

A weaver prosecuted a steward of the Cooks' company in 1488 for 8d owed to him for playing the role of demon in the Cooks' play, a debt that went back to Whit Monday 1486. This raises the possibility that the plays were already being performed at Whitsun, and that the Cooks already staged the Harrowing of Hell as they did in the Whitsun cycle – hence the starring role for the demon. In 1488, however, a barber supplied the Goldsmiths and Masons with six 'coppes' of wax for the Corpus Christi light and play, evidence that performances still took place at the festival, and there was another specific mention of the Corpus Christi play in June 1491, when the stewards of the Goldsmiths and Masons claimed that a mason owed them 20d towards staging it.[88] Between that year and 1521, however, the Corpus Christi play was replaced by the Whitsun plays.

A list of the guilds recorded in a seventeenth-century manuscript and dating from *c*.1500 has been accepted as an ordered list of the companies presenting pageants. It reveals that all but three of the plays included in the Whitsun cycle in 1539–40 already existed. The list begins with the Drapers, who staged the Creation of the World, and ends with the Weavers and Walkers, who staged the Day of Doom. Occasionally the subject of the pageant was appropriate to the guild which performed it: the Drawers of Dee put on Noah's Flood, the Bakers the Last Supper, and the Ironmongers the Crucifixion. By 1500 it seems that the cycle had more or less achieved the form known from surviving plays, although the texts continued to be revised and rewritten up to their final performance in 1575. At some time the cycle was divided into three sections and performed over three days, a change perhaps made in 1531–2 when the plays were mentioned in the plural. They were performed at designated locations, beginning at the abbey gate and moving on to the Pentice and thence through the streets.[89] It could be noted that the first two locations were the setting for performances of the Assumption of Our Lady in the late fifteenth century: the play was performed at the Cross in 1488 and at the abbey gate in 1499.[90] In York the plays were performed in front of inns and the homes of leading citizens but this did not happen at Chester. The Rows perhaps served as convenient viewing galleries.

In the years before the Reformation it was claimed that the Whitsun play originated in the mayoralty of John Arneway, at that time believed to have been the city's first mayor, and the proclamation for the Whitsun plays in 1531–2 ascribed the text to Henry Francis, recorded as a monk of St Werburgh's in 1377–82.[91] Although these traditions had no historical basis they perhaps reflected half-forgotten memories of an association between the mayor and the abbey in an original production.

John Arneway was in fact Chester's fifth mayor and he served for an uninterrupted period of ten years, from 1268–78. During his tenure of office the mayor's powers and influence increased considerably and the mayor became the chief representative of the citizens. In *c.*1274–8 Arneway established two perpetual chantries, one in the abbey where he and his wife were buried, and one in St Bridget's, his parish church. His chantry in St Werburgh's became one of the abbey's most notable chantries and his chantry at St Bridget's was still maintained in the 1540s. John Arneway's name was certainly remembered in the city in the early sixteenth century, as he had doubtless intended.[92] The mass he endowed at St Bridget's was a mass of the Virgin Mary, in whose honour additional services were staged in many English churches during the thirteenth century. Arneway's choice may also have been influenced by an important religious guild dedicated to the Virgin which existed in his day, either the Tailors' fraternity of St Mary attested by *c.*1300, or the guild of St Mary which met in a house close to St Bridget's in 1330–1 and which was almost certainly much older.

The Virgin was always regarded with especial veneration at the abbey. The abbey was referred to as 'of St Mary and St Werburgh' in a late twelfth-century calendar listing the main festivals celebrated during the year, and the Virgin's name was written in capital letters beside her feast days.[93] A Lady chapel was inserted at the east end of the church between 1250 and 1280; her Coronation was carved on one of the misericords and on the abbot's stall in the 1380s; the Assumption featured on the west front of the abbey church in the early sixteenth century.[94] The Assumption of Our Lady was part of the Corpus Christi play cycle and the responsibility of the Worshipful Wives, perhaps a religious guild linked to the fraternity of the Blessed Trinity, the Assumption of Our Lady and St Anne established in 1361 and which may have replaced the earlier guild of St Mary. The play was performed at the Cross for George Stanley, Lord Strange, in 1488, before Prince Arthur in front of the abbey gate in August 1499, and with the Shepherds' play in St John's churchyard in 1516. It was not performed after the Reformation.[95] It was not associated with the craft guilds and perhaps pre-dated their formation. Could it have developed from a procession in honour of the Virgin which took place when the city was governed by the unitary guild merchant in the later thirteenth century? Perhaps the celebration originated during the mayoralty of John Arneway, a mayor closely associated with the abbey and whose name was remembered in the early sixteenth century.[96] If so, this could explain the myths of origin put forward for the Whitsun play in the early sixteenth century.

Chester's mayor was the final arbiter in matters concerning the Corpus Christi celebrations. In 1422 he settled the dispute between the Ironmongers and Carpenters and allocated the individual plays; in 1430 he ruled on the contributions due from the Weavers, Walkers, Chaloners and Shearmen to the light of St Mary and of Corpus Christi.[97] On 3 September 1476 he determined the order of precedence in the Corpus Christi procession. It was most unusual for a precise date to be specified in the documents and the only other known example dates from the early fourteenth century: the city's tailors paid 2s a year to the chamberlain in order that no-one should 'commune' with them on 3 September.[98] It seems unlikely that this was a coincidence and it may hint at a link between an occasion celebrated by the Tailors' fraternity of St Mary in the later thirteenth and early fourteenth century and the Corpus Christi procession and plays of the later medieval period.

CHAPTER TEN

Relationships

A complex network of social relationships linked (and divided) Chester's resident population. Townspeople depended on the support of family, friends, neighbours, fellow parishioners, and those who shared their trade or craft to cope with the routine of daily life. This support was crucial when things went wrong, a not uncommon occurrence among people living close together in cramped accommodation. Conflicting loyalties and competing interests split the community into small social groupings, fragmented on occasion by internal rivalries. These tensions threatened stability but vertical ties of deference and horizontal solidarities acted as a counterbalance and helped to forge bonds which united the various groups. It was vital for strangers to Chester to establish good social relations with the townspeople, whether their stay was short or long. Those without local connections or influence were truly outsiders and gravely disadvantaged if they got into difficulties.

Family

The networks revolving around family and kin were of fundamental importance. In spite of improved job opportunities after 1348–50 most women probably still hoped to marry, aware that as wives they would enjoy enhanced status and security and, if they were fortunate, have the support of a loving husband.[1] Young people in towns may have waited until their mid-twenties before they married, having first served as apprentices or servants for five to ten years. The age-gap separating husband and wife was often small and as young women brought money and skills to the marriage they wielded considerable authority in the household.[2]

The value of marriage to a woman is well illustrated by the experience of the tapster Agnes Filenes who first came to the attention of Chester's authorities in 1484, when she broke the assize of ale by over-charging. In 1487–8 she was named among 33 ale retailers in Foregate Street but by the following year she had married and become known as Agnes Huet *alias* Filenes. Her ambitions increased. She opted to trade as *femme sole*, selling ale, home-baked cakes and wine; among her possessions was a silver-gilt ring. Her husband died within a few years but she soon remarried, continuing to trade as *femme sole* and on a scale that enabled her to supply ale, bread and other foodstuffs to less prosperous women retailers. Unhappily for Agnes her second marriage proved as short as her first; William Chamber was not named in the records after 1496 and had presumably died. Her troubles began almost immediately. She had occasionally been involved in brawls with other alewives and had sometimes been in debt but in January 1497 came the first accusation of brothel-keeping and from then until 1510 it seems that keeping a brothel was her main source of income.[3]

Girls from wealthy families married at a younger age, to older men chosen by their fathers.[4] Marriage ties linked the mercantile élite who dominated town government and the most successful families established links with the local gentry. In 1368 David of Ewloe was granted the wardship and marriage of Elizabeth, daughter of Robert of Strangeways, and married her to his son John while she was under age and without the consent of the lord. Elizabeth was one of the heirs of John Blund and held 23 messuages in Chester worth £12 per year and one third of the manor of Little Neston and Hargrave. After she died John Ewloe remained tenant of her property 'by the curtesy of England' (*per legem Angliae*) until his own death in 1418. John's second wife was another wealthy heiress and as she too died before John he remained tenant of her property as well.[5] These advantageous marriages increased John's wealth and status and he was able to negotiate good matches for his children. In 1398 he agreed that his

FIGURE 10.1. Lamb Row in *c.*1818. Batenham's etching shows the property below St Bridget's at the corner of Cuppin Lane (2–4 Lower Bridge Street) built in the late 16th century. John Ewloe occupied a house on this site in the early 15th century and it passed from his family to William Lely in 1456. Lely was granted permission to enclose a plot of land in Cuppin Lane outside the door of his hall and built a flight of steps on the land. The stairway of the 16th-century house was in the same location. When Lely's daughter married Thomas Hurleton the property came into the possession of the Hurletons.

son Richard should marry the daughter of John Done of Utkinton within four years. The marriage settlement included a payment of £50 by Done and John Ewloe undertook to enfeoff the young couple with lands worth £5 per year once this was paid.[6] John Ewloe's daughter Elizabeth married Richard Hatton and their daughter Katherine married William Walsh, when she was 'upwards' of 14 years of age.[7]

Remarriage was common practice among all sectors of society. Joan, widow of former sheriff Richard Hondeston *alias* Spicer, later married Adam Wotton, mayor in 1434–5. Wotton had also been married before and the daughter of that union married twice, her first husband being William Massey of Coddington, mayor in 1449–50.[8] Margaret, widow of the draper Henry Wiksted murdered in 1487, had married a leading baker by 1489. Each of the three husbands of Elizabeth, daughter and heir of the mercer William Lely, was a draper and all served as sheriff between 1477–8 and 1514–5.[9] Company members married the widows of deceased brethren. Katherine, widow of the butcher Richard Wright, and Matilda, widow of the butcher Richard Hale, both took butchers as second husbands in the early 1490s. Matilda's marriage to Richard Middleton evidently provoked a serious family dispute with the butcher Robert Middleton and his wife. Possibly they resented the intrusion of a new wife with a young son of her own and as the families lived in close proximity near Goss Lane relationships became strained. Each side was bound over to keep the peace towards the other in December 1493, with four butchers acting as their sureties.[10]

In Chester, as in other towns, many marriages proved childless and families commonly died out within two or three generations. Childbirth was fraught with danger and infant mortality was high. In 1508 Piers Whitley voiced typical paternal anxieties when he left his goods to his wife and their unborn

TABLE 10.1. The most popular forenames in 1305–6 and 1476–7.

1305–6	Total	1476–7	Total	1305–6	Total	1476–7	Total
Males	**490**	**Males**	**526**	**Females**	**121**	**Females**	**168**
William	89	John	130	Alice	17	Joanna	34
Richard	73	Thomas	72	Agnes	16	Margaret	21
John	56	William	65	Margaret	11	Agnes	20
Robert	51	Richard	54	Lucy	9	Elena	19
Henry	36	Robert	37	Mabilla	9	Alice	18
Thomas	33	Henry	31	Matilda	7	Elizabeth	12
Roger	24	Roger	20	Cristian	5	Katherine	9
Ranulph	17	Nicholas	17	Emma	5	Margery	8
Hugh	16	Ranulph	15	Felicia	5	Cecily	6
Adam	15	James	10	Juliana	4	Cristian	4
other names (26)	80	other names (31)	75	other names (19)	33	other names (8)	17
'Top four'	55%		61%		44%		56%
'Top ten'	84%		86%		73%		90%

FIGURE 10.2. The 14th-century wooden screen and late 15th- or early 16th-century font of St Andrew's Church, Tarvin. The screen divides the Bruen chapel from the south aisle. The Bruyns (as the family was known in medieval Chester) had close links with the city. They joined the fraternity of St Anne, served as mayor, and married members of the civic élite.

child 'if it please God hit lyve'.[11] Babies were baptised as soon as possible after their birth, sometimes on the same day. It has been suggested that the names chosen for sons were re-used generation after generation, thereby emphasizing the importance of male children to the family and linking the family past and future. Daughters were less important and were therefore named more freely and idiosyncratically. This theory has been challenged. Male personal names were not as restricted as has been claimed and only a very narrow range of forenames was in use for both males and females, possibly because England was the earliest country to get surnames and not so many forenames were needed. The use of names to identify lineage and dynasty has been overstated; it was godparents and not parents who chose names.[12]

One example at Chester is Richard Hondeston who was godfather to Adam Wotton's son Richard in the early fifteenth century, thus creating a spiritual relationship between the families. This proved an impediment when Adam later married Hondeston's widow and in 1422 a papal dispensation was obtained which allowed them to contract their marriage anew and legitimize their offspring.[13] Other examples include John Hawarden who bequeathed 40s to his godson John Birkenhead in 1496, and Nicholas Deykin who left a new white coat to his godson Nicholas Barker in 1518. Both men were probably related to their godsons through marriage and the forenames may well have been family names on the mother's side.[14] This was evidently true of John Dedwood, godfather to John son of James Bruyn of Bruen Stapleford, baptised in Tarvin church in 1444. Dedwood's daughter, wife of John Bruyn, was the baby's aunt; Thomas Dedwood's daughter was the baby's mother.[15] Godparents and godchildren from Cheshire's gentry families invariably shared the same forename.[16]

Ordinary townspeople may have adopted a similar naming pattern but no direct evidence survives. In the years 1392–1499 just 13 of the 65 men admitted to the franchise whose fathers were free at the time of their birth shared their father's forename. Eight were called John, the most common forename in medieval England, and may well have been named after another male relative. Siblings were occasionally given the same name, a duplication intended to counteract infant mortality. John senior and John junior, the sons of Nicholas Monksfield, entered the freedom together in March 1487.[17] Nothing is known about how Chester's parents chose names for their daughters but the most frequently reported female names came from the core group of names popular throughout England and there were no idiosyncratic choices.

The evidence suggests that parents were concerned for their children and made careful provision for their upbringing. The pewterer William Rawson, sheriff in 1466–7, left money to support his sons John and Nicholas; they were to be given meat, drink, clothing and other necessaries 'convenable' for children.[18] In 1499 the former sheriff John Norris appointed his sister Katherine Grosvenor guardian of William his son and heir until he reached the age of 24. The boy was to receive five marks per year for his sustenance and schooling but if he refused to be governed by his aunt he was to have nothing, and he was to inherit his father's lands only if 'he be well gidet and take gode waies'. The barker Richard Broster in 1523 stipulated that after his wife's death his dwelling house was to pass to his son Hugh, provided he was 'well ordered and of good disposition'.[19] John Hope evidently had misgivings about his son and heir Oliver, named as overseer of his will in 1439 but warned not to meddle with it. His fears may have been justified. In May 1439, only a few days after his father's will was proved, Oliver accused his mother of unjustly detaining charters kept in a locked chest and she in turn sued Oliver and his wife for dower of two acres in Claverton.[20]

Wives, children and grandchildren were always uppermost in the minds of testators but they also remembered siblings and their offspring. Young relatives were taken into the household. In 1415 two young girls, described in the court record as relatives and servants of John Hope, were with his wife in the garden of his home when they were assaulted and a spade snatched from one girl's hands. In 1523 Richard Broster made provision for his sister's daughter who lived in the house with him, requesting that she be given £4, her gown, kirtle, hose, shoes and other necessaries such as linen clothes.[21] Favoured apprentices could also be treated as members of the extended family circle.

Parish

Chester's nine parish churches provided fixed points of reference for the community, both for long-established families and also for newcomers, some of whom may have lost contact with their own kinsfolk. The parish boundaries as mapped in 1833 are believed to have been essentially the same as they were in the Middle Ages. The parishes varied in size. Those of St Peter's, St Michael's and St Olave's were entirely intramural, covering seven acres, eight acres and five acres respectively. St Bridget's parish covered 163 acres and extended beyond the walls but not beyond the liberties. St Mary's parish covered the south-western part of the city (excluding the castle and Gloverstone), all the liberties south of the river except for Earl's Eye, and several townships to the north and south of the city. St John's parish was mainly extramural and probably coincided with the bishop's borough and 'Redcliff', an early estate to the east of the Roman fortress. Within the liberties it covered 257 acres.[22] As buildings, the parish churches were very different, ranging from the tiny St Olaves' to the grandiose if somewhat neglected St John's. Some were served by underpaid parochial chaplains and others by rectors. Absenteeism never became a serious problem, even at St Mary's which, as the richest living, was the most vulnerable to abuse. Only seven out of that church's 20 rectors were absentees in the years 1300–1540.[23]

The townspeople showed a conventional piety and owned rosaries of coral, jet or amber beads.[24] In more costly versions the beads were interspersed with larger beads (gauds) of silver; some were entirely of silver and included a silver crucifix. The wealthiest individuals owned rosaries made of gold.[25] From the end of the fifteenth century it became fashionable to own an *Agnus Dei*, an image of the Lamb of God.[26] Prominent citizens obtained licences from the bishop to have oratories in their homes; in the years 1360–85 they included William Whitmore, John Blund and subsequently his widow, and Alexander Bellyetter.[27] Others employed private chaplains or sought papal permission to choose personal confessors who could grant absolution and enjoin penances. In 1431 Thomas Wotton and Robert Hewster and their wives were granted permission to choose a confessor; in 1453 a chaplain agreed to serve the hosteler Thomas Wainfleet for a year.[28] John Hawarden in 1496 asked that a 'convenient' priest be found to attend upon his wife, to be at table with her and to say mass for Hawarden's soul for ten years, duties for which the priest was to receive 13s 4d a year.[29]

Private oratories were not a substitute for the parish church and all parishioners were expected to attend services. The great festivals of the church's year were major celebrations. The elaborate decoration set up in St Mary's at Christmas 1540, complete with holly, candles, gilded moon and stars, had probably long been traditional.[30] A city barber provided two large candles and a torch for the royal chapel at Christmas 1400, charging 6d for making the torch and 1d for the verdigris used to colour it green.[31] Congregations received communion only at Easter and those services were of especial significance. Between Maundy Thursday and Easter Sunday the consecrated bread was kept in an Easter Sepulchre, in many churches no more than a wooden chest placed on a temporary wooden frame but in some a permanent Sepulchre decorated with sculptures, usually in the north wall of the chancel.[32] Nicholas Deykin in 1518 left his best bed covering to be used each year to hang over the Sepulchre at St John's; Margaret Hawarden in 1520 left two twill towels and a small flaxen sheet for the Easter Sepulchre in St Olave's.[33]

All churches received bequests from their parishioners. These included gifts of money: to buy ornaments for St Bridget's, to gild St Thomas's statue in St Peter's, and to provide a 'cote' (sleeveless garment) for the statue of the Blessed Virgin in St Mary's. In 1439 John Hope gave 26s 8d for a window in St Michael's, for his soul and the soul of his brother Robert.[34] Other legacies were practical in nature: lead vessels for the fabric and the steeple; gowns to make vestments; twill or flaxen board-cloths to place on the altar.[35] The cooper Hugh Lake in 1505–6 left St Peter's several dozen lambskins, a pair of gimlets, a bow-stringer, 25 arrows and a box for keeping fire.[36] The numerous candles and torches required by the churches were produced by the city's barbers, who also used wax to prepare unguents for medicinal purposes. Alan the barber served as churchwarden of St Peter's in 1318–19 and perhaps supplied candles at advantageous prices. John the painter, warden at St Mary's in *c.*1346, and the carpenter Donald Sawer, warden of Holy Trinity in *c.*1496, may also have had skills that proved useful to their church.[37] Churchwardens occasionally reflected the occupational character of the parish: Robert the saucemaker churchwarden of St Peter's in 1318–19, Roger the heuster churchwarden of St Mary's in *c.*1346, and the butcher John Smith, churchwarden of St Peter's in *c.*1504–5 for example. St Peter's churchwardens in 1415 were former mayor John of Preston and former sheriff Richard Hatton, who personified the close relations between the church and the civic authorities.[38]

The crucial ceremony of baptism was performed as soon as possible after a child's birth. Family and friends went in procession to the church, the baby in the arms of a female relative. The priest met the group in the church porch and the baptism took place at the font, traditionally located close to the door, with guests holding the basin, ewer and towels for the priest and godparents. The baptism was then recorded in the church 'missal'.[39] Witnesses at proofs of age recalled their role at the baptism or remembered the ceremony for other reasons. Among those who gave evidence at the inquiry into the age of Richard Hatton's daughter Katherine in 1428 were several who remembered that she had been baptised in St Peter's 14 years earlier because they had attended a wedding at the church on the same day. Witnesses at the proof of age of Hugh son of Roger Venables in 1410 included a number of Cheshire gentlemen who were in Chester on the day of his baptism in August 1389 for a day of reconciliation between Sir John [Massey] of Puddington and William Stanley. They were standing near the gates of St Mary's when the baby was carried from church in the arms of his godmother, with his godfather Sir Hugh de Holes and Chester's prioress in attendance.[40]

Wedding ceremonies took place in the church porch. Chaucer's wife of Bath had five husbands 'at the church door', and it was at the church door that one woman in Chester received her dower in the early fourteenth century.[41] The wedding party then entered the church for the nuptial mass. Young people were given money and plate by wealthy relatives to help set them up in married life. John Hatton in 1398 left his nephew and heir silver spoons, a silver mazer and a gold ring towards his marriage; in the early sixteenth century Thomas Spark left his young cousin two gold coins known as 'angelets', one of which was to be kept for her wedding. Poor girls received charitable bequests, generally very small. The rector of Holy Trinity, for example, in 1506 bequeathed 20d to each of twelve poor maidens at their marriage.[42] Fellow parishioners often helped to launch a young couple by holding a 'bride-ale' after the marriage ceremony, a communal event with food, drink, dancing and entertainment, usually accompanied by charitable donations of money.[43] Chester's ruling body frowned on such festivities, considering them likely to lead to drunkenness and rowdy behaviour, and in 1515 forbade townspeople from attending common ales and 'walshe weddings' within the city and beyond the liberties.[44]

St Oswald's and St John's, the two oldest foundations, had burial rights from the start; St Mary's possessed a graveyard by 1328, possibly intended for the burial of prisoners from the castle, and St Michael's and St Peter's had acquired small graveyards by the 1480s. William Mauwer of Handbridge asked to be buried in St Mary's graveyard in 1407 and the following year the master carpenter Robert Scot requested burial in St Oswald's graveyard, leaving money for a chaplain to celebrate masses for his soul.[45] Most surviving wills were made by parishioners whose wealth and status guaranteed burial within the church. In 1396 John the armourer asked to be buried in St Mary's chapel in Holy Trinity, and William Heth in 1401 requested burial in St Michael's church in front of the image of St Michael.[46] Burial near a member of the family was the preferred option, usually beside a husband or wife but on one occasion beside a father-in-law.[47] John Hope's parents and brother were buried in the Carmelite church and in 1439 he asked to be buried close to their grave. The family may have been parishioners of St Michael's but evidently preferred the more fashionable friary church. John Hawarden in 1496 also requested burial in the Carmelite church, doubtless considering his own parish church (St Olave's) too small and poor.[48]

All wealthy testators showed concern for their funerals. These were public as well as private events and gave the deceased a final opportunity for display as the cortège passed through the streets. The arrangements made by John Coly for his funeral in 1413 were typical. He left money to provide garments: black ones to be worn by his wife, relatives and friends and white ones to be worn by the twelve poor men who carried the crucifix, mortuary bell and torches. His bier was placed in front of the great crucifix at Holy Trinity where he was to be buried, and on it stood his best silver bowl; the bowl was to remain in the church in perpetuity and be used for the consecrated bread. The service took place in a church illuminated by torches and candles and Coly left money to the parish priests and clerk who officiated. He left 20s to provide food and drink for those present at his funeral and 20s to buy bread to be distributed to the poor on the same day. This would have caused a crowd to gather, as Coly had probably intended.[49]

There is no evidence at Chester for almsgiving by the parishioners. By the mid fifteenth century churchwardens were required to keep parish boxes for such donations and to distribute the money as they saw fit.[50] The practice is badly documented everywhere and Chester's parishioners may well have been generous. Charity at neighbourhood level also went unrecorded. Parishes and neighbourhoods overlapped and loyalties may have conflicted. St Peter's parish, for example, straddled the city centre, with parishioners drawn from all four main streets. St Bridget's parish lay on the west side of Bridge Street and St Michael's on the east, except for a few burgages on the west sandwiched between detached portions of St Mary's and St Bridget's.

Craft guilds

Fellow guildsmen inevitably established close relationships, sharing as they did the same trading concerns and commonly living in the same neighbourhood or parish. By 1450 more than 20 craft companies existed and the Bakers,

Shoemakers, Tailors and Weavers had separate organizations of journeymen; the journeymen Glovers had been formed by 1492. Members assembled regularly to attend to company business, much of it economic in nature. They determined the length of apprenticeship, enforced trading standards and attempted to prevent men working within the liberties without belonging to the relevant company. In July 1501 a fine of 6d was imposed on members of the Smiths' company who failed to attend a meeting (if warned in advance by the stewards) or who arrived 'after the book was called'. The members promised to obey the aldermen, stewards and elder brethren 'in orderly manner and sort' and agreed that the company officers should arbitrate in cases of 'variance' between the brothers.[51]

The companies were also social and religious organizations. In 1501 members of the Smiths' company were not only fined for non-attendance at meetings but also for failure to attend the funeral of a fellow guildsman. The companies' socio-religious functions may have pre-dated their economic concerns, possibly explaining why they were sometimes termed fraternities in the early fifteenth century. Several companies bore the name of their patron saint and company officers were elected on the saint's feast day. The Tailors were dedicated to the Virgin Mary, the Shoemakers to St Martin and the Smiths to St Eligius (St Loy). In 1521, when the Founderers, Pewterers and Smiths agreed to combine for the Whitsun play and the Corpus Christi procession, they also agreed to maintain a priest in St Loy's chapel. The location of this chapel is not known but a tombstone at St John's carved with a horseshoe, a pair of pincers and a hammer is believed to commemorate a company alderman, possibly Thomas Edyan to whom Prince Arthur gave a silver badge bearing similar emblems in 1499, allegedly for the love he had towards him.[52] Chester's smiths worked outside the walls and it would have been appropriate for their company altar to be in the city's only extra-mural church. The city tanneries were in the eastern suburb and the Tanners maintained a light on the altar of St Mary Calvercroft in the Calvercroft chapel in St John's precinct. The chapel was also known as the White chapel and may have been linked in some way to the 'minster' of St Mary recorded between 1086 and c.1200. It perhaps housed the light dedicated to the Virgin maintained by the Weavers, Walkers, Chaloners and Shearmen. The Carpenters maintained a light in the Carmelite church and it seems likely that most if not all the craft guilds also had a patron saint and a light.

Religious fraternities

The leading men of late medieval Chester shared the same mercantile interests, sat together as aldermen in the common hall, and were often inter-related. They strengthened these close ties by gathering together as fellow members of one of the city's religious fraternities. Almost nothing is known of the guild of St Mary, established by the early fourteenth century and not recorded after the Black Death. The fraternity of St Anne, founded in 1361 and refounded in

1393, became the 'top people's club' in the fifteenth century, with an exclusive membership of 25 or 30 élite citizens and their wives, and some prominent country gentlemen. St George's guild, first mentioned in 1462, was also open to men and women. It was closely associated with city government; the guild altar was in St Peter's church and by 1472–3 the guild chaplain occupied a chamber over the Pentice door. The fraternity of St Ursula, established in 1509, was never popular and proved short-lived.

John Hatton, one of the founders of the fraternity of St Anne, in his will in 1398 asked to be buried in the chapel of St Mary in the collegiate church of St John's. In 1408 the master carpenter Robert Scot bequeathed land to the fraternity and a torch and candle to the chapel of St Mary.[53] The chapel may have been the stone-vaulted and richly carved Lady chapel inserted in the east end of St John's in *c*.1349. The fraternity had close links with the clergy of St John's. Ranulph Scolehall, senior chaplain of the Orby chantry and consequently known as the petty canon, regularly served as warden or master of St Anne's in the years 1396–1421. On 21 August 1404, just a few days after the feast of the Assumption of the Virgin, the members met at his house to approve the accounts and they assembled there again some two weeks later, just before the Nativity of the Virgin (8 September), spending modest amounts on bread, ale, cheese and wine.[54] The seventeenth-century plan of St John's and its precinct depicted the petty canons' houses east of the church and immediately adjoining the building and courtyard which had belonged to St Anne's. Interestingly, important meetings were held 'betwixt the two St Mary's masses' and were not related to the feast of St Anne (26 July). The fraternity established in 1361 was dedicated to the Blessed Trinity, the Assumption of Our Lady and St Anne. Were the female members known as the Worshipful Wives and responsible for staging the Assumption of Our Lady in the play cycle?

Personal relationships

Townspeople constantly turned to support systems based on family, friends, fellow guildsmen, parish clergy and civic officials. The life-changing events of birth, marriage and death were negotiated with the help of close relatives and personal friends. A wider circle provided assistance with matters of daily routine, which ranged from simple tasks like delivering messages to more demanding roles as pledges in law-suits and guarantors of the payment of debts. The urban community was enmeshed in a complex web of personal relationships.

Executors, supervisors and witnesses of wills

Wills were last-minute affairs, often drawn up on the deathbed, but the choice of those who would fulfil the vital duties of executor and supervisor had probably long been decided. These positions of trust were usually reserved for members of the family. Wives invariably acted as executors, although they were commonly named in second place, after a close male relative or the parish priest. John Hawarden in 1496 appointed his brother Humphrey, Doctor of Law, his wife Margaret and his son Thomas. Margaret in her turn in 1520 appointed the prioress, her cousin Richard Grosvenor of Eaton and her son Thomas, now an alderman. Executors were rewarded for their services with handsome bequests.[55] Family connections linking a testator with his executors cannot always be detected and on occasion men perhaps appointed close friends of equal standing. The butchers Henry Procator and Nicholas Fytton, neighbours in Watergate Street near Goss Lane in the early fifteenth century, may be cited as an example. They habitually paid their fines side by side and their two sons became freemen in the autumn of 1419. Friends as well as neighbours, Procator acted as Fytton's executor a few months later and extended his premises when Fytton's widow and son granted him a chamber, shop and cellar adjoining their property.[56] Christopher Marshall and the smith Thomas Bulkeley evidently worked in related trades and in the early 1450s Christopher appointed Thomas his executor. Within months Thomas married the widow.[57]

A sizeable group gathered at the bedside to witness the will; their testimony would have been crucial if the will was disputed. Among them were family members (but not wives), the parish priest and perhaps a chaplain who advised on the wording and possibly wrote out the document as well. Close friends of similar social standing were present and other witnesses who were not named. In 1519 the will of William Rogerson ironmonger was witnessed by the rector of St Peter's, a chaplain, Rogerson's brother-in-law, two city merchants and 'others'. Sir Robert Devyas (probably priest of St Bridget's), a Carmelite friar and a city merchant witnessed Elizabeth Hurleton's will in 1527.[58] Only one inventory dating from the later medieval period survives, listing the goods of mercer Alexander Stanney who died in 1477.[59] Four aldermen acted as appraisers, all of them involved in the textile trade and qualified to value the merchandise. Whether any of the four were related to Stanney is not known. The authorities doubtless preferred impartial appraisers, considering them more likely to give an accurate valuation.

Entry to the franchise

Men were admitted to the franchise by the mayor at a ceremony held in the common hall. Those whose father had been free at the time of their birth paid an entry fine of 10½d and wine; others paid 26s 8d and needed the sponsorship of three or four citizens. Many entrants were sponsored by one or more members of their craft company. The corviser Ranulph Frodsham in November 1471 and the saddler Robert Hamnet in July 1487 were each sponsored by three fellow craftsmen.[60] Other entrants found pledges among members of related crafts: a draper and two walkers sponsored a dyer in July 1485; a pewterer, a founder and an ironmonger sponsored a plumber in January 1488.[61] The master craftsman who had supervised a young man's apprenticeship was doubtless named among his pledges, many of whom had served as company steward. Neighbours also acted as sponsors. In 1470 the serving sheriff Thomas Fernes was one of two Eastgate Street residents who sponsored the corviser John Cholle who lived in Fleshmonger Lane. Fernes himself had begun his career as a corviser and had become a successful merchant.[62]

Newcomers to Chester were sponsored by citizens whom they knew through trading activities. John Hatton and John Overton acted as pledges for David Dewe of Nantwich in 1420; all three were involved in trade with Ireland.[63] Members of Chester's ruling élite found sponsors within their close-knit circle, fellow office-holders who shared their business interests and to whom they often were connected by marriage. Immediately after his election on 15 October 1462, for example, the new mayor Robert Bruyn admitted William Sneyd to the franchise. Both men were drapers, as was Roger Ledsham the first-named pledge, and all three lived in Northgate Street, Sneyd and Ledsham as neighbours on the west side of the street near the Northgate. Sneyd married Ledsham's daughter and served as mayor in 1479–80; their daughter married Roger Hurleton.[64]

Pledges

Hundreds of townspeople and their pledges were named in Chester's court records and in many cases it is possible to understand the relationships that linked them and the processes whereby these social relations were negotiated. In November 1459, for example, the butcher Thomas Waltham prosecuted the glover Richard Coly for a debt of 48s 1d for sheepskins; Coly responded by accusing Waltham of breaking the agreement that Coly was to have the skins of all sheep the butcher slaughtered that year. The two men worked within hailing distance of one another. Waltham occupied the property near St Peter's formerly held by the Doncaster family and Coly rented the shop next to the new stairs at the north-eastern corner of Bridge Street. Waltham's pledge was another butcher from Watergate Street and Coly chose Grono Chaloner, who lived close to the river where Coly rented land.[65]

Townspeople commonly found pledges among their family, friends, neighbours, fellow craftsmen and trading contacts, people who did not have to be paid other than by reciprocal favours. Husbands acted as pledges for their wives, parents for their children, and masters or mistresses for their servants. Craftsmen frequently acted as pledges for their fellows and men working in associated occupations also helped one another: a lorimer was pledge for a saddler, a dosser for a waterleader, a hosteler for a carrier, and a butcher for the cook at the Franciscan friary.[66] Townsmen supported their neighbours. In 1448 John Barker who lived next to the Bars acted as pledge for Gibon Roper who lived and worked nearby.[67]

Townspeople regularly acted as pledges for non-residents and the court records reveal personal links that stretched far beyond the city liberties. Traders who travelled to the city on a regular basis sometimes appointed court officials to act for them but many turned to townsmen whom they knew through business dealings. Chester's butchers often acted as pledges for Welshmen bringing livestock to the city and for those living in settlements on the droving routes. The fishmongers acted as pledges for traders from the Isle of Man.[68] The city's smiths were in regular contact with carters, carriers and long-distance traders, and were an obvious choice when these men required a pledge.[69] Skinners and dyers served as pledges for their counterparts from other towns.[70] Merchants involved in trade with Ireland were named as pledges for men from Drogheda and Dublin, and Chester's wealthiest merchants invariably acted as pledges for the Londoners who supplied luxury goods. When a London grocer sued a Plymouth merchant in Chester's Pentice court in 1488 the alderman Ralph Davenport acted as pledge for the Devonian, whom he knew through the wine trade.[71]

The professional pleaders at the Pentice court offered pledging services for which they were paid and some townsmen also served as pledges in return for payment. The sum of a shilling a week was recorded in the 1450s.[72] Pledges faced risks. Their goods were distrained if a defendant defaulted and they became liable for the fine imposed by the court; they could be committed to the Northgate gaol.[73] If defendants were unable to find pledges their goods and chattels were taken instead: a smith's anvil, a chaplain's gown, a minstrel's horse, and a furbisher's plate cap and sword.[74] Two books were taken from the Carmelite prior in 1443 and the convent cart from the prioress in 1460.[75] Townsmen were understandably reluctant to act for strangers and it was particularly difficult for men who were not known in the city to find pledges. It was common for their horses to be seized to prevent their departure and ships were occasionally taken from men who had arrived by sea.[76] Other securities ranged from eight packs of merchandise worth £30 owned by an Irish trader to a Welshman's cloak.[77] The loss of such belongings was at best inconvenient and at worst ruinous; many defendants were compelled to remain until the lawsuit was resolved.

Indebtedness

Townspeople needed the support of pledges in a whole host of situations but above all when they borrowed money or fell into debt. Indebtedness was a pervasive feature of life in Chester, as in all medieval towns. Many inhabitants, from all levels of society, were bound into a complex web of credit and debt and the Pentice court, like borough courts everywhere, was overwhelmed by debt litigation. In 1431–2, for example, 63 per cent of pleas involved debt and in the 1450s and 1480s the figure was slightly higher.[78] The sums involved were usually small, in 1450 ranging from £6 in bonds of obligation owed to Thomas Wotton to 8d for a pound of currants; the median was 6s 8d. In 1488 the highest claim was £2, the lowest was 6d, and the median was 7s.[79] Some pleas of detention of chattels were also connected with debt, since they involved the refusal to return goods that had not been paid for in full, and some alleged thefts involved the seizure of goods to the value of the claim.

As it was customary for rents and contract wages to be paid at fixed intervals some indebtedness was built into the system. Chester's quarter days were the feasts of the Annunciation (25 March), the Nativity of St John the Baptist (24 June), Michaelmas (29 September) and Christmas (25 December). Rents were due on these days and some salaries were paid quarterly, including those of the priest engaged to celebrate mass at the nunnery for twelve months from Michaelmas 1458.[80] The June and September quarter days coincided with the annual fairs and the influx of visitors and upsurge in trade helped to generate the ready cash needed to pay rents and wages.

Much indebtedness arose because Chester's traders and craftsmen allowed their regular customers to pay late. Cooks were frequently in debt to butchers, tailors to drapers, and shoemakers to barkers for example. Many townsmen routinely extended credit to a wide circle of relatives, neighbours and friends, people who could offer reciprocal favours in return. Much of this credit appears to have been undocumented and informal but occasional evidence indicates that running accounts were kept. In 1439, for example, a woman who had worked as a servant for Thomas Wotton successfully prosecuted a townsman for 9d owed for ale, having produced the bill that recorded the debt. One debt in 1455 was recorded on a bill to which the parties appended their seals.[81]

Credit was commonly extended for only a few weeks. The man who spent 2s 11d on beef, mutton and veal on 20 February 1494 was prosecuted by the butcher for non-payment on 11 March. Other debts, in contrast, were long standing. The son and executor of a city heuster in 1439 prosecuted the citizen who owed more than £8 for dyeing done by his father several years previously.[82] Extended credit allowed large debts to build up. The serjeant John Botiler successfully prosecuted the prioress in October 1451 for a debt of almost £10 for ale, a startling amount at a time when ale cost only 1½d or 2d a gallon.[83] Ordinary townspeople were not given such credit and debts of less than a shilling were common: 7d for meat, 6d for bread, and 10d for three months' rent of a chamber for example.[84] These small claims indicate just how cheap and effective litigation was.

The apparent informality of many credit arrangements is deceptive. Debtors were often required to find a pledge to act as surety and thus safeguard the investment. To provide 'greater security' for the debt owed by a non-resident for wool in 1449 the weaver John Herford agreed to act as pledge. He accordingly became legally liable for the debt and was prosecuted when the debtor failed to pay. In 1495 a city furbisher guaranteed the debt owed by the *femme sole* Elena Buccy to the prominent mercer Henry Port and was himself prosecuted by Port when the woman defaulted. He denied being the pledge.[85]

Some mercantile debts were backed by written instruments. Chester had been granted the right to hold the seal of Statute Merchant by 1291 and was one of the towns where debt recognizances were registered and details kept.

Recognizances acknowledging a debt were made in the city exchequer in the Pentice and enrolled in the Mayors' Books.[86] As in other towns, they declined in number after 1400 and more use was made of the bond, a promise to pay by a certain date.[87] The debts rarely exceeded £50 and the largest amounts were owed by the city's merchants to the London or Coventry merchants who supplied them with dyestuffs and luxury goods.[88] London mercers evidently kept a careful account of the goods they supplied and issued written receipts.[89] Cestrians involved in long-distance trade also kept documentary records, including William Stanmere, mayor in 1452–3. After his death it was suspected that he had been involved in a dubious transaction and a search was made for the relevant debt obligation, kept by him in his 'Tresorye' during his lifetime, then by his widow, and finally by her executor.[90]

Throughout the later medieval period some debts were recorded on wooden tally sticks. These were carved with notches of various sizes and shapes denoting the sums of money involved and the names of the parties were written in ink beside the notches and seals were sometimes attached. The tally was then split down the middle and one half given to each party; the two halves could be reunited as proof of the transaction.[91] In 1319 William (III) of Doncaster attempted to recover £4 12s 0d owed for herring, a debt he was prepared to prove by his tally 'according to city custom'. Thomas of Strangeways, Philip Dunfoul, John of Brickhill, Roger Erneys and John the armourer were among the many citizens who used tallies in the fourteenth century. The vast majority of debts recorded on tallies involved sales of goods: woad, Irish cloth, lambskins, cartloads of lead, and a quarter of barley for example.[92] Tallies continued to be used in the fifteenth century, although in declining numbers, and recorded debts for wool, dyeing cloth and cisterns of ale.[93] The system was not fool-proof. One debtor entered his creditor's house in December 1458 and stole a tally recording a debt of £10 16s 0d; a few months later he returned and cut 40s from another tally made by the two men.[94]

Occasionally items were deposited as pawns. In 1326 a tailor pawned a hood worth 15d to Richard Dunfoul in return for a loan of 10d. The smith Henry Payn claimed in 1481 that the tailor Thomas Croke owed money for a skull cap bought from him but Croke denied the purchase and maintained that Payn had in fact pawned the cap for bread and ale.[95] Nicholas Deykin requested in his will in 1518 that Agnes Smith (perhaps his sister) be given all her plate that lay in pledge with him and he forgave and pardoned all the money it lay for.[96] Another type of arrangement involved payment or part payment in goods. A miller and his wife agreed in 1429 to pay their debt to a tailor partly in silver and partly in wheat, in 1489 a smith paid for ale with two horseshoes, and the following year a woman agreed to care for a child in return for 15d in money and a bedcovering worth 5s.[97]

The shortage of bullion from 1445 until 1465 resulted in an acute shortage of silver coins in England and this created problems until new sources of silver increased the supply in the late 1460s. This perhaps explains why John Sawer paid an instalment of his entry fine in 1464 by working on the new Pentice without wages.[98] A hint that silver coins may have been in short supply in Chester can be found in a plea heard in 1450. Robert Barber, possibly the common usurer named below, prosecuted a chaplain for failing to change a noble as he had promised.[99] Gold nobles had been introduced by Edward III in 1344 in response to the bullion shortage produced by the outbreak of war with France in 1337.[100] Cestrians occasionally quoted prices in nobles in the fifteenth century: five nobles for red wine in 1437 and two nobles for two casks of herring in 1449 for example.[101] In the 1490s and early 1500s gold nobles, some described as old, were used in transactions between wealthy townsmen, including the rector of Holy Trinity and the mayor Henry Port.[102] Such coins were totally impractical for routine purchases. In 1496 John Hawarden's bequests to his wife included 1,750 pennies and old groats, a thicker coin equal to four pence first minted in 1351–2.[103] Pennies were too large for some transactions and could be cut into halves and quarters.

Money-lending was common practice, often for small amounts and for short periods of time. Claims to recover loans were sometimes associated with claims for other debts, revealing that lender and borrower were acquainted, and it seems that traders with ready cash to spare were happy to lend to people they knew.[104] Concerns about the morality of money-lending faded away in England in the late thirteenth century and it was accepted that lenders could levy extra payments to compensate them for the loss of profit on their capital or for the damage they suffered if borrowers were slow to repay. Interest rates below 10 per cent were not considered usurious and in the fifteenth century they were about 5 to 7 per cent.[105] There is no evidence for interest charged on small loans at Chester and the only citizen named as a common usurer was the barber Robert White, presented at an inquiry in 1463. Usurers were perhaps dealt with by the ecclesiastical courts.[106]

Chester's parish clergy and members of the religious houses were regular money-lenders, as were their counterparts elsewhere.[107] They too made loans to people personally known to them: by the parson of St Mary's to a parishioner, by the abbot of St Werburgh's to a female tenant, and by the Carmelite prior to a building worker whose company light burned on an altar in his church.[108] Wealthy men were another source of credit. In 1469 William Paston of Norfolk explained the advantages of money-lending to his sister-in-law, who had received a request for a £20 loan. The request had come from a man who 'hath and may doo for you, and for my nevewe Sir John, in many thynges, and is his kynnesman; and it were a gode frendely dede and no jeopardy nor hurt.' Furthermore, the loan would be made upon sufficient surety and be repaid by the end of the year.[109] Similar considerations induced Chester's wealthiest men to lend money to relatives, friends and business associates. In their wills, as was common practice, they released some of their debtors and bequeathed other debts to kinsmen. Nicholas Deykin in 1518 forgave and pardoned debts owed to him by five individuals and he bequeathed to his brother-in-law 46s 9d owed by a Caernarfon saddler, a debt which may well have proved difficult to collect.[110] Some loans made by prominent citizens were small: a loan of 8d to a cooper by John Cottingham in 1439, for example, and 4s 10d to a shoemaker by Thomas Wotton in 1443. Cottingham and the cooper both lived in Bridge Street and doubtless knew one another; Wotton and the shoemaker were probably also acquainted.[111]

Support in disputes

Anti-social behaviour ranging from petty theft to serious physical assaults was depressingly familiar in late medieval Chester. Pleas of trespass formed a significant proportion of the business handled by the Pentice court, exceeded only by pleas of debt, and numerous breaches of the peace were presented at judicial inquiries in the portmote. All townspeople embroiled in disputes were required to find pledges and again looked to family, friends and work colleagues for support. In 1419 a mother guaranteed the payment of a fine imposed on her daughter and the goldsmith Edward Myddle guaranteed payment of the fines imposed on his servant and on the goldsmith Roger Warmingham.[112] The relationship between Myddle and Warmingham was based on their shared craft and neighbourhood and the two men served together as company stewards in 1424. By that time they may not have been friends. Whenever one was named as plaintiff or defendant the other invariably acted as pledge for the opposing party.[113] Personal animosities were not unusual and the urban community was in a constant state of flux. Relationships could be strengthened by new marriage alliances or fragmented by difficult trading conditions. The resulting tensions threatened peace and stability.

One method used by the authorities to control disorder was the mainprize, a legal instrument which bound an individual or a group of individuals to keep the peace until a specified court session. The subject of the mainprize had not necessarily committed an offence but the town governors evidently had grounds for believing that he or she might offend in the near future. Each subject needed to find three or four men to act as sureties, who would be willing to pay the monetary penalty imposed in the case of default. This was commonly £40 but rose to 100 marks for prominent individuals. The city's aldermen regularly served as sureties, not only for their own circle but also for townsmen of lesser rank, possibly those living in the same quarter of the city. The few councilmen who served as sureties usually acted for men from the administrative division they represented. Other sureties included fellow craftsmen, neighbours and family members. In December 1462, when Robert Buccy was bound over to keep the peace towards the abbot of St Werburgh's until the following portmote, his sureties were the tailors Thomas and Richard Buccy, almost certainly abbey tenants, and two other Northgate Street residents, one of them a councilman. Robert was bound over again in January, March, April and May 1463, and although one or two of his sureties changed each time they either came from Northgate Street or traded as butchers, barkers or saddlers, suggesting a link with the leather workers. Tensions between the abbot and the Buccy family perhaps went back to February 1460, when the abbot accused Thomas and Richard and four other townsmen of abducting Elena, a villein (servile) tenant from his manor of Upton.[114]

In October 1476 the weaver Henry Rathbone was bound over to keep the peace towards the young widow Elizabeth Ledsham, her tenants and her servants. His sureties were two constables, one of them a weaver, from Northgate Street where Elizabeth lived, a shearman and a second weaver. When the mainprize was reissued on 2 December all four sureties were weavers. Six days later Rathbone stole a pewter bowl from Elizabeth and when he was again bound over on 16 December only one weaver supported him. The theft was presented at the 'full portmote' on 13 January 1477, among the Northgate Street entries because the theft had taken place there, and a fine of 12d was imposed. Rathbone was subsequently named among the fine-payers from Bridge Street, where he lived. The weaver who had loyally supported him throughout again served as pledge and guaranteed payment.[115] The tensions may have originated during the lifetime of Elizabeth's husband, the draper Roger Ledsham, and perhaps involved a shop near the Northgate. Ledsham held two shops in that location, later held by his widow; by the 1490s one was occupied by the draper John Rathbone.[116]

Trouble constantly flared up with outsiders. Hostilities between Robert Bagh of Dodleston and Nicholas Monksfield, sheriff in 1459–60, stemmed from a case heard in the Pentice court in April 1455 in which the abbot of Dieulacres (Staffordshire) attempted to recover rent owed by Bagh, and Monksfield acted as the abbot's pledge.[117] The abbey owned lands in Dodleston and the lost field-name 'Munkesfeld' indicates that the Monksfield family originated in the township, where they continued to hold property.[118] In May 1455 Bagh was bound over to keep the peace towards Monksfield and his associates and the mainprize was regularly renewed over several years, certainly until April 1463 and possibly longer. Almost all those who acted as sureties came from Bridge Street, where Monksfield had his home.[119]

Some medieval 'asbos' failed to keep the peace. In December 1500 Otiwell Corbet acted as one of the sureties for the merchant John Pike and his two

FIGURE 10.3. Mainprize of John Man, tailor. In April 1485 John Man was bound over to keep the peace towards Hugh Smyth, his tenants and servants until the next portmote. The aldermen Richard Gerard and Ralph Davenport acted as his sureties.

FIGURE 10.4. The Old Northgate drawn by Randle Holmes in the mid 17th century. Some indicted felons were imprisoned until their case was heard and then brought to the bar of the court by the gaoler. Debtors were imprisoned in the 'franchise house' above the gate.

sons, bound over to keep the peace towards Thomas Monning, Robert Bruyn, and father and son Richard and John Walley, all of them involved in overseas trade. A few weeks later John Walley attacked Corbet in the street and cut off two of his fingers, but was himself mortally wounded by the knife his victim drew in self-defence. This death naturally caused enduring animosity. Corbet was mainprized in March 1502 to keep the peace towards Joanna Walley widow, Richard Walley, Robert Bruyn, Thomas Monning and their wives, tenants and servants. His sureties included men who had acted with him as sureties in 1500.[120] This bitter feud produced long-lasting tensions within the mercantile community.

Bonds issued by the crownmote court were few in number and different in nature. Subjects of the bonds were either indicted felons or individuals taken on suspicion of felony and the sureties undertook to produce the subject at a subsequent court session. In 1415 the sureties were said to be holding the indicted felon in bail, making it explicit that these were bail bonds.[121] The case of John Sandford, a labourer from Macclesfield, may be taken as an example. He was in Chester on Michaelmas day 1492 and allegedly killed a man outside the Northgate with a blow from his pole-axe. The death was investigated at a coroners' inquest in December and the jurors found him guilty. Sandford was mainprized as an indicted felon in March and April, his sureties guaranteeing that he would not leave the city liberties. The bonding clause was expressed as *corpus pro corpore* which meant, in theory, that they could stand trial for felony if he failed to appear. The case came to court in June. Sandford was brought to court by the gaoler, interrogated by the mayor and pleaded not guilty. Twelve jurors were immediately assembled and found him not guilty. The doomsmen acquitted him and declared that the murderer was a mariner from Dover. Sandford was nevertheless mainprized to appear at the following crownmote, this time not *corpus pro corpore* but for £40. Four of the jurors acted as his sureties. A dozen citizens acted as his sureties between December 1492 and June 1493, including an alderman and several councilmen. It seems unlikely that Sandford was linked to them in any way and they were probably chosen from those present in the court.[122]

The experience of the local shearman and his wife taken on suspicion of felony in January 1477 was very different. When they were bound over to appear at the next crownmote session 16 prominent townsmen appeared in person before the mayor in the Pentice and were named as sureties. Among them were several aldermen and councilmen, and a number of textile workers who perhaps wanted to support a fellow craftsman. When the couple duly appeared in the common hall it was found that no-one wished to plead against them and they were instantly dismissed by proclamation.[123] Personal relationships mattered.

Conclusion

The limitations of the available written sources mean that many aspects of Chester's history in the late medieval period can not be studied. The documents that do survive compensate to a considerable degree, and the court records in particular shed welcome light on daily life in the urban community. Chester's court rolls have been placed at the heart of this book (as the endnotes demonstrate) and they allow the ordinary townspeople to emerge from obscurity. The world in which they lived differed markedly from our own but we can recognise real human beings with whom we have much in common.

The clerks who compiled the records were not always very competent. They struggled to spell Welsh names like 'Glwadys' and 'Thlyke' and wrote other names phonetically, providing a lingering echo of local pronunciation: John ffloide, Dulgethle and Kayros (Caerwys) for example. They were sometimes at a loss for the correct Latin word and inserted the English equivalent: *quoddam* mud wall *super communem solum* (a certain mud wall on the common soil).[1] They enlivened the court entries with doodles: a face in the 'C' of Richard Caldecote, official at the Dee Mills and fishery in the 1430s and 1440s, and a man's head with a jaunty cap and ribbons under the crownmote heading during the Michaelmas fair in 1405.[2]

Forenames were regularly shortened, even in the official records. Robert was rendered as Robyn, Henry as Harry, Simon as Symkyn, Joanna as Janet and Margaret as Meg. English diminutives were added to Welsh names and the holders were called Jankin, Jenkin, Daukyn and Hankin.[3] This naming practice reveals the friendships which helped to sustain the community. The townspeople amused themselves by inventing names appropriate to an individual's trade or appearance. Examples include William traylemantle, Robert clubfoot, the tailor Geoffrey Shaperyght, the shoemakers John and William Pynchware, and the smith's servant Thomas Mendynge.[4] Mariners were named Fairweather, Forthewind and Godsendus.[5]

Women given nicknames were always associated with the drink trade: Margaret Flapcake, struck on the head by a bowl filled with ale in a house in Castle Lane in 1324, Joanna Acavite, fined for keeping a brothel in Watergate Street in 1476, and Margery Goodale, presented for selling ale too dear in 1484.[6] The name Rose may have been restricted to poor women who worked as garlandmakers, huxters and ale sellers, and who had much in common with Rose the regrater described by Langland in *Piers Ploughman*. A taverner's daughter named Rose was involved in an affray on Whitsunday in 1399.[7] Was the name bestowed on comely young females who sold ale and wine? The practice of young women keeping taverns and alehouses was denounced in 1540 because it had resulted in brawls and wanton behaviour; the authorities ordered that henceforth no woman aged between 14 and 40 was to keep a tavern or an alehouse.[8]

It is sometimes possible to detect public disapproval. The duplicity of William Stanmere, mayor in 1452–3, was remembered 20 years after his death and the court record referred to him as 'William Stanmere whom God pardon'. The name of Sir John Savage, brother-in-law of the Stanleys and mayor in the years 1484–6, was struck through in the heading of the portmote session held on 22 August 1485, the day of the battle of Bosworth. So too was his title 'knight of the body of the king', evidently deemed inappropriate for a man whose links with the Stanleys may have implicated him in the defeat and death of Richard III. In January 1494 three respectable wives assaulted Alice Wright *alias* Filpot, recently charged with brothel-keeping in association with two married men, and therefore perceived as a threat to traditional family values.[9]

Occasionally we can glimpse close personal relationships. In February 1405 the mayor dispatched a letter 'in right grett hast' to Hugh de Holes at Oxford asking how to proceed in a plea of real estate that threatened the city's liberties. Hugh replied to his 'welbeloved frynds' six days later (a very prompt response from a lawyer) with the welcome news that the case could not be removed to another court. In the 1450s the mercer John Cottingham wrote to his cousin and namesake in London: 'Cosyn, if there be any service that I can doe for you I pray send me word and I shall doe it with all my hart that knows God the which have yow in is keepeinge'.[10] The hierarchical nature of society was apparent in men's wills and children were carefully ranked. The ironmonger William Rogerson in 1519 left his best set of spoons to his son and other sets in descending order to his five daughters. Margery, given the worst dozen spoons and the fourth best salt, was probably the youngest.[11] Signs of affection nevertheless shine through. Testators remembered 'my young cousin Thomas', 'little Jane Golborne' and 'little Margery'. John Norris in 1499 left money to Thomas Hurleton 'by no right but by favour and love for James your son and heir'.[12]

Late medieval Chester was a typical medieval town, its streets filled with refuse and its air reeking with unpleasant smells. The inhabitants included many who were arrogant, self-seeking, dishonest or violent, but many who were striving to make

It seems that no business was transacted at the crownmote court held on 5 October 1405. Under the heading are a series of doodles, including this face.

a decent living for themselves and their families. Among them were migrants who had left their homes and travelled long distances in the hope of a better life; craftsmen who took on extra work in the weeks before Christmas to gain additional income; parents who found the money to provide schooling for their children. Their endeavours allowed progress to be made, and our world has emerged from theirs.

Abbreviations

Add. Ch.	Additional Charter(s)
Add. Ms.	Additional Manuscript(s)
BL	British Library
BPR	*Register of Edward the Black Prince preserved in the Public Record Office*
CCALS	Cheshire and Chester Archives and Local Studies
CCR	*Calendar of the Close Rolls preserved in the Public Record Office*
Cal. Court R.	*Calendar of County Court, City Court, and Eyre Rolls of Chester, 1259-97*
Cal. Lib.	*Calendar of the Liberate Rolls preserved in the Public Record Office*
CPR	*Calendar of the Patent Rolls preserved in the Public Record Office*
CUH	*The Cambridge Urban History of Britain; volume 1: 600-1540*
DKR	*Reports of the Deputy Keeper of the Public Records*
EETS	Early English Text Society
Econ. HR	*Economic History Review*
Harl. Ms.	Harleian Manuscripts
JCAS	*Journal of the Chester Archaeological Society*
RSLC	Record Society of Lancashire and Cheshire
Sel. Court R.	*Selected Rolls of the Chester City Courts*
Sheaf	*The Cheshire Sheaf* [preceded by series number]
SRO	Staffordshire Record Office
THSLC	*Transactions of the Historic Society of Lancashire and Cheshire*
TNA: PRO	The National Archives: Public Record Office, Kew
TRHS	*Transactions of the Royal Historical Society*
VCH	*Victoria County History*

Notes

Chapter 1

1 *The Metrical Chronicle of Robert of Gloucester*, i, 1, 11–19, 21–7, 36–41, 75–86, 141–50, 169–70.

2 C. Dyer, 'How Urban was Medieval England?', 37, 38, 43; C. Dyer, *Making a Living in the Middle Ages*, 187; C. Dyer, 'Small Towns 1270–1540', *CUH*, I, 505–10; G. Rosser, 'Urban Culture and the Church 1300–1540', *CUH*, I, 337.

3 C. Dyer, 'Small Towns 1270–1540', *CUH*, I, 505.

4 C. Dyer, 'How Urban was Medieval England?', 38; C. Dyer, *Making a Living*, 147; C. Dyer, 'The Hidden Trade of the Middle Ages: Evidence from the West Midlands', 292, 299; J. Laughton and C. Dyer, 'Small Towns in the East and West Midlands in the Later Middle Ages: A Comparison', 28–30; C. Dyer, 'The Urbanizing of Staffordshire: The First Phases', 11; C. Dyer, *An Age of Transition?*, 91.

5 D. Palliser, 'Introduction', *CUH*, I, 4–5. See also R. Holt and G. Rosser, 'Introduction: The English Town in the Middle Ages', in R. Holt and G. Rosser (eds), *The Medieval Town: A Reader in English Urban History 1200–1540*, 4; J. Laughton, E. Jones and C. Dyer, 'The Urban Hierarchy of the later Middle Ages: A Study of the East Midlands', 334–5.

6 J. Laughton and C. Dyer, 'Small Towns in the East and West Midlands', 31–2; G. Astill, 'General Survey 600–1300', *CUH*, I, 46–7.

7 C.M. Barron, 'London 1300–1540', *CUH*, I, 396–7; R. Holt, 'Society and Population 600–1300', *CUH*, I, 103–4; C. Dyer, *Making a Living*, 188–90.

8 R. Holt, 'Society and Population 600–1300', *CUH*, I, 82–3; C. Dyer, 'How Urban was Medieval England?', 38–9.

9 J. Kermode, 'The Greater Towns 1300–1540', *CUH*, I, 442–3.

10 C. Dyer, 'The Hidden Trade of the Middle Ages', 283–303; C. Dyer, 'Market Towns and the Countryside', 17–35; C. Dyer, 'A Summing Up', in J.A. Galloway (ed.), *Trade, Urban Hinterlands and Market Integration c.1300–1600*, 104–5.

11 A.J.L. Winchester, *Landscape and Society in Medieval Cumbria*; H.S.A. Fox, 'Medieval Urban Development'; J. Laughton, E. Jones and C. Dyer, 'The Urban Hierarchy of the later Middle Ages', 331–57.

12 C. Dyer, 'Small Towns 1270–1540', *CUH*, I, 507–10; J. Laughton and C. Dyer, 'Small Towns in the East and West Midlands', 24–52.

13 N.J. Higham, *A Frontier Landscape: The North West in the Middle Ages*, 187.

14 M. Beresford and H.P.R. Finberg, *English Medieval Boroughs: A Handlist*, 73–6; M. Beresford, 'English Medieval Boroughs: A Handlist: revisions 1973–81', 59–65.

15 *Extent of the Lordship of Longdendale 1360*, 25–7, 33–5, 39, 49–55. Tintwistle was transferred to Derbyshire in 1974.

16 SRO, D1734/J2268. I am grateful to Paul Booth for this reference.

17 Samantha Letters, *Online Gazetteer of Markets and Fairs in England and Wales to 1516*: updated February 2007 to include information from Paul Booth.

18 G. Ormerod, *History of Cheshire*, I, 137; *A Middlewich Chartulary*, II, xxvi; P. Arrowsmith, *Stockport: A History*, 40.

19 A.M. Tonkinson, *Macclesfield in the Later Fourteenth Century*, 2–3, 10–11, 81. I thank Mike Shaw for providing the figures for Frodsham.

20 P. Morgan, 'Medieval Cheshire', 32.

21 C. Dyer, *Standards of Living*, 265–7; C. Dyer, *Making a Living*, 261–3.

22 G. Ormerod, *History of Cheshire*, II, 875–7; III, 883.

23 J.McN. Dodgson, *The Place-Names of Cheshire*, Part One, 294–5; P. Arrowsmith, *Stockport: A History*, 37.

24 M. Shaw, *Cheshire Historic Towns Survey: Macclesfield Archaeological Assessment* (1999), 4, 5 (unpublished).

25 *CPR*, 1396–9, 591, 592, 593, 597; TNA: PRO, CHES 25/11, m.5d.

26 P. Arrowsmith, *Stockport: A History*, 6, 43–4.

27 *The Household Books of John Howard, Duke of Norfolk*, I, 230.

28 *Gough Map*; *William of Worcester Itineraries*, 331.

29 N. Pevsner and E. Hubbard, *The Buildings of Cheshire*, 286–7; S. Jenkins, *England's Thousand Best Churches*, 63; C. Grossinger, 'Chester Cathedral Misericords', 99, 103–5.

30 A.J. Kettle, 'Religious Houses', in *VCH, Cheshire*, III, 186–7; G. Ormerod, *History of Cheshire*, III, 450.

31 TNA: PRO, CHES 25/11, m.5; SC 6/790/5, m.11; J.McN. Dodgson, *Place-Names of Cheshire*, Part Three, 34–5.

32 TNA: PRO, CHES 25/8, m.15; CHES 25/9, m.122; CHES 25/10, mm.21, 25; CHES 25/11, mm.1d, 15d, 16d, 17, 19, 21d; CHES 25/12, mm.2, 14, 24; CHES 25/15, mm.14, 17–17d, 37d, 38, 48d; CHES 25/16, mm.6, 9, 14.

33 *3 Sheaf*, 30 (1935), 79; 36 *DKR*, 337; CCALS, ZSR 419, m.1.

34 M.J. Bennett, *Community, Class and Careerism*, 113–14, 116–17.

35 TNA: PRO, CHES 25/12, m.19.

36 CCALS, ZMB 5, f.176; ZSB 1, ff.36v, 38v; ZSB 3, f.176; TNA: PRO, CHES 25/12, m.19d; CHES 25/15, m.31; SC 2/258/8, m.1d; P. Arrowsmith, *Stockport: A History*, 42–3.

37 *CPR*, 1272–81, 300; 1281–92, 74–6; P.H.W. Booth, *Financial Administration of the Lordship of Chester*, 92–4, 97.

38 *BPR*, iii, 274; P.H.W. Booth, *Financial Administration of the Lordship of Chester*, 104–5, n.133 on p.115.

39 TNA: PRO, CHES 25/14, m.9d; SC 6/805/7, m.1d; 805/15, m.1d; 806/3, m.1d; 807/3, m.1d; 807/19, m.1d; SRO, D 641/1/2/73, mm.6, 8; S. Davies, *A History of Macclesfield*, 56–8.

40 TNA: PRO, CHES 25/12, mm.22d, 33d; SC 2/256/18, m.1; SC 2/256/19, m.1.

41 TNA: PRO, CHES 25/4, m.27d; CHES 25/12, m.12d. I thank Paul Booth for the reference to the inventory.

42 TNA: PRO, SC 6/783/15, m.3; 786/1, m.1d; 786/6, m.1; 786/7, m.1; 791/3, m.4; 791/5, m.3d.

43 TNA: PRO, SC 6/793/10, m.4; 795/8, m.6; 796/7, m.5; 797/3, m.3; 801/2, m.3d.

44 TNA: PRO, CHES 25/11, m.22; CHES 25/12, m.6; SC 2/255/17, m.1d.

45 I. Brown, *Discovering a Welsh Landscape: Archaeology in the Clwydian Range*, 104–5.

46 M. Beresford, *New Towns of the Middle Ages*, 39–41, 550; D.H. Owen, 'Denbigh', in R.A. Griffiths (ed.), *Boroughs of Mediaeval Wales*, 169; I. Soulsby, *The Towns of Medieval Wales*, 121–3, 135.

47 R.I. Jack, 'Ruthin', in *Boroughs of Mediaeval Wales*, 245–6; I. Soulsby, *The Towns of Medieval Wales*, 232–4.

48 M. Beresford, *New Towns of the Middle Ages*, 551; I. Soulsby, *The Towns of Medieval Wales*, 211–12; BL, Harl. Ms.2074, 45; *CPR*, 1313–17, 287 (Thomas the taverner granted messuage and 60 acres to William Doncaster the elder and his wife).

49 R.A. Griffiths, 'Wales and the Marches', *CUH*, I, 707.

50 R.I. Jack, 'Ruthin', 252–5; R.A. Griffiths, 'Wales and the Marches', *CUH*, I, 707; I. Soulsby, *The Towns of Medieval Wales*, 94–5, 232–4.

51 R.A. Griffiths, 'Wales and the Marches', *CUH*, I, 708; R.I. Jack, 'Ruthin', 260–1.

52 I. Soulsby, *The Towns of Medieval Wales*, 135, 146, 149, 212; D.H. Owen, 'Denbigh', 171–2.

53 R.I. Jack, 'Ruthin', 255–7, 261.

54 CCALS, ZSR 76, m.1d; ZMB 7, f.146v.

55 C.P. Lewis, 'Population', *VCH, Chester*, V, Part 2, 71.

56 BL, Harl. Ms.2158, ff.45v–47v.

57 H. Clarke, S. Dent and R. Johnson, *Dublinia: The Story of Medieval Dublin*, 93. In 1881 a labourer, his family and nine lodgers occupied a property off Lower Bridge Street (Chester Community History and Heritage Newsletter, Spring 2008, 4).

58 C.P. Lewis, 'Introduction', *VCH, Chester*, V, Part 2, 4; 'Population', Part 2, 71–2; A. Dyer, 'Appendix: Ranking Lists of English Medieval Towns', *CUH*, I, 765.

59 J.McN. Dodgson, *The Place-Names of Cheshire*, Part Five (i:i), 6–7.

60 For full details of Roman Chester, see D. Mason, *Roman Chester: City of the Eagles*; D. Mason, *Chester AD 400–1066*, 11–21; T.J. Strickland, 'Roman Chester', *VCH, Chester*, V, Part 1, 9–15.

61 A. Thacker, 'Early Medieval Chester, 400–1230', *VCH, Chester*, V, Part 1, 16–17; D. Mason, *Chester AD 400–1066*, 89–96.

62 A. Thacker, 'Early Medieval Chester, 400–1230', 18–24.

63 A. Thacker, 'Early Medieval Chester, 400–1230', 24–5; N.J. Higham, *A Frontier Landscape: The North West in the Middle Ages*, 169

64 C.P. Lewis notes that there must have been other houses exempt from tax, and the reduction by 205 probably represented a tax concession rather than an actual count of occupied dwellings: *VCH, Chester*, V, Part 2, 71.

65 A. Thacker, 'Early Medieval Chester, 400–1230', 25–33.

66 *Willelmi Malmesbiriensis Monachi*, 308; *Liber Luciani de Laude Cestrie*, 44, 46.

67 A. Thacker, 'The Earls and their Earldom', 13–15.

68 S. Cather, D. Park and R. Pender, 'Henry III's Wall Paintings at Chester Castle', 170–89.

69 *CLR*, 1240–5, 314–24; *Cheshire in the Pipe Rolls*, 81–3.; *Cal. Doc. Irel.*, 1171–1251, 2501, 2503, 2856, 3078, 3190.

70 *Cheshire in the Pipe Rolls,* 78.

71 A. Thacker, 'Later Medieval Chester', *VCH, Chester*, V, Part 1, 34–5; M. Prestwich, *Plantagenet England, 1225–1360*, 146–50.

72 C. Dyer, *Standards of Living*, 176–7.

73 CCALS, ZSR 5, m.5; ZSR 12, m.10; ZSR 23, m.5; ZSR 30, m.2; ZSR 159, m.1d. Purple and violet: ZMB 6, f.119v; ZSB 5, ff.17, 38v; ZSR 419, m.1; ZSR 442, m.1; ZSR 443, m.1d.

74 *Liber Luciani de Laude Cestrie*, 52, 65.

75 R.H. Morris, *Chester in the Plantagenet and Tudor Reigns*, 45–6.

76 D. Mason, *Roman Chester*, 103–4; A. Thacker, 'Economy and Society, 1230–1350', *VCH, Chester*, V, Part 1, 52; CCALS, ZSB 4, f.53.

77 W.G. Hoskins, 'English Provincial Towns in the early Sixteenth Century', 3–4; Beresford and Finberg, *English Medieval Boroughs*, 56.

78 C.P. Lewis and A.T. Thacker (eds), *Victoria County History, A History of the County of Chester*, volume V: *The City of Chester*, Part 1 (Boydell & Brewer, 2003); Part 2 (Boydell & Brewer, 2005).

79 D. Palliser, 'Introduction', *CUH*, I, 7.

80 Cited by R.A. Griffiths, 'The Study of the Mediaeval Welsh Borough', in R.A. Griffiths (ed.), *Boroughs of Mediaeval Wales*, 8.

Chapter 2

1 *CPR*, 1272–81, 169, 198, 199, 208, 209, 212, 219.

2 For full details of the Welsh wars, see J.E. Morris, *The Welsh Wars of Edward I*; M. Prestwich, *Plantagenet England 1225–1360*, 150–64.

3 *Cheshire in the Pipe Rolls*, 126, 131. Clerks of the merchants of Lucca paid £3,000 into the wardrobe at Chester in August 1282: *CPR*, 1281–92, 33.

4 *Annales Cestrienses*, 113.

5 *CCR*, 1279–88, 202–3; TNA: PRO, E 101/684/20.

6 TNA: PRO, E 101/97/2; E 101/97/3.

7 A. Taylor, *Caernarfon Castle and Town Walls*, 10.

8 TNA: PRO, SC 1/45/71.

9 A. Taylor, *Beaumaris Castle*, 8–9; A. Taylor, *Caernarfon Castle and Town Walls*, 11.

10 C. Dyer, *Making a Living in the Middle Ages*, 260.

11 TNA: PRO, E 101/485/25.

12 R.A. Brown, H.M. Colvin and A.J. Taylor, *History of the King's Works*, ii, 611; *Cheshire in the Pipe Rolls*, 173; TNA: PRO, SC 6/771/4, m.5.

13 TNA: PRO, E 101/486/7; E 101/486/17.

14 *CPR*, 1292–1301, 134; TNA: PRO, SC 6/771/4, m.1; E 101/486/17.

15 *CPR*, 1281–1292, 344; *CPR*, 1292–1301, 22, 310, 482.

16 TNA: PRO, CHES 25/1, mm.1, 2d, 3.

17 *CCR*, 1288–96, 515; M. Beresford, *New Towns of the Middle Ages*, 3–4.

18 CCALS, ZSR 2, m.1.

19 TNA: PRO, SC 6/771/1, m.1.

20 *CPR*, 1307–1313, 353; A. Thacker, 'Later Medieval Chester', *VCH, Chester*, V, Part 1, 37–8.

21 C. Dyer, *Standards of Living*, 262, 265–7; C. Dyer, *Making a Living*, 228–33, 262.

22 *CPR*, 1313–1317, 568; *CPR*, 1321–1324, 27, 114, 116.

23 B.E. Harris, 'The Palatinate 1301–1547', *VCH, Cheshire*, II, 10.

24 *CPR*, 1317–21, 200; *CCR*, 1318–23, 12; BL, Harl. Ms.2162, f.22.

25 *CPR*, 1327–30, 153, 183.

26 TNA: PRO, SC 6/771/12, m.1.

27 *CCR*, 1247–51, 465; TNA: PRO, SC 6/771/17, m.1.

28 D. Keene, *Survey of Medieval Winchester*, i, 295.

29 P.H.W. Booth, *Financial Administration of the Lordship of Chester*, 89–91, 128–9; TNA: PRO, SC 6/783/16, m.7.

30 P. Ziegler, *The Black Death*, 191.

31 A.J. Kettle, 'Religious Houses', *VCH, Cheshire*, III, 145 with n.97, 150; D. Jones, *The Church in Chester 1300–1540*, 163, 166, 170, 177, 180; R.V.H. Burne, *The Monks of Chester*, 84.

32 TNA: PRO, SC 6/784/9, mm.2–3.

33 *BPR*, iii, 242–3, 261.

34 *BPR*, iii, 415.

35 TNA: PRO, CHES 25/8, m.57; R.B. Dobson, *The Peasants' Revolt of 1381*, 297–9.

36 M.J. Bennett, *Community, Class and Careerism*, 93–5.

37 TNA: PRO, SC 6/788/1, m.1; SC 6/788/2, m.1.

38 TNA: PRO, E 101/335/1.

39 G. Harriss, *Shaping the Nation: England 1360–1461*, 469–70; P. McNiven, 'The Cheshire Rising of 1400', 379; P. Morgan, *War and Society in Medieval Cheshire 1277–1403*, 194–8; A. Thacker, 'Later Medieval Chester', *VCH, Chester*, V, Part 1, 56.

40 CCALS, ZMB 1, f.14v.

41 P. Morgan, *War and Society*, 196; 36 *DKR*, 433; *CPR*, 1396–99, 402.

42 TNA: PRO, SC 6/774/3, m.1; 36 *DKR*, 18.

43 R.V.H. Burne, *The Monks of Chester*, 107–8; 36 *DKR*, 382.

44 *CPR*, 1391–1396, 522; 36 *DKR*, 124; TNA: PRO, SC 6/774/4, m.1d.

45 R.R. Davies, 'Richard II and the Principality of Chester 1397–9', 256–79; TNA: PRO, SC 6/774/6, m.1; SC 6/774/8, m.1.

46 P. Morgan, *War and Society*, 198–201.

47 36 *DKR*, 224; P. Morgan, *War and Society*, 206.

48 R.R. Davies, 'Richard II and the Principality of Chester', 261.

49 TNA: PRO, SC 6/774/10, m.1d; 36 *DKR*, 376.

50 TNA: PRO, SC 6/774/10, m.1d.

51 R.R. Davies, 'Richard II and the Principality of Chester', 276.

52 *Chronicle of Dieulacres Abbey*, 171–2; *Chronicon Adae de Usk*, 27; TNA: PRO, SC 6/774/10, m.1d.

53 *Translation of a French Metrical History of the Deposition of King Richard the Second*, 172–5.

54 R.R. Davies, 'Richard II and the Principality of Chester', 279.

55 C. Dyer, *Making a Living*, 268, 296.

56 P. McNiven, 'The Cheshire Rising of 1400', 386–96; P. Morgan, *War and Society*, 205–7; TNA: PRO, SC 6/774/13, m.1.

57 TNA: PRO, CHES 25/10, m.1; *CPR*, 1399–1401, 285–6, 385–6.

58 *Calendar of Charter Rolls*, V, 384.

59 I. Soulsby, *The Towns of Medieval Wales*, 233. It has also been claimed that chattels, livestock and cash totalling £2,100 were taken but that only one house was burnt: R.I. Jack, 'Ruthin', 259.

60 J.E. Lloyd, *Owen Glendower: Owen Glyn Dwr*, 36, 56.

61 TNA: PRO, SC 6/774/13, m.1d; SC 6/774/14, m.1d; SC 6/774/15, m.1d; CCALS, ZMR 67, m.1d.

62 CCALS, ZMB 2, f.1v; 36 *DKR*, 226, 230, 247; J.E. Messham, 'The County of Flint and the Rebellion of Owen Glyndwr', 4–5.

63 CCALS, ZSR 114, m.1; TNA: PRO, CHES 25/10, m.8d.

64 CCALS, ZMB 2, ff.1v, 10, 18.

65 I. Soulsby, *The Towns of Medieval Wales*, 149; A. Taylor, *Harlech Castle*, 9.

66 P. McNiven, 'The Men of Cheshire and the Rebellion of 1403', 1–29; P. McNiven, 'Rebellion, Sedition and the Legend of Richard II's Survival', 93–117; P. Morgan, *War and Society*, 213–18.

67 TNA: PRO, CHES 25/10, m.10d; *Chronicle of Dieulacres Abbey*, 177.

68 36 *DKR*, 3.

69 J.G. Messham, 'The County of Flint and the Rebellion of Owen Glyndwr', 14–19.

70 36 *DKR*, 102; TNA: PRO, SC 6/774/15, m.1d; SC 6/775/3, m.1d; 36 *DKR*, 102.

71 TNA: PRO, CHES 29/107, m.17; CHES 25/10, m.17d.

72 J.G. Messham, 'The County of Flint and the Rebellion of Owen Glyndwr', 18; TNA: PRO, CHES 29/109, m.16.

73 TNA: PRO, CHES 25/10, mm.20, 25d; 36 *DKR*, 140; TNA: PRO, SC 6/775/3, m.1d.

74 CCALS, ZMB 2, ff.18, 20, 23v, 50; 36 *DKR*, 114.

75 R.H. Morris, *Chester in the Plantagenet and Tudor Reigns*, 47.

76 CCALS, ZMB 2, ff.62v, 63, 81, 81v, 83, 83v, 84v, 85, 85v, 91.

77 36 *DKR*, 387, 493; CCALS, ZAF 1, f.1.

78 TNA: PRO, CHES 25/11, mm.17–18.

79 TNA: PRO, SC 6/793/6, m.6d.

80 C. Dyer, *Standards of Living*, 263, 267–8; C. Dyer, *Making a Living*, 275–6; G. Ormerod, *History of Cheshire*, I, 233; TNA: PRO, SC 6/795/9, m.8; SC 6/796/4, m.10.

81 R.H. Morris, *Chester in the Plantagenet and Tudor Reigns*, 512; D. Keene, *Survey of Medieval Winchester*, i, 96–8; C. Dyer, *Making a Living*, 298–300.

82 TNA: PRO, SC 6/797/3, m.1d; 797/5, m.1; R.A. Griffiths, *The Reign of Henry VI*, 387–9.

83 TNA: PRO, SC 6/798/1, m.1d; SRO, D 641/2/73, m.13.

84 D. Clayton, *Administration of the County Palatine of Chester 1442–85*, 74–7.

85 TNA: PRO, SC 6/779/7, m.1; D. Clayton, *Administration of the County Palatine of Chester*, 73–90.

86 J. Laughton, forthcoming.

87 TNA: PRO, SC 6/779/7, m.1.

88 CCALS, ZMB 5, ff.49, 49v, 53v–57v, 61–67v.

89 D. Clayton, *Administration of the County Palatine of Chester*, 151.

90 TNA: PRO, SC 6/798/7, mm.1, 6d; *CPR*, 1461–7, 129.

91 TNA: PRO, SC 6/801/2, m.1d; 3 *Sheaf*, 19 (1922), 4.

92 TNA: PRO, SC 6/798/7, m.1; CCALS, ZMB 5, f.71v.

93 TNA: PRO, SC 6/779/10, m.1; D. Clayton, *Administration of the County Palatine of Chester*, 98–9.

94 TNA: PRO, SC 6/798/7, m.1; BL, Harl. Ms.2158, ff.47v, 49, 49v.

95 *Paston Letters and Papers of the Fifteenth Century*, i, 525–6.

96 *The Household Books of John Howard, Duke of Norfolk*, I, 156, 159, 162, 233, 234–5, 237–8, 239–40, 241.

97 TNA: PRO, SC 6/780/2, m.1; SC 6/780/4, m.1.

98 G. Ormerod, *History of Cheshire*, I, 233; J. Thomson, *Transformation of Medieval England*, 207.

99 TNA: PRO, SC 6/799/4, m.1d; SC 6/799/5, m.5; SC 6/780/7, m.1d.

100 TNA: PRO, CHES 25/15, mm.17–17d; 3 *Sheaf*, 22 (1925), 14.

101 *CPR*, 1467–77, 491, 524; 1476–85, 79.

102 CCALS, ZMB 6, f.33v; G. Ormerod, *History of Cheshire*, I, 233.

103 CCALS, ZMB 6, ff.85–7; D. Clayton, *Administration of the County Palatine of Chester*, 113–20, 150–55, 167–9, 176.

104 R.H. Morris, *Chester in the Plantagenet and Tudor Reigns*, 63, 521–4; G. Ormerod, *History of Cheshire*, I, 234.

105 G. Ormerod, *History of Cheshire*, I, 234; BL, Harl.Ms. 2054, f.25.

106 R.H. Morris, *Chester in the Plantagenet and Tudor Reigns*, 524–40.

107 G. Ormerod, *History of Cheshire*, I, 234.

108 C. P. Lewis, 'Introduction', *VCH, Chester*, V, Part 2, 4; A. Dyer, 'Ranking Lists of English Medieval Towns', *CUH*, I, 761, 765.

Chapter 3

1 D. Mason, *Roman Chester: City of the Eagles*, 13–14, 89–91; A. Thacker, 'Topography', *VCH, Chester*, V, Part 1, 206–7; A. Thacker, 'City Walls and Gates', *ibid.*, Part 2, 215, 219.

2 *Polychronicon Ranulphi Higden*, ii, 76–80; A. Gransden, *Historical Writing in England*, II, 44–5.

3 A. Thacker, 'The Early Medieval City and its Buildings', 18; S. Ainsworth and T. Wilmott, *Chester Amphitheatre from Gladiators to Gardens*, 8, 11–12.

4 D. Mason, *Roman Chester*, 162.

5 A. Thacker, 'Topography', *VCH, Chester*, V, Part 1, 207, 210; A. Thacker, 'City Walls and Gates', *ibid.*, Part 2, 215, 223, 224.

6 *Liber Luciani de Laude Cestrie*.

7 TNA: PRO, CHES 25/1, m.4; CCALS, ZMB 6, ff.166v, 169v-170v; ZMB 7, f.2v; ZMB 9(g), f.2.

8 *Charters of the Anglo-Norman Earls of Chester, c.1071–1237*, 1–2, 20–1.

9 BL, Harl. Ms.2158, f.32; J.S. Barrow, 'Water Supply', *VCH, Chester*, V, Part 2, 36.

10 A. Thacker, 'Municipal Buildings', *VCH, Chester*, V, Part 2, 20.

11 CCALS, ZSB 2, f.26v.

12 BL, Harl. Ms.2158, ff.44v-47; CCALS, ZMB 5, ff.41, 69v, 85v, 129v, 181v; ZMB 6, ff.84v, 121.

13 BL, Harl. Ms.2158, ff.31v, 32v, 34, 36, 40; CCALS, ZTAR 1/4.

14 K. Matthews and others, *Excavations at Chester: The Evolution of the Heart of the City*, 9, 15–16, 33.

15 CCALS, ZQCR 2, m.1d; ZMB 3, f.10; ZSR 223, m.1; ZTAR 1/3.

16 R.H. Morris, *Chester in the Plantagenet and Tudor Reigns*, 294; K. Matthews, *Evolution of the Heart of the City*, 33; BL, Harl. Ms.2162, f.86; CCALS, ZSR 22, m.3d; ZQCR 10, m.1.

17 CCALS, ZSR 14, m.2; ZQCR 10, m.1; ZQCR 11, m.1; ZMB 3, ff.101, 102.

18 BL, Harl. Ms.2046, f.33v; Harl. Ms.2020, f.36.

19 CCALS, ZC/Ch/3, 4, 10.

20 K. Matthews, *Evolution of the Heart of the City*, 3–4, 7–9, 33–4; A. Brown (ed.), *The Rows of Chester*, 170.

21 TNA: PRO, CHES 25/1, m.3.

22 BL, Harl. Ms.2162, f.67v; Eaton Ms. 321, m.1; *CPR, 1313–17*, 568; *CPR, 1321–4*, 114; *CPR, 1324–7*, 196; *Talbot Deeds, 1200–1682*, 54.

23 BL, Harl. Ms.2158, f. 45; CCALS, ZTAR 1/4, m.1; TNA: PRO, WALE 29/134.

24 CCALS, ZSB 2, ff.26v, 45v, 87v.

25 CCALS, ZMR 81, m.1d; BL, Harl. Ms.2020, f.424v.

26 3 *Sheaf*, 26 (1929), 75; 3 *Sheaf*, 36 (1941), 31; BL, Harl. Ms.2099, f.310.

27 CCALS, ZSB 3, f.65; ZMR 64, m.1; DCH/DD/1; *Norris Deeds*, 624.

28 J.McN. Dodgson, *Place-Names of Cheshire*, Part Five (1:i), 17–18; CCALS, ZSR 243, m.1.

29 BL, Harl. Ms.2158, ff.45v-46v.

30 CCALS, DVE/CII/21; ZCHD 2/7; *Chester Customs Accounts*, 24–8, 39; BL, Harl. Ms.2020, f.38v; R.H. Morris, *Chester in the Plantagenet and Tudor Reigns*, 250–1.

31 BL, Harl. Ms.2158, ff.34, 36v, 38, 39v, 40v; CCALS, ZTAR 1/3, m.1d.

32 BL, Harl. Ms.2046, f.34v.

33 BL, Harl. Ms.2158, ff.36v, 55v, 57v; TNA: PRO, SC 6/780/5, m.1; J.McN. Dodgson, *Place-Names of Cheshire*, Part Five (1:i), 21.

34 TNA: PRO, CHES 25/8, m.30; CHES 25/10, m.26d; CCALS, ZMB 1, f.60.

35 3 *Sheaf*, 23 (1926), 49–50; BL, Harl. Ms.2158, ff.36v, 38, 41.

36 G. Rosser, *Medieval Westminster*, 145; D. Keene, *Medieval Winchester*, i, 319; CCALS, ZMB 3, f.111v; ZSB 2, f.46.

37 TNA: PRO, SC 6/774/3, m.1; CCALS, ZMR 31, m.2; D. Clayton, *Administration of the County Palatine of Chester*, 163–5, 169–70.

38 3 *Sheaf*, 19 (1922), 72–3; BL, Harl. Ms.2020, f.146v.

39 A. Thacker, 'Topography', *VCH, Chester*, V, Part 1, 207; A. Thacker, 'City Walls and Gates', *ibid.*, Part 2, 223.

40 BL, Harl. Ms.2158, ff.45v, 47; D. Clayton, *Administration of the County Palatine of Chester*, 169–72.

41 CCALS, ZMR 64, m.1d. The spelling Gerrard's Lane occurred in later centuries.

42 CCALS, DCH/DD/3; ZMR 78, m.1; ZMB 2, f.95v; ZMB 5, ff.1, 41v; 3 *Sheaf*, 43 (1948), 6.

43 CCALS, ZMB 5, ff.41, 69v, 85v, 129v, 180v, 181v; ZSPR 12, mm.1d, 4d, 7d.

44 CCALS, ZCHD 2/1; BL, Harl. Ms.2046, f.34v; Dodgson, *Place-Names of Cheshire*, Part Five (1:i), 21. An alternative interpretation locates Corvisers' Row on the west side of Bridge Street: A. Thacker, 'The Rows', *VCH, Chester*, V, Part 2, 230–1.

45 BL, Harl. Ms.2158, f.32; CCALS, ZSB 2, ff.22, 43, 88v; ZSB 3, ff.24v, 45v, 86v.

46 TNA: PRO, CHES 25/1, m.4; CCALS, ZSR 22, m.7d.

47 TNA: PRO, WALE 29/291.

48 CCALS, ZMB 2, ff.12v, 68, 82; ZMB 3, ff.93, 94v, 96, 96v.

49 CCALS, ZMB 9, ff.32v-33; ZSB 1, f.172v; ZSB 2, f.51; ZSB 4, ff.14, 37, 61v, 62, 107v, 138v, 140v; ZSR 403, m.1; ZSR 412, mm.1, 1d; ZSR 442, m.1d; ZSR 459, m.1; T. O'Neill, *Merchants and Mariners in Medieval Ireland*, 31–40.

50 A. Brown (ed.), *The Rows of Chester*, 90, 93, 182; BL, Harl. Ms.2037, ff.309v, 310.

51 CCALS, ZSB 2, ff.6, 8; ZSB 3, f.39v; ZSB 6, f.10.

52 BL, Harl. Ms.2158, ff.32, 33, 34, 38v, 52v; CCALS, ZMR 42, m.1; ZMR 46, m.1; ZMR 48, m.1; ZMR 62, m.1d; ZMR 75, m.1; ZMR 78, m.1; ZMR 81, m.1; ZMR 98, m.3.

53 BL, Harl. Ms.2079, f.14; CCALS, ZMR 75, m.1; ZMR 81, m.1; ZMR 98, m.3.

54 A. Thacker, 'Early Medieval Chester', *VCH, Chester*, V, Part 1, 32; A. Thacker, 'The Churches and other Religious Bodies', *ibid.*, Part 2, 141, 158.

55 TNA: PRO, CHES 29/108, m.15d.

56 *The Past Uncovered* (Chester Archaeology Quarterly Newsletter, Summer 1998), 1–2; BL, Harl. Ms.2158, f.38v.

57 CCALS, ZMB 2, f.62; ZMB 5, ff.41, 69v, 85v, 129v; ZMB 6, ff.4v, 34v; ZMB 7, ff.2v, 156.

58 BL, Harl. Ms.2158, f.45v; CCALS, ZMB 2, f.58v; ZMB 6, f.3v; ZSR 1, ff.118, 139.

59 W.F. Irvine, 'Chester in the Twelfth and Thirteenth Centuries', 17.

60 CCALS, ZTAR 1/3; ZTAR 1/4; BL, Harl. Ms.2158, ff.32, 36, 37, 38, 39v, 43, 51v, 55, 57v.

61 TNA: PRO, CHES 25/1, mm.2d, 3.

62 BL, Harl. Ms.2020, f.73 (plot measured 2½ ells by 2½ ells); Harl. Ms.2158, ff.33, 42, 51v, 55v; TNA: PRO, SC 6/779/10, m.1.

63 A. Thacker, 'The Rows', *VCH, Chester*, V, Part 2, 234; CCALS, ZMR 62, m.1.

64 CCALS, ZTAR 1/3.

65 D. Keene, 'Suburban Growth', 97–8, 115–16.

66 *The Canon's Yeoman's Prologue*, lines 104–9.

67 J.McN. Dodgson, *Place-Names of Cheshire*, Part Five (1:i), 79; C. Phythian-Adams, *Desolation of a City*, 174–5.

68 D. Keene, 'Suburban Growth', 118.

69 CCALS, ZMB 2, ff.26, 59; ZMB 3, ff.45v, 46; DCH/DD/10.

70 CCALS, ZMB 3, f.32; ZSB 5, f.61; ZTAR 1/4; BL, Harl. Ms.2158, ff.55, 57.

71 CCALS, ZSB 2, f.45v; ZSB 3, ff.20, 64v, 95v; ZSB 4, f.53; ZSB 5, f.111; BL, Harl. Ms.2061, f.3; 3 *Sheaf*, 36 (1941), 9.

72 TNA: PRO, SC 6/792/1, m.1; SC 6/792/3, m.2; CCALS, ZSR 12, m.6d; ZSR 21, m.1d.

73 D. Keene, 'Suburban Growth', 110, 116; *Cal. Court R.*, 157; CCALS, ZMB 2, f.27; ZMR 64, m.1d; ZSB 5, f.111.

74 CCALS, ZMB 1, ff.34v, 55, 60v.

75 M. Kowaleski, *Medieval Exeter*, 181; C. Dyer, *Standards of Living*, 198; C. Dyer, *Making a Living*, 224.

76 CCALS, ZMB 2, ff.45v, 46.

77 CCALS, ZMB 6, ff.166v-170.

78 CCALS, ZSB 1, f.69; ZMB 4, f.37v; ZCHD/4/1; 3 *Sheaf*, 36 (1941), 22–3.

79 W.F. Irvine, 'Chester in the Twelfth and Thirteenth Centuries', 35, 39, 40–1; CCALS, DCH/DD/7, no.3.

80 TNA: PRO, CHES 25/1, m.3.

81 BL, Harl. Ms.2020, ff.36, 38; CCALS, ZCHD/4/1; ZMB 3, f.11.

82 BL, Harl. Ms.2158, ff.32v, 33, 34v, 36, 51, 55, 57; CCALS, ZTAR 1/1; 1/3.

83 J.McN. Dodgson, *Place-Names of Cheshire*, Part Five (1:i), 53–4.

84 BL, Harl. Ms.2099, f.325; CCALS, ZMB 6, f.79v.

85 W.F. Irvine, 'Rental of St Mary's Nunnery in 1526', 105–9; CCALS, ZSR 128, m.2.

86 D. Mason, *Roman Chester*, 107–8; TNA: PRO, E 101/545/25, mm.1, 1d, 5, 9, 10; CCALS, ZMUR/1, m.3; C.P. Lewis, 'Open Spaces and Parks', *VCH, Chester*, V, Part 2, 303.

87 TNA: PRO, E 101/486/10, m.1; E 101/486/12, m.1; E 101/545/25, mm.3, 9.

88 A.J. Kettle, 'Religious Houses', *VCH, Cheshire*, III, 127; ZSR 90, m.1d; ZSR 300, m.1d; ZSR 387, m.1d.

89 CCALS, ZSB 1, f.122; ZMB 4, f.72v.

90 *Annales Cestrienses*, 87–9.

91 3 *Sheaf*, 29 (1934), 39, 52–3; CCALS, ZCHD/7/1.

92 CCALS, ZSB 2, f.45v; ZTAR 1/3, m.1; ZTAR 1/4, m.1; ZMUR 1, m.3; BL, Harl. Ms.2158, ff.51v, 55v, 57v.

93 TNA: PRO, E 101/488/2, m.1d; E 101/488/7, mm.1d, 2.

94 *Chartulary or Register of St Werburgh's Abbey*, II, 274; *Cheshire in the Pipe Rolls*, 210; TNA: PRO, SC 6/771/2, m.7.

95 *Chartulary or Register of St Werburgh's Abbey*, II, 348–9; CCALS, ZSR 12, m.6; ZSB 1, f.139; WS 1628 Eaton.

96 CCALS, ZSB 1, f.139; ZSB 2, ff.6v, 23, 44, 88; ZSB 3, f.25; ZSB 5, f.19; ZSR 454, m.1; BL, Harl. Ms.2020, f.35v; Harl. Ms.2079, f.48.

97 R.H. Morris, *Chester in the Plantagenet and Tudor Reigns*, 402, 530, 556–7; M. Kowaleski, *Medieval Exeter*, 143–7.

98 CCALS, ZSR 104, m.1d; ZSR 121, m.1; BL, Harl. Ms.2046, f.27.

99 R.H. Morris, *Chester in the Plantagenet and Tudor Reigns*, 557–8.

100 TNA: PRO, E 101/488/2; E 101/545/125; SC 6/774/10; 774/13; 774/14; 780/4; CCALS, ZMB 1, f.61v.

101 *Cal. Court R.*, 156; J.McN. Dodgson, *Place-Names of Cheshire*, Part Five (1:i), 59, 62.

102 BL, Harl. Ms.2158, ff.44v, 47; CCALS, ZMB 1, f.16v; ZMB 2, f.19v.

103 D. Mills, 'Plays, Sports, and Customs before 1700', *VCH, Chester*, V, Part 2, 253.

104 C.P. Lewis, 'Introduction', *VCH, Chester*, Part 2, 1; C.P. Lewis, 'Local Government Boundaries', *ibid.*, 9–10.

105 BL, Harl. Ms.2061, f.3; CCALS, ZSR 300, m.1d.

106 CCALS, ZSR 280, mm.1, 1d; ZSR 311, m.1; ZSR 322, m.1d; ZSR 351, m.7d; ZSR 391, m.1; ZSR 400, m.1d.

Chapter 4

1 J. Schofield and G. Stell, 'The Built Environment 1300–1540', *CUH*, I, 371–2. For St Werburgh's, see A. Thacker, 'Major Buildings', *VCH, Chester*, V, Part 2, 184–95.

2 R.H. Morris, *Chester in the Plantagenet and Tudor Reigns*, 512, 521–2.

3 I thank Simon Ward for the acreage for Chester; J. Kermode, 'The greater towns', *CUH*, I, 442.

4 R.H. Morris, *Chester in the Plantagenet and Tudor Reigns*, 510; CCALS, ZMB 2, f.94.

5 CCALS, ZMUR 1, m.3; ZMB 4, f.53v.

6 A. Thacker, 'City Walls and Gates', *VCH, Chester*, V, Part 2, 213, 215, 218–19.

7 BL, Harl. Ms.2020, f.35v; Harl. Ms.2158, f.49v.

8 *CPR*, 1272–81, 311; 36 *DKR*, 31 March 1395.

9 CCALS, ZMUR 1, m.3; ZMUB 1, f.9.

10 P.J. Davey, *Chester Northgate Brewery: Interim Report* (Grosvenor Museum Excavations, 1973), 15–17.

11 J.McN. Dodgson, *The Place-Names of Cheshire*, Part Five (1:i), 12; CCALS, ZCHD/8/1.

12 CCALS, ZCHD/4/2; BL, Harl. Ms.2020, f.38v.

13 Information from Simon Ward of Chester Archaeology. I am grateful to him and his colleague Julie Edwards for help with the physical evidence.

14 D.F. Petch, 'The Roman Period', *VCH, Cheshire*, I, 174; T.J. Strickland, 'Roman Chester', *VCH, Chester*, V, Part 1, 11, 13; D. Mason, *Roman Chester: City of the Legions*, 108.

15 A. Thacker, 'Bridges and River Crossings', *VCH, Chester*, V, Part 2, 77–8; *Annales Cestrienses*, 107; 3 *Sheaf*, 21 (1924), 32–3.

16 TNA: PRO, SC 6, 771/19, m.1; 783/15, m.1; 783/16, m.1d; 783/17, m.1; 784/2, m.1; 784/3, m.1; 784/5, mm.1d, 5.

17 *BPR*, iii, 275.

18 TNA: PRO, SC 6/772/19, m.1d; R.H. Morris, *Chester in the*

Plantagenet and Tudor Reigns, 503; *CPR*, 1385–9, 529.

19 CCALS, ZMB 1, f.16v; ZMB 2, f.19v.

20 CCALS, ZSB 4, ff.32v, 51; 3 *Sheaf*, 29 (1934), 74.

21 For full details of the castle buildings, see A. Thacker, 'Castle', *VCH*, *Chester*, V, Part 2, 204–13.

22 *Cheshire in the Pipe Rolls*, 210–11; TNA: PRO, E 101/486/7; E 101/486/17.

23 TNA: PRO, E 101/487/5, mm.1, 1d; SC 6/771/19, m.1d.

24 TNA: PRO, E 101/488/2, m.1; E 101/488/7, m.1; CHES 25/8, m.34.

25 S. Cather, D. Park and R. Pender, 'Henry III's Wall Paintings at Chester Castle', 170–89; *Cheshire in the Pipe Rolls*, 166, 177, 209.

26 TNA: PRO, E 101/487/5, m.1.

27 TNA: PRO, SC 6/774/10, m.1; E 101/545/25, mm.1d, 9.

28 TNA: PRO, SC 6/779/8, m.1; E 101/488/2, m.1; E 101/488/7, m.1d.

29 TNA: PRO, E 101/486/17, m.1; SC 6/771/4, m.5; SC 6/771/7, m.3.

30 TNA: PRO, SC 6/774/13, m.1; SC 6/774/14, m.1d; SC 6/774/15, m.1; SC 6/775/3, m.1.

31 TNA: PRO, SC 6/779/4, m.1; SC 6/779/6, m.1; SC 6/779/8, m.1.

32 TNA: PRO, E 101/488/2, mm.1, 1d; E 101/488/4, m.1d; E 101/488/7, mm.1, 1d; SC 6/774/8, m.1.

33 TNA: PRO, SC 6/780/7, m.1d; E 101/317/37, m.1.

34 TNA: PRO, CHES 25/15, m.15d.

35 C.P. Lewis, 'Introduction', *VCH*, *Chester*, V, Part 1, 3, 7; A. Thacker, 'Topography', *ibid.*, 212.

36 TNA: PRO, E 101/545/25, m.9.

37 For detailed treatment of the mills and fisheries, see A. Thacker, 'Mills and Fisheries', *VCH*, *Chester*, V, Part 2, 104–13.

38 *CCR*, 1288–96, 182–3.

39 *Cheshire in the Pipe Rolls*, 156; TNA: PRO, E 101/486/10, m.1; E 101/486/12, m.1.

40 TNA: PRO, SC 6/774/3, m.1d; 790/1, m.4; 790/3, m.3; 790/5, m.4; CHES 25/8, m.41.

41 TNA: PRO, CHES 25/10, m.22.

42 A.D. Carr, *Medieval Anglesey*, 108–9, 116; TNA: PRO, SC 6/774/14, m.1d; 775/4, m.1d; 775/5, m.1d.

43 TNA: PRO, SC 6/780/4, m.1; SC 6/785/9, m.1d.

44 TNA: PRO, SC 6/797/1, m.7.

45 TNA: PRO, SC 6/771/19, m.1; SC 6/784/5, m.3; SC 6/794/1, m.1d.

46 TNA: PRO, SC 6/789/10, m.3; SC 6/790/1, m.3; SC 6/793/6, m.6.

47 TNA: PRO, SC 6/788/2, m.3; SC 6/788/4, m.3; SC 6/788/6, m.3; SC 6/788/8, m.3; SC 6/789/6, m.3.

48 TNA: PRO, CHES 25/10, m.10.

49 TNA: PRO, SC 6/799/8, m.4d; SC 6/800/7, m.4; SC 6/801/1, m.4d.

50 TNA: PRO, E 101/486/10, m.1.

51 TNA: PRO, SC 6/784/6, m.1d; SC 6/789/10, m.3; SC 6/790/1, m.3; 36 *DKR*, 88.

52 *CPR*, 1391–6, 4; 36 *DKR*, 543; TNA: PRO, SC 6/790/5, m.4; SC 6/790/7, m.4.

53 TNA: PRO, E 101/545/25, mm.7d, 10.

54 TNA: PRO, SC 6/798/9, m.6d; 799/1, m.7d; 800/1, m.4d; 800/5, m.4d; 801/1, m.4.

55 TNA: PRO, SC 6/HENVII/1520, m.6d.

56 S. Ward, *Excavations at Chester, the Lesser Medieval Religious Houses*; S. Ward, 'Recent Work at St John's and St Werburgh's'; S. Ward, 'The Friaries in Chester: Their Impact and Legacy'; A. Thacker, 'The Early Medieval City and its Buildings'; A. Thacker, 'Cathedral and Close', *VCH*, *Chester*, V, Part 2, 185–95; A. Thacker, 'Sites and Remains of Medieval Religious Houses', *ibid.*, 240–6.

57 3 *Sheaf*, 19 (1922), 4; 3 *Sheaf*, 23 (1926), 37–8; C. Grossinger, 'Chester Cathedral Misericords', 104.

58 *Chartulary of St Werburgh's*, II, 463–4, 468–70; 3 *Sheaf*, 36 (1941), 9.

59 *English Benedictine Kalendars after 1100*, I, 95; N. Orme, *Medieval Schools*, 65.

60 A. Thacker, 'Religion, 1230–1550', *VCH*, *Chester*, V, Part 1, 88; A. Thacker, 'Cathedral and Close', *ibid.*, Part 2, 196; S-B. Maclean, 'Marian Devotion in post-Reformation Chester', 237–56.

61 R.V.H. Burne, *Monks of Chester*, 136–7; *Obits of St Werburgh's Abbey*, 91; CCALS, ZMB 8, f.60; ZSR 358, m.1d; ZSR 383, m.1d.

62 Information from Simon Ward; CCALS, ZSR 14, m.2d.

63 R.V.H. Burne, *Monks of Chester*, 61–2; A.J. Kettle, 'Chester Abbey', *VCH*, *Cheshire*, III, 142.

64 See S. Ward, *Lesser Medieval Religious Houses*, for full discussion of the buildings.

65 BL, Harl. Ms.1991, ff.152–7v.

66 A.J. Kettle, 'Religious Houses', *VCH*, *Cheshire*, III, 147; 3 *Sheaf*, 17 (1920), 69–70.

67 *Lancashire and Cheshire Wills and Inventories* (1860), 7.

68 J. Barrow, 'Churches, Education and Literacy in Towns 600–1300', *CUH*, I, 144–5.

69 S. Ward, 'Friaries in Chester', 121–3; A.J. Kettle, 'Religious Houses', *VCH*, *Cheshire*, III, 171–8.

70 S. Ward, 'Friaries in Chester', 128; J.H.E. Bennett, 'The Grey Friars of Chester', 28–9.

71 S. Ward, 'Friaries in Chester', 125–7.

72 CCALS, ZMR 42, m.1d.

73 3 *Sheaf*, 36 (1941), 54.

74 3 *Sheaf*, 17 (1920), 69–70; 3 *Sheaf*, 36 (1941), 9; *Lancashire and Cheshire Wills and Inventories* (1860), 7.

75 A.J. Kettle, 'Religious Houses', *VCH*, *Cheshire*, III, 176–7.

76 J. Barrow, 'Churches, Education and Literacy in Towns 600–1300', *CUH*, I, 142–3; C. Rawcliffe, *Leprosy in Medieval England*, 108; A.J. Kettle, 'Religious Houses', *VCH*, *Cheshire*, III, 178–84.

77 36 *DKR*, 46, 144, C. Rawcliffe, *Leprosy in Medieval England*, 213–14, 226, 307, 308–13, 322, 329–30, 343–51.

78 A.J. Kettle, 'Religious Houses', *VCH*, *Cheshire*, III, 127; BL, Harl. Ms.2079, f.14; J.McN. Dodgson, *Place-Names of Cheshire*, Part Five (1:i), 18–19, 36–7.

79 A. Thacker, 'The Churches and other Religious Bodies', *VCH*, *Chester*, V, Part 2, 125–59.

80 CCALS, ZSR 330, m.1.

81 3 *Sheaf*, 23 (1926), 49–50; *Talbot Deeds*, *1200–1682*, 99.

82 G. Ormerod, *History of Cheshire*, II, 41, 666; 3 *Sheaf*, 18 (1921), 92; 3 *Sheaf*, 17 (1920), 69–70.

83 TNA: PRO, E 134/36 Chas 2/Mich 3.

84 3 *Sheaf*, 17 (1920), 69–70; *Lancashire and Cheshire Wills and Inventories* (1860), 6–12.

85 BL, Harl. Ms.2057, ff.125–7; CCALS, ZMB 5, f.104v.

86 CCALS, ZTAR, 1/4, m.1; BL, Harl. Ms.2158, ff.36, 37v, 39, 40v, 55, 57.

87 G. Ormerod, *History of Cheshire*, I, 233–4.

88 *3 Sheaf*, 15 (1918), 23; CCALS, ZMR 75, m.1d.

89 TNA: PRO, WALE 29/291; G. Ormerod, *History of Cheshire*, I, 197, 198, 262; CCALS, ZSR 290, m.1d; ZSR 325, m.1.

90 *Chartulary of St Werburgh's*, II, 469–70; 37 *DKR*, 779; BL, Harl. Ms.2067, ff.43v-44; G. Ormerod, *History of Cheshire*, I, 340. The Hurleton family name had by then been changed to Hurleston.

91 *3 Sheaf*, 36 (1941), 59; *Catalogue of Ancient Deeds*, vi, C 5282.

92 *Lancashire and Cheshire Wills and Inventories* (1860), 6–12.

93 *Chartulary of Chester Abbey*, II, 467; *3 Sheaf*, 28 (1933), 92; CCALS, uncalendared Sneyd family papers: 310, 311, 312.

94 CCALS, ZMB 1, ff.16v, 41v; ZMB 5, f.174v; R.H. Morris, *Chester in the Plantagenet and Tudor Reigns*, 525–6.

95 CCALS, ZMB 1, ff.41, 48v, 49, 49v; ZMB 5, f.176; ZMB 6, ff.36-36v, 79v; ZSB 1, ff.131, 155.

96 CCALS, ZMB 2, ff.69, 103v; ZMB 5, f.18; ZSR 196, m.1d; BL, Harl. Ms.2158, f.215.

97 BL, Harl. Ms.2158, ff.31v, 32v-33, 34.

98 D. Jones, *Church in Chester*, n.3 on p.98; BL, Harl. Ms.2063, f.113; Harl. Ms.2158, ff.49v-50; CCALS, ZSR 216, m.1 (reference to the chaplain of St George of Chester in 1431).

99 CCALS, ZMB 6, f.33v; A. Thacker, 'Municipal Buildings', *VCH, Chester*, V, Part 2, 20.

100 For full discussion of the Rows, see A. Brown (ed.), *The Rows of Chester*; A. Thacker, 'The Rows', *VCH, Chester*, V, Part 2, 225–39; R. Harris, 'The Origins of the Rows', 132–51.

101 TNA: PRO, CHES 25/1, m.3; SC 6/771/5, m.14.

102 D. Keene, 'Shops and Shopping in Medieval London', 38–40.

103 BL, Add. Ch.49997, 50004.

104 CCALS, ZSR 6, m.10; ZSR 22, m.4; ZSR 26, m.3d; ZSR 35, m.5d; ZSR 45, m.2; ZSR 51, m.2; BL, Harl. Ms.2162, f.90v.

105 CCALS, ZMR 48, m.1.

106 TNA: PRO, SC 6/784/5, m.5; CCALS, DVE 1/C11/21; BL, Harl. Ms.2046, f.28v; Harl. Ms.2158, ff.32, 34, 40, 41.

107 A. Brown (ed.), *The Rows of Chester*, 15–18; R.C. Turner, 'Shop, Stall and Undercroft in 'The Rows' of Chester', 162.

108 CCALS, ZSR 10, m.1; ZSR 11, m.1d; ZQCR 4, m.1d; TNA: PRO, CHES 25/8, m.30.

109 A. Brown (ed.), *The Rows of Chester*, 44, 51; CCALS, ZSB 3, f.27v.

110 CCALS, ZQSF/36, n.57.

111 CCALS, ZMB 1, f.15v. (ZMB 2, f.4: attack with pole-axe in Margery Walsh's cellar in Bridge Street).

112 TNA: PRO, SC 6/771/4, m.5; 771/9, m.1; 774/6, m.1d; 774/10, m.1d; 774/14, m.1d.

113 CCALS, ZMB 1, ff.14v, 59v; ZSB 3, f.71v; *3 Sheaf*, 36 (1941), 17; BL, Harl. Ms.2091, f.56; D. Keene, *Medieval Winchester*, i, 274–5; ii, 1426.

114 CCALS, ZMB 1, f.14v.

115 CCALS, ZMR 3, m.2d.

116 TNA: PRO, CHES 25/1, m.3; CCALS, ZMR 3, m.2d; ZQCR 5, m.1.

117 BL, Harl. Ms.2158, f.33v; CCALS, ZCHD 2/3, ZCHD 2/7.

118 CCALS, ZMR 52, m.1; TNA: PRO, SC 6/784/5, m.5.

119 BL, Harl. Ms.1994, ff.34–6. In 1650 former abbey property in Parsons Lane included small houses with one or two rooms above and below stairs and a tiny garden plot: TNA: PRO, E 317 Chester 6A.

120 TNA: PRO, SC 6/784/9, mm.1, 3; SC 6/784/11, m.2. Mention was made of a seld, shop, cellar and stallboard.

121 A. Brown (ed.), *The Rows of Chester*, 27, 54, 176–7.

122 CCALS, ZSB 2, f.86; ZTAR 1/4, m.1d; *Lancashire and Cheshire Wills and Inventories* (1860), 6–12.

123 TNA: PRO, CHES 25/12, mm.6–6d; *3 Sheaf*, 11 (1914), 1.

124 A. Brown (ed.), *The Rows of Chester*, 25–7, 54; BL, Harl. Ms.2158, f.50.

125 CCALS, ZMB 3, f.65v; ZSB 3, ff.19v, 20v, 69v, 70; BL, Harl. Ms.2037, f.309v.

126 D. Keene, *Medieval Winchester*, i, 173; TNA: PRO, E 101/488/2, m.1; E 101/488/7, m.1d.

127 TNA: PRO, SC 6/784/5, m.5d; CCALS, ZSR 366, mm.1, 1d.

128 TNA: PRO, E 101/488/2, m.1; E 101/545/25, mm.3, 9, 10; CCALS, ZSR 457, m.1d; ZQCR 11, m.1.

129 A. Thacker, 'Economy and Society, 1230–1350', *VCH, Chester*, V, Part 1, 52; CCALS, ZSB 4, f.53.

130 I thank Simon Ward and Julie Edwards for this information.

131 A. Brown (ed.), *The Rows of Chester*, 64–5, 178–9.

132 CCALS, ZSR 87, m.1d; ZSR 196, m.1; ZSR 377, m.1d; ZSR 443, m.1d; ZSR 460, m.1d; ZSB 3, f.85v; *Lancashire and Cheshire Wills and Inventories* (1884), 1–4; S. Thrupp, *Merchant Class of Medieval London*, n.117 on p.139.

133 CCALS, ZSB 4, f.96v; D. Keene, *Medieval Winchester*, i, 177–8.

134 CCALS, ZSR 312, m.1d; ZSR 333, m.1d; ZSR 423, m.1; ZSR 476, m.1d; J.H.E. Bennett, 'Hospital and Chantry of St Ursula', 100.

135 R. Marks, 'Window Glass', 277; I. Archibald (forthcoming).

136 TNA: PRO, E 101/488/2, m.1; E 101/545/25, mm.6, 9.

137 CCALS, ZSB 2, f.86; BL, Harl. Ms.2158, ff.36v, 38, 39v, 41.

138 *Lancashire and Cheshire Wills and Inventories* (1860), 6–12.

139 TNA: PRO, WALE 29/291; *3 Sheaf*, 17 (1920), 105; *3 Sheaf*, 36 (1941), 9; CCALS, ZSB 5, ff. 40v-41.

140 *Lancashire and Cheshire Wills and Inventories* (1884), 1–4; CCALS, ZSR 459, m.1d.

141 CCALS, ZSR 91, m.1d; ZSR 158, m.1; ZSR 167, m.1d; ZSR 230, m.1d; ZSR 303, m.1; ZSR 413, m.1; ZSB 2, f.100v.

142 J. Schofield and G. Stell, 'The Built Environment 1300–1540', *CUH*, I, 377–8.

143 S. Ward, 'The Friaries in Chester', 125; A. Thacker, 'Cathedral and Close', *VCH, Chester*, V, Part 2, 194.

144 CCALS, ZMB 1, f.16; ZMB 2, ff.19, 19v, 40, 41; ZSB 3, ff.21v, 40, 64v, 66v, 93v; ZSB 4, ff.74, 94v; ZSB 5, ff.84, 88v, 111, 133. Information from Simon Ward.

145 TNA: PRO, CHES 25/10, m.22.

146 TNA: PRO, CHES 25/1, m.3; BL, Harl. Ms.2162, f.64v; CCALS, ZSB 3, f.21v; ZQCR 4, m.1.

147 S. Ward, *Excavations at 12 Watergate Street*, 45, 59.

148 A.J. Kettle, 'Religious Houses', *VCH, Cheshire*, III, 171; CCALS, ZSB 2, f.26v; *CPR*, 1413–16, 256.

149 R.H. Morris, *Chester in the Plantagenet and Tudor Reigns*, 99; J. Harvey, *Mediaeval Gardens*, 64, 84.

150 *Cheshire in the Pipe Rolls*, 117; TNA: PRO, SC 6/784/5, m.1; SC 6/771/19, m.1.

151 TNA: PRO, SC 6/771/22, m.1; SC 6/774/4, m.1.

152 TNA: PRO, E 101/486/7, m.1; SC 6/771/1, m.1.

153 J. Harvey, *Mediaeval Gardens*, 4, 78–9, 84; *Chartulary of St Werburgh's*, II, 467.

154 CCALS, ZSR 216, m.1d; ZSR 280, m.1; ZSR 284, mm.1, 1d; ZSR 456, m.1d.

155 CCALS, ZSR 159, m.1; ZSR 268, m.1; ZSR 298, m.1; ZSR 408, m.1d; BL, Harl. Ms.2020, f.18v.
156 J. Greig, 'Plant Remains', 59–62.
157 CCALS, ZMR 63, mm.1, 1d; D. Keene, *Medieval Winchester*, i, 152.
158 CCALS, ZSR 351, m.4d; TNA: PRO, CHES 25/16, m.8.
159 BL, Harl. Ms.2158, f.63v; TNA: PRO, SC 6/800/1, m.1d; SC 6/800/6, m.1d.
160 CCALS, ZSB 3, ff.93v, 94v, 95, 95v, 96v.
161 A. Brown (ed.), *The Rows of Chester*, 178–9; BL, Harl. Ms.2037, ff.309v, 310.

Chapter 5

1 CCALS, ZMB 3, f.8; ZSR 239, mm.1, 1d.
2 P. McClure, 'Patterns of Migration', 167–82; D. Keene, *Medieval Winchester*, i, 371–9; C. Dyer, *Making a Living*, 193–4.
3 C. Dyer, *Making a Living*, 40, 193.
4 TNA: PRO, SC 6/771/10, m.1; CCALS, ZMR 52, m.1; R.V.H. Burne, *Monks of Chester*, 208.
5 C. Dyer, *Making a Living*, 201.
6 CCALS, ZSR 166, m.1d; ZSR 316, m.1d; ZSR 401, m.1d.
7 R. Holt and G. Rosser, 'Introduction', in R. Holt and G. Rosser (eds), *The Medieval Town*, 10; H. Swanson, 'Illusion of Economic Structure', 39–43; H. Swanson, *Medieval Artisans*, 106; R. Holt, 'Gloucester', 185–9.
8 CCALS, ZSB 1, ff.115–18; ZSB 2, ff.4–6v, 20–3, 63–5, 88–90v; ZSB 3, ff.99–100v.
9 CCALS, ZSB 1, ff.115, 118, 136, 139, 158, 162; ZSB 2, ff.4, 6v, 63v, 65; ZSB 3, ff.6, 8, 25.
10 CCALS, ZMB 1, f.9; ZMB 3, f.105v; ZAF 1, f.15v.
11 CCALS, ZMB 5, ff.2v–4v, 72–3, 155–6, 166–166v; ZMB 6, ff.60–1, 123–6; ZMB 7, ff.45–6, 160–1.
12 CCALS, ZMB 2, f.14v; ZMB 6, ff.85v, 86v, 87, 125; ZMB 7, f.7v; ZMB 9(a), f.12; 9(b), f.10v.
13 CCALS, ZSR 121, m.1; ZSR 223, m.1d; ZSR 338, m.1; ZSR 364, m.1d; C. Dyer, *Standards of Living*, 232–3.
14 BL, Harl. Ms.2099, no.13; TNA: PRO, WALE 29/291.
15 R.B. Dobson, 'Admissions to the Freedom', 11.
16 CCALS, ZMB 4, ff.7, 35, 42; ZMB 5, ff.69v, 72, 109v, 129v, 166v; ZMB 6, ff.4, 34; ZMB 7, f.6; ZMB 9(e), f.13.
17 CCALS, ZMB 5, f.87; ZMB 7, f.6; ZMB 9(e), f.13; ZSB 4, ff.51, 53v, 98; ZSB 5, ff.63v, 93.
18 *Sel. Court R.*, lxv; TNA: PRO, WALE 29/134; CCALS, ZMB 3, f.25; ZMB 4, f.13; ZMB 5, ff.88, 186v, 187; ZMB 9, f.9v; ZTAR 2/29; ZTAB 4; BL, Harl. Ms.2158, ff.14v, 75.
19 E.M. Veale, 'Craftsmen and the Economy of London', 124; D. Keene, *Medieval Winchester*, i, 81.
20 CCALS, ZMR 62, m.1d; ZMR 91, m.1; R.H. Morris, *Chester in the Plantagenet and Tudor Reigns*, 525, 533.
21 CCALS, ZSR 191, m.1; ZSR 262, m.1; ZSR 341, m.1d; ZSR 359, m.1; ZSR 453, m.1d; TNA: PRO, WALE 29/291; 3 *Sheaf*, 17 (1920), 69–70, 105; 3 *Sheaf*, 23 (1926), 37–8; 3 *Sheaf*, 36 (1941), 9.
22 CCALS, ZMB 6, f.119v; ZSB 3, f.20; ZSB 4, ff.42, 84v, 115; ZSR 360, m.1d; ZSR 419, m.1; ZSR 442, m.1; ZSR 443, m.1d; ZSR 458, m.1d.
23 3 *Sheaf*, 14 (1917), 8; 3 *Sheaf*, 15 (1918), 23.
24 C. Dyer, *Standards of Living*, 88–9; S. Thrupp, *Merchant Class of Medieval London*, 148; J. Thomson, *Transformation of Medieval England*, 403–5.

25 CCALS, ZSR 334, m.1; ZSR 359, m.1.
26 CCALS, ZSR 158, m.1; ZSR 273, m.1d; ZSR 334, m.1; ZSR 354, m.1d; ZSR 372, m.1d; ZSR 470, m.1.
27 CCALS, ZSR 52, m.1d; ZSR 84, m.1; ZSR 281, m.1; ZSB 3, ff.20, 45.
28 BL, WALE 29/291; Harl. Ms.2067, f.43v. The Hurleton family later changed the name to Hurleston.
29 CCALS, ZSR 223, m.1d.
30 CCALS, ZMB 2, f.57.
31 CCALS, ZSR 247, m.1; other examples: ZSR 108, m.1d; ZSR 183, m.1; ZSR 294, m.1d.
32 *The Book of Margery Kempe*, 9–10.
33 CCALS, ZSR 21, m.9; other examples: ZSR 36, m.5; ZSR 37, m.4d.
34 J. Laughton, 'Women in Court', 93.
35 CCALS, ZSR 366, mm.1, 1d; ZSR 370, m.1d; ZSR 384, m.1.
36 TNA: PRO, E 101/317/37, m.1; SC 2/255/15, m.1; SC 6/782/2, m.1.
37 BL, Harl. Ms.2158, ff.55v, 57v; TNA: PRO, SC 6/782/2, m.1; SC 6/782/7, m.1.
38 CCALS, ZSR 280, m.1; ZSR 304, m.1d (Hope); ZSR 302, m.1d; ZSR 304, m.1; ZSR 305, m.1d; ZSR 311, m.1; ZSR 312, m.1 (Wotton); *Register of the Guild of the Holy Trinity* (Armourer).
39 *Prologue*, lines 378–80.
40 CCALS, ZSR 142, m.1; ZSR 289, m.1; ZSR 386, m.1; ZSR 413, m.1; ZSR 452, m.1d; ZSB 4, ff.20, 42v.
41 CCALS, ZSR 381, m.1d.
42 *Lancashire and Cheshire Wills and Inventories* (1860), 6–12.
43 TNA: PRO, CHES 25/11, mm.7, 9, 17, 17d.
44 R. Horrox, 'The Urban Gentry in the Fifteenth Century', 22–44; 3 *Sheaf*, 29 (1934), 74.
45 G. Ormerod, *History of Cheshire*, I, 169; II, 504–8.
46 TNA: PRO, SC 6/796/3, m.13; SC 6/797/1, m.2; CCALS, ZSR 313, m.1; ZMB 6, ff.3v, 4, 34.
47 *CPR, 1441–6*, 1; 37 *DKR*, 359.
48 37 *DKR*, 131, 132; TNA: PRO, CHES 25/15, m.15d; CHES 29/187, m.5; CCALS, ZSB 4, f.95v; ZSR 451, m.1; ZSR 458, m.1d.
49 *CPR, 1461–7*, 129; 3 *Sheaf*, 19 (1922), 4; 3 *Sheaf*, 23 (1926), 37–8; CCALS, ZMB 5, ff.76v, 176; ZMB 6, ff.4, 84; ZSB 3, f.38v.
50 TNA: PRO, CHES 25/11, m.9; CHES 25/12, mm.1, 6; CHES 29/127, m.27d; CHES 29/129, m.1d.
51 TNA: PRO, CHES 25/12, mm.13, 16, 16d; G. Ormerod, *History of Cheshire*, II, 833, 842.
52 TNA: PRO, SC 6/795/8, m.1d; SC 6/797/1, m.1d.
53 CCALS, ZMB 5, ff.88, 112v. William Stanley esquire was regularly named in the Pentice court rolls.
54 R.N. Swanson, *Church and Society*, 82.
55 BL, Harl. Ms.2162, f.404; G. Ormerod, *History of Cheshire*, II, 379.
56 M.J. Bennett, 'Lancashire and Cheshire Clergy', 6, 22.
57 A.J. Kettle, 'Religious Houses', *VCH, Cheshire*, III, 138; R.V.H. Burne, *Monks of Chester*, 99–101.
58 TNA: PRO, CHES 25/11, m.7; *Calendar of Papal Letters*, VII, 1417–1431, 126.
59 E. Danbury, 'The Intellectual Life of the Abbey of St Werburgh', 112–14.
60 TNA: PRO, CHES 25/10, mm.33, 35; A. Gransden, *Historical Writing in England*, II, 48.
61 TNA: PRO, SC 6/793/5, m.6d (43 quarters); C. Dyer, *Standards of Living*, 263.

62 CCALS, ZSR 154, m.1; ZSR 292, m.1; ZSR 301, m.1; ZSR 374, m.1d; TNA: PRO, SC 2/255/15, m.1.

63 CCALS, ZSR 123, m.3; ZSR 126, m.2d; ZSR 161, m.1; ZSR 383, m.1; ZSR 424, m.1d. The abbey's wool was taken to Boston fair in the 1280s: A.J. Kettle, *VCH, Cheshire*, III, 137.

64 CCALS, ZSR 337, m.2d; ZSB 3, f.106; ZSB 4, ff.14, 19, 37v, 54; ZSB 5, f.59v.

65 CCALS, ZMB 3, f.2; ZMB 5, ff.8v, 158v; ZMB 6, ff.8, 25; ZSB 2, ff.45v, 86v, 87v.

66 TNA: PRO, CHES 29/165, m.18; CHES 25/16, m.15d.

67 M.J. Bennett, 'Lancashire and Cheshire Clergy', 22. For the nunnery, see A.J. Kettle, 'Religious Houses', *VCH, Cheshire*, III, 146–50.

68 CCALS, ZMR 58, m.1d.

69 E. Power, *Medieval English Nunneries*, 6–17.

70 *BPR*, iii, 310; TNA: PRO, CHES 25/4, m.15.

71 CCALS, ZSR 256, m.1d; ZSR 287, m.1d; ZSR 294, m.1; ZSR 295, m.1d.

72 CCALS, ZSR 313, m.1d; ZSR 318, m.1; ZSR 321, m.1; *Processional of the Nuns of Chester*, 27.

73 For the friaries, see A.J. Kettle, 'Religious Houses', *VCH, Cheshire*, III, 171–8.

74 CCALS, ZSB 1, f.132; ZSB 4, f.111; ZSB 5, f.6; ZSR 130, m.1d; ZSR 186, m.1.

75 CCALS, ZMB 5, f.74; ZSR 203, m.1; ZSR 253, m.1d; ZSR 311, m.1.

76 *3 Sheaf*, 24 (1927), 4–5.

77 D. Jones, *Church in Chester*, 96–8.

78 CCALS, ZSR 123, m.1d; ZSR 174, m.1; ZSR 265, m.1d; ZSR 315, m.1.

79 CCALS, ZMUR 1, f.3; ZMB 5, f.182.

80 CCALS, ZSR 264, m.1d; *3 Sheaf*, 18 (1921), 93.

81 BL, Harl. Ms.2158, f.32; CCALS, ZSR 334, m.1.

82 CCALS, ZSR 245, m.1; ZSR 311, m.1; ZSR 420, m.1d.

83 *3 Sheaf*, 36 (1941), 54; CCALS, ZSR 259, m.1d; ZSR 277, m.1d; ZSR 289, m.1d; ZSR 321, m.1d; ZMB 2, f.2.

84 D. Jones, *Church in Chester*, 97.

85 M.J. Bennett, 'Lancashire and Cheshire Clergy', 23–4.

86 BL. Harl. Ms.2158, ff.32, 35v, 36v, 38; CCALS, ZTAR 2/23, m.2.

87 CCALS, ZSR 283, m.1d; ZMB 4, f.66v; D. Jones, *Church in Chester*, 175.

88 D. Jones, *Church in Chester*, 168, 169–70; BL, Harl. Ms.2158, f.32; CCALS, ZSR 222, m.1d; ZSR 237, m.1d. Henry del Hey was also rector of West Kirby but was regularly named in the city records.

89 CCALS, ZMB 4, f.45; ZSR 165, m.1d; ZSR 170, m.1; ZSR 174, m.1d; ZSR 177, m.1d; ZSR 190, m.1d; ZSR 196, m.1; ZSR 204, m.1d; ZSR 261, m.3; ZSR 264, m.1d.

90 CCALS, ZSR 155, m.1d; ZSR 182, m.1; ZSR 184, mm.1, 1d; ZSR 186, m.1d; ZSR 196, m.1; ZSR 198, m.1; ZSR 219, m.1; ZSR 277, m.1.

91 P. Nightingale, 'The English Parochial Clergy as Investors and Creditors', 89–105; D. Jones, *Church in Chester*, 29, 172; CCALS, ZSR 352, m.1d; ZSR 433, m.1.

92 BL, WALE 29/291; *3 Sheaf*, 14 (1917), 8; *3 Sheaf*, 36 (1941), 59.

93 *3 Sheaf*, 55 (1960), 47–8, 48–9, 50–1.

94 CCALS, ZSR 156, m.1d; ZSR 175, m.1; ZSR 301, m.1; ZSR 302, m.1d; *3 Sheaf*, 17 (1920), 69–70.

95 CCALS, ZSR 142, m.1; ZSR 327, m.1d; ZSR 356, m.1; ZSR 381, m.1d; ZMB 1, f.153v; BL, Harl. Ms.2067, f.45.

96 A. Thacker, 'Early Medieval Chester, 400–1230', *VCH, Chester*, V, Part 1, 19–22.

97 *Liber Luciani de Laude Cestrie*, 65.

98 CCALS, ZSR 6, mm.4, 10d; ZSR 16, m.3; ZSR 28, m.4.

99 *3 Sheaf*, 36 (1941), 62–3; *3 Sheaf*, 29 (1934), 54; CCALS, ZMR 63, m.1d.

100 TNA: PRO, SC 11/99, m.1; CCALS, ZMB 6, f.169v.

101 CCALS, ZSR 220, m.1; ZSR 226, m.1; TNA: PRO, CHES 25/8, m.15d.

102 CCALS, ZMB 1, f.26v; ZMB 2, f.3; ZSB 1, f.154; ZSB 3, f.96; ZSB 4, f.31v.

103 CCALS, ZSB 4, f.121v; OED, sv. goddard. Was it a corruption of the French *godet*, a drinking cup?

104 *3 Sheaf*, 36 (1941), 9; CCALS, ZMB 3, f.56v; ZSR 153, m.1d; ZSR 157, m.1; ZSR 170, m.1d.; ZSR 171, m.1d; ZSR 172, m.1d. Hatton's ship: ZMB 3, ff.93, 94v, 96, 96v.

105 *3 Sheaf*, 29 (1934), 40; CCALS, ZMB 5, ff.45v, 85v, 109v; ZSB 3, ff.77, 79, 81v; ZSR 366, m.1.

106 A. Cosgrove, 'The Emergence of the Pale', 553; R.A. Griffiths, *Reign of Henry VI*, 134–5, 168; *CPR, 1436–41*, 281.

107 CCALS, ZMB 3, f.12v; ZMB 4, f.41v; ZSB 1, f.138; ZSB 2, f.8.

108 J.R. Dickinson, *Lordship of Man under the Stanleys*, 76.

109 J. Laughton, 'Historical Commentary on Meols', 417.

110 CCALS, ZSB 2, f.21; ZSB 3, f.39v; ZSB 4, f.31; ZSR 349, m.1d; ZSR 385, m.1d; ZSR 452, m.1d; ZSR 463, m.1

111 CCALS, ZSR 332, m.1d; ZSR 337, m.1; ZSR 338, m.1; ZSR 351, m.2; ZSR 363, m.1; ZSR 385, m.1; ZSR 390, m.1d.

112 CCALS, ZSR 385, m.1d.

113 CCALS, ZSB 1, ff.167, 167v; ZSB 2, ff.59, 68, 70v, 71v; ZSR 356, m.1d.

114 CCALS, ZSB 1, f.172v; ZSB 2, f.51.

115 CCALS, ZSB 4, ff.14, 37, 41, 62, 79, 140v; ZSR 403, m.1; ZSR 412, mm.1, 1d; ZSR 442, m.1d; ZSR 451, m.1.

116 CCALS, ZTAR 1/5, mm.1, 1d; ZMB 9, ff.32v-33; OED, sv. skene.

117 E.M. Veale, 'Craftsmen and the Economy of London', 124.

118 C. Dyer, *Making a Living*, 201; C. Phythian-Adams, *Desolation of a City*, 134; C. Dyer, *Standards of Living*, 196.

119 TNA: PRO, WALE 29/291; CCALS, ZMR 75, m.1.

120 C. Dyer, *Standards of Living*, 240–1.

121 A.J. Kettle, 'Religious Houses', *VCH, Cheshire*, III, 135, 136, 138, 144, 149, 178–84.

122 C. Dyer, *Standards of Living*, 247.

123 J. Bennett, 'Conviviality and Charity', 19–41; CCALS, ZMB 7, f.1.

124 TNA: PRO, SC 11/890.

125 *The Household Books of John Howard, Duke of Norfolk*, I, 240.

126 *3 Sheaf*, 36 (1941), 9; *Lancashire and Cheshire Wills and Inventories* (1860), 6–12.

127 *3 Sheaf*, 18 (1921), 93.

128 CCALS, ZMB 1, f.16; ZMB 2, f.19v; C. Dyer, *Standards of Living*, 252.

129 CCALS, ZMB 4, f.34; ZSB 1, f.122; ZSB 4, f.99v; ZSB 5, ff.61, 63.

Chapter 6

1 For city government in the medieval period, see *VCH, Chester*, V, Part 1, 28, 38–44, 58–63.

2 CCALS, ZCH 13; R.H. Morris, *Chester in the Plantagenet and Tudor Reigns*, 490–3.

3 CCALS, ZMB 1, ff.16, 38v-39; ZMB 2, ff.20, 50.

4 CCALS, ZMB 1, f.62v.

5 CCALS, ZMR 61, m.1d; ZMR 69, m.1d; ZMB 1, f.16v.

6 CCALS, ZMB 1, ff.16–16v; ZAF 1, f.2.

7 BL, Harl. Ms.2020, f.73.

8 CCALS, ZAF 1, f.2; ZMB 2, f.94; ZMUR 1.

9 CCALS, ZMB 1, ff.9, 42; ZMB 2, f.48v; ZMB 3, ff.25, 105; ZMB 4, ff.45–6.

10 CCALS, ZSR 231, m.1; ZSR 239, m.1; ZSR 254, m.1d; ZSR 263, m.1; TNA: PRO, CHES 25/12, m.39; SC 6/779/4, m.1.

11 CCALS, ZMB 4, f.67v.

12 CCALS, ZMB 6, f.34v.

13 CCALS, ZMB 5, f.46v; ZMB 6, ff.3v, 33v; BL, Harl. Ms.2158, f.44.

14 R.H. Morris, *Chester in the Plantagenet and Tudor Reigns*, 218.

15 BL, Harl. Ms.2158, f.47v; CCALS, ZMB 8, f.97.

16 CCALS, ZCH 32; ZMB 9 (a), ff.2–4.

17 BL, Harl. Ms.2158, ff.31, 42v, 44, 48, 48v, 60, 61, 63.

18 BL, Harl. Ms.2158, ff.31v-34v, 36–7, 43–43v, 44, 54v.

19 BL, Harl. Ms.2158, ff.44–47v, 48v-50.

20 C.P. Lewis, 'Municipal Prisons', *VCH, Chester*, V, Part 2, 32.

21 R.H. Morris, *Chester in the Plantagenet and Tudor Reigns*, 556–7.

22 ZCHB 2, f.76; BL, Harl. Ms.2020, f.22v (customary tenants in 1437–8).

23 CCALS, ZMB 5, f.180v; ZMB 6, f.33v.

24 CCALS, ZMB 6, ff.3v, 34v; ZSB 3, f.63.

25 CCALS, ZMB 6, ff.166v-170v; ZMB 9, ff.2–2v.

26 *The Ledger Book of Vale Royal*, 52.

27 CCALS, ZTAR 1/8; ZCHD 2/1; BL, Harl. Ms.2158, ff. 31v, 32, 34, 36v, 38, 43v, 52v, 55v; Harl. Ms.2093, f.205.

28 BL, Harl. Ms.2158, ff.32, 34v, 56; CCALS, ZSB 1, f.68v.

29 BL, Harl. Ms.2158, ff.48v, 49, 52, 55v, 56, 57v, 62; CCALS, ZTAR 1/3; ZTAR 1/4.

30 BL, Harl. Ms.2158, ff.36v, 43v, 52, 53, 55v, 62, 63v, 63v, 64v; Harl. Ms.2162, f.75; CCALS, ZSB 2, ff.85, 89; ZSB 3, f.21v.

31 C.P. Lewis, 'Craft Guilds', *VCH, Chester*, V, Part 2, 114–19.

32 BL, Harl. Ms.2054, f.64; 3 *Sheaf*, 30 (1935), 26.

33 BL, Harl. Ms.2115, f.163; TNA: PRO, SC 6/771/3, m.8; SC 6/771/5, m.14.

34 CCALS, ZMR 7, m.4; ZSR 110, m.1d; ZSR 130, m.1d.

35 CCALS, ZMB 3, f.60; ZSR 110, m.1d; ZSR 235, m.1d; ZSR 453, m.1d.

36 CCALS, ZSR 145, m.1; ZSR 146, m.1; ZSR 147, m.1; ZSR 165, m.1d; ZSR 166, m.1d.

37 *BPR*, iii, 428, 486.

38 CCALS, ZG 7/23; ZSR 145, m.1; ZSR 146, m.1; ZSR 151, m.1d; ZSR 153, mm.1, 1d; ZSR 156, mm.1, 1d; ZSR 160, m.1d; ZSR 165, m.1d; ZSR 166, m.1d.

39 CCALS, ZSR 183, m.1; ZSR 203, m.1; ZSR 232, m.1d; ZSR 236, m.1; ZSR 239, m.1d.

40 CCALS, ZSR 248, m.1d; ZSR 251, m.1; ZSR 261, m.1d; ZSR 272, m.1d. (A possible reference to an association of skinners in 1412–13: ZMB 2, f.108).

41 CCALS, ZSR 310, m.1; ZSR 314, m.1d; ZSR 342, m.1; ZMB 6, f.30.

42 CCALS, ZSR 389, m.1; C.P. Lewis, 'Craft Guilds', *VCH, Chester*, V, Part 2, 124.

43 CCALS, ZMR 85, m.1; BL, Harl. Ms.2054, f.23.

44 CCALS, ZSR 366, m.1d; ZSR 382, m.1; ZSR 387, m.1d; ZSR 467, m.1.

45 TNA: PRO, CHES 25/8, m.34; BL, Harl. Ms.2054, ff.41v-42; CCALS, ZG 7/19.

46 CCALS, ZMB 7, f.159; ZMB 8, f.128; ZMB 9(g), f.5; ZMB 10, f.2v; ZMB 11, f.3.

47 BL, Harl. Ms.2054, ff.41v-42.

48 CCALS, ZG 7/19.

49 CCALS, ZMB 6, ff.30–30v.

50 CCALS, ZSR 222, m.1d; ZSR 238, m.1d; ZSR 247, m.1; ZSR 373, m.1; ZSR 419, m.1d; ZSR 467, m.1d (tailors); ZSR 427, m.1; ZSR 459, m.1; ZSR 461, m.1d (bakers); ZSR 469, m.1d; ZSR 476, m.1; ZSR 477, m.1 (smiths); ZSR 433, m.1d; ZSR 441, m.1 (weavers); ZSR 366, m.1d; ZSR 462, m.1d (skinners).

51 CCALS, ZSR 302, m.1.

52 CCALS, ZMB 3, f.60; ZSR 150, m.1; ZSR 166, m.1d; ZSR 302, m.1.

53 3 *Sheaf*, 36 (1941), 54; CCALS, ZSR 330, m.1.

54 CCALS, ZMB 5, f.216; ZSR 358, m.1.

55 BL, Harl. Ms.2158, f.32, 33v.

56 BL, Harl. Ms.2158, ff.39, 39v, 40, 62, 63v; ZTAR 1/4, m.1d; ZTAR 1/8. Some sources name the Merchants and not the Mercers as tenants of the carriage house in Grey Friars Lane.

57 BL, Harl. Ms.2158, f.41v; CCALS, ZMR 37, m.1d.

58 N. Orme, *Medieval Schools*, 65; *Chartulary of St Werburgh's*, II, 469.

59 D. Keene, *Medieval Winchester*, i, 318; S. Thrupp, *Merchant Class of Medieval London*, 30–1 (tailors' company included many members with no connections to the trade but attracted by the lavish expenditure).

60 CCALS, ZSR 61, m.6.

61 *BPR*, iii, 408–9.

62 *CPR*, 1391–6, 248–9; *CPR*, 1396–9, 156–7; *CPR*, 1408–13, 242–3; TNA: PRO, SC 11/890–1; BL, Harl. Ms.2061, ff.35–59.

63 TNA: PRO, SC 11/890; CCALS, ZSR 158, m.1.

64 3 *Sheaf*, 36 (1941), 9, 54.

65 TNA: PRO, SC 11/890.

66 CCALS, ZSR 216, m.1; BL, Harl. Ms.2063, f.113.

67 CCALS, ZTAR 1/4, m.1; BL, Harl. Ms.2158, ff.36, 37v, 39, 40v, 55, 57.

68 CCALS, ZMB 5, f.176.

69 3 *Sheaf*, 17 (1920), 69; 3 *Sheaf*, 19 (1922), 4; BL, Harl. Ms.2037, ff.309v, 310v.

70 CCALS, ZMB 12, f.4; ZMB 13, f.2.

71 A. Thacker, 'Economy and Society, 1230–1350', *VCH, Chester*, V, Part 1, 55.

72 CCALS, ZMB 5, ff.69v, 109v, 130, 181v; ZMB 6, ff.4v, 34v.

73 TNA: PRO, SC 6/793/2, m.1; SC 6/797/3, m.1d.

74 CCALS, ZCR 352.

75 CCALS, ZMB 2, f.50; ZMB 6, ff. 34, 37.

76 CCALS, ZMB 1, f.23; ZMB 4, ff.68, 69; ZMB 7, f.11v.

77 CCALS, ZAF 1, f.1; BL, Harl. Ms.2158, f.49v.

78 BL, Harl. Ms.2158, ff.46v, 47; CCALS, ZMB 8, f.97.

79 BL, Harl. Ms.2158, ff.31, 42v, 44, 50v; CCALS, ZMB 5, f.46v; ZAB 1, f.43.

80 S. Thrupp, *Merchant Class of Medieval London*, 86.
81 CCALS, ZAB 1, f.43.
82 3 *Sheaf*, 17 (1920), 105.
83 A.M. Kennett (ed.), *Archives and Records of the City of Chester*, 31.
84 CCALS, ZCH 32.
85 CCALS, ZSR 239, m.1; ZSR 267, m.1d; ZMB 5, f.85v; ZMB 6, ff.3, 33, 88.
86 Matthew Johnson: CCALS, ZMB 5, f.153; ZMB 6, ff.33v, 34v, 84; ZMB 7, ff.81, 158; ZMB 8, f.60; 3 *Sheaf*, 18 (1921), 92. Edmund Farrington: CCALS, ZMB 5, f.185v; ZMB 6, ff.3v, 34v, 83v; ZMB 7, ff.3v, 81v, 158; ZMB 8, f.60, 125v; ZMB 9, f.2; ZSR 480, m.1d.
87 G. Ormerod, *History of Cheshire*, II, 729–31, 737, 761; TNA: PRO, SC 6/795/6, m.1d; CCALS, ZSR 237, m.1d; ZSR 248, m.1d; ZSR 276, m.1; ZSR 293, m.1; ZSR 300, m.1.
88 TNA: PRO, CHES 29/166, m.25.
89 S. Thrupp, *Merchant Class of Medieval London*, 191–206; M. Kowaleski, 'Commercial Dominance of a Medieval Provincial Oligarchy', 378–81.
90 A. Thacker, 'Economy and Society, 1230–1350', *VCH, Chester*, V, Part 1, 53; G. Ormerod, *History of Cheshire*, II, 826; TNA: PRO, SC 6/771/7, m.1.
91 TNA: PRO, SC 6/793/8, m.1d; 36 *DKR*, 153–4, 176; CCALS, ZMR 64, mm.1–1d; ZMR 81, m.1.
92 3 *Sheaf*, 17 (1920), 105; BL, Harl. Ms.2158, ff.38, 52, 56v; G. Ormerod, *History of Cheshire*, II, 821.
93 R. Britnell, *Growth and Decline in Colchester*, 130.
94 CCALS, ZMB 5, ff.88, 129v, 186v, 187; ZMB 6, ff.84, 84v, 121; ZMB 7, f.3v; ZMB 9(a), f.9v; 9(e), f.11v.
95 A. Thacker, 'Law Courts', *VCH, Chester*, V, Part 2, 20–5.
96 BL, Harl. Ms.2162, ff.58, 93; Harl. Ms.2057, ff.125–7.
97 CCALS, ZMB 1, ff.16–16v.
98 CCALS, ZMB 1, ff.5–5v, 6v–7v.
99 CCALS, ZSR 6, mm.2, 4.
100 CCALS, ZSB 2, ff.39v, 85, 90v.
101 TNA: PRO, CHES 25/1, mm.1–3.
102 CCALS, ZQCR 8, m.1; ZQCR 11, m.1.
103 CCALS, ZMB 1, f.16; ZMB 7, f.1; ZSB 5, f.61.
104 CCALS, ZMB 7, f.1; ZMB 9(d), f.29v; ZSB 5, f.92v.
105 BL, Harl. Ms.2158, ff.48v, 63; S. Thrupp, *Merchant Class of Medieval London*, 24–5.
106 CCALS, ZSB 6 (a), f.11v.
107 *Liber Luciani de Laude Cestrie*, 65; *BPR*, iii, 161, 271; *CPR*, 1446–52, 261.
108 D. Clayton, *Administration of the County Palatine of Chester*, 215–16, 241, 268–70; M.J. Bennett, *Community, Class and Careerism*, 162–91; P. Morgan, *War and Society in Medieval Cheshire*, 6–8.
109 M.J. Bennett, 'A County Community: Social Cohesion amongst the Cheshire Gentry, 1400–25', 25–8; E. Powell, 'Arbitration and the Law in England in the Late Middle Ages', 52–3; R.A. Griffiths, *The Reign of Henry VI*, 595–7.
110 CCALS, ZMB 1, f.16; ZMB 2, f.19v; ZAF 1, f.3; BL, Harl. Ms.2054, f.20.
111 CCALS, ZSR 424, m.1.
112 CCALS, ZMB 3, ff.23, 68v; ZMB 4, ff.49v, 66v; ZMB 5, f.13v; ZSR 243, m.1; ZSR 245, m.1; ZSR 289, m.1d; ZSR 331, m.1; ZSR 405, m.1.
113 CCALS, ZMB 5, f.182; ZSR 364, m.1.
114 CCALS, ZMB 6, ff.127–64; ZMB 7, ff.83–94, 98–117.
115 CCALS, ZMB 7, ff.69–71v, 146v–149v.
116 CCALS, ZMB 4, f.61; ZMB 6, ff.53v, 54; ZMB 7, f.142v.
117 CCALS, ZMB 6, ff.50–51v, 158v; ZMB 8, f.73v.
118 CCALS, ZMB 6, ff.37, 53; *Lancashire and Cheshire Wills and Inventories* (1884), 1–4.
119 CCALS, ZSR 5, m.3d; ZSR 6, m.5d; ZSR 12, m.10.
120 CCALS, ZSR 284, m.1; ZSB 4, ff.97–99v.
121 CCALS, ZMB 5, ff.59v–60; ZMB 7, ff.152v–153; ZSB 2, f.60v; ZSB 3, f.97v.
122 CCALS, ZMB 7, ff.75v, 79; TNA: PRO, CHES 25/16, m.3d.
123 CCALS, ZSB 3, f.19v; TNA: PRO, CHES 25/16, m.12.
124 CCALS, ZSB 3, ff.66v, 95v, 98; ZSR 363, m.1; ZSR 365, m.1d; ZSR 375, m.1d; TNA: PRO, CHES 25/16, m.12.
125 CCALS, ZMB 1, ff.55v–56; R.H. Morris, *Chester in the Plantagenet and Tudor Reigns*, 405–8.
126 TNA: PRO, CHES 25/11, mm.7, 8, 9, 17–18.
127 *Catalogue of Ancient Deeds*, IV (1902), A 10383; 3 *Sheaf*, 22 (1925), 67.
128 TNA: PRO, CHES 25/12, mm.2, 2d, 3.
129 37 *DKR*, 790; TNA: PRO, CHES 25/12, mm.13, 16, 16d; CHES 25/13, m.1d.
130 A.J. Kettle, 'Religious Houses', *VCH, Cheshire*, III, 147; CCALS, ZSR 205, m.1; ZSR 208, m.1; ZSR 245, m.1; TNA: PRO, CHES 25/16, m.19d.
131 A. Thacker, 'Fairs', *VCH, Chester*, V, Part 2, 100–1.
132 *BPR*, iii, 178, 185, 190, 360–1, 399–400.
133 G. Rosser, 'Conflict and Political Community in the Medieval Town', 20–42.
134 TNA: PRO, CHES 29/110, mm.4d, 7d. 13.
135 TNA: PRO, CHES 25/12, m.17d; CHES 25/15, m.39; CHES 29/187, mm.5, 5d, 6, 8, 8d.
136 CCALS, ZMB 6, f.101; ZCH 32; R.H. Morris, *Chester in the Plantagenet and Tudor Reigns*, 133–5.
137 CCALS, ZMB 1, f.19v; ZMB 3, f.84; ZMB 4, f.47v.
138 CCALS, ZMB 2, ff.5, 110; ZMB 3, ff.79, 84, 101v; ZSB 1, ff.132, 132v; ZSB 3, f.96.
139 CCALS, ZSR 5, mm.3, 3d, 4; ZSR 6, m.4; BL, Harl. Ms.2162, ff.71v, 79.
140 CCALS, ZSB 1, f.136v; ZSPR 1, f.16v; ZMB 5, f.103v; ZCHB 2, ff.71, 80v–81.
141 BL, Harl. Ms.2046, f.33.
142 TNA: PRO, CHES 25/1, m.3; *Sel. Court R.*, 183.
143 TNA: PRO, CHES 25/8, m.16; CHES 25/10, mm.33d, 36d; CHES 29/108, m.15d.
144 TNA: PRO, CHES 25/11, m.15; BL, Harl. Ms.2020, f.18.
145 TNA: PRO, CHES 25/12, mm.6–6d; 3 *Sheaf*, 11 (1914), 1.

Chapter 7

1 D. Keene, *Winchester*, i, 250; E.M. Veale, 'Craftsmen and the Economy of London in the fourteenth century', 127.
2 J. Laughton, E. Jones and C. Dyer, 'Urban Hierarchy in the Later Middle Ages', 343–4.
3 *English Historical Documents*, III, *1189–1327*, 882; A. Thacker, 'Early Medieval Chester, 400–1230', *VCH, Chester*, V, Part 1, 24, 29.
4 CCALS, ZSR 143, m.1; ZSR 226, m.1; ZSR 467, m.1d; ZSB 2, f.26.
5 TNA: PRO, CHES 25/12, m.13; CCALS, ZSR 148, m.1d; ZSR

151, m.1; ZSR 196, m.1d; ZSR 207, m.1d; ZMB 4, f.35.

6 TNA: PRO, E 101/486/12, m.1; SC 6/790/10, m.4; CHES 25/10, m.10; CHES 25/11, m.8d; Eaton Hall, Ch.321.

7 *Willelmi Malmesbiriensis Monachi*, 308.

8 CCALS, ZSR 123, m.3d; ZSR 135, m.1d; ZSR 143, m.1; TNA: PRO, CHES 25/10, m.10.

9 TNA: PRO, CHES 38/26/3, mm.1, 2–2d. I thank Dr J. Galloway for this reference.

10 TNA: PRO, CHES 25/11, mm.1, 5, 8, 22; CHES 25/12, mm.18d, 38d; CHES 25/13, m.1.

11 TNA: PRO, CHES 25/10, m.33; CHES 25/12, mm.4, 38d; CHES 25/14, m.3d.

12 CCALS, ZSR 1, m.1d; ZMB 1, f.40; ZMB 3, f.15; ZMB 7, f.156; ZMB 8, f.128; ZMB 9 (g), f.5.

13 3 *Sheaf*, 49 (1954), 16–17, 18, 19.

14 CCALS, ZSB 4, f.75; J.McN. Dodgson, *Place-Names of Cheshire*, Part Five (1:i), 68–9.

15 CCALS, ZMB 1, ff.5–7v, 37v; ZMB 2, ff.35v–36v; ZMB 3, f.50v; ZMB 7, f.2 ; ZSR 226, m.1; ZSR 385, m.1; ZSR 387, m.1d (tarts); ZSR 388, m.1d (tarts); ZSR 406, m.1.

16 CCALS, ZSR 135, m.1d; ZSR 145, m.1; ZSR 147, m.1; ZSR 287, m.1d; purchase of peas: ZSR 126, m.2d; ZSR 158, m.1d; ZSR 164, m.1; ZSR 167, m.1d; ZSR 191, m.1d (and beans).

17 C. Dyer, *Standards of Living*, 199; *Records of Early English Drama: Cheshire including Chester*, I, 67.

18 CCALS, ZSR 360, m.1d; ZSR 388, m.1d; ZSR 427, m.1d.

19 P.H.W. Booth and J.P. Dodd, 'The Manor and Fields of Frodsham, 1315–74', 42–4; P.H. Booth, '"Farming for Profit" in the Fourteenth Century', 79–80; C. Dyer, 'English Diet in the Later Middle Ages', 213–14; R. Britnell, *Growth and Decline in Colchester*, 198–9.

20 CCALS, ZSR 14, m.2; ZSR 314, m.1d; ZMB 1, f.2; ZQCR 10, m.1; ZQCR 4, m.1.

21 CCALS, ZMB 2, f.78; ZMB 3, f.62; ZMB 4, f.7; ZSB 5, f.139v.

22 CCALS, ZMB 6, f.122; ZMB 7, ff.120, 156; ZMB 9 (e), f.12; ZMB 11, m.3.

23 CCALS, ZSB 2, f.8; ZSB 3, f.40.

24 CCALS, ZSR 200, m.1; ZSR 371, m.1; ZSR 248, m.1d; ZSR 232, m.1; ZSR 237, m.1.

25 CCALS, ZMB 3, f.16; ZSB 2, f.43.

26 CCALS, ZMR 64, m.1d; ZMR 72, m.1; ZMR 78, m.1; ZSR 126, m.2d.

27 CCALS, ZQCR 5, 10, 11; ZMB 1, f.16; ZSB 3, f.60v; ZSB 4, f.32v; ZSB 5, f.35.

28 CCALS, ZSB 2, f.40; BL, Harl. Ms.2158, ff.36, 37v, 43, 51v, 57.

29 CCALS, ZSR 135, m.1d; ZSR 170, m.1; ZSR 244, m.1d; ZSR 281, m.1; ZSR 349, m.3.

30 CCALS, ZMB 4, ff.7, 72; ZSR 163, m.1d.

31 CCALS, ZSR 385, m.1d; ZSR 388, m.1d; ZSR 427, m.1d; ZMB 4, f.7.

32 CCALS, ZSR 161, m.1; ZSR 177, m.1; ZSR 195, m.1d; ZSR 209, m.1d; ZSR 239, m.4d; ZSR 289, m.1d; ZSR 298, m.1d.

33 CCALS, ZSR 171, m.1; ZSR 262, m.1d; ZSR 264, m.1d; ZSR 272, m.1; ZSR 304, m.1; ZSR 315, m.1d; ZSR 329, m.1.

34 C. Dyer, *Standards of Living*, 58; M. Kowaleski, *Medieval Exeter*, 307.

35 J. Mc.N. Dodgson, *Place-Names of Cheshire*, Part One, 24–5; Part Four, 169; P.H. Sawyer, 'Translation of the Cheshire Domesday', folio 263v.

36 *BPR*, iii, 304; TNA: PRO, SC 6/793/8, m.1d; SC 6/794/1, m.1d; SC 6/799/1, m.1d.

37 TNA: PRO, SC 6/788/2, m.3; SC 6/789/8, m.3; SC 6/793/3, m.6.

38 TNA: PRO, SC 6/789/8, m.3; SC 6/789/10, mm.3, 4; SC 6/792/3, m.5d.

39 R.H. Morris, *Chester in the Plantagenet and Tudor Reigns*, 554–8.

40 CCALS, ZMB 2, ff.17, 37v, 38v, 42, 80; ZMB 3, f.97; ZSB 1, ff.54, 57v.

41 CCALS, ZSB 3, f.86v.

42 CCALS, ZCHD 2/1; BL, Harl. Ms.2046, f.34v; J. McN. Dodgson, *Place-Names of Cheshire*, Part Five (1:i), 31.

43 CCALS, ZSB 2, f.8; ZSB 3, ff.21v, 60v, 65v, 94v; ZSB 4, f.53v.

44 CCALS, ZSB 3, f.3v; ZSB 4, ff.13, 16v, 19, 32v, 44v, 94v; ZMB 4, f.53v.

45 CCALS, ZSR 127, m.1d; ZSR 129, m.2d; ZSR 135, m.1; ZSR 143, m.1d; ZSR 165, m.1d; ZSR 168, m.1d; ZSR 234, m.1d; ZSR 242, m.1d; ZMB 3, f.86v; ZSB 1, f.75; *Calendar of Moore Deeds*, no.1028; D. Keene, *Medieval Winchester*, i, 273.

46 CCALS, ZSB, f.27v; ZMB 2, f.97; ZSR 6, m.8; ZSR 130, m.1d; ZSR 359, m.1.

47 TNA: PRO, CHES 25/1, m.4; CCALS, ZSR 22, m.7d.

48 BL, Harl. Ms.2091, f.24v; CCALS, ZSR 330, m.1d.

49 CCALS, ZSB 3, f.37; ZMB 4, ff.24, 34, 53; ZSR 228, m.1d; ZSR 261, m.3; ZSR 267, m.1; ZSR 285, m.1; M. Kowaleski, *Medieval Exeter*, 316; D. Keene, *Medieval Winchester*, i, 277, 278.

50 CCALS, ZMB 1, f.36; ZMB 3, f.62v; ZMB 4, f.27; ZSB 2, f.24; ZSB 3, f.70v; ZSB 4, f.12.

51 CCALS, ZSR 14, m.2; ZMB 2, ff.27, 59, 92; ZQCR 4, m.1; ZQCR 10, m.1; ZQCR, 11, m.1.

52 CCALS, ZMB 3, ff.60v, 101, 102; ZTAR 1/3, m.1; BL, Harl. Ms.2158, ff.36, 43, 51v, 55, 57.

53 CCALS, ZSB 1, f.52v; G. Rosser, *Medieval Westminster*, 128–9.

54 CCALS, ZSR 135, m.1d; ZSR 170, m.1; ZSR 266, m.1d; ZSR 281, m.1; ZSR 346, m.2; ZSR 349, m.3; ZSR 359, m.1; ZSR 408, m.1d.

55 CCALS, ZSR 14, m.2; ZSR 170, m.1; ZQCR 4, m.1; ZQCR 10, m.1; ZQCR 11, m.1.

56 K. Matthews, *Excavations at Chester*, 51, 56.

57 CCALS, ZSR 21, m.4; ZSR 26, m.1d; ZSR 52, m.2; ZMB 2, ff.25, 28; ZMB 3, ff.60v, 100v, 101.

58 CCALS, ZMB 5, f.69v; ZSR 260, m.1; ZSR 282, m.1d; ZSR 314, m.1d.

59 CCALS, ZSR 314, m.1d; ZSR 344, m.1d; ZSR 348, m.1; ZSR 349, m.3; ZSR 350, m.1.

60 C. Dyer, *Standards of Living*, 64; J.M. Bennett, 'The Village Alewife', 31, n.7; *Records of Early English Drama: Cheshire including Chester*, I, 67.

61 CCALS, ZMB 2, ff.51, 51v; ZSB 3, ff.39v, 67 (wheat); ZSR 123, m.4d; ZSR 207, m.1; ZSR 244, m.1; ZSR 306, m.1; ZSR 365, m.1; ZSR 383, m.1; ZSR 386, m.1d; ZSR 399, m.1d; ZSR 407, m.1d; ZSR 448, m.1; ZSR 457, m.1d (barley and oats).

62 For brewing in Chester, see J. Laughton, 'The Alewives of Later Medieval Chester'.

63 CCALS, ZMB, 4, f.34; ZSB 1, ff.41, 42v; ZSB 2, f.63v; ZSB 4, ff.5–7, 27–8.

64 CCALS, ZMB 2, f.57; ZSB 4, ff.94–94v, 110v-111; ZMB 6, ff.166v-8, 169v-70v.

65 CCALS, ZSB 3, ff.20, 64v, 91v, 92v; ZSB 3, f.32v.

66 CCALS, ZSR 87, m.1; ZSR 89, m.1; ZSR 115, m.1; 36 *DKR*, 105, 119, 474.

67 K.P. Wilson, 'The Port of Chester in the Fifteenth Century', 6, 14; *Chester Customs Accounts*, 20–45.

68 CCALS, ZMB 2, ff.72, 93v; ZSR 239, m.4d; ZMB 1, f.16v; TNA: PRO, CHES 25/11, m.5.

69 CCALS, ZMB 3, ff.35, 58; ZSR 142, m.1; ZSR 249, m.1; *Chester Customs Accounts*, 35, 38–42.

70 CCALS, ZSR 163, m.1; ZSR 247, m.1; ZSR 369, m.1; ZSR 405, mm.1, 1d; SRO, D 641/1/2/73, mm.2d, 5d; BL, Harl. Ms.2057, f.23.

71 CCALS, ZSR 119, m.1d; TNA: PRO, SC 11/890.

72 CCALS, ZMB 1, f.14v; ZMR 75, m.1; BL, Harl. Ms.2158, f.56.

73 Ireland: Statute Rolls of the Parliament, 233, 433.

74 G. Ormerod, *History of Cheshire*, I, 288; CCALS, ZSR 118, m.1; ZSR 123, mm.2d, 3; ZSR 135, m.1; ZSR 143, m.1; ZSR 168, m.1; ZMB 2, f.100v; ZMB 3, f.98v.

75 CCALS, ZSR 222, m.1; ZSR 270, m.1; ZSR 340, m.1; ZSR 351, m.4d; ZSR 373, m.1d; ZSR 426, m.1; ZSR 453, m.1d; ZSR 454, m.1d; ZSR 459, m.1d.

76 CCALS, ZSR 66, m.1d; ZSR 69, m.1d; ZSR 106, m.1d; ZSR 108, m.1d; ZSR 110, m.1d; D. Keene, *Medieval Winchester*, i, 299–300; P. Walton, 'Textiles', 324.

77 CCALS, ZMB 3, f.97v; ZSR 113, m.1; ZSR 245, m.1; ZSR 310, m.1d.

78 CCALS, ZSR 213, m.1d; ZSR 240, m.1; ZSR 245, m.1d; ZSR 250, m.1; ZSR 263, m.1d.

79 TNA: PRO, CHES 25/10, m.33d; CCALS, ZSR 318, m.1d; ZSR 407, m.1d.

80 CCALS, ZSR 289, m.1d; ZSR 319, m.1.

81 CCALS, ZSR 119, m.1; ZSR 136, m.1; ZSR 138, m.1.

82 CCALS, ZSR 338, m.1; ZSR 352, m.1; ZSR 371, m.1d; ZSR 372, m.1d; ZSR 455, m.1.

83 CCALS, ZSR 351, m.6; ZSR 376, m.1d.

84 CCALS, ZSR 321, m.1d; ZSB 3, f.59; 3 *Sheaf*, 18 (1921), 92.

85 CCALS, ZSR 155, m.1; ZSR 205, m.1; ZSR 226, m.1d; ZSR 243, m.1; ZSR 311, m.1d; ZSR 351, m.1d; ZMB 3, f.101v; ZMB 7, f.152v; P. Walton, 'Textiles', 335.

86 CCALS, ZSR 121, m.1; ZSR 138, m.1; ZSR 144, m.1d; ZMR 83, m.1d; ZSR 241, m.1d.

87 D. Garner, *Archaeology in the Park*, 18–19.

88 CCALS, ZSR 179, m.1d; ZMB 4, f.53.

89 CCALS, ZSR 230, m.1; ZSR 351, m.6; ZSR 363, m.1; ZSR 475, m.1d; ZSR 476, m.1; P. Walton, 'Textiles', 334.

90 CCALS, ZSR 159, m.1; ZSR 191, m.1; ZSR 230, m.1; ZSR 236, m.1d; ZSR 237, m.1d; ZSR 356, m.1; ZSR 360, m.1d; ZSR 372, m.1d.

91 CCALS, ZSR 259, m.1; ZSR 288, m.1; ZSR 346, m.2d; ZSR 373, m.1d; shears: ZSR 318, m.1d; ZSR 378, m.1d; ZSR 462, m.1; tools in shop in 1507: ZSR 483, m.1d.

92 CCALS, ZSR 251, mm.1, 1d; ZSR 258, m.1d; ZSR 267, m.1d; ZSR 276, m.1; ZSR 287, m.1d; ZSR 288, m.1d; ZSR 289, m.1; ZSR 295, m.1; ZSR 306, m.1; ZSR 320, m.1.

93 TNA: PRO, SC 6/790/5, m.4; SC 6/790/7, m.4.

94 TNA: PRO, SC 6/798/9, m.6; 799/1, m.7d; 799/9, m.4d; 800/4, m.4d; 801/1, m.4d; CCALS, ZSR 279, m.1; ZSR 292, m.1d.

95 CCALS, ZSR 325, m.1d; ZSR 357, m.1d; ZSR 462, m.1; ZSR 485, m.1.

96 CCALS, ZQCR 7; ZMB 2, ff.26, 26v, 59; ZMB 3, ff.45–45v, 60v, 98v-100; ZMB 4, f.4v; ZSB 1, ff.39v, 42, 52, 64–66v, 118.

97 CCALS, ZMB 3, f.106v; ZSR 197, m.1d.

98 CCALS, ZSR 154, m.1; ZSR 236, m.1d; ZSR 304, m.1; ZSR 337, m.1d; ZSR 338, m.1; ZSR 448, m.1; ZMB 2, f.72; ZSR 304, m.1; ZSR 421, mm.1, 1d; ZSR 425, m.1; TNA: PRO, CHES 25/15, m.7.

99 CCALS, ZSR 344, m.1.

100 CCALS, ZSR 135, m.1; ZSR 153, m.1; ZSR 158, m.1; ZSR 233, m.1d; ZSR 239, m.1; ZSR 408, m.1d.

101 CCALS, ZSR 123, m.4d; ZSR 129, m.2d; ZSR 140, m.1; ZSR 162, m.1d; ZSR 171, m.1; ZSR 396, m.1d; ZSR 418, m.1d.

102 TNA: PRO, SC 6/771/12, m.1; SC 6/771/17, m.1.

103 CCALS, ZSR 154, m.1d; ZSR 188, m.1d; ZSR 290, m.1.

104 CCALS, ZMB 5, f.83; ZSB 2, f.37v; ZSR 128, m.1; ZSR 129, m.2; ZSR 317, m.1d; ZSR 359, m.1.

105 *Lancashire and Cheshire Wills and Inventories* (1884), 1–4; CCALS, ZSR 334, m.1; ZSR 351, m.3; ZSR 362, m.1d; ZSR 365, m.1; ZSR 367, m.1; ZSR 368, m.1; ZSR 384, m.1; ZSR 386, m.1; ZSR 403, m.1; ZSR 452, m.1; ZSR 410, m.1d; ZSR 419, m.1; ZSR 452, m.1.

106 CCALS, ZSR 129, m.2.

107 E. Crowfoot, F. Pritchard and K. Staniland, *Textiles and Clothing*, 75–6; CCALS, ZSR 310, m.1; ZSR 361, m.1d.

108 CCALS, ZSB 4, f.50v; ZSR 462, m.1d; 3 *Sheaf*, 14 (1917), 8.

109 3 *Sheaf*, 28 (1933), 92; 3 *Sheaf*, 29 (1934), 46; *Chester Plea Roll*, 169; TNA: PRO, CHES 25/1, m.3.

110 CCALS, ZAB 1, f.34; D. Garner, *Archaeology in the Park*, 11.

111 CCALS, ZSR 261, m.3; ZSB 3, f.65v; DCH/DD/7.

112 J. Cherry, 'Leather', 295–7; M. Shaw, 'A Late 15th- to 17th-century Tanning Complex at Northampton', 107.

113 *BPR*, iii, 50, 428, 472, 486; TNA: PRO, SC 6/787/2, m.1.

114 TNA: PRO, CHES 25/12, m.32d; CCALS, ZSR 239, m.2; ZSR 243, m.1; ZSR 244, m.1d.

115 3 *Sheaf*, 26 (1929), 36; S. Ward, *Chester City Ditches*, 18, 21.

116 CCALS, ZSR 161, m.1; ZSR 262, m.1; ZSR 289, m.1d.

117 CCALS, ZSR 178, m.1; ZSR 314, m.1d; ZSB 5, f.59v.

118 36 *DKR*, 21, 275, 325, 459; CCALS, ZSR 299, m.1.

119 CCALS, Company Minute Book (1737–1959), 6 January 1797.

120 TNA: PRO, E 315/47/139; E 326/3474; SC 6/787/2, m.1; CCALS, ZSR 150, m.1; ZSR 224, m.1.

121 J. Cherry, 'Leather', 308; D. Keene, *Medieval Winchester*, i, 289; CCALS, ZSR 122, m.1d; ZSR 217, m.1; ZSR 283, m.1.

122 CCALS, ZSB 3, f.65v; BL, Harl. Ms.2099, f.309; Harl. Ms.2158, f.40; S. Ward, *Chester City Ditches*, 19.

123 CCALS, ZSR 139, m.1; ZSR 238, m.1; ZSR 244, m.1; ZSR 246, m.1d; ZSR 289, m.1d; ZSR 307, m.1; ZSR 296, m.1d; ZSR 414, m.1; ZSR 419, m.1d; ZSR 421, m.1; ZSR 452, m.1d.

124 CCALS, ZSR 282, m.1d; ZSR 387, m.1d.

125 CCALS, ZMB 6, ff.50–51v; ZSR 429, m.1; J. Cherry, 'Leather', 309.

126 CCALS, ZSR 129, m.2; ZSR 190, m.1d; ZSR 198, m.1; ZSR 227, m.1; ZSR 229, m.1d; ZSR 270, m.1d.

127 CCALS, ZSR 129, m.2; ZSR 177, m.1d; ZSR 198, m.1; ZSR 223, m.1; ZSR 229, m.1d; ZSR 448, m.1.

128 CCALS, ZSR 90, m.1d; ZSR 93, m.1; ZSR 96, m.1d; ZSR 114, m.1; 36 *DKR*, 298.

129 CCALS, ZSR 285, m.1d; ZSR 391, m.1; ZSR 445, m.1d.

130 CCALS, ZSR 169, m.1d; ZSR 177, m.1; ZSR 203, m.1; ZSR 390, m.1; ZSR 446, m.1; J. Cherry, 'Leather', 311; *The Household Books of Sir John Howard, Duke of Norfolk*, I, 182 (6d to the saddler for stuffing).

131 CCALS, ZSR 169, m.1d; ZSR 206, m.1d; ZSR 220, m.1; ZSR 282, m.1; ZSR 295, m.1d.

132 CCALS, ZSR 282, m.1; ZSR 401, m.1d; ZSR 417, m.1; ZSR 444, m.1d; ZSR 447, m.1d.

133 BL, Add. Ch.50152; TNA: PRO, SC 6/771/5, m.14.

134 CCALS, ZSR 59, m.1; ZSR 90, m.1; ZSR 121, m.1d.

135 *CPR*, 1399–1401, 299; CCALS, ZSR 21, m.9d; ZSR 235, m.1; ZSR 270, m.1.

136 CCALS, ZSR 175, m.1d; ZSR 250, m.1d.

137 BL, Harl. Ms.2020, f.22v; CCALS, ZMUB 1, f.9.

138 TNA: PRO, SC 6/779/8, m.1; 780/2, m.1; 780/8, m.1; 782/1, m.1; 782/2, m.1; 782/7, m.1.

139 TNA: PRO, SC 6/774/8, m.1.

140 CCALS, ZSR 173, m.1d; ZSR 263, m.1d; ZSR 370, m.1; ZSR 376, m.1d.

141 CCALS, ZSR 234, m.1; ZSR 307, m.1d; ZSR 315, m.1d; ZSR 334, m.1d; ZSR 337, m.2d.

142 CCALS, ZSR 163, m.1; ZSR 180, m.1d; ZSR 203, m.1; ZSR 451, m.1d; ZSR 453, m.1d; ZSR 459, m.1d.

143 BL, Harl. Ms.2046, f.26 (it measured 10 x 6 royal virgates).

144 CCALS, ZSR 51, m.2; ZMR 81, m.1d; BL, Harl. Ms.2020, f.56v.

145 CCALS, ZTAR 1/3, m.1d; ZTAR 1/4, m.1d; BL, Harl. 2158, ff.36v, 38, 40v.

146 CCALS, ZSB 3, f.27v; TNA: PRO, SC 6/774/8, m.1; SC 6/782/1, m.1.

147 *Charters of the Anglo-Norman Earls*, 32–4; D. Keene, *Medieval Winchester*, i, 285; CCALS, ZSR 55, m.1d; ZSR 115, m.1; ZSR 123, m.4 (parmenters); ZSR 12, m.6; ZSR 262, m.1; ZSR 386, m.1 (costly furs).

148 CCALS, ZSR 23, m.3d; ZSR 42, m.3; ZSR 61, m.6.

149 CCALS, ZSR 6, m.3d; ZSR 36, m.4d; ZSR 153, m.1d; ZSR 245, m.1.

150 CCALS, ZSB 1, ff.127, 147, 152, 172; ZSR 180, m.1d: ZMB, 3, f.56.

151 BL, Harl. Ms.2020, f.36; Harl. Ms.2158, ff.32, 32v, 34; CCALS, ZCHD/4/1; ZSB 2, f.44.

152 3 *Sheaf*, 23 (1926), 49–50; BL, Add. Ch.75178; J. McN. Dodgson, *Place-Names of Cheshire*, Part Five (1:i), 50.

153 CCALS, ZSR 117, m.1; ZSR 119, m.1; TNA: PRO, CHES 25/10, m.26d.

154 CCALS, ZSR 386, m.1d; ZSR 457, m.1; ZSR 466, m.1d. Fur worth 40s: ZSR 158, m.1.

155 CCALS, ZMUR 1, m.3; TNA: PRO, E 101/488/2, mm.1, 3d.

156 CCALS, ZSR 121, m.1; ZSR 132, m.1; ZSR 322, m.1; ZSR 390, m.1d; TNA: PRO, E 101/488/2, m.1; BL, Harl. Ms.2158, f.49v.

157 CCALS, ZSB 5, f.32; ZSR 470, m.1d.

158 CCALS, ZMUR 1, m.3; BL, Harl. Ms.2158, ff.49v-50.

159 CCALS, ZSR 175, m.1d; ZSR 180, m.1.

160 A. Brown (ed.), *The Rows of Chester*, 51, 53, 67, 69, 70, 73, 168, 175–6, 183.

161 BL, Harl. Ms.2158, f.50.

162 G. Ormerod, *History of Cheshire*, II, 41; CCALS, ZSR 236, m.1.

163 CCALS, ZSB 3, f.93v; ZSB 4, f.9v; ZSB 5, f.33; ZSR 237, m.1; ZSR 265, m.1; BL, Harl. Ms.2037, f.209v.

164 TNA: PRO, E 101/487/5, m.1; E 101/488/2, m.1; E 101/545/25, mm.3, 5.

165 TNA: E 101/486/15; J.M. Lewis, 'Roof Tiles: Some Observations and Questions', 4.

166 TNA: PRO, E 101/545/25, m.9; CCALS, ZSR 366, m.1; ZMB 8, f.46.

167 CCALS, ZSB 4, f.53; information from Julie Edwards.

168 CCALS, ZSB 4, f.53; ZSR 362, m.1d; ZSR 363, m.1; ZSR 391, m.1d.

169 CCALS, ZSR 312, m.1d; S. Ward, 'Friaries in Chester', 125.

170 TNA: PRO, SC 6/771/4, m.5; BL, Harl. Ms.2158, f.48v; CCALS, ZSR 445, m.1d.

171 R. Marks, 'Window Glass', 277, 280; *Calendar of Documents, Ireland, 1252–1284*, 420.

172 R.J. Charleston, 'Vessel Glass', 256.

173 TNA: PRO, E 101/488/2, m.1; E 101/545/25, mm.6, 9.

174 CCALS, ZSR 104, m.1; ZSR 238, m.1d; R. Marks, 'Window Glass', 267–9.

175 I. Archibald, forthcoming.

176 CCALS, ZSR 142, m.1d; ZSR 288, m.1; ZSR 300, m.1.

177 A. Thacker, 'Economy and Society, 1230–1350', *VCH, Chester*, V, Part 1, 55.

178 TNA: PRO, SC 6/779/4, m.1.

179 CCALS, ZQCR 11.

180 Chester Archaeology, Lists of finds of metalwork/iron.

181 CCALS, ZSR 143, m.1d; ZSR 321, m.1d; ZSR 359, m.1d; ZSR 413, m.1d; TNA: PRO, SC 6/772/11, m.1.

182 *Chartulary of Chester Abbey*, II, 348–9; CCALS, ZSR 12, m.6; ZSR 51, m.6d; ZSR 140, m.1d; ZSR 161, m.1; ZSR 251, m.1d; ZSR 259, m.1; ZMB 3, f.99v; TNA: PRO, CHES 25/11, m.21.

183 CCALS, ZSR 289, m.1d; ZSR 429, m.1d.

184 CCALS, ZSR 196, m.1; WS 1628 Eaton (tools in smithy at corner of Bag Lane in 1628).

185 CCALS, ZSR 87, m.1d; ZSR 196, m.1; ZSR 227, m.1d; ZSR 363, m.1d; ZMUR 1, m.3.

186 CCALS, ZSR 12, m.6d; ZSR 230, m.1d; ZSR 233, m.1d; ZSR 237, m.1d; ZSR 239, m.3d; ZSR 292, m.1d.

187 CCALS, ZSR 138, m.1d; ZSR 267, m.1; ZSR 270, m.1; ZSR 272, m.1d; ZSR 273, m.1d; ZSR 296, m.1d; ZSR 307, m.1; ZSR 389, m.1.

188 *The Reeve's Tale*, lines 75–9.

189 CCALS, ZSR 90, m.1; ZSR 106, m.1; ZSR 117, m.1; ZSR 155, m.1; BL, Harl. Ms.2020, f.36; Harl. Ms.2099, f.35; TNA: PRO, WALE 29/158.

190 CCALS, ZMB 4, f.40v; ZSR 190, m.1; D. Keene, *Medieval Winchester*, i, 280.

191 CCALS, ZSR 411, m.1; ZSR 423, m.1; ZSR 447, m.1; ZSR 454, m.1; ZSR 461, m.1.

192 CCALS, ZSB 5, f.110v.

193 CCALS, ZSR 68, m.1; ZSR 247, m.1; ZSR 259, m.1; ZSR 277, m.1; ZSR 386, m.1.

194 CCALS, ZSR 183, m.1; ZSR 193, m.1; ZSR 294, m.1d.

195 TNA: PRO, E 101/488/2, m.1; E 101/488/7, mm.1, 1d; E 101/545/25, mm.1, 5d; 9; *BPR*, i, 100.

196 CCALS, ZSR 12, m.8; ZSB 2, ff.60v, 101v; ZSB 3, f.59v (armourers); ZSB 3, f.68v; ZSR 463, m.1d (brigandmakers).

197 CCALS, ZSR 178, m.1; ZSB 1, f.39v.

198 CCALS, ZSR 126, m.2; ZSR 129, m.2; ZSR 135, m.1d; ZSR 242, m.1; ZSR 297, m.1; ZSR 320, m.1d; ZSR 329, m.1d; ZSR 351, m.1d; ZSR 377, m.1d; ZSR 401, m.1; ZSR 433, m.1d; ZSR 455, m.1.

199 CCALS, ZSR 245, m.1d.

200 CCALS, ZSR 189, m.1d; ZSR 228, m.1; ZSR 231, m.1d.

201 *The Past Uncovered*, February 2003, 1.

202   CCALS, ZSR 161, m.1; ZSR 214, m.1; ZSR 227, m.1; ZMB 4, f.53v.

203   CCALS, ZSR 153, m.1d; ZSR 157, m.1; ZSR 224, m.1d; ZSR 227, m.1d.

204   CCALS, ZSR 351, mm.6d, 7; ZSR 358, m.1; ZSR 394, m.1; ZSR 403, m.1; ZSR 471, m.1; ZSB 4, ff.13v, 18v, 74, 138v; BL, Harl. Ms.2158, f.51; *Chester Customs Accounts*, 37.

205   *Lancashire and Cheshire Wills and Inventories* (1884), 1–4.

206   CCALS, ZSR 189, m.1; ZSR 191, m.1; ZSR 242, m.1; ZSR 243, m.1.

207   CCALS, ZSR 104, m.1; ZSR 128, m.1; ZSB 1, f.158; ZSB 2, f.45v; ZMB 5, f.20v.

208   TNA: PRO, SC 6/780/2, m.1; CCALS, ZSR 318, m.1d; ZSR 324, m.1d; ZSR 391, m.1.

209   A. Thacker, 'Economy and Society, 1230–1350', *VCH, Chester*, V, Part 1, 52.

210   CCALS, ZSB 3, f.64v; ZTAR 1/3, 1/4; ZSB 3, f.21v; BL, Harl. Ms.2158, f.36; *Talbot Deeds*, 203.

211   CCALS, ZSR 156, m.1; ZSR 440, m.1.

212   CCALS, ZSR 177, m.1; ZSR 191, m.1d; ZSR 360, m.1d; ZSR 424, m.1; ZSB 3, f.59v.

213   CCALS, ZSR 136, m.1; ZSR 381, m.1d; ZSR 419, m.1; ZSR 438, m.1; ZSR 467, m.1.

214   CCALS, ZSR 155, m.1d; M. Campbell, 'Gold, Silver and Precious Stones', 117.

215   TNA: PRO, SC 6/771/7, m.3; SC 6/779/6, m.1.

216   CCALS, ZSR 239, m.4; BL, Harl. Ms.2054, f.42.

217   CCALS, ZSR 124, m.1; ZSR 191, m.1d; ZSR 243, m.1d; ZSR 380, m.1; ZSR 381, m.1d; A. Brown (ed.), *The Rows of Chester*, 177, 183.

218   CCALS, ZMB 1, ff.4v, 8v.

219   CCALS, ZSR 2, m.6; ZSR 9, m.3d; ZSR 11, mm.1, 2; ZSR 12, m.6; ZMB 2, f.59.

220   *3 Sheaf*, 43 (1948), 7, 8.

221   H. Swanson, *Medieval Artisans*, 101–4; TNA: PRO, SC 6/774/14, m.1d; SC 6/774/15, m.1d; SC 6/775/3, m.1d; CCALS, ZMB 3, f.105v.

222   TNA: PRO, SC 6/780/5, m.1d; J. Munby, 'Wood', 400; R. Hardy, *Longbow: A Social and Military History*, 53.

223   CCALS, ZSR 42, m.1; ZSR 44, m.1; ZSR 128, m.3; ZSR 165, m.1d; ZSR 294, m.1d; ZSR 297, m.1; ZSR 321, m.1.

224   *The Household Books of John Howard, Duke of Norfolk*, I, 234–5; CCALS, ZSR 326, m.1.

225   CCALS, ZSR 44, m.1; ZSR 123, m.4; ZSR 312, m.1; ZSR 364, m.1.

226   CCALS, ZSR 238, m.1d; ZSR 326, m.1; ZSR 357, m.1d; TNA: PRO, SC 6/779/10, m.1.

227   CCALS, ZSR 273, m.1d; *Prologue*, lines 104–5.

228   TNA: PRO, SC6/774/14, m.1d; SC 6/774/15, m.1d; SC 6/775/4, m.1d; CCALS, ZMB 4, f.40v.

229   CCALS, ZSR 370, m.1d.

230   *The Household Books of John Howard, Duke of Norfolk*, I, xxii-iii; II, 295.

231   CCALS, ZQCR 11, m.1.

232   CCALS, ZSR 269, m.1d; ZMB 1, f.30; ZMB 3, ff.56v, 60v, 72v; TNA: PRO, E 101/545/25, m.9; SC 6/774/10, m.1d.

233   CCALS, ZSB 4, ff.138v, 139v, 147v, 151v; ZSB 5, f.17v; ZSR 449, m.1.

234   CCALS, ZSR 172, m.1d.

235   *BPR*, iii, 409; CCALS, ZSR 311, m.1; ZSR 320, m.1d; ZSR 330, m.1d; ZSR 345, m.1; ZSR 349, m.3.

236   CCALS, ZMB 1, f.61v; ZSR 264, m.1d; ZSR 322, m.1d; ZSR 378, m.1d; TNA: PRO, SC 6/774/14, m.1d; SC 6/779/5, m.1d; SC 6/780/4, mm.1, 1d; E 101/545/25, m.1.

237   CCALS, ZMUR 1, m.3; TNA: PRO, E 101/488/7, mm.1d, 2.

238   CCALS, ZMR 95, m.1; ZSR 190, m.1d; ZSR 198, m.1; ZSR 228, m.1; ZSR 250, m.1; ZSR 263, m.1d; ZSR 264, m.1; ZSR 275, m.1d.

239   CCALS, ZSR 277, m.1d; ZSR 290, m.1d; ZSR 301, m.1d; ZSR 302, m.1; ZSR 303, m.1d; ZSR 304, m.1; ZSR 317, m.1; ZSB 1, f.114.

240   A. Thacker, 'Economy and Society, 1230–1350', *VCH, Chester*, V, Part 1, 53–4; *Letters of Edward Prince of Wales: 1304–5*, 56.

241   CCALS, ZSR 153, m.1d; ZSR 157, m.1; ZSR 162, m.1d; ZSR 173, m.1d; ZSR 205, m.1d; ZSR 223, m.1d; ZSR 228, m.1d; ZSR 246, mm.1, 1d; ZSR 250, m.1; ZSR 276, m.1; ZMB 4, f.45; *Calendar of Papal Letters, vii, 1417–31*, 219; G. Ormerod, *History of Cheshire*, II, 729–31, 761.

242   *Lancashire and Cheshire Wills and Inventories* (1884), 1–4; *Chester Customs Accounts*, 36–44.

243   CCALS, ZSR 197, m.1d; ZSR 223, m.1d; ZSR 298, m.1; ZSR 300, m.1d; ZSR 387, m.1d; ZSR 418, m.1.

244   TNA: PRO, WALE 29/291; *3 Sheaf*, 17 (1920), 69–70.

245   CCALS, ZSR 214, m.1d; ZSR 240, m.1; ZSR 380, m.1d.

246   J. Laughton, 'The Alewives of Later Medieval Chester'; J.M. Bennett, *Ale, Beer and Brewsters in England: Women's Work in a Changing World*; CCALS, ZMB 2, f.57; ZSB 3, ff.21v, 66, 69, 92, 92v, 93; ZSR 214, m.1; ZSR 231, m.1; ZSR 234, m.1d; ZSR 351, m.1d.

247   CCALS, ZSR 167, m.1d; ZSR 223, m.1d; ZSR 247, m.1d; ZSR 263, m.1; ZSR 272, m.1; ZSR 295, m.1d; ZSR 309, m.1d; ZMB 4, f.40v.

248   CCALS, ZSR 35, m.6; ZSR 61, m.5; ZSR 196, m.1d; ZSR 278, m.1d; ZSR 289, m.1d; ZSR 356, m.1d; ZSR 360, m.1; ZSR 366, m.1d; ZSR 388, m.1d; ZSR 391, m.1; ZSR 451, m.1; ZMB 2, ff.26, 27, 58v; ZMB 3, ff.10, 45v; ZSB 5, f.110v.

249   CCALS, ZSR 44, m.5; ZSR 47, m.1; ZSR 71, m.1; ZSR 136, m.1; ZSR 162, m.1; ZSR 515, m.5d; ZSR 244, m.1; ZSR 254, m.1; ZSR 366, m.1d; ZMB 3, f.7v; ZSB 2, f.5v.

250   CCALS, ZSR 44, m.4d; ZSR 366, m.1d.

251   CCALS, ZSR 6, m.4d; ZMB 7, f.1.

252   TNA: PRO, E 101/545/25, mm.3, 3d, 5, 6, 9, 10.

253   CCALS, ZSB 1, f.156v; ZSB 2, f.8.

254   CCALS, ZSB 2, f.85; ZSB 3, ff.19v, 20, 20v, 37v, 64; ZSB 4, ff.8, 92.

255   CCALS, ZSB 3, ff.20, 20v, 37v, 39v; ZSB 4, ff.9v, 76, 111v; ZSB 6, f.10.

256   CCALS, ZSB 2, f.25v; ZSB 3, ff.3, 64, 65v, 66; ZSB 4, ff.9v, 31v, 92; ZSB 5, ff.34v, 35, 59–61v.

257   CCALS, ZSB 3, ff.37, 37v, 39v.

258   CCALS, ZSB 2, f.8; ZSB 3, ff.20v, 39v; ZSB 6, f.10.

259   CCALS, ZSB 4, f.8v; ZSB 5, ff.61v, 84, 88, 92v, 140v; ZSB 6, f.10.

Chapter 8

1   *Map of Great Britain c.1360 known as the Gough Map*.

2   TNA: PRO, WALE 29/291; SC 6/787/5, m.3; CCALS, ZMR 75, m.1; *3 Sheaf*, 17 (1920), 69–70; *3 Sheaf*, 22 (1925), 62; *3 Sheaf*, 23 (1926), 37–8; C. Dyer, *Standards of Living*, 249.

3   Borthwick Institute, Probate Register V, f.362. I thank Dr J. Kermode for this reference.

4   CCALS, ZSR 111, m.1; ZSR 301, m.1.

5   TNA: PRO, E 101/620/24, mm.1, 4.

6   CCALS, ZSR 267, m.1d; ZSR 359, m.1d.

7   CCALS, ZSR 247, m.1; ZSR 311, m.1; ZSR 318, m.1; ZSR 515, m.1d; ZMB 1, f.60v; ZMB 3, f.37.

8   CCALS, ZSR 193, m.1; ZSR 197, m.1d; ZSR 357, m.1d.

9   CCALS, ZSR 80, m.1; ZSR 96, m.2; ZSR 163, m.1; ZSR 170, m.1; ZSR 201, m.1; ZSR 210, m.1; ZSR 420, m.1d.

10 CCALS, ZSR 158, m.1; ZSR 163, m.1; ZSR 306, m.1; ZSR 367, m.1; ZSR 443, m.1.

11 A. Thacker, 'Fairs', *VCH, Chester*, V, Part 2, 100–1.

12 BL, Add. Ch. 49,997, 50,004.

13 CCALS, ZMR 3, m.2d; ZSR 35, m.5d; ZSR 51, m.2.

14 CCALS, ZSR 81, m.2d; ZSR 135, m.1; ZSR 166, m.1d; ZSR 261, mm.1, 2; ZSR 308, m.1; ZSR 349, m.3; ZSR 351, m.4d; ZSR 360, m.1d; ZSR 375, m.1d; ZSR 377, m.1; ZSR 387, m.1d; ZSR 391, m.1d; ZSR 400, m.1; ZSR 401, m.1; ZSR 407, m.1d; ZSR 449, m.1.

15 CCALS, ZSR 283, m.1d; TNA: PRO, CHES 29/167, m.23.

16 CCALS, ZSR 288, m.1d; ZSR 351, m.7d; ZSR 359, m.1d; ZSR 417, m.1d; ZSR 418, m.1; ZSR 424, m.1d; ZSR 427, m.1.

17 CCALS, ZSR 420, m.1; ZSR 423, m.1d; ZSR 425, m.1.

18 D.L. Farmer, 'Marketing the Produce of the Countryside, 1200–1500', 339–40; *BPR*, i, 19; CCALS, ZSR 160, m.1; ZSR 400, m.1d.

19 TNA: PRO, CHES 25/15, m.16d; CHES 29/165, m.15d.

20 *Willelmi Malmesbiriensis Monachi*, 308; *Polychronicon Ranulphi Higden*, ii, 78.

21 CCALS, ZSR 157, m.1; ZSR 158, m.1; ZSR 164, m.1d; ZSR 165, mm.1, 1d; ZSR 244, m.1; ZSR 284, m.1; ZSR 352, m.1d; ZSR 402, m.1d.

22 P.H.W. Booth and J.P. Dodd, 'The Manor and Fields of Frodsham, 1315–74', 42–6; P. Morgan, 'Medieval Cheshire', 34; CCALS, ZSR 112, m.1; ZSR 136, m.1; ZSR 155, m.1d; ZSR 156, m.1d; ZSR 227, m.1; ZSR 254, m.1; ZSR 261, m.3d; ZSR 268, m.1d; ZSR 383, m.1; ZSR 413, m.1.

23 *Chartulary of Chester Abbey*, I, 201; CCALS, ZSR 175, m.1.

24 CCALS, ZSR 115, m.1d; ZSR 128, m.1d; ZSR 322, m.1d; ZSR 411, m.1; TNA: PRO, CHES 29/111, m.21.

25 BL, Harl. Ms.2158, ff.49v-50; 36 *DKR*, 21, 275, 325.

26 TNA: PRO, E 101/488/7, m.1d; SC 6/790/1, m.2d; 791/5, m.3; 791/7, m.3; 791/10, m.3; CHES 25/110, m.26.

27 TNA: PRO, SC 6/798/4, m.6; BL, Harl. Ms.2046, f.28v.

28 TNA: PRO, SC 6/790/1, m.2d; SC 6/791/5, m.3; SC 6/792/3, m.3.

29 P.H. Sawyer and A. Thacker, 'The Cheshire Domesday', *VCH, Cheshire*, I, 353, 362; TNA: PRO, SC 6/796/3, m.13; SC 6/801/8, m.2d; G. Ormerod, *History of Cheshire*, II, 542.

30 CCALS, ZMB 1, f.20; ZSB 3, f.94; ZSR 220, m.1d; E. Davey, 'Very Plenteous in Fish – A Survey of Fisheries in Wirral', 40–6.

31 CCALS, ZSR 159, m.1; ZSR 191, m.1; ZSR 194, m.1; ZSR 205, m.1; ZSR 230, m.1; ZSR 259, mm.1, 1d; ZSR 297, m.1; ZSR 316, m.1; ZSR 321, m.1; ZSR 344, m.1; ZSR 349, m.3; ZSR 370, m.1; ZSR 371, m.1d; ZSR 372, m.1d; ZSR 377, m.1; ZSR 389, m.1.

32 CCALS, ZSR 81, m.2d; ZSR 129, m.2d; ZSR 134, m.1; ZSR 168, m.1; ZSR 281, m.1; ZSR 282, m.1d; ZSR 283, m.1; ZSR 307, m.1; ZSR 318, m.1d; ZSR 367, m.1; ZSR 385, m.1.

33 CCALS, ZSR 122, m.1; ZSR 197, m.1; ZSR 239, m.4; ZSR 362, m.1; ZSR 374, m.1; ZSR 402, m.1d.

34 TNA: PRO, CHES 25/15, m.23; CHES 29/137, m.35d. Other cattle thefts at Eccleston: CHES 25/12, mm.6, 36d; 25/14, m.6; 25/15, m.2d; 25/16, m.4.

35 *Itinerary of John Leland*, iii, 68, 71, 73; CCALS, ZSR 135, m.1d; ZSR 136, m.1; ZSR 155, m.1d; ZSR 187, m.1.

36 TNA: PRO, E 101/486/10, m.1; E 101/486/12, m.1; E 101/486/15, m.1; E 101/486/17, m.2; SC 6/771/1, m.1; SC 6/771/4, m.5.

37 TNA: PRO, SC 6/772/3, m.1; 772/15, m.1; 774/13, m.1; 775/3, m.1; 780/7, m.1.

38 TNA: PRO, SC 6/772/15, m.1; SC 6/774/6, m.1.

39 CCALS, ZSR 186, m.1; ZSR 191, m.1; ZSR 210, m.1d; ZSR 245, m.1. Carters: CCALS, ZSB 2, f.6; ZSB 4, f.32v; ZSR 190, m.1d.

40 CCALS, ZSR 198, m.1d; ZSR 224, m.1d; ZSR 228, m.1; ZSR 289, m.1d; ZSR 429, m.1d.

41 CCALS, ZSR 174, m.1; ZSR 245, m.1; TNA: PRO, E 101/488/2, m.1; SC 6/779/7, m.1d; BL, Harl. Ms.2091, ff.56–56v; C. Dyer, *Standards of Living*, 73.

42 CCALS, ZSR 351, mm.7d, 8d; ZSR 454, m.1.

43 TNA: PRO, SC 6/771/1, m.1; SC 6/772/14, m.1.

44 C.J. Williams, 'The Mining Laws in Flintshire and Denbighshire', 62; D. Pratt, 'Minera: Township of the Mines', 114–54; *Account of Master John de Burnham the Younger*, lxxvii.

45 TNA: PRO, SC 6/771/1, m.1; SC 6/771/4, m.1; SC 6/771/6, m.1; SC 6/771/7, m.1.

46 TNA: PRO, SC 6/774/15, m.1; SC 6/775/3, m.1; SC 6/775/4, m.1; 36 *DKR*, 213.

47 TNA: PRO, SC 6/771/2, m.6.

48 R.H. Morris, *Chester in the Plantagenet and Tudor Reigns*, 555; TNA: PRO, SC 6/774/10, m.1d.

49 CCALS, ZMB 2, f.59; ZMB 3, ff.16, 105v.

50 CCALS, ZMB 2, ff.37, 40, 48v, 72v, 93v; ZMB 3, ff.34, 35, 58, 58v, 61v, 62v, 63v, 86v, 95v.

51 CCALS, ZSR 143, m.1d; ZSR 374, m.1.

52 CCALS, ZSR 104, m.1; ZSR 143, m.1d; ZSR 312, m.1; ZSR 314, m.1d; ZSR 373, m.1d; ZSR 380, m.1; ZSB 4, f.93v; 3 *Sheaf*, 30 (1935), 26.

53 CCALS, ZMB 1, f.9; ZMB 2, f.73.

54 CCALS, ZSB 1, ff.29v, 30v, 33v, 38v, 71, 78, 79; ZSB 2, ff.66v, 70, 92; ZSB 3, ff.5, 48, 56v, 74v, 77, 78, 79, 79v, 80v, 82v; ZSB 4, f.102v; ZSR 365, m.1d; ZSR 369, m.1; ZCAM 1, f.16.

55 CCALS, ZSR 219, m.1d.

56 A.J. Kettle, 'Birkenhead Priory', *VCH, Cheshire*, III, 128, 129.

57 M.J. Bennett, *Community, Class and Careerism*, 13; 3 *Sheaf*, 11 (1914), 1.

58 CCALS, ZSB 2, f.12v; ZSB 4, ff.15v, 16, 63, 81v; C.N. Parkinson, *Rise of the Port of Liverpool*, 18–20.

59 H. Swanson, *Medieval Artisans*, 101–4. In 1379 25% of Sheffield's population were listed as metalworkers; already the town was becoming a centre of knife-making: C. Dyer, *Making a Living*, 321.

60 TNA: PRO, SC 6/774/14, m.1d; SC 6/774/15, m.1d; SC 6/775/4, m.1d.

61 CCALS, ZMB 3, ff.100v, 105v; ZMB 4, ff.7, 40v; ZSR 162, m.1d; ZSR 264, m.1; ZSR 265, m.1d.

62 CCALS, ZSR 128, m.4d; ZMB 2, f.82.

63 P.J.P. Goldberg, *Women, Work and Life Cycle in a Medieval Economy*, 75; CCALS, ZMB 4, f.26; ZSB 1, f.133v; ZSB 3, f.63.

64   CCALS, ZSR 290, m.1d; ZSR 483, m.1d; TNA: PRO, CHES 25/15, m.53; CHES 29/187, m.2; SC 6/800/10, m.6d.

65   CCALS, ZSR 255, m.1d; ZSR 256, m.1.

66   CCALS, ZMB 1, f.36; ZMB 3, f.62v; ZMB 4, f.27; ZSB 1, ff.139v, 163; ZSB 2, ff.7, 24, 46; ZSB 3, ff.25v, 70v; ZSB 4, f.12; ZSB 5, f.47v.

67   CCALS, ZSR 109, m.1; ZSR 123, m.1; ZSR 130, m.1d; ZSR 195, m.1d; ZSR 245, m.1d; ZSR 277, m.1d; ZSR 334, m.1.

68   CCALS, ZSR 311, m.1; ZSR 315, m.1d; ZSR 337, m.1; ZSR 359, m.1d.

69   CCALS, ZSR 190, m.1; ZSR 231, m.1d; ZSR 237, m.1d; ZSR 243, m.1; ZSR 245, m.1d; ZSR 249, m.1; ZSR 376, m.1; ZMB 4, f.40v; ZSB 1, f.38v.

70   J. Greig, 'Plant Remains', 61.

71   CCALS, ZSR 124, mm.1, 1d; ZSR 136, m.1; ZSR 160, m.1d; ZSR 190, m.1; ZSR 206, m.1d; ZSR 220, mm.1, 1d; ZSR 316, m.1; ZSB 3, f.101.

72   CCALS, ZSR 166, m.1; ZSR 206, m.1; ZSR 228, m.1d; ZSR 240, m.1d; ZSR 316, m.1; ZSR 327, m.1; ZSR 353, m.1; ZSR 394, m.1d; ZSB 2, f.37v; ZMB 3, f.56.

73   *Register of the Guild of the Holy Trinity*, 26, 28, 30, 31, 35, 36, 59, 65, 68, 91.

74   CCALS, ZMB 1, f.60v; ZMB 3, ff.35, 58, 58v, 95v.

75   CCALS, ZSR 160, m.1d; ZMB 3, ff.61v, 95v, 96v, 97v; ZSB 1, ff.30v, 31 (draper Richard Sharp); ZSR 220, m.1, ZMB 3, f.92v (John Bristow, who evidently dealt in fish).

76   CCALS, ZMB 2, f.82v; ZMB 3, ff.58, 95; ZSR 315, m.1d; ZSR 316, m.1; ZSR 327, m.1; ZSR 353, m.1; ZSR 357, m.1d; ZSR 359, m.1d; ZSR 394, m.1d; BL, Harl. Ms.2091, f.57; K.P. Wilson, 'The Port of Chester', 89–93.

77   D. Keene, 'Medieval London and its Region', 101–5; D. Keene, 'Small Towns and the Metropolis: the Experience of Medieval England', 236, 237.

78   CCALS, ZSB 2, f.53; ZSR 107, m.1d; ZSR 156, m.1d; ZSR 204, m.1d; ZSR 210, m.1; ZSR 238, m.1d; ZSR 261, m.3; ZSR 324, m.1d.

79   CCALS, ZSB 1, f.155; ZSB 2, f.44v.

80   CCALS, ZSB 2, ff.9, 33v, 34v, 47, 68v–74v; ZSB 3, ff.11, 28v–29, 31v, 49v, 52, 102v, 111v.

81   CCALS, ZMB 5, f.180; J.T. Gilbert, *A History of the City of Dublin*, I, 324–5, 420–5. John Wells was warden of the Grocers' Company in 1417–18: P. Nightingale, *A Medieval Mercantile Community*, 378–9.

82   CCALS, ZSR 111, m.1d; ZSR 115, m.1d; ZSR 261, m.2; ZSR 351, m.3d; ZSR 360, m.1d; ZSR 413, m.1d; *CPR*, 1405–8, 254; *CPR*, 1416–1422, 347.

83   CCALS, ZSR 256, m.1d; ZSR 261, mm.2, 3; ZSR 273, m.1; ZSR 276, m.1d; ZMB 4, f.22v; ZMR 96, m.1.

84   CCALS, ZMB 4, f.22v; ZSR 273, m.1; ZSR 277, m.1d; ZSR 320, m.1; S. Thrupp, *Merchant Class of Medieval London*, 371, 373–4, 375–6.

85   CCALS, ZTAR 1/4, m.1d; BL, Harl. Ms.2158, ff.54, 55v, 57v, 61.

86   BL, Harl. Ms.2158, f.49v; *Lancashire and Cheshire Wills and Inventories* (1884), 1–4; 3 *Sheaf*, 23 (1926), 37–8; CCALS, ZSR 193, m.1.

87   36 *DKR*, 126; CCALS, ZSR 129, mm.2, 2d; ZSR 136, m.1d; ZSR 139, m.1; ZSR 140, m.1; ZSR 142, m.1; ZMB 3, f.56.

88   CCALS, ZSB 1, ff.30v, 57v; ZMB 4, f.26v; ZMUR 1, mm.1, 2d.

89   CCALS, ZMB 3, ff.85v, 95; ZMB 4, f.24v; ZSB 1, ff.127, 128v, 147v, 172v.

90   BL, Harl. Ms.2046, f.33v.

91   *Liber Luciani de Laude Cestrie*, 46.

92   G. Ormerod, *History of Cheshire*, I, 185.

93   S. Ward, 'The Course of the River Dee at Chester', 9–10; *Itinerary of John Leland*, iii, 91.

94   CCALS, ZCH 8; ZCH 32; R.H. Morris, *Chester in the Plantagenet and Tudor Reigns*, 498, 529–30.

95   *BPR*, iii, 415–16; R.H. Morris, *Chester in the Plantagenet and Tudor Reigns*, 511–12, 516, 518, 521.

96   TNA: PRO, SC 6/771/2, m.8; SC 6/771/9, m.1.

97   *Chester Customs Accounts*, 20–45.

98   J. Laughton, 'Historical Commentary on Meols', 415–17.

99   *Chester Customs Accounts*, 2–5, 8–9, 143.

100 CCALS, ZSB 4, ff.102–104v, 106–108v, 137–144v; *Chester Customs Accounts*, 132–42.

101 CCALS, ZSB 1, ff.127, 167, 168v; ZSB 2, f.80; ZMB 5, f.104v; TNA: PRO, SC 6/779/10, m.1d. For the types of vessel using Chester's port, see J. Laughton, 'The Port of Chester', 68–9.

102 *The Past Uncovered*, Spring 1999, 3.

103 P.H.W. Booth, *Burton in Wirral*, 10; TNA: PRO, CHES 25/10, m.20; CHES 25/15, m.31.

104 CCALS, ZMB 6, f.83.

105 CCALS, ZSR 400, m.1d; ZSR 401, m.1d; ZSR 454, m.1d; ZSR 467, m.1d.

106 CCALS, ZSR 52, m.1d; ZSR 370, m.1; ZSR 410, m.1d; ZSB 3, f.102v.

107 CCALS, ZSR 287, m.1; ZSR 311, m.1; ZSR 400, m.1; ZSR 465, m.1d.

108 CCALS, ZSB 4, ff.138v, 139v, 147v, 151v; ZSR 449, m.1.

109 TNA: PRO, SC 6/774/15, m.1d; CCALS, ZSR 381, m.1; *Letters and Papers of Henry VIII*, volume I, Part 2, 1513–14, 2977.

110 *Willelmi Malmesbiriensis Monachi*, 308; *Liber Luciani de Laude Cestrie*, 46; *Metrical Chronicle of Robert of Gloucester*, 149.

111 *CPR*, 1313–17, 470, 568; *CPR*, 1321–24, 27.

112 *CPR*, 1391–6, 17; CCALS, ZMB 2, ff.40v, 41, 42, 51; ZMB 3, f.112v; ZSB 1, f.31v; *Chester Customs Accounts*, 110–13, 115.

113 E.M. Carus Wilson, 'The Overseas Trade of Bristol', 199; T. O'Neill, *Merchants and Mariners in Medieval Ireland*, 27.

114 *The Libelle of Englyshe Polycye*, lines 656–64.

115 CCALS, ZSR 6, m.3d; ZSR 36, m.4d; ZSR 108, m.1d; ZSR 153, m.1d; ZSR 245, m.1; ZSR 314, m.1d.

116 W. Childs and T. O'Neill, 'Overseas Trade of Ireland', 500, 503–4.

117 CCALS, ZMB 2, ff.80–82v; ZMB 3, ff.63–63v, 92v–95; ZSB 1, ff.55v-58; ZSB 4, ff.138–44v; ZSR 22, m.7d; ZSR 32, m.2d; ZSR 33, m.3d; ZSR 37, m.1; *Chester Customs Accounts*, 103–16, 132–42.

118 CCALS, ZMB 3, ff.93v, 95; ZSB 1, f.33; ZSB 4, ff.140v, 141v, 148v, 149; ZSR 312, m.1d; *Chester Customs Accounts*, 132, 133, 134.

119 CCALS, ZMB 6, ff.36–7.

120 CCALS, ZMB 3, ff.34, 93v, 97v; ZSB 1, f.125; ZSB 2, f.32v; ZSB 3, f.53v.

121 CCALS, ZSR 412, m.1d; ZSR 442, m.1d; ZSR 465, m.1.

122 CCALS, ZSR 12, mm.4, 6; ZSR 44, m.2d.

123 CCALS, ZMB 3, f.31v; ZSB 4, ff.143v, 148v; ZSR 367, m.1d; W. Childs and T. O'Neill, 'Overseas Trade of Ireland', 502; E.M. Carus Wilson, 'The Overseas Trade of Bristol', 199.

124 CCALS, ZMB 2, f.72; ZMB 3, f.75; ZMB 5, f.214v.

125 E.M. Carus Wilson, 'The Overseas Trade of Bristol', 199; CCALS, ZSB 2, ff.97v, 98, 99v; ZMB 5, f.177; ZSB 4, f.148; *Chester Customs Accounts*, 132.

126 *Chester Customs Accounts*, 103–16.

127 CCALS, ZMB 2, ff.40, 48v, 72v, 93v; ZMB 3, ff.62v, 63v, 86v, 105v.

128 CCALS, ZMB 2, f.72v; ZMB 3, ff.34, 35, 58, 58v, 61v, 70v, 95v, 105v; ZSB 1, f.62v; ZSR 157, m.1.

129 E.M. Carus Wilson, 'The Overseas Trade of Bristol', 200; W. Childs and T. O'Neill, 'Overseas Trade of Ireland', 508.

130 CCALS, ZMB 2, ff.40, 41, 82; ZMB 3, ff.58, 95v, 100v; ZMB 4, ff.7, 26; ZSB 1, ff.24, 24v, 37v, 54v, 70v, 133v; ZSB 3, f.63; ZSR 160, m.1d.

131 CCALS, ZMB 5, f.180; BL, Harl. Ms.2091, ff.57–8.

132 CCALS, ZMB 3, ff.56v, 93, 94v, 96, 96v; TNA: PRO, CHES 29/166, m.8; CHES 29/167, m.3; W. Childs and T. O'Neill, 'Overseas Trade of Ireland', 520.

133 3 *Sheaf*, 29 (1934), 40.

134 BL, Harl. Ms.368, f.161.

135 CCALS, ZSR 126, m.1d; ZSR 159, m.1d; ZSR 376, m.1d; ZSR 466, m.1.

136 A.D. Carr, *Medieval Anglesey*, 110–11.

137 *Calendar of Deeds and Papers of the Moore Family*, no.1028; CCALS, ZSR 363, m.1d; ZSR 408, m.1; ZSR 421, m.1; ZSR 457, m.1d.

138 CCALS, ZSR 285, m.1d; ZSR 287, m.1d; ZSB 1, ff.126, 127, 168v; TNA: PRO, SC 6/779/5, m.1; A.D. Carr, *Medieval Anglesey*, 110.

139 A.D. Carr, *Medieval Anglesey*, 108–9; TNA: PRO, SC 6/772/19, m.1d; SC 6/774/10, m.1d; SC 6/775/5, m.1d; SC 6/780/4, m.1.

140 CCALS, ZSR 306, m.1; ZSR 311, m.1.

141 A. Thacker, 'Early Medieval Chester, 400–1230', *VCH, Chester*, V, Part 1, 20.

142 CCALS, ZSR 454, m.1d.

143 TNA: PRO, WALE 29/291; J. Laughton, 'Historical Commentary on Meols', 417.

144 J.R. Dickinson, *The Lordship of Man under the Stanleys*, 1, 4–6; M.J. Bennett, *Community, Class and Careerism*, 130–1, 217, 220; CCALS, ZMB 3, f.33v.

145 CCALS, ZSB 1, f.108v; ZSB 2, ff.49, 52, 68; ZSB 3, ff.11, 14, 29, 30v, 75, 77v, 81, 107, 112; ZSB 4, ff.14, 15, 18v, 37, 40, 41.

146 CCALS, ZSR 318, m.1d; ZMB 6, f.81.

147 CCALS, ZSB 3, ff.42, 81, 106v, 112; ZSB 4, ff.18v, 41, 59, 81, 103.

148 CCALS, ZSB 2, ff.72, 73v; ZSB 4, ff.37, 40, 58v, 128v, 141, 149v.

149 CCALS, ZSB 4, ff.128, 128v; E.M. Carus Wilson, 'The Overseas Trade of Bristol', 194.

150 36 *DKR*, 4, 105, 119, 474.

151 TNA: PRO, SC 6/772/11, m.1; SC 6/774/14, m.1d; SC 6/775/4, m.1d.

152 CCALS, ZSB 2, ff.50v, 51.

153 CCALS, ZSB 3, f.102v; ZSB 4, f.34v.

154 *Chester Customs Accounts*, 132, 135, 137, 138, 139, 142.

155 *Chester Customs Accounts*, 37–40.

156 CCALS, ZMB 4, ff.8, 72v; ZSB 1, f.135v; ZSR 282, m.1; ZSR 299, m.1; ZSR 316, m.1d.

157 CCALS, ZSR 288, m.1d.

158 CCALS, ZMB 3, ff.65, 101, 111v; ZMB 4, f.30; ZSB 3, ff.71v, 78v, 81v.

159 CCALS, ZMB 7, f.142v; ZSB 4, f.110; ZSR 447, m.1d.

Chapter 9

1 *Liber Luciani de Laude Cestrie*, 10, 63; D. Jones, *Church in Chester*, 111; N. Orme, *Medieval Schools*, 63–4, 67, 351; 36 *DKR*, 243.

2 *BPR*, iii, 310.

3 N. Orme, *Medieval Schools*, 111, 129, 283–5.

4 CCALS, ZSR 264, m.1d.

5 S. Thrupp, *Merchant Class of Medieval London*, 156–8; D. Keene, *Medieval Winchester*, i, 394; C. Dyer, *An Age of Transition?*, 125.

6 TNA: PRO, CHES 25/12, m.12d; CCALS, ZSR 81, m.2d; N. Orme, *Medieval Schools*, 360, 362, 366.

7 CCALS, ZSR 239, m.1d.

8 CCALS, ZMB 5, ff.184v, 189v; ZMB 6, ff.4v, 34v, 84v. His widow occupied a messuage in Watergate Street in 1506: 3 *Sheaf*, 23 (1926), 37–8.

9 CCALS, ZSR 349, m.2; ZSR 372, m.1; ZSB 4, f.9v.

10 CCALS, ZSR 126, m.2d; ZSR 179, m.1d; N. Orme, *Medieval Schools*, 66.

11 S. Thrupp, *Merchant Class of Medieval London*, 159; N. Orme, *Medieval Schools*, 32–3.

12 CCALS, ZSR 169, m.1; ZSR 294, m.1d; ZSR 337, m.3d.

13 R.R. Davies, 'Richard II and the Principality of Chester, 1397–9', n.5 on p.259.

14 M. Campbell, 'Gold, Silver and Precious Stones', 148; H. Taylor, 'Notes upon some Early Deeds relating to Chester and Flint', 171–2, 178. Other examples: BL, Harl. Ms.2037, f.79; Harl. Ms.2054, f.42; TNA: PRO, E 101/486/10, m.1d.

15 CCALS, ZSR 332, m.1.

16 CCALS, ZSR 229, m.1; ZSR 356, m.1; S. Thrupp, *Merchant Class of Medieval London*, 163.

17 TNA: PRO, CHES 25/15, m.15d; A. Gransden, *Historical Writing in England*, II, 127.

18 TNA: PRO, CHES 25/10, mm.33, 35; S. Thrupp, *Merchant Class of Medieval London*, 161–2.

19 CCALS, ZSR 56, m.1; ZSR 96, m.1d; ZSR 319, m.1; ZSR 238, m.1d; ZSR 337, m.1; ZSR 356, m.1.

20 CCALS, ZSR 458, m.1; ZMB 7, f.146v; ZSB 5, f.88.

21 CCALS, ZSR 454, m.1d; 3 *Sheaf*, 15 (1918), 23.

22 CCALS, ZSR 6, m.11; ZSR 22, m.4; ZSR 37, m.1; ZSR 42, m.1; ZSR 43, m.1; ZSR 74, m.1d; ZSR 94, m.1; ZSR 138, m.1d; ZSR 283, m.1d; ZSR 295, m.1.

23 CCALS, ZSR 23, m.3; ZSR 300, m.1; ZSR 381, m.1d; ZSR 447, m.1d; ZSR 466, m.1d.

24 3 *Sheaf*, 3 (1899–1900), 70.

25 CCALS, ZSR 164, mm.1, 1d; ZSR 300, m.1; ZSR 349, m.3; ZSR 366, m.1; ZSR 377, m.1; ZSR 396, m.1d; ZSR 414, m.1.

26 CCALS, ZSR 374, m.1; ZSR 469, m.1d; ZMR 64, m.1; ZMR 71, m.1.

27 CCALS, ZSR 188, m.1d; ZSR 244, m.1d; ZSR 269, m.1; ZSR 284, m.1.

28 CCALS, ZSR 283, m.1d; ZSR 300, mm.1, 1d; ZSR 301, m.1d; ZSR 330, m.1.

29 *Prologue*, lines 427–30.

30 CCALS, ZSR 308, m.1; ZSR 367, m.1; ZSR 458, m.1; ZMB 7, f.6. Thomas Monksfield grocer was mentioned in 1451: CHES 29/157, m.10.

31 CCALS, ZMB 6, f.61.

32 C. Phythian-Adams, *Desolation of a City*, 74–9.

33 CCALS, ZG 7/19.

34 CCALS, ZMB 3, ff.81, 82v; ZMB 4, ff.12v, 57; ZMB 5, ff.55, 93, 172; ZMB 7, f.65; ZMB 9, f.15v.

35 CCALS, ZMB 1, f.25; ZMB 2, f.19; ZSB 1, ff.131, 155; ZSB 2, f.25v; ZSB 3, ff.20v, 66; ZSB 4, ff.8, 50, 53v, 96.

36 CCALS, ZMB 3, f.44; ZSB 1, f.123v.

37 CCALS, ZMB 9, f.29v.

38 TNA: PRO, E 101/486/10, m.1; E 101/488/7, m.1.

39 CCALS, ZSR 278, m.1d.

40 C. Dyer, *An Age of Transition?*, 128–9, 132, 232–8.

41 C. Dyer, *An Age of Transition?*, 131, 132.

42 TNA: PRO, E 101/486/10, m.1; E 101/488/2, m.1d; E 101/488/4, m.1d; E 101/488/7, m.1; E 101/545/25, m.1.

43 TNA: PRO, SC 6/774/8, m.1; SC 6/774/14, m.1; SC 6/780/1, m.1; SC 6/780/2, m.1; SC 6/780/4, m.1.

44 TNA: PRO, E 101/545/25, mm.3, 3d, 6, 7, 9, 10; SC 6/774/10, m.1d.

45 C. Phythian-Adams, *Desolation of a City*, 78–9; TNA: PRO, E 101/486/10, m.1; E 101/486/12, m.1; E 101/487/5, mm.1, 1d.

46 *Records of Early English Drama: Cheshire including Chester*, I, lvii; J.McN. Dodgson, *Place-Names of Cheshire*, Part Five (1:i), 73.

47 *Cal. Court R.*, 156.

48 *The Household Books of John Howard, Duke of Norfolk*, I, 234–5.

49 CCALS, ZSR 426, m.1d; BL, Add. Ms.11335, f.23.

50 *Cal. Court R.*, 205; CCALS, ZMB 1, f.54v.

51 *Liber Luciani de Laude Cestrie*, 61; J.McN. Dodgson, *Place-Names of Cheshire*, Part Five (1:i), 9.

52 CCALS, ZSB 4, f.49; R. H. Morris, *Chester in the Plantagenet and Tudor Reigns*, 333.

53 CCALS, ZSB 5, f.5; ZSB 6, f.11v; ZAB 1, ff.64–5.

54 TNA: PRO, CHES 25/12, m.1d; CHES 25/16, mm.7, 19, 19d, 24d.

55 TNA: PRO, CHES 25/15, mm.15d, 36d; CHES 25/16, m.3.

56 *Chartulary of St Werburgh's Abbey*, II, 469–70.

57 CCALS, ZSR 258, m.1; ZSR 454, m.1d.

58 CCALS, ZSR 456, m.1; ZSR 459, m.1d; ZSR 460, m.1d; *Records of Early English Drama: Cheshire including Chester*, I, 67.

59 *Letters and Papers of Henry VIII*, xiii (I), 477.

60 *Processional of the Nuns of Chester*.

61 M.F. Bukofzer, 'Popular and Secular Music in England (to *c*.1470)', 117.

62 *Prologue*, 91, 95, 565–6.

63 CCALS, ZSR 89, m.1; ZSR 91, m.1d; ZSR 113, m.1; ZSR 116, m.1d; ZSR 128, m.1; ZSR 135, m.1; ZSR 157, m.1d; ZSR 195, m.1d; ZSR 229, m.1; ZSR 239, m.3d; ZSR 261, m.3; ZSR 320, m.1d; ZSR 348, m.1; ZSR 358, m.1d; ZSR 389, m.1; ZMB 7, f.60v.

64 CCALS, ZSR 89, m.1; ZSR 122, m.1; ZSR 128, m.1; ZSR 197, m.1; ZMB 1, f.60; ZMB 7, f.142v; ZMB 8, f.75; ZSB 1, f.40v.

65 D. Mills, 'Plays, Sports, and Customs before 1700', *VCH, Chester*, V, Part 2, 254; TNA: PRO, SC 6/801/5, m.1; CCALS, ZSR 41, m.3; ZMB 2, f.51.

66 CCALS, ZSB 3, ff.67v, 69; ZSB 4, ff.7, 33v; ZSB 6, f.10v; ZMB 8, f.75; ZSR 413, m.1d; ZSR 425, m.1.

67 CCALS, ZSR 223, m.1; ZSR 283, m.1d; ZSR 461, m.1d.

68 CCALS, ZSR 360, m.1d; ZSR 515, m.18d; ZSB 4, f.6v.

69 CCALS, ZSR 304, m.1; ZSR 313, mm.1, 1d; ZSR 325, m.1; ZSR 351, m.8; ZMB 6, f.44; ZSB 5, f.136v.

70 BL, Harl. Ms.2150, f.108; Harl. Ms.2091, f.56.

71 CCALS, ZSR 288, m.1; ZSR 294, m.1d.

72 E. Danbury, 'Intellectual Life of St Werburgh's', 114; CCALS, ZMB 4, f.37v; ZSB 1, f.69.

73 CCALS, ZSR 391, m.1d; ZMB 9, f.5.

74 M. James, 'Ritual, Drama and Social Body in the Late Medieval English Town', 4–5.

75 CCALS, ZMB 1, ff.55v-56.

76 M. James, 'Ritual, Drama and Social Body', 5, 10, 18.

77 CCALS, ZMB 5, f.216; ZMB 6, ff.30–30v.

78 CCALS, ZG 7/23.

79 CCALS, ZSR 145, m.1; ZSR 146, m.1; ZSR 147, m.1; ZSR 150, m.1; ZSR 151, m.1d; ZSR 153, m.1d; ZSR 156, m.1. Specific mention of the light or play: ZSR 149, m.1; ZSR 153, m.1; ZSR 160, m.1; ZSR 161, m.1.

80 Information from Professor David Mills; M. James, 'Ritual, Drama and Social Body', 6.

81 *Records of Early English Drama: Cheshire including Chester*, II, 897.

82 CCALS, ZSR 224, m.1d; ZSR 262, m.1d.

83 CCALS, ZSR 213, m.1.

84 CCALS, ZSR 229 m.1d; ZSR 236, mm.1, 1d; ZSR 239, m.2; ZSR 248, m.1d; ZSR 261, m.1.

85 BL, Harl. Ms.2158, ff.32, 32v, 33, 33v.

86 BL, Harl. Ms.2158, ff.36v, 37, 38v, 39, 39v, 40, 41, 51, 52v, 55v, 56, 58, 62, 62v, 63v, 64, 64v, 65; CCALS, ZTAR 1/3, m.1d; ZTAR 1/4, m.1d.

87 37 *DKR*, 140; TNA: PRO, CHES 2/144, m.7.

88 CCALS, ZSR 356, m.1; ZSR 358, m.1; ZSR 383, m.1d.

89 *Records of Early English Drama: Cheshire including Chester*, I, xxxii, xli, 65–6; II, 886–92.

90 G. Ormerod, *History of Cheshire*, I, 233, 234.

91 D. Mills, 'Plays, Sports, and Customs before 1700', *VCH, Chester*, V, Part 2, 249–50.

92 *Chartulary of Chester Abbey*, II, 466–70; 37 *DKR*, 779; A. Thacker, 'Medieval Parish Churches', *VCH, Chester*, V, Part 2, 137.

93 *English Benedictine Kalendars after 1100*, I, 95–111.

94 C. Grossinger, 'Chester Cathedral Misericords', 99, 101; S-B. Maclean, 'Marian Devotion in post-Reformation Chester: Implications of the Smiths' "Purification" Play', 237–56.

95 G. Ormerod, *History of Cheshire*, I, 233, 234; D. Mills, 'Plays, Sports, and Pastimes before 1700', *VCH, Chester*, V, Part 2, 249.

96 For a full discussion, see J. Laughton, forthcoming.

97 CCALS, ZG 7/23; ZMR 85, m.1.

98 TNA: PRO, SC 6/771/3, m.8; SC 6/771/5, m.14; CCALS, ZMB 5, f.216.

Chapter 10

1 C. Dyer, *Standards of Living*, 229–30; C. Dyer, *Making a Living*, 276–7, 280–1; M. Kowaleski, 'The History of Urban Families', 58.

2 J. Goldberg, 'Female Labour, Service and Marriage', 23–8; M. Kowaleski, 'The History of Urban Families', 54–5.

3 J. Laughton, 'The Alewives of Later Medieval Chester', 204–5.

4 M. Kowaleski, 'The History of Urban Families', 48, 54–6.

5 TNA: PRO, SC 6/786/8, mm.7, 7d; SC 6/793/8, m.1d; BL, Harl. Ms.2037, ff.209–210v; J.H. Baker, *An Introduction to English Legal History*, 310.

6 TNA: PRO, SC 6/786/8, m.7d; 36 *DKR*, 153–4.

7 G. Ormerod, *History of Cheshire*, II, 379.

8 *Calendar of Papal Letters*, VII, 1427–47, 219; G. Ormerod, *History of Cheshire*, II, 731.

9   CCALS, ZSR 367, m.1d; ZSR 465, m.1d; ZSR 466, m.1d; ZSR 469, m.1.

10 CCALS, ZSR 384, m.1; ZMB 7, ff.166, 166v.

11 3 *Sheaf*, 14 (1917), 73.

12 This discussion is based on a seminar paper delivered to the Cambridge Group for the History of Population and Social Structure by Professor R. Smith on 3 March 1992. See also J. Bennett, *Women in the Medieval English Countryside: Gender and Household in Brigstock before the Plague*; P. Franklin, 'Normans, Saints and Politics: Forename-choice among Fourteenth-century Gloucestershire Peasants'; E.B. DeWindt, *Land and People in Holywell-cum-Needingworth*; S. Smith-Bannister, *Naming and Naming Patterns in England, 1538–1700*.

13 *Calendar of Papal Letters*, VII, 1427–47, 219.

14 3 *Sheaf*, 14 (1917), 8; 3 *Sheaf*, 17 (1920), 69–70.

15 G. Ormerod, *History of Cheshire*, II, 319, 322.

16 G. Ormerod, *History of Cheshire*, II, 126, 203, 239, 506; III, 394, 575, 657.

17 CCALS, ZMB 7, f.6.

18 CCALS, ZMB 7, ff.40v-41.

19 3 *Sheaf*, 12 (1915), 37; 3 *Sheaf*, 14 (1917), 37–8; 3 *Sheaf*, 22 (1925), 62.

20 CCALS, ZMB 3, f.3v; ZSR 240, m.1d; TNA: PRO, CHES 25/11, mm.17d-18; 3 *Sheaf*, 17 (1920), 105; G. Ormerod, *History of Cheshire*, II, 821.

21 CCALS, ZMB 3, f.3v; 3 *Sheaf*, 14 (1917), 37–8.

22 For full discussion of the parish boundaries, see *VCH, Chester*, V, part 2, 12–14, 133–56.

23 D. Jones, *Church in Chester*, 30–5.

24 M. Campbell, 'Gold, Silver and Precious Stones', 138.

25 CCALS, ZSR 155, m.1d; ZSR 158, m.1d; ZSR 175, m.1d; ZSR 177, m.1; ZSR 193, m.1; ZSR 419, m.1; ZSR 452, m.1d; ZSB 4, ff.21, 115v; ZSB 5, f.182.

26 CCALS, ZSR 458, m.1; ZSB 4, f.115v; ZSB 5, ff.157, 157v.

27 3 *Sheaf*, 55 (1960), 46–8, 48–9, 50–1.

28 *Calendar of Papal Letters*, VII, 1427–47, 362; CCALS, ZSR 301, m.1.

29 3 *Sheaf*, 17 (1920), 69–70.

30 J.P. Earwaker, 'The Ancient Parish Books of the Church of St Mary-on-the-Hill, Chester', 141.

31 G. Ormerod, *History of Cheshire*, I, 354.

32 C. Platt, *The Parish Churches of Medieval England*, 41.

33 3 *Sheaf*, 14 (1917), 8; *Lancashire and Cheshire Wills and Inventories* (1860), 6–12.

34 3 *Sheaf*, 15 (1918), 23; 3 *Sheaf*, 17 (1920), 69–70, 105; 3 *Sheaf*, 19 (1922), 4.

35 TNA: PRO, WALE 29/291; 3 *Sheaf*, 14 (1917), 37–8; 3 *Sheaf*, 17 (1920), 69–70; 3 *Sheaf*, 18 (1921), 92; *Lancashire and Cheshire Wills and Inventories* (1860), 6–12.

36 CCALS, ZSB 5, f.17v.

37 CCALS, ZSR 22, m.3d; ZSR 59, m.1; ZSR 419, m.1d.

38 CCALS, ZSR 22, m.3d; ZSR 59, m.1; ZSB 5, f.17v; 3 *Sheaf*, 4 (1902), 29–30.

39 G. Ormerod, *History of Cheshire*, II, 126, 239, 319, 774; III, 255–6.

40 G. Ormerod, *History of Cheshire*, II, 379, 667.

41 BL, Harl. Ms.2020, f.24.

42 BL, Harl. Ms.2067, f.39v; 3 *Sheaf*, 17 (1920), 105; 3 *Sheaf*, 18 (1921), 93; 3 *Sheaf*, 36 (1941), 9.

43 J.M. Bennett, 'Conviviality and Charity', 20–1, 31–3.

44 CCALS, ZMB 7, f.1; R.H. Morris, *Chester in the Plantagenet and Tudor Reigns*, 334–5.

45 3 *Sheaf*, 5 (1903), 38; 3 *Sheaf*, 36 (1941), 54.

46 TNA: PRO, WALE 29/291; *Catalogue of Ancient Deeds*, VI (1915), C 5282.

47 3 *Sheaf*, 13 (1916), 90–1; 3 *Sheaf*, 14 (1917), 8, 37–8; 3 *Sheaf*, 23 (1926), 37–8; BL, Harl. Ms.2067, f.43v.

48 3 *Sheaf*, 17 (1920), 69–70, 105.

49 CCALS, ZMR 75, m.1; R.H. Morris, *Chester in the Plantagenet and Tudor Reigns*, 350–1.

50 C. Dyer, *Standards of Living*, 248.

51 BL, Harl. Ms.2054, f.23.

52 BL, Harl. Ms.2054, ff.20, 30; R.H. Morris, *Chester in the Plantagenet and Tudor Reigns*, 64; G. Ormerod, *History of Cheshire*, I, 322–3.

53 3 *Sheaf*, 36 (1941), 9, 54.

54 TNA: PRO, SC 11/890; 3 *Sheaf*, 36 (1941), 7, 24, 32, 45, 46; *CPR*, 1408–13, 242.

55 3 *Sheaf*, 17 (1920), 69–70, 105; *Lancashire and Cheshire Wills and Inventories* (1860), 6–12.

56 TNA: PRO, CHES 29/108, m.15d; CCALS, ZMB 2, ff.29, 78; ZMB 3, ff.56v, 57; ZMR 64, m.1d; ZMR 78, m.1; ZSR 126, m.2d.

57 CCALS, ZSR 302, m.1; ZSR 306, m.1d.

58 3 *Sheaf*, 13 (1916), 90–1; BL, Harl. Ms.2067, f.44.

59 *Lancashire and Cheshire Wills and Inventories* (1884), 1–4.

60 CCALS, ZMB 5, f.155v; ZMB 7, f.7.

61 CCALS, ZMB 6, ff.87v, 123.

62 CCALS, ZMB 5, f.166.

63 CCALS, ZMB 2, f.105v.

64 CCALS, ZMB 5, f.72; ZMR 90, m.1; BL, Harl. Ms.2158, f.45v; G. Ormerod, *History of Cheshire*, III, 492.

65 CCALS, ZSR 315, m.1d; ZTAR 1/3; BL, Harl. Ms.2158, f.40v; 3 *Sheaf*, 43 (1948), 6.

66 CCALS, ZSR 71, m.1d; ZSR 178, m.1; ZSR 239, mm.1d, 3; ZSR 242, m.1d; ZSR 245, m.1; ZSR 337, m.1d; ZSR 339, m.1d; ZSR 353, m.1d; ZSR 357, m.1.

67 CCALS, ZSR 261, m.3; ZSR 263, m.1d.

68 CCALS, ZSR 152, m.1; ZSR 230, m.1; ZSR 261, m.3; ZSR 282, m.1; ZSR 303, m.1; ZSR 349, m.3d; ZSR 362, m.1; ZSR 380, m.1 (butchers); ZSR 277, m.1d; ZSR 300, m.1; ZSR 356, m.1d; ZSR 378, m.1d (fishmongers).

69 CCALS, ZSR 239, m.4; ZSR 267, m.1; ZSR 290, m.1d; ZSR 322, m.1; ZSR 356, m.1d; ZSR 357, m.1d; ZSR 385, m.1; ZSR 399, m.1; ZSR 412, mm.1, 1d; ZSR 420, m.1; ZSR 423, m.1; ZSR 429, mm.1, 1d.

70 CCALS, ZSR 156, m.1d; ZSR 157, m.1; ZSR 193, m.1d.

71 CCALS, ZSR 111, m.1d; ZSR 124, m.1; ZSR 156, m.1d; ZSR 170, m.1d; ZSR 265, m.1d; ZSR 289, m.1; ZSR 353, m.1d; *Chester Customs Accounts*, 36, 37.

72 CCALS, ZSR 295, m.1.

73 CCALS, ZSR 163, m.1d; ZSR 215, m.1; ZSR 268, m.1d; ZSR 283, m.1d; ZSR 307, m.1d; ZSR 346, m.2; ZSR 350, m.1; ZSR 470, m.1d.

74 CCALS, ZSR 164, m.1; ZSR 178, m.1; ZSR 196, m.1; ZSR 214, m.1; ZSR 227, m.1d; ZSR 242, m.1; ZSR 251, m.1d.

75 CCALS, ZSR 245, m.1; ZSR 321, m.1.

76 CCALS, ZSR 130, m.1; ZSR 153, m.1; ZSR 155, m.1d; ZSR 157, m.1; ZSR 164, m.1; ZSR 169, m.1; ZSR 187, m.1d; ZSR 214, m.1; ZSR 216, m.1d; ZSR 284, m.1d; ZSR 287, m.1d; ZSR 324, m.1d; ZSR 515, m.6.

77 CCALS, ZSR 160, m.1d; ZSR 333, m.1d.
78 J. Laughton, 'Aspects of medieval Chester', 276.
79 CCALS, ZSR 281–284; ZSR 353–360.
80 CCALS, ZSR 318, m.1.
81 CCALS, ZSR 239, m.3; ZSR 305, m.1. References to schedules, accounts and paper bills: ZSR 241, m.1d; ZSR 246, mm.1, 1d; ZSR 274, m.1; ZSR 284, m.1d; ZSR 297, m.1; R. Britnell, *Growth and Decline in Colchester*, 103; M. Kowaleski, *Medieval Exeter*, 205.
82 CCALS, ZSR 239, m.4; ZSR 404, m.1.
83 CCALS, ZSR 287, m.1d. Prices of ale: ZSR 223, m.1; ZSR 349, mm.2, 3d; ZSR 353, m.1.
84 CCALS, ZSR 175, m.1d; ZSR 268, m.1; ZSR 302, m.1.
85 CCALS, ZSR 267, m.1; ZSR 287, m.1d; ZSR 413, m.1d.
86 CCALS, ZMB 2, ff.30, 33v, 54, 55, 86v, 100; ZMB 3, ff.54, 80v, 81; ZMB 5, f.113v.
87 C. Dyer, *Making a Living*, 216; R. Britnell, *Growth and Decline in Colchester*, 104–5.
88 CCALS, ZSR 21, m.7; ZSR 111, m.1d; ZSR 220, m.1d.
89 CCALS, ZMB 6, f.165v; ZSR 115, m.1d; ZSR 261, m.1.
90 CCALS, ZMB 6, f.36v; ZSR 128, m.4; ZSR 179, m.1d; ZSR 218, m.1; ZSR 367, m.1; ZSR 478, m.1d; ZSR 480, m.1; ZSR 515, m.17d.
91 M.T. Clanchy, *From Memory to Written Record*, 95–6.
92 CCALS, ZSR 12, m.4; ZSR 13, m.1d; ZSR 22, mm.5, 9; ZSR 26, m.1d; ZSR 55, m.1.
93 CCALS, ZSR 135, m.1; ZSR 152, m.1d; ZSR 318, m.1d.
94 CCALS, ZSR 316, m.1; ZSR 325, m.1.
95 CCALS, ZSR 36, m.6; ZSR 338, m.1.
96 3 *Sheaf*, 14 (1917), 8.
97 CCALS, ZSR 171, m.1d; ZSR 368, m.1; ZSR 374, m.1.
98 BL, Harl. Ms.2158, f.50; P. Nightingale, *A Medieval Mercantile Community*, 568; C. Dyer, *An Age of Transition?*, 175–6.
99 CCALS, ZSR 283, m.1d.
100 P. Nightingale, *A Medieval Mercantile Community*, 175.
101 CCALS, ZSR 233, m.1; ZSR 278, m.1d.
102 CCALS, ZSR 350, m.1; ZSR 406, m.1d; ZSR 455, m.1; ZSR 460, m.1d.
103 3 *Sheaf*, 17 (1920), 69–70.
104 CCALS, ZSR 6, m.6d; ZSR 319, m.1; ZSR 325, m.1d; ZSR 462, m.1.
105 P. Nightingale, 'The English Parochial Clergy as Investors', 89–90; C. Dyer, *Making a Living*, 327; C. Dyer, *An Age of Transition?*, 177–8.
106 CCALS, ZSB 2, f.26.
107 P. Nightingale, 'The English Parochial Clergy as Investors', 90; C. Dyer, *An Age of Transition?*, 186.
108 CCALS, ZSR 168, m.1; ZSR 311, m.1; ZSR 362, m.1d.
109 *Paston Letters and Papers of the Fifteenth Century*, 170.
110 3 *Sheaf*, 14 (1917), 8.
111 CCALS, ZSR 239, m.1d; ZSR 245, m.1d.
112 CCALS, ZMB 3, f.65.
113 CCALS, ZSR 153, m.1; ZSR 156, mm.1, 1d; ZSR 160, m.1d.
114 CCALS, ZMB 5, ff.74v, 76, 78, 78v; TNA: PRO, CHES 29/165, m.18.
115 CCALS, ZMB 6, ff.41v, 43, 43v, 44v; ZSB 3, ff.67, 69.
116 BL, Harl. Ms.2158, ff.36v, 38, 39v.
117 CCALS, ZSR 305, m.1.
118 G. Ormerod, *History of Cheshire*, II, 864–5; J.McN. Dodgson, *Place-Names of Cheshire*, Part Four, 159; TNA: PRO, CHES 25/15, m.13d; CCALS, ZSR 367, m.1.
119 CCALS, ZMB 5, ff.9, 9v, 11, 11v, 12, 30v, 48v, 51, 53, 54v, 78v.
120 CCALS, ZMB 9(a), ff.32v-33, 36; ZMB 9(b), f.8.
121 CCALS, ZMB 3, ff.18, 18v, 19.
122 CCALS, ZMB 7, ff.150, 151, 152–153v.
123 CCALS, ZMB 6, ff.58–58v.

Conclusion

1 CCALS, ZSR 220, m.1; ZSR 226, m.1; ZSR 278, m.1d; ZSB 3, f.67; TNA: PRO, CHES 25/8, m.15d; SC 6/6/771/1, m.1.
2 TNA: PRO, SC 6/796/9, m.7; CCALS, ZMB 2, f.34v.
3 CCALS, ZMB 2, f.28; ZMB 3, f.15; ZMB 7, f.42v; ZSB 2, f.59; ZSR 274, m.1; BL, Harl. Ms.2158, ff.46–46v.
4 CCALS, ZSR 5, mm.3, 4d; ZSR 217, m.1d; TNA: PRO, CHES 25/12, m.31d; CHES 25/15, m.37.
5 CCALS, ZSR 23, m.1d; ZSB 2, f.93v; ZSB 4, f.107v.
6 CCALS, ZSR 32, m.1d; ZSB 3, ff.39v, 92v.
7 CCALS, ZMB 1, f.60; ZMB 2, f.52v; ZMB 3, f.75v; ZMB 5, f.180; ZSB 4, ff.9v, 75, 155, 160v; ZSB 2, f.40; ZSR 61, m.5; ZSR 119, m.1.
8 CCALS, ZAB 1, f.70.
9 CCALS, ZMB 6, ff.36–36v, 104v; ZSB 4, f.31v.
10 BL, Harl. Ms.2046, f.33v; Harl. Ms.2057, f.156v.
11 3 *Sheaf*, 13 (1916), 90–1.
12 3 *Sheaf*, 22 (1925), 62.

Select Bibliography

Manuscript Sources

Public Record Office

CHES 25	Chester County Court: Indictment Rolls and Files
CHES 29	Chester County Court: Plea Rolls
E 101	Exchequer: Accounts, Various
SC 1	Special Collections: Ancient Correspondence
SC 2	Special Collections: Court Rolls
SC 6	Special Collections: Ministers' and Receivers' Accounts
SC 11	Special Collections: Rentals and Surveys
WALE 29	Palatinate of Chester: Ancient Deeds, Series F

Cheshire and Chester Archives and Local Studies

County Records

DCH	Cholmondeley of Cholmondeley: Estate, Family and Personal Papers
DVE	Vernon of Kinderton: Estate, Family and Personal Papers
WS	Wills and Probate Records: Supra Series

Chester City Records

ZAB	Assembly Books
ZAF	Assembly Files
ZCAM	Muragers' Account Book
ZCH	Charters
ZCHC	Charities
ZCHD	Corporation Deeds
ZCR 63	J.P. Earwaker (antiquary): Private Records
ZG	Guild Records
ZMB	Mayors' Books
ZMR	Portmote Court Rolls
ZMUB	Muragers' Account Books
ZMUR	Muragers' Account Roll
ZQCR	Crownmote Court Rolls
ZSB	Sheriffs' Books
ZSP	Passage Court Rolls
ZSR	Pentice Court Rolls
ZSRE	Pentice Court: Estreats of Fines
ZTAR	Treasurers' Account Rolls and Rentals

Staffordshire Record Office

D 641	Stafford Manuscripts

Printed Primary Sources

Accounts of the Chamberlains and Other Officers of the County of Chester, 1301–60, ed. R. Stewart-Brown (RSLC, 59, 1910).

Account of Master John de Burnham the Younger, Chamberlain of Chester, 1361–2, ed. P.H.W. Booth and A.D. Carr (RSLC, 125, 1991).

Annales Cestrienses, or the Chronicle of the Abbey of St Werburg at Chester, ed. R.C. Christie (RSLC, 14, 1886).

The Book of Margery Kempe, ed. S.B. Meech and H.E. Allen (EETS, old series, 212, 1940).

Calendar of Chester City Council Minutes 1603–1642, ed. M.J. Groombridge (RSLC, 106, 1956).

Calendar of the Close Rolls preserved in the Public Record Office (HMSO).

Calendar of County Court, City Court and Eyre Rolls of Chester, 1259–97, ed. R. Stewart-Brown (Chetham Society, 84, 1925).

Calendar of the Moore Family Deeds and Papers, ed. J. Brownbill (RSLC, 67, 1913).

Calendar of the Norris Deeds (Lancashire), 12th to 15th century, ed. J.H. Lumby (RSLC, 93, 1939).

Calendar of the Patent Rolls preserved in the Public Record Office (HMSO).

Calendar of the Recognizance Rolls of the Palatinate of Chester from the earliest times to the end of the reign of Henry IV, Report of the Deputy Keeper of the Public Records, 36, Appendix II (London, 1875).

Calendar of the Recognizance Rolls of the Palatinate of Chester from the beginning of the reign of Henry V to the end of the reign of Henry VIII, Report of the Deputy Keeper of the Public Records, 37, Appendix II (London, 1876).

The Charters of the Anglo-Norman Earls of Chester, c.1071–1237, ed. G. Barraclough (RSLC, 126, 1988).

The Chartulary or Register of the Abbey of St Werburgh, Chester, ed. J. Tait (2 volumes, Chetham Society, 79, 1920; 82, 1923).

Cheshire in the Pipe Rolls, 1158–1301, ed. R. Stewart-Brown and M.H. Mills (RSLC, 92, 1938).

Chester Customs Accounts, 1301–1566, ed. K.P. Wilson (RSLC, 111, 1969).

The Chronicle of Adam of Usk, 1377–1421, ed. C. Given-Wilson (Oxford, Clarendon Press, 1997).

Chronicle of Dieulacres Abbey, 1381–1403, ed. M.V. Clarke and V.H. Galbraith (Bulletin of the John Rylands Library, 14, 1930), 164–81.

Chronicon Adae de Usk, AD 1377–1404, ed. E.M. Thompson (London, 1904).

A Descriptive Catalogue of Ancient Deeds in the Public Record Office (HMSO).

English Benedictine Kalendars after 1100, Volume One: Abbotsbury-Durham, ed. F. Wormald (Henry Bradshaw Society, 77, 1939).

English Historical Documents, III, *1189–1327*, ed. H. Rothwell (London, 1975).

Extent of the Lordship of Longdendale 1360, ed. J. Harrop, P. Booth and S. Harrop (RSLC, 140, 2005).

The Household Books of John Howard, Duke of Norfolk, 1462–1471, 1481–1483, ed. A. Crawford (Alan Sutton for Richard III & Yorkist History Trust, 1992).

The Itinerary of John Leland in or about the years 1535–1543, ed. L. Toulmin Smith (5 volumes, London, 1964).

Lancashire and Cheshire Wills and Inventories from the Ecclesiastical Court, Chester, ed. G.J. Piccope (Chetham Society, first series 51, 1860).

Lancashire and Cheshire Wills and Inventories, ed. J.P. Earwaker (Chetham Society, new series 3, 1884).

The Ledger Book of Vale Royal Abbey, ed. J. Brownbill (RSLC, 68, 1914).

Letters and Accounts of William Brereton of Malpas, ed. E.W. Ives (RSLC, 116, 1976).

Letters of Edward Prince of Wales 1304–5, ed. H. Johnstone (Roxburghe Club, Cambridge, 1931).

Letters & Papers, Foreign and Domestic, of the Reign of Henry VIII (HMSO).

The Libelle of Englyshe Polycye: A Poem on the Use of Seapower, 1436, ed. G. Warner (Oxford, 1926).

Liber Luciani de Laude Cestrie and *Obits of St Werburgh's Abbey*, ed. M.V. Taylor (RSLC, 64, 1912).

The Map of Great Britain c.1360 known as the Gough Map, Bodleian Library facsimile (Oxford, 1958).

The Metrical Chronicle of Robert of Gloucester, ed. W.A. Wright (Rolls Series, 86, 1887).

A Middlewich Chartulary compiled by William Vernon in the Seventeenth Century, ed. J. Varley (2 volumes, Chetham Society, 105, 1941; 108, 1944).

Paston Letters and Papers of the Fifteenth Century, ed. N. Davis (2 volumes, Oxford, 1971, 1976).

Polychronicon Ranulphi Higden Monachi Cestriensis, ed. C. Babington and J.R. Lumby (9 volumes, Rolls Series, 1865–86).

The Processional of the Nuns of Chester, ed. J.W. Legg (Henry Bradshaw Society, 18, 1899).

Records of Early English Drama: Cheshire including Chester, ed. E. Baldwin, L.M. Clopper and D. Mills (2 volumes, The British Library and University of Toronto Press, University of Toronto Press Incorporated, 2007).

Register of Edward the Black Prince (HMSO, London, 1930–3).

Register of the Guild of the Holy Trinity, Coventry, ed. M.D. Harris, (Dugdale Society, 13, 1935).

Selected Rolls of the Chester City Courts: Late Thirteenth and Early Fourteenth Centuries, ed. A. Hopkins (Chetham Society, 3rd series 2, 1950).

Talbot Deeds, 1200–1682, ed. E.E. Barker (RSLC, 103, 1953).

Translation of a French Metrical History of the Deposition of Richard II, ed. J. Webb (Archaeologia, 20, 1824).

Willelmi Malmesbiriensis Monachi de Gestis Pontificum Anglorum, ed. N.E.S.A. Hamilton (Rolls Series, 1870).

William Worcestre, Itineraries, ed. J.H. Harvey (Oxford, 1969).

Secondary Works (general)

Baker, J.H., *An Introduction to English Legal History* (3rd edition, London, 1990).

Barrell, A.D.M., Davies, R.R., Padel, O.J. and Smith, L.B., 'The Dyffryn Clwyd court roll project, 1340–52 and 1389–99: a methodology and some preliminary findings', in Z. Razi and R. Smith (eds), *Medieval Society and the Manor Court* (Oxford, 1996), 260–97.

Barron, C.M, 'The 'Golden Age' of Women in Medieval London', *Reading Medieval Studies*, 15 (1989), 35–58.

Barron, C.M., 'London 1300–1540', in D. Palliser (ed.), *CUH*, I, 600–1540 (Cambridge, 2000), 395–440.

Bennett, J.M., 'The Village Alewife: Women and Brewing in Fourteenth-Century England', in B.A. Hanawalt (ed.), *Women and Work in pre-Industrial Europe* (Bloomington, 1986), 20–36.

Bennett, J.M., 'Conviviality and Charity in Medieval and Early Modern England', *Past & Present*, 134 (1992), 19–41.

Bennett, J.M., *Ale, Beer and Brewsters in England: Women's Work in a Changing World, 1300–1600* (Oxford, 1996).

Beresford, M. and Finberg, H.P.R., *English Medieval Boroughs: A Handlist* (Newton Abbot, 1973).

Beresford, M., 'English Medieval Boroughs: A Handlist: Revisions, 1973–81', *Urban History Yearbook* (1981), 59–65.

Beresford, M., *New Towns of the Middle Ages: Town Plantation in England, Wales and Gascony* (2nd edition, Gloucester, 1988).

Blair, J. and Ramsay, N. (eds), *English Medieval Industries: Craftsmen, Techniques, Products* (London, 1991).

Britnell, R.H., *Growth and Decline in Colchester, 1300–1525* (Cambridge, 1986).

Britnell, R.H., *The Commercialisation of English Society 1000–1500* (Cambridge, 1993).

Brown, R.A., Colvin, H.M. and Taylor, A.J., *The History of the King's Works*, 1–2, 7: *The Middle Ages* (2 volumes, London, 1963).

Brown, I., *Discovering a Welsh Landscape: Archaeology in the Clwydian Range* (Bollington, 2004).

Bukofzer, M.F., 'Popular and Secular Music in England (to c.1470)', in Dom Anselm Hughes and G. Abraham (eds),

The New Oxford History of Music, III: *Ars Nova and the Renaissance, 1300–1540* (London, 1960), 107–33.

Campbell, M., 'Gold, Silver and Precious Stones', in J. Blair and N. Ramsay (eds), *English Medieval Industries* (London, 1991), 107–66.

Carr, A.D., 'Medieval Fisheries in Anglesey', in *Maritime Wales,* 3 (Gwynedd Archives Society, 1978), 5–8.

Carr, A.D., *Medieval Anglesey* (Anglesey Antiquarian Society, Llangefni, 1982).

Carus-Wilson, E.M., 'The Overseas Trade of Bristol', in E. Power and M.M. Postan (eds), *Studies in English Trade in the Fifteenth Century* (London, 1933).

Chaloner, J., *A Short Treatise on the Isle of Man* (The Manx Society, 10, 1864).

Charleston, R.J., 'Vessel Glass', in J. Blair and N. Ramsay (eds), *English Medieval Industries* (London, 1991), 237–64.

Cherry, J., 'Leather', in J. Blair and N. Ramsay (eds), *English Medieval Industries* (London, 1991), 295–318.

Childs, W. and O'Neill, T., 'Overseas Trade of Ireland', in A. Cosgrove (ed.), *A New History of Ireland,* II: *Medieval Ireland, 1169–1534* (Oxford, 1987), 492–524.

Clanchy, M.T., *From Memory to Written Record: England 1066–1307* (Cambridge, 1979).

Clarke, H., Dent, S. and Johnson, R., *Dublinia: The Story of Medieval Dublin* (Dublin, 2002).

Cooke, J., *Wakeman's Handbook of Irish Antiquities* (Dublin, 1903).

Cosgrove, A., 'The Emergence of the Pale' in A. Cosgrove (ed.), *A New History of Ireland,* II: *Medieval Ireland, 1169–1534* (Oxford, 1987), 533–56.

Crowfoot, E., Pritchard, F. and Staniland, K., *Textiles and Clothing c.1150–1450*, Medieval Finds from Excavations in London, 4 (London, 1992).

Davies, R.R., *The Revolt of Owain Glyn Dŵr* (Oxford, 1995).

DeWindt, E.B., *Land and People in Holywell-cum-Needingworth* (Toronto, 1971).

Dickinson, J.R., *The Lordship of Man under the Stanleys: Government and Economy in the Isle of Man, 1580–1704* (Chetham Society, 41, 1996).

Dobson, R.B., 'Admissions to the Freedom of the City of York in the later Middle Ages', *Economic History Review,* 2nd series 26 (1973), 1–21.

Dobson, R.B., *The Peasants' Revolt of 1381* (2nd edition, London, 1983).

Dobson, R.B., 'Mendicant Ideal and Practice in Late Medieval York', in P.V. Addyman and V.E. Black (eds), *Archaeological Papers from York presented to M.W. Barley* (York, 1984), 109–22.

Dyer, A., 'Appendix: Ranking Lists of English Medieval Towns', in D. Palliser (ed.), *CUH,* I, *600–1540* (Cambridge, 2000), 747–70.

Dyer, C., 'English Diet in the Later Middle Ages', in T.H. Aston, P.R. Coss, C. Dyer and J. Thirsk (eds), *Social Relations and Ideas: Essays in Honour of R.H. Hilton* (Cambridge, 1983), 191–216.

Dyer, C., *Standards of Living in the Later Middle Ages: Social Change in England c.1200–1520* (Cambridge, 1989).

Dyer, C., *Everyday Life in Medieval England* (London, 1994).

Dyer, C., 'Gardens and Orchards in Medieval England', in C. Dyer, *Everyday Life in Medieval England* (London, 1994), 113–31.

Dyer, C., 'The Hidden Trade of the Middle Ages: Evidence from the West Midlands', in C. Dyer, *Everyday Life in Medieval England* (London, 1994), 283–303.

Dyer, C., 'Market Towns and the Countryside', *Canadian Journal of History,* 31 (1996), 17–35.

Dyer, C., 'How Urban was Medieval England?', *History Today,* 47 (1997), 37–43.

Dyer, C., 'Small Towns 1270–1540', in D. Palliser (ed.), *CUH,* I, *600–1540* (Cambridge, 2000), 505–37.

Dyer, C., 'A Summing Up', in J.A. Galloway (ed.), *Trade, Urban Hinterlands and Market Integration c.1300–1600* (Centre for Metropolitan History Working Papers Series, 3, 2000), 103–9.

Dyer, C., *Making a Living in the Middle Ages: The People of Britain 850–1520* (London, 2002).

Dyer, C., 'Small Places with Large Consequences: the Importance of Small Towns in England, 1000–1540', *The Bulletin of the Institute of Historical Research,* 75 (2002), 1–24.

Dyer, C., 'The Urbanizing of Staffordshire: The First Phases', *Staffordshire Studies,* 14 (2002), 1–31.

Dyer, C., *An Age of Transition? Economy and Society in England in the Later Middle Ages* (Oxford, 2005).

Farmer, D.L., 'Marketing the Produce of the Countryside, 1200–1500', in E. Miller (ed.), *The Agrarian History of England and Wales,* III, *1348–1500* (Cambridge, 1991), 324–430.

Fox, H.S.A., 'Medieval Urban Development', in R. Kain and W. Ravenhill (eds), *An Historical Atlas of South-West England* (Exeter, 1999), 424–31.

Franklin, P., 'Normans, Saints and Politics: Forename-choice among Fourteenth-century Gloucestershire Peasants', *Local Population Studies,* 36 (1986), 19–26.

Geddes, J., 'Iron', in J. Blair and N. Ramsay (eds), *English Medieval Industries* (London, 1991), 167–88.

Gilbert, J.T., *A History of the City of Dublin* (3 volumes, Dublin, 1861).

Goldberg, J., 'Female Labour, Service and Marriage in the Late Medieval Urban North', *Northern History,* 22 (1986), 18–38.

Goldberg, J., 'Marriage, Migration, Servanthood and Life-Cycle in Yorkshire Towns of the Later Medieval Ages', *Continuity and Change,* 1 (1986), 141–69.

Goldberg, J., *Women, Work and Life Cycle in a Medieval Economy: Women in York and Yorkshire c.1300–1520* (Oxford, 1992).

Gransden, A., *Historical Writing in England,* II, *c.1307 to the Early Sixteenth Century* (London, 1982).

Grenville, J., *Medieval Housing* (London, 1997).

Griffiths, R.A., *Boroughs of Mediaeval Wales* (Cardiff, 1978).

Griffiths, R.A., 'The Study of the Mediaeval Welsh Borough', in R.A. Griffiths (ed.), *Boroughs of Mediaeval Wales* (Cardiff, 1978), 1–17.

Griffiths, R.A., *The Reign of Henry VI* (Stroud, 1998).

Griffiths, R.A., 'Wales and the Marches', in D.M. Palliser (ed.), *CUH*, I, *600–1540* (Cambridge, 2000), 681–714.

Griffiths, R.A., 'After Glyn Dŵr: An Age of Reconciliation?', *Proceedings of the British Academy*, 117 (2002), 139–64.

Griffiths, Rhidian, 'Prince Henry and Wales, 1400–1408', in M. Hicks (ed.), *Profit, Piety and the Professions in Later Medieval England* (Gloucester, 1990), 51–61.

Hardy, R., *Longbow: A Social and Military History* (Stroud, 2006).

Harriss, G., *Shaping the Nation: England 1360–1461* (Oxford, 2005).

Harvey, J., *Mediaeval Gardens* (London, 1981).

Harvey, P.D.A. (ed.), *The Hereford World Map: Medieval World Maps and their Context* (The British Library, 2006).

Hatcher, J., 'The Great Slump of the Mid-Fifteenth Century', in R. Britnell and J. Hatcher (eds), *Progress and Problems in Medieval England: Essays in Honour of Edward Miller* (Cambridge, 1996), 237–72.

Hinton, D.A., *Gold and Gilt, Pots and Pins: Possessions and People in Medieval Britain* (Oxford, 2005).

Holt R. and Rosser G. (eds), *The Medieval Town: A Reader in English Urban History 1200–1540* (London, 1990).

Holt, R., 'Society and Population 600–1300', in D. Palliser (ed.), *CUH*, I, *600–1540* (Cambridge, 2000), 79–104.

Horrox, R., 'The Urban Gentry in the Fifteenth Century', in J.A.F. Thomson (ed.), *Towns and Townspeople in the Fifteenth Century* (Gloucester, 1988), 22–44.

Hoskins, W.G., 'English Provincial Towns in the Early Sixteenth Century', *TRHS*, 5th series 6 (1956), 1–19.

Jack, R.I., 'Ruthin', in R.A. Griffiths (ed.), *Boroughs of Mediaeval Wales* (Cardiff, 1978), 244–61.

James, M., 'Ritual, Drama and Social Body in the Late Medieval English Town', *Past & Present*, 98 (1983), 3–29.

Jenkins, S., *England's Thousand Best Churches* (London, 1999).

Jones, M.K., 'Sir William Stanley of Holt: Politics and Family Allegiance in the Late Fifteenth Century', *The Welsh History Review*, 14 (1988), 1–22.

Keene, D., *Survey of Medieval Winchester* (2 volumes, Oxford, 1985).

Keene, D., 'Medieval London and its Region', *The London Journal*, 14 (1989), 99–111.

Keene, D., 'Shops and Shopping in Medieval London', in L. Grant (ed.), *Medieval Art, Architecture and Archaeology in London* (British Archaeological Association, Conference Transactions, 10, 1990), 29–46.

Keene, D., 'Suburban Growth', in R. Holt and G. Rosser (eds), *The Medieval Town: A Reader in English Urban History 1200–1540* (London, 1990), 97–119.

Keene, D., 'Small Towns and the Metropolis: the Experience of Medieval England', in J-M. Duvosquel and E. Thoen (eds), *Peasants and Townsmen in Medieval Europe* (Ghent, 1995), 223–38.

Kermode, J., 'The Greater Towns 1300–1540', in D. Palliser (ed.), *CUH*, I, *600–1540* (Cambridge, 2000), 441–65.

Kowaleski, M., 'The Commercial Dominance of a Medieval Provincial Oligarchy: Exeter in the Later Fourteenth Century', *Medieval Studies*, 46 (1984), 355–84.

Kowaleski, M., 'The History of Urban Families in Medieval England', *Journal of Medieval History*, 14 (1988), 47–63.

Kowaleski, M., *Local Markets and Regional Trade in Medieval Exeter* (Cambridge, 1995).

Laughton, J. and Dyer, C., 'Small Towns in the East and West Midlands in the Later Middle Ages: A Comparison', *Midland History*, 24 (1999), 24–52.

Laughton, J., Jones, E. and Dyer, C., 'The Urban Hierarchy in the Later Middle Ages: A Study of the East Midlands', *Urban History*, 28 (2001), 331–57.

Laughton, J. and Dyer, C., 'Seasonal Patterns of Trade in the later Middle Ages: Buying and Selling at Melton Mowbray, Leicestershire, 1400–1520', *Nottingham Medieval Studies*, 46 (2002), 162–84.

Lewis, J.M., 'Roof Tiles: Some Observations and Questions', *Bulletin of the Medieval Pottery Research Group*, 11 (1987), 3–14.

Lloyd, J.E., *Owen Glendower: Owen Glyn Dwr* (Oxford, 1931).

McClure, P., 'Patterns of Migration in the Late Middle Ages: The Evidence of English Place-Name Surnames', *Economic History Review*, 32 (1979), 167–82.

Macgregor, A., 'Antler, Bone and Horn', in J. Blair and N. Ramsay (eds), *English Medieval Industries* (London, 1991), 355–78.

Maddern, P., ' 'Best Trusted Friends': Concepts and Practices of Friendship among Fifteenth-Century Norfolk Gentry', in N. Rogers (ed.), *England in the Fifteenth Century: Proceedings of the 1992 Harlaxton Symposium* (Stamford, 1994), 100–17.

Marks, R., 'Window Glass', in J. Blair and N. Ramsay (eds), *English Medieval Industries* (London, 1991), 265–94.

Masschaele, J., *Peasants, Merchants and Markets. Inland Trade in Medieval England, 1150–1350* (New York, 1997).

Messham, J.E., 'The County of Flint and the Rebellion of Owen Glyndwr in the records of the earldom of Chester', *Flintshire Historical Society Publications*, 23 (1967–8), 1–34.

Miller, E. and Hatcher, J., *Medieval England: Towns, Commerce and Crafts, 1086–1348* (Harlow, 1995).

Morris, J.E., *The Welsh Wars of Edward I* (Oxford, 1901).

Munby, J., 'Wood', in J. Blair and N. Ramsay (eds), *English Medieval Industries* (London, 1991), 379–405.

Nightingale, P., *A Medieval Mercantile Community: The Grocers' Company and the Politics and Trade of London 1000–1485* (New Haven and London, 1995).

Nightingale, P., 'The English Parochial Clergy as Investors and Creditors in the first half of the Fourteenth Century', in P.R. Schofield and N.J. Mayhew (eds), *Credit and Debt in Medieval England c.1180–c.1350* (Oxbow Books, Oxford, 2002), 89–105.

O'Neill, T., *Merchants and Mariners in Medieval Ireland* (Dublin, 1987).

Orme, N., *Medieval Schools from Roman Britain to Renaissance England* (New Haven and London, 2006).

Owen, D.H., 'Denbigh', in R.A. Griffiths (ed.), *Boroughs of Mediaeval Wales* (Cardiff, 1978), 164–87.

Palliser, D. (ed.), *The Cambridge Urban History of Britain*, I, *600–1540* (Cambridge, 2000).

Palliser, D., 'Introduction', *CUH*, I, *600–1540* (Cambridge, 2000), 3–15.

Parkinson, C.N., *The Rise of the Port of Liverpool* (Liverpool, 1952).

Phythian-Adams, C., 'Urban Decay in Late Medieval England', in P. Abrams and E.A. Wrigley (eds), *Towns in Society: Essays in Economic History and Historical Sociology* (Cambridge, 1978), 159–85.

Phythian-Adams, C., *Desolation of a City: Coventry and the Urban Crisis of the Late Middle Ages* (Cambridge, 1979).

Platt, C., *The Parish Churches of Medieval England* (London, 1981).

Powell, E., 'Arbitration and the Law in England in the Late Middle Ages', *TRHS*, 5th series 33 (1983), 49–67.

Powell, E., 'Settlement of Disputes by Arbitration in Fifteenth-Century England', *Law and History Review*, 2 (1984), 21–43.

Power, E., *Medieval English Nunneries, c.1275–1535* (Cambridge, 1922).

Pratt, D., 'The Medieval Borough of Holt', *Transactions of the Denbighshire Historical Society*, 14 (1965), 9–74.

Pratt, D., 'Minera: Township of the Mines', *Transactions of the Denbighshire Historical Society*, 25 (1976), 114–54.

Prestwich, M., *Plantagenet England: 1225–1360* (Oxford, 2005).

Rawcliffe, C., *Leprosy in Medieval England* (Woodbridge, 2006).

Reynolds, S., *An Introduction to the History of English Medieval Towns* (Oxford, 1977).

Rosser, G., *Medieval Westminster 1200–1540* (Oxford, 1989).

Rosser, G., 'Conflict and Political Community in the Medieval Town: Disputes between Clergy and Laity in Hereford', in T.R. Slater and G. Rosser (eds), *The Church in the Medieval Town* (Aldershot, 1998), 20–42.

Rosser, G., 'Urban Culture and the Church 1300–1540', in D. Palliser (ed.), *CUH*, I, *600–1540* (Cambridge, 2000), 335–69.

Rubin, M., *Corpus Christi: The Eucharist in Late Medieval Culture* (Cambridge, 1991).

Slater, T., 'The Urban Hierarchy in Medieval Staffordshire', *Journal of Historical Geography*, 11 (1985), 115–37.

Schofield, J. and Stell, G., 'The Built Environment 1300–

1540', in D. Palliser (ed.), *CUH*, I, *600–1540* (Cambridge, 2000), 371–93.

Shaw, M., 'The Excavation of a late 15th- to 17th-Century Tanning Complex at The Green, Northampton', *Post-Medieval Archaeology*, 30 (1996), 63–127.

Smith-Bannister, S., *Naming and Naming Patterns in England 1538–1700* (Oxford, 1997).

Soulsby, I., *The Towns of Medieval Wales: A Study of their History, Archaeology and Early Topography* (Chichester, 1983).

Swanson, H., 'The Illusion of Economic Structure: Craft Guilds in Late Medieval English Towns', *Past & Present*, 121 (1988), 29–48.

Swanson, H., *Medieval Artisans: An Urban Class in Late Medieval England* (Oxford, 1989).

Swanson, R.N., *Church and Society in Late Medieval England* (Oxford, 1989).

Taylor, A., *Caernarfon Castle and Town Walls* (Fourth edition, Cadw, Cardiff, 1997).

Taylor, A., *Harlech Castle* (Third edition, Cadw, Cardiff, 1997).

Taylor, A., *Beaumaris Castle* (Fourth edition, Cadw, 1999).

Taylor, H., *Historical Notices with Topographical Gleanings Descriptive of the Borough and County Town of Flint* (London, 1883).

Thomson, J.A.F., *The Transformation of Medieval England 1370–1529* (London, 1983).

Thrupp, S., *The Merchant Class of Medieval London* (University of Michigan, 1989).

Veale, E.M., 'Craftsmen and the Economy of London in the Fourteenth Century', in R. Holt and G. Rosser (eds), *The Medieval Town: A Reader in English Urban History 1200–1540* (London, 1990), 120–39.

Walton, P., 'Textiles', in J. Blair and N. Ramsay (eds), *English Medieval Industries* (London, 1991), 319–54.

Williams, C.J., 'The Mining Laws in Flintshire and Denbighshire', *Bulletin of the Peak District Mines Historical Society*, 12 (1994), 62–8.

Winchester, A.J.L., *Landscape and Development in Medieval Cumbria* (Edinburgh, 1987).

Ziegler, P., *The Black Death* (London, 1969).

Secondary Works (Chester and Cheshire)

Arrowsmith, P., *Stockport: A History* (Stockport, 1997).

Bennett, J.H.E., 'The Grey Friars of Chester', *JCAS*, 24 (1921), 5–85.

Bennett, J.H.E., 'The Hospital and Chantry of St Ursula', *JCAS*, 32 (1938), 98–129.

Bennett, M.J., 'The Lancashire and Cheshire Clergy, 1379', *THSLC*, 124 (1972), 1–30.

Bennett, M.J., 'A County Community: Social Cohesion among the Cheshire Gentry, 1400–25', *Northern History*, 8 (1973), 24–44.

Bennett, M.J., 'Sources and Problems in the Study of Social Mobility: Cheshire in the Later Middle Ages', *THSLC*, 128 (1979 for 1978), 59–95.

Bennett, M.J., 'Sir Gawain and the Green Knight and the Literary Achievement of the North-West Midlands: the Historical Background', *Journal of Medieval History*, 5 (1979), 63–88.

Bennett, M.J., ' "Good Lords" and "King-Makers": the Stanleys of Lathom in English Politics, 1385–1485', *History Today*, 31 (1981), 12–17.

Bennett, M.J., *Community, Class and Careerism: Cheshire and Lancashire Society in the Age of Sir Gawain and the Green Knight* (Cambridge, 1983).

Bennett, M.J., *Richard II and the Revolution of 1399* (Stroud, 1999).

Booth, P.H.W. and Dodd, J.P., 'The Manor and Fields of Frodsham, 1315–74', *THSLC*, 128 (1979 for 1978), 27–57.

Booth, P.H.W., ' "Farming for Profit" in the Fourteenth Century: The Cheshire Estates of the Earldom of Chester', *JCAS*, 62 (1980 for 1979), 73–90.

Booth, P.H.W., *The Financial Administration of the Lordship and County of Chester 1272–1377* (Chetham Society, 28, 1981).

Booth, P.H.W., *Burton in Wirral* (Burton, 1984).

Brown, A. (ed.), *The Rows of Chester: The Chester Rows Research Project* (English Heritage Archaeological Report, 16, 1999).

Burne, R.V.H., *The Monks of Chester: The History of St Werburgh's Abbey* (London, 1962).

Cather, S., Park, D. and Pender, R., 'Henry III's Wall Paintings at Chester Castle', in A. Thacker (ed.), *Medieval Archaeology, Art and Architecture at Chester* (The British Archaeological Association Conference Transactions, 22, 2000), 170–89.

Clayton, D.J., *The Administration of the County Palatine of Chester 1442–85* (Chetham Society, 35, 1990).

Coward, B., *The Stanleys: Lords Stanley and Earls of Derby, 1385–1672: the Origins, Wealth and Power of a Landowning Family* (Chetham Society, 30, 1983).

Danbury, E., 'The Intellectual Life of the Abbey of St Werburgh, Chester, in the Middle Ages', in A. Thacker (ed.), *Medieval Archaeology, Art and Architecture at Chester* (The British Archaeological Association Conference Transactions, 22, 2000), 107–20.

Davey, E., 'Very Plenteous in Fish – A Survey of Fisheries in Wirral', *Cheshire History*, 43 (2003–2004), 40–6.

Davey, P. (ed.), *Northgate Street Brewery: Interim Report* (Grosvenor Museum Excavations, Chester, 1973).

Davies, R.R., 'Richard II and the Principality of Chester 1397–9', in F.R.H. Du Boulay and C.M. Barron (eds), *The Reign of Richard II: Essays in honour of May McKisack* (London, 1971), 256–79.

Davies, S. (ed.), *A History of Macclesfield* (Manchester, 1961).

Dodgson, J.McN., *The Place-Names of Cheshire* (6 volumes, English Place-Name Society, volumes 44–8, 54, 74, Cambridge, 1966–70, 1981, 1996–7).

Earwaker, J.P., 'The Ancient Parish Books of the Church of St Mary-on-the-Hill, Chester, *JCAS*, 2 (1888), 132–48.

Garner, D., *Archaeology in the Park: Grosvenor Park Chester 2007* (Chester City Council, 2007).

Greig, J., 'Plant Remains', in S. Ward, *Excavations at Chester: 12 Watergate Street 1985* (Grosvenor Museum Archaeological Excavation and Survey Report, 5, Chester City Council, 1988), 59–69.

Grossinger, C., 'Chester Cathedral Misericords: Iconography and Sources', in A. Thacker (ed.), *Medieval Archaeology, Art and Architecture at Chester* (The British Archaeological Association Conference Transactions, 22, 2000), 98–106.

Harris, R.B., 'The Origins of the Chester Rows', in A. Thacker (ed.), *Medieval Archaeology, Art and Architecture at Chester* (The British Archaeological Association Conference Transactions, 22, 2000), 132–51.

Higham, N.J., *A Frontier Landscape: The North West in the Middle Ages* (Bollington, 2004).

Irvine, W.F., 'Chester in the Twelfth and Thirteenth Centuries', *JCAS*, 10 (1904), 13–52.

Irvine, W.F., 'Rental of St Mary's Nunnery, 1526', *JCAS*, 13 (1907), 105–9.

Jones, D., *The Church in Chester, 1300–1540* (Chetham Society, 7, 1957).

Kennett, A. (ed.), *Archives and Records of the City of Chester* (Chester, 1985).

Kettle, A.J., 'Religious Houses', in *VCH*, *Cheshire*, III (Oxford, 1980), 132–50, 171–84.

Laughton, J., 'Women in Court: Some Evidence from Fifteenth-Century Chester', in N. Rogers (ed.), *England in the Fifteenth Century* (Stamford, 1994), 89–99.

Laughton, J., 'The Alewives of Later Medieval Chester', in R.E. Archer (ed.), *Crown, Government and People in the Fifteenth Century* (Stroud, 1995), 191–208.

Laughton, J., 'The Port of Chester in the Later Middle Ages', in P. Carrington (compiler), *'Where Deva Spreads Her Wizard Stream': Trade and the Port of Chester* (Chester Archaeology: Occasional Paper No 3, Chester City Council, 1996), 66–71.

Laughton, J., 'Economy and Society, 1350–1500', in *VCH*, *Chester*, V, Part 1 (Boydell & Brewer, 2003), 64–78.

Laughton, J., 'Historical Commentary on Meols in the Later Medieval Period', in D. Griffiths, R.A. Philpott and G. Egan, *Meols: The Archaeology of the North Wirral Coast* (Oxford University School of Archaeology: Monograph 68, 2007), 412–22.

Lewis, B.J., *Welsh Poetry and English Pilgrimage: Gruffudd ap Maredudd and the Rood of Chester* (Aberystwyth, 2005).

Lumiansky, R.M. and Mills, D., *The Chester Mystery Cycle: Essays and Documents* (Chapel Hill, 1983).

McNiven, P., 'The Cheshire Rising of 1400', *Bulletin of the John Rylands Library*, 52 (1969–70), 375–96.

McNiven, P., 'The Men of Cheshire and the Rebellion of 1403', *THSLC*, 129 (1980 for 1979), 1–29.

McNiven, P., 'Rebellion, Sedition and the Legend of Richard II's Survival', *Bulletin of the John Rylands Library*, 76 (1994), 93–117.

MacLean, S-B, 'Marian Devotion in post-Reformation Chester: Implications of the Smiths' "Purification" Play', in T. Scott and P. Starkey (eds), *The Middle Ages in the North-West* (Oxford, Leopard's Head, 1995), 237–56.

Mason, D., *Roman Chester: City of the Eagles* (Stroud, 2001).

Mason, D., *Chester AD 400–1066: From Roman Fortress to English Town* (Stroud, 2007).

Matthews, K. and others, *Excavations at Chester: The Evolution of the Heart of the City: Investigations at 3–15 Eastgate Street 1990/1* (Archaeological Service Excavation and Survey Reports No 8, Chester City Council, 1995).

Mills, D., 'The Chester Mystery Plays and the Limits of Realism', in T. Scott and P. Starkey (eds), *The Middle Ages in the North-West* (Oxford, Leopard's Head, 1995), 221–36.

Morgan, P., *War and Society in Medieval Cheshire, 1277–1403* (Chetham Society, 34, 1987).

Morgan, P., 'Medieval Cheshire', in A.D.M. Phillips and C.B. Phillips (eds), *A New Historical Atlas of Cheshire* (Chester, 2002), 28–37.

Morris, R.H., *Chester in the Plantagenet and Tudor Reigns* (Chester, ?1894).

Ormerod, G., *The History of the County Palatine and City of Chester* (revised and enlarged edition by T. Helsby, London, 1882).

Palliser, D.M. (compiler), *Chester: Contemporary Descriptions by Residents and Visitors* (Chester, 2nd edition, 1980).

Pevsner, N. and Hubbard, E., *The Buildings of England: Cheshire* (London, 1971).

Roberts, S.J., *A History of Wirral* (Chichester, 2002).

Sawyer, P.H., 'Translation of the Cheshire Domesday', *VCH, Cheshire*, I (Oxford, 1987), 342–70.

Taylor, H., 'Notes upon some early deeds relating to Chester and Flint' (*JCAS*, 2, 1888), 149–85.

Taylor, H., 'Some Early Medieval Goldsmiths in Chester', *JCAS*, 4 (1892), 178–85.

Taylor, H., 'Ten Early Chester Deeds, 1270–1490', *JCAS*, 10 (1904), 104–16.

Thacker, A., 'The Earls and Their Earldom', *JCAS*, 71 (1991), 7–21.

Thacker, A., 'The Early Medieval City and its Buildings', in A Thacker (ed.), *Medieval Archaeology, Art and Architecture at Chester* (The British Archaeological Association Conference Transactions 22, 2000), 16–30.

Tonkinson, A.M., *Macclesfield in the Later Fourteenth Century: Communities of Town and Forest* (Chetham Society, 42, 1999).

Turner, R.C., 'Shop, Stall and Undercroft in 'The Rows' of Chester', in P. Addyman and S.P. Roskams (eds), *Medieval Europe,* I: *Urbanism* (York, 1992), 161–6.

Victoria County History of Cheshire, I, ed. B.E. Harris assisted by A.T. Thacker (Oxford University Press, 1987).

Victoria County History of Cheshire, II, ed. B.E. Harris (Oxford University Press, 1979).

Victoria County History of Cheshire, III, ed. B.E. Harris (Oxford University Press, 1980).

Victoria County History of Cheshire, V, part 1, ed. C.P. Lewis and A.T. Thacker (Boydell & Brewer, 2003).

Victoria County History of Cheshire, V, part 2, ed. C.P. Lewis and A.T. Thacker (Boydell & Brewer, 2005).

Ward, S., *Excavations at Chester: 12 Watergate Street 1985; Roman Headquarters Building to Medieval Row* (Grosvenor Museum Archaeological Excavation and Survey Reports, 5, Chester City Council, 1988).

Ward, S., *Excavations at Chester: The Lesser Medieval Religious Houses* (Grosvenor Museum Archaeological Excavation and Survey Reports, 6, Chester City Council, 1990).

Ward, S., *Chester City Ditches: A Slice of History* (Chester Archaeological Service: Guidebook No 1, 1992).

Ward, S., 'The Course of the River Dee at Chester' in P. Carrington (compiler), *'Where Deva spreads her Wizard Stream': Trade and the Port of Chester* (Chester Archaeology: Occasional Paper No 3, Chester City Council, 1996), 4–11.

Ward, S., 'Recent Work at St John's and St Werburgh's', in A. Thacker (ed.), *Medieval Archaeology, Art and Architecture at Chester* (The British Archaeological Association Conference Transactions, 22, 2000), 45–56.

Ward, S., 'The Friaries in Chester, Their Impact and Legacy', in A. Thacker (ed.), *Medieval Archaeology, Art and Architecture at Chester* (The British Archaeological Association Conference Transactions, 22, 2000), 121–31.

Wilson, K.P., 'The Port of Chester in the Fifteenth Century', *THSLC*, 117 (1966), 1–15.

Unpublished Dissertations

Holt, R.A., 'Gloucester: an English Provincial Town during the Later Middle Ages', Ph.D. dissertation, University of Birmingham (1987).

Laughton, J., 'Aspects of the Social and Economic History of Late Medieval Chester', Ph.D. dissertation, University of Cambridge (1994).

Wilson, K.P., 'The Port of Chester in the Later Middle Ages', Ph.D. dissertation, University of Liverpool (1965).

Index